Balanced Scorecards & Operational Dashboards with Microsoft® Excel®

Second Edition

Ron Person

WILEY

John Wiley & Sons, Inc.

Balanced Scorecards & Operational Dashboards with Microsoft® Excel®, Second Edition

Published by
John Wiley & Sons, Inc.
10475 Crosspoint Boulevard
Indianapolis, IN 46256
www.wiley.com

Copyright © 2013 by Tor Consulting, Inc., Santa Rosa, California

Published by John Wiley & Sons, Inc., Indianapolis, Indiana
Published simultaneously in Canada

ISBN: 978-1-118-51965-3
ISBN: 978-1-118-51967-7 (ebk)
ISBN: 978-1-118-61084-8 (ebk)
ISBN: 978-1-118-61089-3 (ebk)

Manufactured in the United States of America

10 9 8 7 6 5 4 3 2 1

For general information on our other products and services please contact our Customer Care Department within the United States at (877) 762-2974, outside the United States at (317) 572-3993 or fax (317) 572-4002.

Wiley publishes in a variety of print and electronic formats and by print-on-demand. Some material included with standard print versions of this book may not be included in e-books or in print-on-demand. If this book refers to media such as a CD or DVD that is not included in the version you purchased, you may download this material at http://booksupport.wiley.com. For more information about Wiley products, visit www.wiley.com.

Library of Congress Control Number: 2012951872

*My deepest love and gratitude to my family for their support
and understanding.
I missed you and our time together during both editions of this book.
All my love to Barb, Annika, Rohan, Marjorie, and Anne.*

Credits

Executive Editor
Carol Long

Project Editor
Sydney Jones Argenta

Technical Editors
Jim Coffey
Michael Alexander

Production Editor
Christine Mugnolo

Copy Editor
Gayle Johnson

Editorial Manager
Mary Beth Wakefield

Freelancer Editorial Manager
Rosemarie Graham

Associate Director of Marketing
David Mayhew

Marketing Manager
Ashley Zurcher

Business Manager
Amy Knies

Production Manager
Tim Tate

Vice President and Executive Group Publisher
Richard Swadley

Vice President and Executive Publisher
Neil Edde

Associate Publisher
Jim Minatel

Project Coordinator, Cover
Katie Crocker

Compositor
Jeff Wilson,
Happenstance Type-O-Rama

Proofreader
Nancy Carrasco

Indexer
Johnna VanHoose Dinse

Cover Image
© Goodshot / Jupiter Images

Cover Designer
Ryan Sneed

About the Author

Ron Person is a Sr. Consultant for Business Optimization for Sitecore. Sitecore is recognized as the innovation leader in software that helps organizations engage customers with online and offline marketing. Ron continues to use processes described in the first sections of this book to help Sitecore's partners and customers reach their business objectives.

In the 27 years prior to joining Sitecore Ron helped organizations create a competitive advantage through strategic execution and a culture of high-performance.

Ron worked with mid-sized organizations with revenues of $25 to $500 million. His clients in the United States and internationally have included hospitals, banks, biotech companies, medical device manufacturers, and financial services firms, spanning a diversity of organizations such as:

- Medtronic CardioVascular
- Bethanie Group (Western Australia's largest elder care and hospital system)
- Wells Fargo Center for the Arts
- U.S. Army Corps of Engineers
- U.S. Naval Undersea Warfare Center

Prior to consulting in performance improvement Ron has been:

- A manager of competitive analysis for a Fortune 500 corporation
- One of Microsoft's first twelve consulting partners
- The founder or co-founder of four companies, two of them high-tech
- The author of 26 business and computer books, including four international bestsellers with almost 4 million copies in print

He has personally conducted workshops for thousands of business people and has spoken before conferences and groups such as Vistage (the world's leading Chief Executive organization), Microsoft technical conferences, the American Society for Quality, APICS (the Association for Operations Managers), the Project Management Institute, PIHRA (the Professionals in Human Resources Association), and the American Association of Homes and Services for the Aging.

Ron's education and credentials include:

- Certification by the Balanced Scorecard Collaborative, the educational division of the founders of Balanced Scorecard, Drs. Kaplan and Norton. Only a few independent consultants each year pass this rigorous training and examination.

- Member of the California Awards for Performance Excellence™ Board of Examiners, 2008 (California's Malcolm Baldridge award for excellence in organizational performance)

- A Six Sigma Black Belt

- An M.B.A. in marketing and finance with highest honors

- An M.S. in physics

- Training as a facilitator for strategic planning by the Institute for Cultural Affairs and the Center for Strategic Facilitation

Ron supports his readers and subscribers through his website **Critical To Success** at www.criticaltosuccess.com. His website is dedicated to helping business owners, managers, and professionals improve their personal and organizational performance. Ron's website contains:

- Tips
- Tricks
- Tools
- Techniques
- Tutorials
- Toolkits

About the Technical Editors

Jim Coffey has lead Strategy and Strategy Execution engagements using the Balanced Scorecard for a wide variety of public and private sector clients, including the US Army, the FBI, FedEx, Crown Castle, and the USC LA County Hospital. In addition to his strategy work, Jim does executive coaching and organizational development consulting to help organizations successfully navigate the cultural aspects of strategy execution.

Previously, Jim was a manager with PricewaterhouseCoopers (PwC). While there, he led numerous project teams responsible for process reengineering, cost estimates, and market competitive analysis. Prior to PwC, he worked in the power industry as a nuclear power plant performance evaluator with the Institute of Nuclear Power Operations and as a start-up engineer with General Electric Nuclear.

As a result, Jim has:

- Over twenty years of experience supervising personnel, managing multiple diverse technical programs with budgetary, planning, and customer interface responsibility

- Over fifteen years' experience in organizational strategy management and performance improvement efforts using Balanced Scorecard/Strategic Performance Measurement System methodologies; including managing, aligning and linking multiple organizational performance projects and initiatives

- Extensive experience using automated, web-based Balanced Scorecard Collaborative/Strategic Performance Measurement certified applications and tools for scorecard development and reporting

Education: MBA from the University of Chicago; Bachelor of Science in Engineering from The Ohio State University

Michael Alexander is a Microsoft Certified Application Developer (MCAD) and author of several books on advanced business analysis with Microsoft Access and Excel. He has more than 16 years of experience consulting and developing Office solutions. Michael has been named a Microsoft MVP for his ongoing contributions to the Excel community. Visit him at www.datapigtechnologies.com.

Acknowledgments

With the second edition of this book I continue to realize how we help each other expand our knowledge, improve our lives, and improve our world. I am very grateful for the opportunity to have worked with so many outstanding people. It is to the many high energy, hardworking, and spirited people I've worked with that I dedicate this book.

I want to thank Michael Seifert, CEO of Sitecore, and Lars Petersen, Head of Sitecore's Business Optimization Services for the opportunity to work with a global group of dynamic, intelligent people who are changing the way the world does business.

James Coffey deserves praise for not just reviewing the sections on strategy and Balanced Scorecard, but also for adding depth that comes from his years of experience in Balanced Scorecard consulting and working for the Palladium Group, Drs. Kaplan and Norton's consultancy.

Michael Alexander had the difficult job of reviewing the technical sections that covered three versions of Excel. His experience added to those sections. Michael's expertise in Excel and Access is visible in his books for John Wiley & Sons as well as his consulting website, DataPig Technologies.

Having been a consultant for almost 30 years, I realize that one of the responsibilities of a consultant is collecting and filtering ideas that help clients, and then putting the best ones into practice in ways that make them productive and beneficial. There are many people and sources who have built the foundation of the ideas presented in this book. Here are a few I would like to thank.

Thank you to Drs. Kaplan and Norton of the Palladium Group for furthering the advancement of management science with Balanced Scorecards and Strategy Maps.

Each year, a few consultants complete the Balanced Scorecard certification program delivered through the Balanced Scorecard Collaborative, the educational division of the Palladium Group. Thank you to Edward A. Barrows, Jr., independent consultant and former Vice President of Balanced Scorecard Collaborative, a Palladium company, and Karen A. DiMartino, Manager, Advisory Services, for conducting excellent Balanced Scorecard certification programs.

The consulting profession can often be lonely, and the opportunities to develop our professional skills are neglected as we help clients and spend time with family. Many people have committed extra time to developing the professional skills of consultants, and we consultants owe them a debt of gratitude. Throughout the years I've enjoyed their camaraderie and shared learning. A few of these people in northern California are:

- Harry Chapman, Bay Area Consulting Group, founder of the Bay Area Consultants Network
- Rogene Baxter, the Bridgewater Group, former president of the Institute of Management Consultants, Northern California Chapter
- Jane Stallman, Center for Strategic Facilitation

After having written more than 20 books, I wasn't sure I wanted to write again, but working with a great team from Wiley Publishing has made it easy to get back in the saddle. Thanks to:

- Jim Minatel, Associate Publisher, for proposing and expanding on the second edition
- Carol Long, Executive Editor, for working out all the business details
- Sydney Jones Argenta, Project Editor, for being so easy to work with while maintaining an even flow of work. She seemed to magically make the work flow.

There have been many people who have reviewed this book, but the responsibility for accuracy and the descriptions of real-world business solutions lie with me. If you, the reader, find an error or something about which you have a question, please contact me through www.criticaltosuccess.com.

To Your Best Performance,

Ron

Contents

Introduction

This book is a guide to how your organization can create a competitive advantage by successfully executing strategy and accelerating performance. You must begin with a vision held by and communicated through leadership to every employee. That vision is achieved when employees work in concert, knowing how they contribute to strategic success and operational performance. A Strategy Map and Balanced Scorecard are the tools you need to gather the information that shows you how you can achieve strategic success. Operational maps and operational dashboards are the tools and measures that show you how to accelerate operational success.

Since I wrote the first edition of this book, the world has undergone significant change. With continued globalization and the global recession, it's even more apparent that winning organizations possess two attributes. They must be flexible enough to pivot in new directions, and they must focus on their core strategic strengths:

- Winning organizations continually monitor their performance and are willing to pivot with a better strategy. To monitor their performance, they need operational dashboards that measure the Critical Few operational metrics specific to their organization.

- Winning organizations must focus their people, processes, and technology. To do that, they need a Balanced Scorecard that helps the organization stay aligned with its core strategic strengths.

As I move between organizations of all types, I am continuously amazed at the cultural differences between winners and those that just get by. The culture I see in winning organizations is one of high energy, proactive execution, and continuous learning. In general, everyone is aligned with the key strategic and operational objectives. When an effort works, it's leveraged. When an effort doesn't work, time isn't spent on blaming. Instead, everyone works to improve performance. This attitude comes from the leadership and the people, but the tools that identify performance are operational dashboards and Balanced Scorecards.

I enjoy, and am continually heartened by, the 10 to 20 e-mails per week from readers. Among these is the occasional request for a list of generic metrics. This piques my curiosity, because one of my main reasons for writing this book was to emphasize the importance of the Critical Few objectives and metrics. The Critical Few are specific to your organization. The best way I've found to identify them is to use the group brainstorming and mapping processes described in this book. Don't pick metrics from a generic list! Use the processes described here to identify the Critical Few objectives, identify their drivers and success measures, and then look for metrics to measure their performance.

After 30 years as a road warrior consultant, I have amassed a huge performance-improvement toolkit. I want to share with as many people and organizations as possible this collection of tips, tools, and techniques. If you'd like to benefit from this collection, I welcome you to. Go to `http://www.criticaltosuccess.com`.

To your best performance!

Ron

Success through Strategic Execution and Accelerating Operational Performance

Business horror stories repeat themselves. We've all seen the numbers that define the stories:

- 90 percent of corporate strategies fail to achieve their expected results.

- 80 percent of projects are late or over budget.

- 70 percent of mergers fail to exceed the value of the original companies.

Those are pretty uncomfortable statistics. On the other hand, some organizations succeed well beyond expectations. One famous bank merger achieved a 19-fold profit increase in three years. One hotel chain increased its profit margin 3 percent over the industry average in three years. What is the difference between the terrible failures and the huge successes?

Whether at the macro level of executing your strategy and aligning your company or at the micro level of creating a project team that meets deadlines, a few core principles remain the same:

- Create a "burning platform" that moves people away from business as usual.

- Identify the objectives most critical to success.

- Define the initiatives that will make those objectives succeed.
- Select the Critical Few metrics that track performance and alignment.
- Create a culture of measurable high performance while breaking down silos.
- Maintain and sustain the high-performance culture.

Some of my clients who have been through the processes described in this book have said the following:

- "Our leadership team had the best strategic discussions they have ever had."
- "The budget process was significantly easier than in any previous year."
- "This process is changing our entire culture to keep up with our high growth."

Who This Book Will Help

This book is built to be a practical guide; it doesn't contain much theory. Many other books describe theory and case studies for Balanced Scorecards, Six Sigma, Lean, and other performance-improvement methods. This book is intended to be a guide for the people who take action. It will help you map your future, identify the Critical Few metrics, implement the Balanced Scorecard, and create operational dashboards.

This book has three different audiences: the executive sponsor or operations manager, facilitators and consultants, and software developers.

Executive Sponsor

Balanced Scorecards and performance-improvement programs don't succeed without an executive sponsor. Members of the executive leadership team and the senior managers who are team leaders should scan Parts I and II of this book to understand the time frames and commitments involved in creating success.

Members of the executive leadership team who have heard the term Balanced Scorecard may not know what it takes to drive strategic success with a Balanced Scorecard. They can scan Part I to see what is involved. It takes time and commitment from the executive leadership team.

Two telephone calls from senior managers remind me that many do not know what is involved in creating a Balanced Scorecard or how it affects an organization when implemented correctly. In one call, the manager said, "We're having a two-day corporate retreat for the executive leadership team. Could you do a Balanced Scorecard for us in two hours?"

Another call illustrated the business buzzword effect. It was from a manager whose division executive had heard about a Balanced Scorecard being used at a pharmaceutical competitor. He had been assigned to put together a Balanced Scorecard for the division within the next week.

Neither of these cases had executive commitment or the time frames necessary to create a Balanced Scorecard that drives success and creates a culture of high performance.

Facilitators and Consultants

Facilitators and consultants are vital to creating a Balanced Scorecard or operational dashboard. They are the guides who help the executive leadership team and managers through sticky spots. When discussions get too easy because no one is asking the hard questions, the facilitator must be able to step in and ask probing questions that put a tough issue in the spotlight so that it will be addressed. It is imperative, especially in the case of strategic Balanced Scorecards, to have a consultant who has no agenda and who is politically impartial.

Software Developers

The majority of Balanced Scorecards and operational dashboards are created in Microsoft Excel. You don't need to be an Excel Visual Basic guru to build them when you know the correct combination of worksheet functions. Part III describes most of the building blocks for creating and maintaining powerful scorecards and dashboards.

BUILD A SCORECARD OR DASHBOARD YOU CAN MAINTAIN

Part III covers the methods and tools necessary for building powerful decision-making aids in three different versions of Excel. But there is more to building them than just a few techniques. Make sure your Excel developer knows how to build systems that can be easily maintained and updated. Whether you use an internal or external developer, make sure he or she documents the system and shows others how to maintain it.

Additional skills the software developer needs are the ability to interview users to discover their needs, understand what is critical in a business process, design user interfaces, build maintainable architectures, and integrate live data.

How This Book Is Organized

This book has three parts. Part I covers the steps and processes required for building a Balanced Scorecard to execute strategy. Part II introduces the basics of mapping operational processes and identifying critical metrics. Part III shows intermediate-to-advanced Excel users techniques specific to creating dashboards.

Part I

Part I describes the journey of building and rolling out the Strategy Map and Balanced Scorecard. It is used by over 50 percent of Fortune 1000 companies and more than 70 percent of international corporations. It begins with an overview of the tools commonly used to develop organizational strategy. A chapter is devoted to building the Strategy Map, the diagram that visually defines the strategic themes on which the organization will focus and the objectives that will drive success. The next chapter describes how the Strategy Map must be converted into an action plan that details the initiatives to reach success and the metrics required to keep those initiatives on track and on time. Once the metrics are defined, the Balanced Scorecard can be developed and used—not just as a dashboard for strategic progress, but as a core mechanism to guide ongoing strategy meetings. The last chapter of Part I describes some of the communication and rollout processes necessary to communicate the change.

Part II

The three chapters in Part II describe a few methods of mapping operations. These include process maps and economic value maps, as well as how to use them to identify the Critical Few metrics that drive an operation and measure its success.

Part III

Part III gives many specific examples of how to use Excel 2003, 2007, and 2010 to build Balanced Scorecards and operational dashboards. Excel is the most widely used business analysis and graphics tool in the world; the majority of Balanced Scorecards and operational dashboards in the world are built using Excel. Scorecards and dashboards in Excel do not need to use Visual Basic for Applications, but they do need a good architecture, and they require a few little-known worksheet functions.

Free Resources That Extend This Book

There is much more to executing strategy and creating high performance than will fit in this book. You can find newsletters, articles, tools, video demonstrations, and software at http://www.criticaltosuccess.com.

Download Free Excel Sample Files

The Excel training examples featured in Part III are available for free download. Go to my website or the publisher's website:

    http://www.criticaltosuccess.com

    http://www.wiley.com/go/scorecardsanddashboardswithexcel2E

Free Balanced Scorecard and Operational Dashboard Tips, Tools, and Tutorials

Staying ahead of the competition and keeping your organization performing at its highest level is an ongoing process. To get a jump start on improving your execution and performance advantage, go to http://www.criticaltosuccess .com for additional tips, tools, tutorials, and videos.

While you are at the Critical To Success website, be sure to sign up for the newsletter. It will keep you up to date with the best tips to help you grow as a business owner, manager, or professional.

Videos and Online Tutorials

No book can convey all the lessons learned through years of experience. Some processes and techniques are just too difficult to convey completely in text. And many tips, templates, and toolkits just can't fit in this book.

To learn more about the video and online tutorials to help you and your organization improve, go to http://www.criticaltosuccess.com.

Part

I

Strategic Performance with Balanced Scorecards

In This Part

Accelerating Strategic Performance

The essence of strategy is choosing what not to do.
—**Michael Porter**

The rate of change in the business world is accelerating. To get ahead—in fact, just to keep up—organizations of all types must accelerate their strategic performance.

They have to work with better performance, more precise focus, and better strategic alignment. For this to happen, all parts of the organization must clearly understand and be firmly aligned with strategic goals.

In the last two decades, a strategic management system has been developed that enables organizations to achieve the clarity and alignment necessary to accelerate strategic performance. That system is the Balanced Scorecard.

Managing with a 500-Year-Old System

Until recently, organizations have used the same accounting system to track assets and value production that was used 500 years ago in Venice, Italy. In 1494, Fra Luca Pacioli, Franciscan monk and friend of Leonardo da Vinci, wrote *Everything about Arithmetic, Geometry, and Proportions* (see Figure 1.1). It was the first best-selling business book to come off of Gutenberg's printing press.

Luca Pacioli's Portrait, Gallery of Museum of Capodimonte, Naples

Figure 1.1: Over 500 years ago, Fra Luca Pacioli, on the left, documented the double-entry accounting system we still use today.

What made his book a best-seller throughout Europe was that it contained detailed instructions on how the merchants of Venice kept their accounts using double-entry accounting. The book included sections on

- Modern accounting cycles
- Double-entry accounting
- Journals and ledgers
- Assets, liabilities, capital, income, and expenses
- Closing
- Trial balances

The book blazed through the halls of commerce in Europe because, for the first time, it gave business people a way to value their tangible assets and measure how they were producing value. But what is surprising is that we still use the same accounting system used by the merchants of Venice 500 years ago.

The Failure of Modern Management Systems

Research by Margaret Blair of the Brookings Institute into the market value of corporations listed in the Compustat database shows that the market value of U.S. corporations has shifted significantly from tangible to intangible assets. As shown in Table 1.1, in the ten years from 1982 to 1992, the contribution of intangible assets to market value rose from 32 percent to 68 percent. Subsequent studies from multiple sources estimate that since 1998, intangible assets' contribution to corporate value is approximately 85 percent.[1]

Table 1.1: The Growth of Intangible Asset Contribution to Corporate Value

YEAR	INTANGIBLE ASSETS	TANGIBLE ASSETS
1982	32%	68%
1992	68%	32%
1998	85%	15%

More recent research reflected in the Ocean Tomo 300 Patent Index shows that 80 percent of the market value of companies in the United States' Standard & Poor's 500 Index is due to intangible assets for the period from 2005 to 2010.

How can intangible assets such as people, processes, patents, and data be monitored and managed effectively using a 500-year-old system designed for use with tangible assets?

Ram Charan, international consultant and coauthor of *Execution*,[2] wrote an article in *Fortune* magazine titled "Why CEOs Fail." In writing about highly experienced, well-known CEOs who lead their companies into failure, he said, "In the majority of cases—we estimate 70 percent—the real problem isn't the high-concept boners the boffins love to talk about. It's bad execution."[3]

Charan goes on to write that most CEOs are hard-working, experienced, brilliant people. His research found one problem common to all the failures:

> *Yes, strategy matters. A good, clear strategy is necessary for success—but not sufficient for survival. So look again at all those derailed CEOs on the cover [of the magazine]. They're smart people who worried deeply about a lot of things. They just weren't worrying enough about the right things: execution, decisiveness, follow-through, delivering on commitments.*

So executives and managers face two serious problems. First, the source of value production has switched from tangible assets that can be monitored with current accounting systems to intangible assets that are difficult to manage. Second, most corporations fail at executing their strategy.

A Modern Strategic Management System

In 1992 Harvard professor Robert Kaplan and consultant David Norton published the article "The Balanced Scorecard—Measures that Drive Performance" in the *Harvard Business Review*.[4] The ideas in this article sowed the seeds of a strategic management system to translate strategy into action, to monitor strategic execution, and to align organizations around strategy.

Initial attempts to use the Balanced Scorecard seemed to either propel organizations to success or burden them with administrative overhead and dismal results. The difference between failure and success was often in the selection of metrics used to measure strategic execution. In 2000, Kaplan and Norton published another article in the *Harvard Business Review* titled "Having Trouble with Your Strategy? Then Map It."[5] This article outlined how to build a visual map that shows the objectives and causal links necessary to execute a strategy. These causal links enabled executives to identify the key metrics that drive success. These two ideas, the Strategy Map and the Balanced Scorecard, combined with more recent developments, have built a strategic management system that is an important part of modern business management.

The Strategy Map represents how an organization will execute its strategy. The Strategy Map shows the objectives needed to execute the strategy and the causal links between objectives. The Strategy Map is a tool for clear communication and helps identify the "critical few" metrics to monitor strategic execution. You can learn more about Strategy Maps in Chapter 4.

The Balanced Scorecard is part of a system that translates strategy into action. The Balanced Scorecard gives a balanced view in four perspectives of how well an organization is driving execution and how successful the results are. The four perspectives in the Balanced Scorecard and Strategy Map give executives a more balanced view of their organizations. They go beyond financial measures to include finance, customer and marketplace, internal operations, and learning and growth. These categories include people, culture, intellectual property, and IT infrastructure.

The Strategy Map and Balanced Scorecard can take one to three years to fully implement in an organization, but the results can be impressive. A Balanced Scorecard helps you do the following:

- **Clarify strategy.** The discussions and thought that go into developing the Strategy Map bring clarity and understanding to the executive team in terms of the strategy and interplay between departmental silos. The graphical Strategy Map pinpoints for employees how they contribute to strategic success.

- **Translate strategy into action and execute it.** The Strategy Map, combined with an Action Plan and Implementation Plan, give everyone a clear road map showing how the strategy will be translated into action. The Balanced Scorecard is used to stay on track and to monitor execution.

- **Align business units around the strategy.** Most organizations develop "silos," functional departments or divisions that are more concerned with their own success than they are with achieving success for the entire organization. But developing the Strategy Map and Action Plan requires that the walls between silos come down. Focusing on Strategic Themes that cross functional boundaries forces departments to work together, breaking down silos even more.

- **Communicate the strategy to all levels.** The process of cascading the Balanced Scorecard through the organization gives each level the opportunity to contribute to organizational success. It allows executives to communicate with functional managers about how to achieve strategic goals. It allows functional managers to provide feedback to executives about capability and capacity.

- **Monitor and manage strategic execution.** Research has shown that most executive staff members spend less than 10 percent of their time monitoring strategy and execution. Instead of leading through strategy, executive staff members often become embroiled in operational performance, something better left to managers. Using the Balanced Scorecard as an agenda gives executive meetings a central focus on strategic leadership.

Why Use a Balanced Scorecard?

Building a Strategy Map and Balanced Scorecard for an organization follows much the same process as taking a trip to a specific location. To take a trip you need to do the following:

- Select a destination.
- Agree on the type of trip.
- Agree on the route.
- Map the route.
- Plan time and resources.
- Travel.
- Stay on course.

Leading a business in our high-speed world isn't that different from flying a jet. Imagine boarding a small jet, pausing at the entry, and asking the pilot a few questions:

You: "What is our destination?"

Pilot: "The crew got together and talked about a destination. We couldn't agree, so we decided to go somewhere out West. If something better comes up while we're en route, we might change direction."

You: "What route will we be taking?" (Maybe I'll still go. It sounds adventurous, although it could be a waste of time and fuel. It shouldn't be too dangerous.)

Pilot: "Well, we aren't sure about the exact route, but I've been that general direction before, so I don't need maps. I'm experienced."

You: "I notice that your cockpit dashboard seems a bit sparse. There aren't any flight instruments—just stacks of paper. How will you monitor the flight?" (This is starting to sound a bit iffy. The pilot may be experienced, but how will she communicate her experience to the copilot, the flight engineer, the flight attendants, the ground crew, other aircraft, and the Federal Aviation Administration?)

Pilot: "Well, we're comfortable with the detail of printed reports. While we're in flight, I can request a short stack of printed reports that tell me the airspeed, altitude, attitude, and heading. The copilot gets a larger stack with operational data about radio settings, fuel, hydraulics, and technical details. We have to ask for the data, but it takes only a few minutes to get new reports. So we're in pretty good shape as long as everything stays stable and we don't have mechanical, weather, or crew problems."

You: "Sounds like quite an adventure you're about to embark on. Sorry I won't be able to go with you."

This metaphor isn't that far from how some organizations manage. Many start-ups and high-tech companies define their strategy as going after "targets of opportunity." I've actually heard executives of high-tech start-ups proclaim that having a strategy puts up boundaries. They feel their business changes too fast for any type of strategy. This seems especially true for companies making the organizational leap from small company (less than $50 million) to big company (over $100 million).

It is possible to be agile while having strategic objectives that cement the organization. For example, Eric Ries in his book *The Lean Startup* (Crown Business, 2011) describes the concept of Minimum Viable Product that evolves with agile adaptation to customer needs. At market failure points the lean startup method demands that a business pivot in a new direction. But nowhere does that prevent a business from having an overarching strategy and objectives. In fact, objectives such as minimum viable products, agile development, and pivots can be critical strategic objectives in themselves. They are objectives on which you want to build a culture. Without the use of strategic and operational dashboards to monitor customer and development metrics, high-tech companies can drive themselves crazy chasing customers and wasting resources.

Although the idea of a pilot flying by referring only to printed reports seems outlandish, consider how many organizations manage while looking only at financial reports. Financials show only lagging results from efforts that may be from months before. Doing this is almost the same as flying using printed reports alone.

Recent research confirms that executives and managers with over ten years' experience in an industry can have a good gut instinct for making decisions, but how can they communicate that gut instinct to the hundreds or thousands of people they must lead and manage? How can employees and managers without such experience understand the strategy and make good decisions?

The Strategy Map gives an organization an excellent visual tool to explain what is important for strategic success and how and where in the strategy each employee contributes. Executives and managers at multiple levels can use the Balanced Scorecard to monitor whether they are actually driving strategic success. If the results aren't happening as planned, the Strategy Map, Strategic Objectives, and Balanced Scorecard need to be revised until the organization has a valid model of what works.

Building a Balanced Scorecard

The activities for planning a trip listed in the preceding section correspond to similar activities in building a Strategy Map and Balanced Scorecard, as shown in Table 1.2.

Table 1.2: Building a Balanced Scorecard Is a Journey

TRAVEL	BALANCED SCORECARD	INTENT
Select a destination.	Destination Statement	State in one page what your organization wants to be at the end of your strategic horizon.
Agree on the type of trip.	Strategic Themes	Your trip's journey might have a theme of speed or low cost. Your Balanced Scorecard might have Strategic Themes such as customer intimacy or operational excellence. How you execute your Strategic Themes differentiates you from your competitors.

Continued

Table 1.2 *(continued)*

TRAVEL	BALANCED SCORECARD	INTENT
Agree on the route.	Executive and Division Alignment	Leaders, managers, and employees must all be going in the same direction.
Map the route.	Strategy Map	Identify the route and objectives that will get you to your destination.
Plan time and resources.	Action Plan and Implementation Plan	Identify the measures, metrics, and initiatives, and who is accountable.
Travel.	Prioritize, budget, and act	Execute the strategy.
Stay on course.	Balanced Scorecard	Monitor your Balanced Scorecard to make sure your organization is on track.

Does the Balanced Scorecard Guarantee Business Success?

No killer methodology guarantees success in business. The Strategy Map and Balanced Scorecard do not guarantee success. Organizations can still fail by having the wrong strategy, by having a poorly built Strategy Map and Balanced Scorecard, by failing to use the Balanced Scorecard after it is implemented, or by failing to modify the Balanced Scorecard if their hypothesis of what works is wrong.

I occasionally meet consultants and executives who proclaim, "We tried a Balanced Scorecard and it didn't work." Their perception may be true. Some research shows that approximately 30 percent of Balanced Scorecard attempts fail.

There are many reasons for failure, and the Balanced Scorecard fails in companies for a variety of reasons. Here are some of the most common:

▪ **Lack of senior executive commitment:** An executive at the highest level in the strategic business unit must sponsor the Balanced Scorecard. Without the commitment of the senior executive, managers and employees feel that the Balanced Scorecard is just another "management fad of the month." The senior executive must make a case for change in the organization that will light a fire under everyone.

- **Lack of a case for change:** Organizations are difficult to change. The Balanced Scorecard is used to create a culture of high performance, translating strategy into action. Without a driving need for change, and an organization-wide awareness of the need, the Balanced Scorecard will become just another performance management system that will fade.

- **Lack of an experienced consultant or facilitator:** Developing and implementing a Balanced Scorecard is difficult. It is critical to use an experienced facilitator or consultant to guide initial development and to train internal facilitators and managers who can carry on the work. You are betting the strategic success of your organization on this effort. You don't want to use a general business consultant who has read a book or a *Harvard Business Review* article on Balanced Scorecards. There are many traps to avoid, and you want someone who knows how to do so.

- **Too many metrics:** Too many metrics can create a confusing model of what drives strategic success. The Balanced Scorecard becomes an Operational Dashboard.

- **The wrong metrics:** Using the wrong metrics drives performance in the wrong direction.

- **Fear of measurement:** People in some organizations fear being measured. This fear could stem from many different causes, some of them valid. The way to approach this fear is that the Balanced Scorecard and operational performance are not there to identify and punish the poor performers. Rather, they are there to identify high performance and share the best practices that created the high performance. Handling this depends on the skill and practices of management.

- **Too long to develop:** Taking too long drains motivation and results in the loss of key resources and momentum.

- **Cultural mismatch:** Organizations with a cultural norm of low performance or organizations with dictatorial executives require a major cultural change before implementing a Balanced Scorecard.

Some executives and consultants have asked me if the Balanced Scorecard replaces Six Sigma, if it's more productive than Lean, or if it coordinates projects better than a Project Management Office. A Balanced Scorecard does not replace any of these. It works as a strategic management system that acts as an envelope to keep Six Sigma and Lean projects aligned with strategy. It works with accounting, budgeting, and the Project Management Office to optimize them for the organization, rather than just for individual silos.

Some organizational cultures just don't work well with a Balanced Scorecard. For example, some nonprofits, such as hospitals, work well with Balanced

Scorecards and can use them to significantly increase their efficiency and performance. Other nonprofits, such as social service organizations, seem to have a great deal of difficulty working with measures and metrics. Often this is because they feel they provide intangible benefits, which are not measurable. Some for-profit high-tech companies, especially start-ups, feel that their business changes too rapidly to have any strategy. Their strategy is to go after any opportunity. Other for-profit high-tech companies, such as medical device manufacturers, have a focus that benefits greatly from a Balanced Scorecard.

I've seen organizations that have a cultural mismatch with a Balanced Scorecard and have no desire to change. Some of these organizations seem to have a culture of self-inflicted low performance. In particular, one director of an umbrella social services organization comes to mind. As part of a group of pro bono senior consultants, I volunteered to help the organization increase productivity and manage staffing problems. When our pro bono group presented our findings, along with numerous no-cost and low-cost solutions, the director scolded us: "We are here to help people. We are not your Silicon Valley corporation concerned with measuring, planning, and performance." Those of us on the consulting team who gathered later for an After-Action Review felt sad for the organization's young clients. The director had the attitude that her organization couldn't increase performance and care for people at the same time. By enabling low performance under her management, she was abandoning many children who might have gotten a head start on education. Low performance with no desire to change meant that many low-income families weren't being served by the health and education clinic under her control.

Does the Balanced Scorecard Really Work?

The now-famous quote "What gets measured gets done" is most often attributed to management guru Peter Drucker. Although it seems to be an obvious truth, a more direct proof of the value of Balanced Scorecards is their acceptance and use among corporations worldwide. Bain & Company, an international consulting firm, does an annual survey on management tools among its 6,200-plus large corporate clients. Approximately 50 percent of the surveyed clients use a Balanced Scorecard, with an almost 80 percent satisfaction level. This makes the Balanced Scorecard one of the most widely used strategic tools and places it within the cluster of tools that garner high levels of satisfaction.

Although the Bain & Company survey shows the pervasive use of the Balanced Scorecard, many organizations don't talk much about their success to the press. But successes that have been publicized cover a wide range of industries:

- Duke Children's Hospital reduced costs by $30 million and increased net margin by $50 million in two to three years while increasing patient and staff satisfaction.

- Delta Dental of Kansas, the largest dental benefits provider in the state, is a 90-employee company that saw its revenues jump from $63 million in 2001 to $172 million in 2006 (a 173 percent increase) while increasing employees' satisfaction with and understanding of their jobs.[6]

- Crown Castle International, the world's largest owner of telecom infrastructure, needed a strategic shift from its acquisition strategy in 2001 to a strategy of operational excellence in 2003. Even as its competitors faced meltdown, it saw cash flow rise from a negative $300 million to a positive $100 million, and its stock price beat market indices by more than 300 percent.[7]

- Keycorp, one of the nation's largest bank financial services organizations, has cascaded its four strategic themes through all 19,000 employees.[8] The Key Corporate and Investment Banking Group (KCIB) improved its return on equity (ROE) by 28.8 percent in three years, and its vendor satisfaction ratings also improved. In three years, its ratings went from 45–74 percent to 86–93 percent.

Do Small and Midsized Businesses Benefit from the Balanced Scorecard?

Executives of small and midsized businesses (SMBs) may have the impression that the Strategy Maps and Balanced Scorecards are for large corporations only. Actually, small and midsized businesses may find that Balanced Scorecards are easier for them to implement and that the payoff comes quicker. Of the Balanced Scorecard Hall of Fame winners, 20 percent are small and midsized businesses.

SMBs may have even more to gain from Strategy Maps and Balanced Scorecards than large organizations because of their limited resources. SMBs in particular have to make sure that they focus their efforts, provide better services, and drop projects that aren't aligned with strategy. The Balanced Scorecard is designed to align an organization around a focus and to make it easier to identify projects that aren't within that focus.

Communication and decision-making within SMBs can improve as well. With fewer layers of management and fewer employees, a Strategy Map makes communication even easier and faster. Also, strategic issues can come to light faster when the Balanced Scorecard is incorporated into normal executive team meetings.

Many SMBs are opportunity-driven. SMBs providing high value in growing niches will see opportunity everywhere. Maintaining a focused strategic direction can be as difficult as walking a kid in a straight line through a toy store. This is where a Balanced Scorecard can help. In the article "Why the BSC Is

Just as Effective for Small and Medium-Sized Firms," Tom Lefebvre, director of Strategic Planning for the Alaska Native Tribal Health Consortium (ANTHC), says that the Balanced Scorecard "has provided a framework that has created absolute clarity of our strategy and ultimate vision." Because of the Balanced Scorecard, ANTHC has increased its cash flow and has seen an 80 percent drop in nursing turnover.[9]

Strategic plans in all organizations usually become far too complex to implement. This is where the Balanced Scorecard can help. By working through the Balanced Scorecard process, from Strategy Map to Balanced Scorecard to Action Plan to Implementation Plan, it becomes obvious which initiatives and projects contribute to strategy and how they must be scheduled and budgeted over time.

The work of developing a Balanced Scorecard is intense in an SMB in which everyone wears multiple hats. This is where an experienced consultant can help facilitators and managers get up to speed quickly and reduce the burden. Write-ups from the Balanced Scorecard Hall of Fame winners show that the first year of development is hard work, the second year gets easier, and the third year is even easier—with benefits coming in.

Is the Balanced Scorecard Worth Developing?

Is the Balanced Scorecard worth developing in your organization? It takes dedication and work, but ask yourself these questions:

- Would we be more successful if the executive team focused more on strategic leadership and less on operational problems?
- Would we be more successful if our executives and managers used Strategy Maps as a forum to constructively breach the walls between silos?
- Would our managers be more knowledgeable about what drives their business if they had to define the critical few metrics that drive and measure success?
- Would our employees be more proactive and satisfied if they understood how they affect strategic success?

If your answers to these questions are yes—if changes such as these would increase the success of your organization and its people—you should find out how you can implement your Balanced Scorecard.

Summary

The rate of change in the world of business is accelerating. The only way for organizations to succeed is to execute their strategy. If your organization wants to succeed, you have to translate your strategy into action, aligning your organization with strategic objectives and making sure that every employee knows how he or she contributes to strategic success. The most powerful tools you can find for building a culture of high performance are the Strategy Map and Balanced Scorecard. Creating them and building a high-performance culture isn't easy, but it is a journey that can lead to organizational success.

Notes

1. M. Blair, *Ownership and Control: Rethinking Corporate Governance for the Twenty-First Century* (Washington, D.C.: Brookings Institution, 1995).

2. L. Bossidy and R. Charan, *Execution: The Discipline of Getting Things Done* (New York, New York: Crown Business, 2002).

3. R. Charan and G. Colvin, "Why CEOs Fail," *Fortune* 139, no. 12 (June 21, 1999).

4. R. Kaplan and D. Norton, "The Balanced Scorecard—Measures that Drive Performance," *Harvard Business Review*, January 1992.

5. R. Kaplan and D. Norton, "Having Trouble with Your Strategy? Then Map It," *Harvard Business Review*, September 2000.

6. Delta Dental of Kansas, "Balanced Scorecard Hall of Fame Report 2007," Harvard Business School Publishing and Balanced Scorecard Collaborative, 2007: 17.

7. Crown Castle International, "The Balanced Scorecard Hall of Fame Profile Series," Harvard Business School Publishing and Balanced Scorecard Collaborative, 2005.

8. "KeyCorp Honors Its Top Technology Suppliers," Actuate Corporation, February 26, 2004, http://www.actuate.com/company/news.

9. M. Bognanno, "Why the BSC Is Just as Effective for Small and Medium-Sized Firms," *Balanced Scorecard Report*, January–February 2008.

CHAPTER 2

Developing Your Strategic Foundation

Plans are nothing; planning is everything.
—Dwight D. Eisenhower

The most widely used management tool is strategic planning. Bain & Company, an international consulting firm, does an annual survey of more than 8,000 international clients. Since the early 1990s, this survey has shown strategic planning to be one of the most frequently used and highly rated management tools.

Before you can begin developing a Balanced Scorecard, you must start with a strategic foundation. For most organizations this foundation has the following components:

- Mission, vision, and values
- Assessment of internal and external environment
- Strategy formulation
- Strategic Destination Statement

Any search of Amazon.com will point you to many books on business strategy. This topic has at least 10 schools of thought, and most business executives have their own preferences and opinions that guide their development of strategy. Because so much information on strategic planning is available, this chapter won't attempt to describe how you should formulate your own business strategy. But it gives you some background on the basic tools needed for developing strategy in preparation for your Balanced Scorecard.

You must remember one thing as you develop your strategy: What differentiates you from your competition is how well you execute your strategy. You may develop a great strategy, but it will fail if you can't, or don't, execute it. The Balanced Scorecard is your tool for strategic execution.

Developing Your Strategic Foundation

The members of the executive leadership team are the leaders of your organization. The leadership team should lay the company's foundation by defining its mission, vision, and values.

Most business people recognize the need for an organization to have a mission, vision, and values, but confusion often results over what these elements are. You know confusion is present when it is hard to tell the difference between the three. Descriptions about beliefs and values show up in a vision statement, and descriptions of an organization's future appear in a mission statement.

Lacking clarity in your mission, vision, and values makes it difficult to create a successful strategy. Alice and the Cheshire Cat discussed the reasons for knowing where you want to go in Lewis Carroll's *Alice's Adventures in Wonderland*:

"Would you tell me, please, which way I ought to go from here?"

"That depends a good deal on where you want to get to," said the Cat.

"I don't much care where—," said Alice.

"Then it doesn't matter which way you go," said the Cat.

"—so long as I get SOMEWHERE," Alice added as an explanation.

"Oh, you're sure to do that," said the Cat.

If you want your organization to achieve a specific future goal, create clear and concise mission, vision, and value statements. You also need a clear, concise, and precisely quantified Strategic Destination Statement, which is described near the end of this chapter.

To keep your mission, vision, and values clear and concise, use these questions as clarifiers:

Mission: What do we do? Why do we exist?

Vision: What do we want to be? (Notice that this is not about doing. It is about being in the future.)

Values: What do we believe? How do we act?

The Strategic Destination Statement is similar to the vision statement. It details the specifics of what the organization will be, who its customers will be, the time frame for accomplishing these things, and how it will get there.

Mission

The mission statement says what you do as an organization—why you exist. The most memorable mission statements are short and inspiring.

I remember accompanying a senior engineer through one high-tech plant. As we walked the halls, I asked him about the company's mission and vision statement. He stopped and pulled from his shirt pocket a threefold laminated card. It detailed the company's mission, vision, and values in all their 12-paragraph, nine-point glory. Putting on his glasses, he began to read. He had to read through only the first three paragraphs with a smile before I got his message. Everyone was expected to carry around the mission, vision, and values, but they were so large, cumbersome, and convoluted that no one could remember them.

Compare that to a mission statement attributed to Walt Disney:

We make people happy.

To see examples of both good and bad mission statements, go to `http://www` `.missionstatements.com`.

Vision

A vision statement inspires an organization to be more than it is now. Vision statements are all about what the organization will be in the future, not what it will do to get there. We'll leave the doing and the details to the Strategic Destination Statement, described later.

The time frame for your vision statement depends on the speed of change in your industry. If you are in a rapidly changing industry, your vision statement may have a short strategic horizon of a few years. If you are in a stable industry, your strategic horizon may be 10 years. Most organizations use a strategic horizon of three to five years.

Vision statements should inspire their audience with a big, glorious picture of what could be. Those big, glorious pictures are BHAGs—big, hairy, audacious goals. BHAGs were first described by best-selling authors James Collins and Jerry Porras, who wrote about them for the *Harvard Business Review* in their 1996 article "Building Your Company's Vision."[1] They later expanded on the concept in their book *Built to Last: Successful Habits of Visionary Companies.*[2]

In *Built to Last*, Collins and Porras illustrate how a clear and compelling vision serves as a catalyst to inspire people to reach new heights. Their book describes the differences between 18 companies inspired by BHAGs and 18 other companies.

Jon Katzenbach and Douglas Smith describe this same big vision in *The Wisdom of Teams*[3] as the catalytic force necessary to create a high-performance team. They show how high performance and exceptional effort don't happen in organizations or teams until a "timely crisis" occurs. Teams and companies need a big, almost insurmountable goal that can be achieved only through extraordinary effort.

Developing Your Vision

One strategy I use to help an organization imagine its BHAG or vision is guided imagery. This process helps people relax and allows their imaginations to go beyond their normal limits. Then you guide the group through an experience using nonjudgmental statements. Counselors, meditators, and therapists have used it for decades.

Before initiating this process, consider the company's culture and your own experience. Using this process with a group of English barristers might be completely different from using it with a group in a California organic foods grocery chain. Individuals who are uncomfortable relaxing into this process can participate at whatever level they feel comfortable. For participants who are practiced in meditation or self-hypnosis, it can be as relaxing and invigorating as a mini vacation.

In this process, you lead your "visionary" group on a trip into the future. On that trip, they envision and experience the organization in the future. Upon returning to the present, each person writes down the four or five most important new "ways of being" they saw in the future. These can then be used as the source for a vision statement.

Before you begin, you must know what your strategic horizon is. How far out will this vision be? Most organizations use three to five years for the horizon.

Choose a room with comfortable chairs and tables for writing. Decrease the illumination slightly by closing any shades or blinds and turning down the lights. One wall needs a smooth surface or large whiteboard on which you will capture the vision with a giant notepad of the sort typically used for group meetings.

The visioneering team should have six to eight senior executives with cross-functional positions and 10 or more years of experience in the industry. The whole process may take two to three hours.

Before you begin, remind everyone that the vision is not "what we will do," but rather "what we will be in *x* years."

Begin with a warmup discussion about envisioning the future and BHAGs. You may want to use examples from experience or from books such as *Built to Last* or *Good to Great*. In one instance, a group started with a movie on how nearly impossible visions have become realities. The movie included clips from John

F. Kennedy's speech about putting a man on the moon and clips from Martin Luther King's "I Have a Dream" speech.

Remember to leave time between statements as you guide people with your voice. It is very uncomfortable to participate in a guided imagery session that feels rushed because the guide is moving on to the next scene before the participants are ready to. You must think about what will work for the person seeing the guided images.

One client's visioneering session took place at headquarters on an upper floor of a large office building. I dimmed the lights, had everyone put down their pens, and gave them the option of closing their eyes if they felt comfortable doing so. I then proceeded to guide them on a bus trip to see their company, PerformCo., in the future. Clients told me later that they called this the "Magic Bus."

My soft "tour guide" voice followed a script something like this:

"We are going on a trip into the future to see what PerformCo. has become. While you are on this trip, watch and listen for important points you want to remember.

"We will be traveling through offices and seeing presentations. You will have a chance to read important items on whiteboards. You may even see a newspaper headline or overhear a conversation. Remember what is important to you about PerformCo's future.

"Let's begin the trip.

"Imagine that you are standing in front of an elevator that will take us down to a bus that will transport us to PerformCo x years in the future.

"The elevator doors open. You step in, and the doors swoosh shut. You feel the elevator sway slightly as it moves down. You look up and see the floor numbers count down to the bottom floor. As it goes down each floor, you feel more and more relaxed and comfortable, yet your mind feels awake. 10, 9, 8, … ." (Count down slowly and in a soft voice.)

"We're at the bottom floor. The doors open, and a bus is waiting for us outside. The bus opens its doors, and we get on." (Wait for a moment as people get on the bus in their minds.)

"As the bus starts, the driver says, 'We're going x years into the future. We will be stopping at a couple of locations, including the PerformCo office. I will be here to take you back when you're ready.'

"You feel the bus move rapidly forward, and the windows fog. The bus slows and stops.

"We have just arrived at one of PerformCo's newest locations.

"The doors swoosh open. As you step off the bus, you can feel the wind blowing against your face. You hear the crunch of small stones under your feet.

"You stand outside and look at the building. What is your impression?

"Look around you. Notice the building. Notice the people. How do they feel about being here?

"You walk to the front door, open it, and walk inside.

"The reception area has a directory board. Notice the divisions and departments on the board. Has the organizational structure changed?" (Pause so that people can visualize and remember what they imagine. Take longer than you think they will need.)

"Let's walk down the hall.

"A group of customers are in the hallway. They don't notice you. You overhear them talking about PerformCo. What are they saying?" (Pause.)

"You continue walking. Looking into a lounge area, you see PerformCo employees and customers gathered around a table. What are they doing? What is their attitude toward each other?

"You've walked full circle and are coming back to reception. A *Wall Street Journal* is lying open. The special-interest story is about PerformCo. What does it say?" (Pause.)

"*Beep beep.* The bus is waiting outside.

"You walk out to the bus.

"The driver says, 'Now we're going to one of our premiere locations. It's a real model for the industry.'

"The windows fog and the bus rumbles. Then the windows clear and the bus stops.

"You exit and walk into the building. As you enter, you see a hallway leading to offices, so you walk that way.

"You wander the hallways, remembering how things look.

"You come across two employees in the hall. They are talking about why they work here. You overhear what they are saying.

"As you continue walking, you see an open room with someone giving a presentation to a roomful of people. There are slides on a screen.

"The speaker says, 'These are the three accomplishments that have driven our success in the last x years.' You watch as a slide with three bulleted items comes up. Read what the slide says. Remember it." (Pause.)

"*Beep beep.* The bus is waiting outside.

"You hurry to the exit.

"The bus driver says, 'I hope you've enjoyed your trip. You are a lucky group of people. Not many get to take this trip. But now it's time to return.'

"The bus begins moving. The windows fog, and then they clear.

"You are back at your building. You know you will remember the most important things you saw and heard.

"The bus doors open. You step forward. As you step down from the bus, a cool breeze brushes your face. You feel energized and refreshed. You enter the elevator and watch the floor numbers count up. As the elevator goes up, you feel more and more refreshed and energized. 1, 2, 3 … 10. The memories from your trip are very clear."

Quietly and individually, have everyone write on a notepad the most important things they saw and heard on the trip. This is a personal list. Later, the participants will select the most important of their recollections.

Pass out large 8-by-6-inch Post-it Super Sticky Notes from 3M or similar large sticky notes. These should be the type without lines, with the adhesive on the long side. You'll want about 40 cards for the entire group. If your group has eight people, that equals five cards per person. Have them write down one idea per card, using only five to seven words. Write in large block letters so that everyone can read it when it is posted on the wall. Emphasize that people should write only one idea on each card, or they will write long paragraphs with multiple ideas. If this happens, just rewrite the card before you post it.

As the facilitator, you should now use an affinity diagram process to get dynamic discussions going about the content of the cards as you post them on the wall. Collect a few cards and post them. (Learn more about using affinity diagram processes on my website: http://www.criticaltosuccess.com). Let the team group and regroup them into affinity groups with common intent. Add more cards to the wall, and group or regroup. The important thing to realize is that the intent of each of these groups of cards will form your vision statement.

After you have reorganized and discussed the groups of cards and everyone is satisfied with the groupings, give each group a concise name.

The names of each of these groups will become the core of your vision statement. The actual construction of a final statement is best left to a small group of two or three people who are good wordsmiths. If you attempt to write a strategy statement with a group of more than three people, you will be in for a long, tedious process that will devolve your vision statement into nothing more than a boring platitude.

Developing a vision statement in this way may not create a vision statement with quantitative, finely detailed goals. But it can capture the BHAG and create an inspirational vision.

You will use the work here to move forward to a Strategic Destination Statement like that described near the end of this chapter. It is the Strategic Destination Statement that precisely defines what your organization will be at a specific time in the future, who your customers will be, and not only what your value proposition for them will be, but also how you will deliver it. Getting to a precise Strategic Destination Statement is critical, because it is your springboard to your Strategy Map and Balanced Scorecard.

Values

Values are the things that the people in the organization believe in. Values determine how people act, what their ethics are, and what their behaviors are as they go about their business. Value statements come from the people and from what their leadership values. Values exist in the culture and are promoted by the leaders. It is rare that values can be instilled through training classes and workshops.

Upon returning from business trips, I sometimes go out of my way to stop at a Nordstrom department store here in northern California. On one side trip I stopped to look for a tie and ended up buying a pair of dress pants, a couple of shirts, and a tie that wasn't the one I'd originally wanted. The pants needed some alteration and were shipped to my home. The whole process took about 30 minutes, and I enjoyed the conversation with the young clerk who helped me.

Almost two months later, I stopped at the same Nordstrom, hoping to find the tie I had originally been looking for. As I walked toward the men's department, the same young clerk stepped forward and greeted me by name. It had been two months since we had talked for a scant 30 minutes, yet he remembered my name. This type of caring for people—not "customers"—isn't learned through a value statement. It is in the culture of the organization, and the culture re-creates itself as the organization hires new people who fit the culture. The value statement comes from the culture and how its leaders live and act.

It isn't hard to find examples of value statements on the web. Here are some examples from famous organizations:

- Science-based innovation
- Profit, but profit from work that benefits humanity
- No cynicism
- Nurturing and promulgation of "wholesome American values"
- Fanatical attention to consistency and detail

Examine your value statement to make sure that it includes your beliefs and how you act.

Developing Your Strategic Assessment

Strategic assessment is the evaluation of how and where your organization fits into its environment. This is a Darwinian "fit." Your strategy must find the fit that will enable your organization to prosper and grow while fending off voracious competitors.

In your strategic assessment, you must evaluate external opportunities and threats. Define how you can take advantage of those external opportunities and neutralize or sidestep the threats. Many tools and models are used in this process. Here are some of the most popular:

- A PESTEL analysis evaluates large-scope external threats.

- Porter's 5 Forces model is widely used to assess near-scope industry and competitive threats.

- A SWOT analysis evaluates your organization's strengths, weaknesses, opportunities, and threats from an internal perspective.

This section briefly describes these tools. More information is available in strategic planning books and on the Web. Additional references and whitepapers are available at my website, http://www.criticaltosuccess.com.

Defining Your External Environment by Using PESTEL

You can use PESTEL, also called PEST or STEP, with groups to assess the external environment, pressures, and threats that may affect your organization's business. It is a good process for shifting from an inward to an outward focus. PESTEL reminds people of the external forces outside their control that they must plan for. You should use a PESTEL analysis along with an industry analysis such as Porter's 5 Forces and an internally focused analysis such as SWOT.

PESTEL considers the external influences of the following environments:

- **Political:** Election changes, public policy shifts, war, tax changes, terrorism

- **Economic:** Consumer confidence, inflation, economic growth and trends (regional, national, and international), government funding, new business formation rates, job growth, unemployment, exchange rates, foreign competition, tariff changes

- **Social:** Demographics of the workforce and the target customer, fashion and lifestyle shifts, population movements, immigration and emigration, occupational trends and needs, economic profiles, health shifts

- **Technological:** New production methods, new fuels and energy sources, communication methods and channels, increased obsolescence rates, production equipment and processes, outsourcing

- **Environmental:** Environmental regulations, public opinion, environmental risk/accidents, recycling

- **Legal:** Employment law, industry law and lawsuits, consumer protection law, international law and regulations

PESTEL has advantages and disadvantages. A team of informed managers or analysts can quickly complete a PESTEL by doing little more than searching online through the *Wall Street Journal*, trade magazines, and business archives such as EBSCOhost. But the results so garnered are general impressions of external influences. For small and midsized businesses, this is probably sufficient. Conducting an in-depth, quantitative external market analysis requires dedicated market analysts and can take weeks or longer—and cost a lot.

In surging markets that have raised the prosperity of all companies in an industry, a PESTEL analysis can help the team realize that their fortunes will change when the environment changes. For example, a change in the governing political party may result in a tax policy change that will affect their client's ability to purchase.

PESTEL is also useful in quickly evaluating a new market your organization is considering. Although you may not be worried about competitors or functional replacements, PESTEL may reveal other external conditions.

To perform a PESTEL, do the following:

1. Select one person to research each PESTEL topic prior to the meeting. Each "expert" should present a 5-to-10-minute review of the key factors that might affect the organization.

2. Have individuals brainstorm what they think are the most impactful and probable factors.

3. Post and discuss how the most critical factors will affect the organization.

4. Create a one- or two-page table of these factors, with weightings on impact and probability.

The one downside of doing this with a team of close executives and managers is that they have all drunk the same Kool-Aid. It can be enlightening to have an outsider give a contrasting opinion.

Defining Your Industry Environment with Porter's 5 Forces

I remember the first time I read Michael Porter's seminal book *Competitive Strategy: Techniques for Analyzing Industries and Competitors.*[4] Like Balanced Scorecards, it was a slap-your-forehead type of experience. His book and its analysis of the growth and death of industries and competitive positioning was probably one of the kick starts that moved me to become one of Microsoft's first 12 consultants. Porter's models used framework and structure to make competitive analysis and strategic positioning easy to understand.

> **NOTE** Porter's 2000 article "What Is Strategy?," available from *Harvard Business Review* through Amazon, is a must-read for anyone needing a base in strategy.[5]

Porter's 5 Forces model analyzes the industry and competition surrounding a business. It helps you understand how consumers and competitors affect each other in the market. Unlike PESTEL, which looks at the large external environment, 5 Forces looks only at internal and marketplace factors that directly affect an organization.

Here are the 5 Forces and some of their factors that affect businesses:

- **Substitute products:** How much power can your consumers exert by switching? Products that can easily be substituted affect your ability to raise prices. Switching is affected by how easily buyers switch, the perceived differences between products, and product quality or features. When more products are close to you, you are less able to raise prices.

- **Entry of new competitors:** How likely are new competitors to enter the market? If you earn a high margin on your products, competitors are more likely to move into your area. Prevent new entrants by raising barriers to entry via methods such as registering patents or controlling distribution channels.

- **Competitive rivalry:** How much power do you have compared to your rivals? Each industry has its own model of competition. Some resort to intense price cutting; others expand advertising and promotion.

- **Consumer bargaining power:** How easily can consumers lower prices? Consumers can affect pricing when they have competitive pricing information, when there are few consumers and many competitors (switching costs), and when they can easily find substitute products.

- **Supplier bargaining power:** How easily can suppliers raise prices? Suppliers can affect pricing when the product they supply is rare or unique, when supplier switching costs are high, and when there are few suppliers and many competitors.

You can use the same facilitation methods as those for PESTEL to identify the 5 Forces for your organization.

Defining Your Strengths and Weaknesses with the Balanced Scorecard SWOT

Whereas the PESTEL and Porter's 5 Forces look outside your organization, SWOT looks within. SWOT is the tool most business people use for strategic analysis. SWOT stands for

- **Strengths:** Where your organization is strong
- **Weaknesses:** Where your organization is weak
- **Opportunities:** Where your organization has great potential
- **Threats:** Where your organization could be at risk

An important point to remember is that a SWOT must be done with a specific strategy in mind. It is against this strategy that you compare your strengths, weaknesses, opportunities, and threats. This may mean that you have to use a process of defining a "straw strategy," developing a SWOT, revising the "straw strategy," reanalyzing the SWOT, and so forth until you create a viable strategy.

If you are in a rapidly evolving marketplace and are using the product/service development methods described in *Lean Startup* by Eric Reis (Crown Business, 2011), you need to do a new SWOT at each *pivot* point—points where you need to reinvent your organization.

Many consultants do a SWOT with just four columns—one for each letter—and a long bullet list under each letter. You can add greater depth and insight to your SWOT by building it around the four perspectives used in a Balanced Scorecard. Doing so also generates a lot of discussion among the executive team. The four perspectives are

- Financial
- Customer
- Internal operations
- Learning and growth

These perspectives are described in detail in Chapter 4.

Begin your SWOT session by creating a grid on the wall. Use large 8-by-6-inch 3M Post-it Super Sticky Notes for table headers. Build your grid with large cell areas, and arrange headers like this:

	STRENGTHS	WEAKNESSES	OPPORTUNITIES	THREATS
Financial				
Customer				
Internal Operations				
Learning and Growth				

Guide the executive team through individual brainstorming, and have them write down their individual thoughts on the sticky notes. You might want to use a different color Post-it for each vertical column. Allow the executive team to decide where they want to put notes, but limit the number of notes per individual so that they must set priorities. Doing so also keeps the table from becoming too crowded. The group should discuss each note and decide where to place it.

When this is done correctly, you should end up with a lot of discussion, new understanding, and a color "heat map" that identifies areas you should focus on or avoid.

Developing Your Strategic Destination Statement

The useful *Harvard Business Review* article "Can You Say What Your Strategy Is?" by David Collis and Michael Rukstad (April 2008)[6] outlines multiple strategy tools. One of these tools illustrates a way to build a Strategic Destination Statement. The Strategic Destination Statement is like a vision statement with specific details of what will be achieved in a specific time frame with specific offerings to specific customer profiles. The Strategic Destination Statement is essential to developing a well-constructed Strategy Map.

With mission, vision, and values as a base, and having completed the external and internal analysis described earlier in this chapter, your executive leadership team should be ready to develop its Strategic Destination Statement.

Begin by showing your team a sample Strategic Destination Statement. A finished one might look like this:

> *PerformCo will expand to have offices in the top 10 markets in California and remain in the top quartile of private investment firms. By 20xx it will offer a portfolio of green technology investments for clients who have a net worth of $1 million to $10 million, who want to make an environmental contribution, who expect better-than-average returns, and who can tolerate moderate risk. We will differentiate ourselves through our close contacts and expertise in green technology.*

An experienced facilitator will be able to use the following structure to get the executive leadership team to agree on a structured statement. It is critical that you get agreement on and commitment to the Destination Statement. Going forward at this point without a solid Destination Statement can be a waste of time and endanger your strategic success.

PerformCo Strategic Destination Statement

PerformCo will (action)	Expand
to (result)	have offices in the top 10 markets in California and remain in the top quartile of private investment firms
by (time frame)	20*xx*
by (method)	offering a portfolio of green technology investments
for (customer)	clients with a net worth of $1 million to $10 million, who want to make an environmental contribution, who expect better-than-average returns, and who can tolerate moderate risk
through (means)	our close contacts and expertise in green technology

At the end of facilitation, you should have a structure similar to this with notes that focus on the most important concepts. There will usually be too much information to fit in a single paragraph, but a few wordsmiths can use this to craft a Strategic Destination Statement.

After writing the first edition of this book, I found that the Strategic Destination Statement was an eye-opener. Chief executives were having a human resources manager distribute the blank destination statement to their executive team to fill out. The anonymous results were then returned to the CEO. In every case the CEO found wildly varying differences in where each executive thought the organization was heading. With that lack of clarity on the part of the leadership team, imagine how much more misdirection occurs as the message passes down through the organization's silos and layers. Perform this exercise, and you'll see a lot of surprises.

Summary

Developing a winning strategy requires external, industry, and internal assessments. Omitting one of these assessments could be costly and might result in a flawed strategy that is dangerous to the organization's future. All the methods described in this chapter can be completed in a couple of half-day exercises by an experienced facilitator working with the executive leadership team. These methods are appropriate for small to midsized organizations that do not have the time or resources needed to conduct in-depth, lengthy market and competitive analyses.

The Strategic Destination Statement that you develop after your assessments is the destination for your Strategy Map. The next few chapters guide you through developing your Strategy Map.

Notes

1. J. Collins and J. Porras, "Building Your Company's Vision," *Harvard Business Review*, September 1996.

2. J. Collins and J. Porras, *Built to Last: Successful Habits of Visionary Companies* (New York, New York: Collins Business, 2004).

3. J. Katzenbach and D. Smith, *The Wisdom of Teams* (New York, New York: Collins Business, 1994).

4. M. Porter, *Competitive Strategy: Techniques for Analyzing Industries and Competitors* (New York, New York: Free Press, 1980).

5. M. Porter, "What Is Strategy?" *Harvard Business Review*, February 2000.

6. D. Collis and M. Rukstad, "Can You Say What Your Strategy Is?" *Harvard Business Review*, April 2008.

CHAPTER 3

Preparing to Build Your Balanced Scorecard

If I had six hours to chop down a tree, I'd spend the first hour sharpening the axe.
—Abraham Lincoln

The Balanced Scorecard is how you execute your strategic plan. The level of your organization's success depends on how well you implement it. For good implementation, you need a good foundation, and that foundation depends on both your Balanced Scorecard's purpose and your levels of planning and commitment.

Why Use a Balanced Scorecard?

You need to know your organization's purpose for implementing a Balanced Scorecard before you begin developing one. It takes intense, hard work to develop a Balanced Scorecard and make it part of your organization's culture. If the Balanced Scorecard isn't driven by the organization's core purpose, its power to guide your organization will become a lower priority, and people will lose commitment as they face daily crises.

The Balanced Scorecard is not a tool of performance management. It is a tool to translate strategy into action, to remove silos, and to promote a culture of high performance. A lot happens during the development and implementation of a Balanced Scorecard. Extra work is required of executives and managers, the walls between silos are reduced or eliminated, new channels of communication are opened, the value placed on performance changes, and much more.

Organizations don't change easily. In a cultural version of Newton's first law, they are bound by their inertia. I've seen small organizations of fewer than a hundred people have as much difficulty changing as large organizations. So why go through all the work, intensity, and effort that the Balanced Scorecard requires? Because the Balanced Scorecard has proven to be one of the most effective tools for translating strategy into action, aligning the entire organization around that strategy, and monitoring the execution of strategy.

Before you begin developing a Balanced Scorecard, you must know the purpose of doing that in your organization. You must clearly understand why the CEO and executive sponsor want to implement a Balanced Scorecard. The purpose could be driven by internal or external pressures. Some reasons might be as follows:

- **Internal**:
  - A new CEO wants to implement a new strategy and align the culture with that strategy.
  - Two organizations are merging and need to create common cultures, visions, and processes.
  - Silos in the organization are so strong and pervasive that they are pulling the organization apart.
  - The Board of Directors and stockholders demand increased performance.
- **External**:
  - Demographic changes threaten to detrimentally affect the workforce.
  - Competitors are releasing new products that threaten your position.
  - Customer needs and buying patterns are changing.
  - Global economic changes are forcing the organization to focus on local defensible areas with a high return.

Be clear on the purpose of the Balanced Scorecard so that you know what to emphasize and where to spend your resources. For example, suppose you believe that the purposes of the Balanced Scorecard are to significantly increase performance at all levels and to build a permanent culture change of high performance. You would incorporate the following in your Balanced Scorecard implementation:

- Development of a culture of high performance
- Development of a human resources (HR) plan for Strategic Job Analysis
- Development of performance methods such as Six Sigma or Lean
- Cascading scorecards down to the personal level
- Expectations of significant high-performance results in one to three years

If instead your CEO and executive sponsor want to use the Balanced Scorecard as a vehicle to reduce departmental silos and increase horizontal and vertical communication, you would focus on the following:

- Creating an easy-to-understand Strategy Map posted in communal areas
- Hosting ongoing "town hall" meetings to communicate and gather feedback
- Building interdepartmental teams that optimize results for the organization, not for silos
- Achieving near-term results

One of my clients exactly fit this last profile. As a large nonprofit center for the performing arts, it needed to develop a strategy for easily communicating with donors, employees, and the community. It faced serious strategic issues. Highly profitable Indian casinos were bringing in big-time entertainment but making no social contribution to the community, and there was the possibility of a new facility. We used the Balanced Scorecard, coupled with group facilitation methods, to capture needs and capabilities from employees; to involve multiple levels of management in participative strategic planning; and to develop an easily communicable strategic plan, Strategy Map, and Implementation Plan. The organization's purpose was involvement, clarity, and communication, and it felt that its purpose was met without needing to develop detailed metrics.

Is Your Organization Ready for the Balanced Scorecard Journey?

Not all organizations are capable of developing and implementing a Balanced Scorecard. Certain things are critical to success. If your organization lacks these key elements, you will find it significantly more difficult to succeed.

Senior Executive Commitment

Commitment from the senior executive for the business unit implementing the Balanced Scorecard is paramount. Without that commitment, the Balanced Scorecard almost certainly will fail.

It shouldn't be surprising that this is of utmost importance. The Standish Group's research as reported in the CHAOS Report of tens of thousands of IT projects found that the biggest single cause of project management failure was lack of executive commitment. And the Balanced Scorecard is not a one-off project; it requires ongoing commitment. Implementing a Balanced Scorecard requires an organizational culture change. And that requires vision and leadership at the highest level. Without it, you are almost guaranteed to fail.

Although this is true, I have seen Balanced Scorecards successfully implemented within business units or functional departments, such as IT, within a large organization. These can be very successful. Kaplan and Norton have examples of how these internal scorecards spread upward and outward within some organizations. Still, the leadership of the unit implementing the Balanced Scorecard has to be committed to its success.

Experienced Facilitator or Consultant

When talking with many executives and other consultants, I sometimes hear them claim that they tried building a Balanced Scorecard but dropped it partway in, or that it failed shortly after launch. On closer examination, I usually discover that there was no high-level executive commitment, or that the Balanced Scorecard was done as a "project" by someone with no experience.

To develop and implement a Balanced Scorecard, you need one or more internal or external consultants and facilitators who have experience in numerous areas:

- Facilitation skills with senior executives
- Strategic planning
- The Balanced Scorecard, Strategy Map, and Implementation Plans
- Process-mapping skills
- Business metrics
- Working with IT to develop software
- Training your managers and facilitators in how to continue developing the Balanced Scorecard

You may want to use an experienced consultant or facilitator from outside your organization. Outside consultants or facilitators have added advantages:

- They bring cross-industry knowledge and metrics
- They ask questions about the elephant in the room—the major issue no one wants to address
- They have no internal agendas

Make sure that any consultant or facilitator has experience with this type of work and with facilitating executive teams. Many "generic" business consultants do "strategic planning" but have only the most superficial knowledge of Balanced Scorecards. This is more than a two-day executive retreat. Check referrals.

Executive Sponsor Commitment

A Balanced Scorecard must have an executive sponsor who will take responsibility for bringing it to fruition. The executive sponsor works with the internal or external consultant or facilitator to motivate her peers and to make resources available.

Executive Time and Commitment

Senior executives must devote time upfront to developing the Strategy Map and Action Plan. They must also be able to motivate and commit an experienced manager to the core team that will turn those initiatives into action.

The Balanced Scorecard also acts as an agenda for frequent executive reviews of strategy. In too many organizations the executive team reviews strategy annually. Organizations driven by the Balanced Scorecard often do partial strategic assessments monthly and in-depth reviews quarterly. These more frequent assessments take from one to three hours rather than a "too late" annual review that takes days. It is important, however, to remain focused on the strategy. How well are you executing it? Will you achieve your strategic goals and not let the discussion devolve into resolving operational details that are more appropriately addressed elsewhere?

If you are in a rapidly changing business environment or work in a start-up with new products and services, I highly recommend *Lean Startup* by Michael Ries (Crown Business, 2011). Ries discusses pivoting the organization when metrics show that basic assumptions about the business and customer needs are wrong. These pivot meetings are real-time strategy meetings.

Participative Culture with Open Communication

A viable Balanced Scorecard can exist only in a culture of communication and participation. A Balanced Scorecard that is developed in isolation and sent "down the hill" becomes just another top-down directive that won't last.

"The Silent Killers of Strategy Implementation," an article in the summer 2000 edition of *Sloan Management Review*,[1] describes six things that can kill the execution of strategy. Three of those six killers are brought about by failure to openly communicate and participate.

A Balanced Scorecard has a greater chance of success when built in a participative environment with a flow of communication between executives, managers, and employees. Without feedback from employees, the strategic initiatives won't be built on a realistic foundation of capacity and capabilities. Using group facilitation and feedback provided by representatives of all employees concerning methods of accomplishing initiatives and projects builds commitment.

You Must Make Your Case for Change

The Balanced Scorecard will create change in your organization, and few organizations change easily. To make that change happen, and to keep the organization from reverting to old ways, the CEO and executive team must make a strong case for change and then communicate it and live it continually.

Building a case for change has the greatest effect when the executive team members build the case themselves. You can guide them in filling out a change state table like the one shown in Table 3-1. Begin with the current state, and then ask the executives what they think the future state and impact will be if the organization doesn't change.

Table 3-1: A Sample Change State Table

CURRENT STATE	FUTURE STATE	IMPACT
Few available skilled banking officers	Predation on current employees; higher salaries required; more training needed for existing officers	Limits expansion plans; increases salary costs; loss of private clients
Loss of high-net-worth clients	Increased loss with flux in bank officers; lack of personal knowledge of clients	Increased loss of high-net-worth clients to banks with experienced and stable staff; pressure for closer customer relationships
Competitors' websites are easier to use for customer data access	Clients will migrate to private banks with better communication and data access that give timely information and integration with personal investment tools	Increased loss of high-net-worth clients

Guiding the executive team through the current and future states and letting them come to their own conclusions about the impact can light the fires that create a "burning platform" for change.

Jon Katzenbach and Douglas Smith write in their best-seller *The Wisdom of Teams*[2] that high-performance teams arise in the face of timely critical issues. The same is true when adopting the Balanced Scorecard to change your own organization.

Even if you don't face a "timely critical issue," you need to develop one to prepare and protect yourself. Your business may be stable now, but with the pressures and changing currents of global markets, global competition, financial instability, and the Internet, you won't have to wait long for a timely critical issue.

One of my international clients had been growing at over 20 percent per year. It was at the top of its industry and felt in control. It had completed a well-done risk map of the current state. Going through the change state exercise and pinpointing the impact let all executives feel in their gut what they intellectually saw in the risk map. They were facing a perfect storm in the near future. Although they were in a calm spot at the moment, they foresaw the following:

- Government funding, a major source of revenue, was at a change point. A change in government policy would severely detract from revenue.

- Real estate values were skyrocketing, and the company had used that fact to its advantage, but now building contractor rates were also skyrocketing. If the real estate market collapsed, the company's clients wouldn't have the liquidity to buy products and services.

- Skilled staff members were becoming hard to find. The industry sector had the lowest unemployment rates in history. The company depended on licensed professionals, people difficult to find and retain. The future looked even worse.

Within months of completing this exercise, the company was hit by two of the three weather fronts in its perfect storm. The federal policies came under review, which could affect the company's revenue sources. Then the new HR director revealed that employee retention was much worse than previously thought, and that the latest demographics research showed that hiring problems would worsen significantly. The client's work on its change state table, Strategy Map, and Implementation Plans gave it months of advance preparation for its perfect storm.

Motivating Executives

The CEO and the executive team need to know the results that the Balanced Scorecard can produce, how it can change their culture, and the roles they must play to make it work. The Balanced Scorecard gives everyone in the organization a common direction and understanding. However, it is the leadership from executives and the daily empowerment from managers that give staff and employees the confidence and power to make their own decisions and actions leading to strategic success.

Mid-level managers and employees need lasting commitment and vision from their leaders. Leaders need to continually emphasize that the Balanced Scorecard is the tool that will be used to manage strategic execution.

Perhaps this is best illustrated by the following story. I was enjoying an early breakfast with eight project managers employed by one of the largest insurance companies in the U.S. The conversation turned to managing and sustaining change. At that point, the head of the Project Management Office stopped the conversation cold when she said, "I wish we could get the executives to stop flying on planes."

A non sequitur like that made everyone turn to find out where she was going next. She paused, took a sip of coffee, and said, "Don't you see? Every time an executive flies on a plane, they read the latest business book. When they get back, we change direction again." We all grimaced at the painful truth and laughed loud enough to be heard throughout the restaurant.

So how do you motivate the executive staff? How do you get them committed to staying the course? Here are some seed ideas:

- Results are the voice executives hear and believe. You need to show results from similar companies. Do an Internet search for "balanced scorecard hall of fame" to find examples of companies in similar industries. You also can search using an industry term to find success stories, such as "hospitals balanced scorecard." Make sure that you research the continued success of the example organizations you use. Some users of Balanced Scorecards have failed, not because of the Balanced Scorecard, but because they did not choose the right strategy or had operational failures.

- Gather quotes and testimonials from CEOs and senior executives. Don't just proclaim that the Balanced Scorecard is wonderful. Also reveal how much work it takes, and how the culture will change.

- Reveal how the Balanced Scorecard can fail. About 30 to 50 percent of organizations that start a Balanced Scorecard don't successfully implement it the first time. The Bank of Tokyo failed on its first attempt but became a Balanced Scorecard Hall of Fame winner on its second attempt. There are many reasons for failure, and you must be ready to address them.

- Educate executives on the overall process of how their organization can be affected.

- Let executives know the initial and ongoing time and resource commitments required of them and the people they commit to the Balanced Scorecard.

- Let executives hear from other executives. As a consultant certified by Kaplan and Norton on Balanced Scorecard consulting, I have shown video testimonials from CEOs and senior executives who have used and implemented the Balanced Scorecard.

The job of the CEO and senior executives is to lead with vision. The people who follow them need to see a level of commitment in the actions of their leaders that demonstrates that the Balanced Scorecard will remain and be used. Such actions need to be seen and communicated continually to be believed and to create change in the culture.

One of the most important jobs for the CEO, executive sponsor, and Balanced Scorecard consultant is creating the case for change and motivation so that the majority of the members of the executive leadership team will work for a successful Balanced Scorecard.

Building Balanced Scorecard Teams

A single knowledgeable individual can build a good, descriptive Balanced Scorecard, but it is rare for a Balanced Scorecard built like this to succeed. Without the insights and commitment of executives, mid-level managers, and line personnel, the Balanced Scorecard is viewed as an "executive-level" directive that loses momentum over time. At best, it becomes an executive dashboard—and it won't drive culture change or successful execution of strategy.

Building and rolling out a Balanced Scorecard requires at least three levels of teams. The executive team is composed of senior executives, who translate the strategy into a Strategy Map with its strategic objectives and causal links between objectives. They begin developing the Action Plan that defines how those objectives will be measured and what Strategic Initiatives are necessary to reach the objectives. The Strategic Theme team then works with what the executive team has developed and creates a plan for making it happen. The Strategic Theme team further develops the Action Plan, completing the metrics and Strategic Initiatives and working with managers to define what projects are necessary in the initiatives. An experienced Balanced Scorecard leader should guide each of the teams, gathering feedback, facilitating meetings, and helping in the rollout and with communication.

The team's composition, the number of participants, and their roles will vary between organizations. Large organizations with multiple divisions will have a team in each division or business unit. Small to midsized businesses may build a Balanced Scorecard with just one team and one or two facilitators.

Here is a breakdown of the teams and their participants, roles, and products when developing the Balanced Scorecard:

Executive Team

Participants

> Six to eight senior executives in the strategic business unit or their designated representative

Role

> Translate strategy into objectives.

Define what drives the business model.

Act as Strategic Theme sponsors to monitor Core Team results.

Output

Strategy Map

Action Plan

Leadership for the Strategic Theme team

Commitment

Education session

Three half-day workshops

If an executive becomes a Strategic Theme sponsor, she chairs a monthly meeting with her Strategic Theme team.

Strategic Theme Teams

Participants

Strategic Theme managers

One manager for each Strategic Theme. There are usually two or three Strategic Themes.

This is a good role for executives or managers being groomed for higher and broader experience, because it gives them insight into all aspects of the organization.

Team members

Composed of two to five members with wide cross-functional experience. Beware of overloading in one functional area. Usually this occurs in the area of finance. These people are experienced with managing initiatives and projects across the company.

Role and Output

Complete Action Plan that defines initiatives.

Complete Metric Definitions that define measures and metrics.

Develop projects to accomplish initiatives.

Report to Strategic Theme sponsor.

Compare existing projects and budgets to the new Strategic Initiatives, projects, and budgets.

Commitment

Education session

Bi-monthly meetings to coordinate development within the Strategic Theme team

Project development meetings with managers

Facilitators and Consultants

Participants

Consultant (internal or external)

Experienced in guiding the strategy process and developing the Balanced Scorecard

Experienced in developing executive motivation

Trained in using the Balanced Scorecard

Able to train facilitators in Balanced Scorecard development

Facilitators and trainers

Experience in facilitating

Trained to teach the Balanced Scorecard

Trained in using the Balanced Scorecard as an agenda for strategy review meetings

Role and Output

Consultant

Guide executives through Strategy Map and Balanced Scorecard development.

Guide the Strategic Theme Team through Action Plan development.

Have access to a large library of background resources.

Propose and develop metrics.

Work with IT to select or develop software.

Facilitate

Gather feedback from managers and employees.

Brainstorm ideas.

Do process mapping.

Plan.

Facilitate and host the rollout and communication plan.

Commitment

Be available to aid Strategy Theme teams, project planning teams, communication rollout, frontline feedback, and capability assessments.

Background Research

Before starting work on the Balanced Scorecard, before doing interviews, and before the first meeting, the consultant or facilitator leading the Balanced Scorecard process must have 30,000-foot knowledge of all aspects of the organization and its environment. Part of the consultant or facilitator's job is to act as the "outsider" who asks questions, probing accepted industry "truths" and revealing the elephants in the room. Asking these questions is sometimes easier and more acceptable if done by an outsider who isn't expected to have detailed knowledge of the organization and industry. The consultant or facilitator should not be drinking the Kool-Aid in the corporate punch bowl.

There are many sources where you can get broad industry knowledge as well as internal knowledge of a company. I usually allocate a couple of weeks to do reading and research before beginning interviews and workshops.

The critical sources for review are as follows:

- Mission, vision, and value statements
- Strategic plans
- Operational plans
- Annual and quarterly reports
- High-level financial reports
- Key financial metrics
- Key operational metrics
- SWOT analysis, if separate from strategic plans
- Risk analyses or heat maps
- Organization charts with names and contact information for key participants
- Expansion plans

Additional materials for review are as follows:

- Morningstar analysis on public companies
- Consultants' reports or surveys
- HR and employee surveys
- Hiring demographics and environment
- Customer satisfaction surveys
- Competitive analysis
- Industry analyst reports
- Trade journals for environmental conditions

- Benchmark reports
- Trade websites
- Key competitors' websites

Interviewing Executives

Executive interviews are your opportunity to get input from individual executives about their views of the future, what they understand to be the key objectives for the organization and their divisions, and where barriers in the existing organization exist. It is your chance to identify ways in which divisions may not be aligned toward common goals. This can also reveal how silos are creating suboptimal successes, stopping the larger organization short of success.

The executive interview is also your chance to learn what metrics and criteria executives watch and use when making strategic and tactical decisions. These metrics and how they are analyzed and compared will help you later in selecting metrics and designing dashboards.

One test I frequently use at an interview is asking to see the reports or metrics that are most important to a particular executive's decision-making. Often these can be reduced to a few critical pages—the pages or data that the executive wants to see first thing each morning.

In one of my first jobs as a product manager fresh out of business school, I was put on a "Tiger Team" to reduce the paper glut filling the corners in offices throughout the Fortune 500 company I worked for. Reams of computer printouts from reports generated weekly were piled everywhere. After interviewing executives and managers, the team learned that most managers used only a few key numbers—and, at most, a few pages—from the two- or three-inch stack of paper they received weekly. We reduced wasted time, increased the speed of decision-making, and saved thousands of trees by rebuilding reports around the few pieces of data important to each manager. Although the advent of online dashboards has almost eliminated the need for printed reports, the fundamental problem still exists. Even with online dashboards, managers can be overwhelmed by "infoglut" and distracted from the critical few metrics.

Most of my executive interviews focus on metrics and how they are used to make decisions and take about an hour. Always schedule at least an hour between interviews to give yourself time to rewrite notes and refresh your brain. If I don't schedule time between interviews, I lose facts and forget insights.

Some interviewers work in a two-person team. One person is the interviewer and maintains eye contact and rapport, and the other person takes the quiet role of scribe.

I usually do my interviews on-site and solo, although doing phone interviews is sometimes necessary. I prepare a list of about eight questions and keep it in front of me while taking just a few notes that will jog my memory later in case my voice recorder fails. Immediately after the interview, I rewrite my notes. Of course, I let the executive being interviewed know ahead of time that I will be asking her about which key metrics she uses for decision-making. This usually results in her showing me how she uses a couple of key pages containing metrics and charts. I always ask for copies.

In the past I used a small portable digital voice recorder that ran for many hours on one AAA battery. It is small and unobtrusive. After a few minutes, the executive and I don't even notice it on the table. When the interview is over, I plug the recorder into my laptop and download the recording as an MP3 file. That makes it easy to play back the interview while I transcribe it on my laptop. A digital recorder with these capabilities costs between $50 and $150 and is well worth the expense.

In large groups, such as team facilitations, I use both the digital voice recorder and a conference room microphone from Jabra that connects to my laptop. By running Camtasia from TechSmith, an amazing video-capture program, I can capture the comments of everyone in the room while running a PowerPoint presentation on my laptop. This allows me to record comments from anywhere in the room and keep them in synch with the PowerPoint. This makes it easy to go back and review what was said.

Make sure that any recorder you get has a microphone plug size that will fit a telephone adaptor in case you need to conduct an interview by phone. For about $25, you can buy a phone adaptor that enables you to connect to a land-line (but not portable) phone. Of course, the law requires you to notify the other person that you are recording the interview.

Be sure to take a few memory reminder notes even if you are using a voice recorder. A journalist told me a nightmarish story of a time when she conducted a long and hard-to-get interview. Wanting to pay close attention, she took no notes, depending solely on her trusty cassette recorder. When she left the interview, she found that her recorder had failed. She panicked and forgot some of what happened during the interview.

You will probably get through only six to eight questions in an hour, so be sure that you put the most important questions at the top of your list. Keep the interview brisk and on target.

This interview could be important to the future of the company. Be friendly, but don't open with questions about the desktop picture of the family at Disneyland or get into a discussion about why there is a golf trophy or mounted halibut tail on the wall. Executives are busy and bottom-line-oriented.

Think through and rehearse your most important questions beforehand. Although you will have time for only six or eight questions, you have many to choose from. Here are some of the questions you might ask:

- Have you had experience with the Balanced Scorecard before?
- What are your organization's most important strategic objectives?
- How does your division contribute to those objectives?
- How does your division define success?
- Where has your division been most successful?
- What made your division successful in that objective?
- What is your vision for increasing your success in the next three to five years?
- Do you see large trends or shifts changing your industry?
- Where are the barriers to the organization's success?
- Which competitor is most dangerous over the long term, and why?
- Which metrics do you watch that show or drive success?
- Do you compare sets of metrics when making decisions?
- Is there a metric or alert you watch that signals a future problem?
- What in the business keeps you awake at night?
- Because I know your time is limited, is there someone in your organization I can talk to if I need clarification?

Summary

The Balanced Scorecard has an impressive record of helping organizations execute their strategy, but without a burning case for change you may be unable to sustain momentum.

The most important factors for success are

- Commitment from the senior executive
- Guidance from an internal or external consultant experienced in Balanced Scorecards (not just an executive consultant)
- A burning case for change—one that makes everyone in the organization understand why change is necessary

Notes

1. M. Beer and R. Eisenstat, "The Silent Killers of Strategy Implementation," *Sloan Management Review* 41, no. 4 (summer 2000): pp 29–40.

2. J. Katzenbach and D. Smith, *The Wisdom of Teams* (New York, New York: McGraw-Hill, 2005).

Step-by-Step to Building Your Strategy Map

Change is the law of life. And those who look only to the past or present are certain to miss the future.

—John F. Kennedy
U.S. President
1917–1963

You know where you want to go. You've completed your vision and Strategic Destination Statement, and now you face translating your strategy into action. The first step is to create a Strategy Map.

Without a Strategy Map, your Balanced Scorecard will be an executive scorecard. It will report on measures important to the executive, but it will not give you an accurate view of how the entire organization is driving and succeeding at its Strategic Objectives.

There are four reasons you need to create a Strategy Map even if you never build a Balanced Scorecard. First, early versions of Balanced Scorecards had a low success rate because the metrics they monitored were often chosen from the metrics currently in use, which may not have been the metrics that drove strategy. Second, in most organizations, few managers and employees have a clear and concise concept of their organization's strategy. In fact, research shows that less than 10 percent of employees have a clear understanding of their organization's strategy, and 50 percent of executives spend virtually no time on strategic discussion.[1] Third, without a clear, concise model of what drives your strategy, you have no feedback about which drivers are working and which are not. Finally, when the objectives on the Strategy Map are broken into initiatives and projects, it's easy to identify strategic funding during the budget process.

What Is a Strategy Map?

A Strategy Map is a visual representation of what your executive team believes will drive your strategy. Just as a road map shows the path to a destination, a Strategy Map shows which chain of objectives will lead to successfully executing your strategy.

Figure 4.1 shows a Strategy Map for a medical device manufacturer. Like the Balanced Scorecard, which it reinforces, a Strategy Map usually has four perspectives. (Perspectives are described in more detail in the section "Perspectives: Monitoring Your Strategy from Different Points of View.") The perspectives shown in Figure 4.1 fit most for-profit corporations. From the top of the map down, they are as follows:

- Financial
- Customer and marketplace
- Internal operations
- Learning and growth (composed of human capital, culture, and IT infrastructure)

These perspectives appear as horizontal bands on the map.

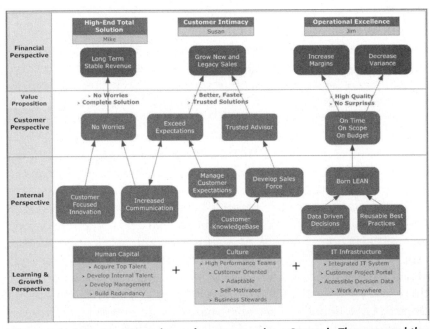

Figure 4.1: A Strategy Map shows four perspectives, Strategic Themes, and the objectives used to execute those Strategic Themes.

As shown in Figure 4.2, the perspectives for different types of organizations may differ from the basic model described by Kaplan and Norton. Figure 4.2 shows the Strategy Map for the U.S. Federal Bureau of Investigation. As a government bureau, the FBI does not drive toward a financial perspective. Instead, it wants to accomplish its mission, so "FBI Mission" is its top perspective. The stewardship of finances is at the bottom and describes how the FBI will acquire and manage its finances. This structure of perspectives with mission topmost is common for nonprofits and government organizations. Each organization must define its own perspectives, but I don't recommend varying greatly from the standard model.

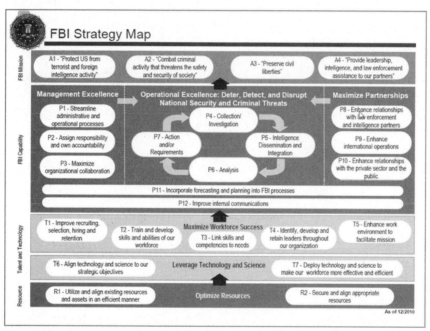

Figure 4.2: The perspectives of your Strategy Map may vary depending on your type of organization.

A good strategy has to focus itself on thrusts that satisfy customer needs. It must have the resources and capabilities to execute them and be able to defend them against competitors. These focused efforts are Strategic Themes. They appear on the Strategy Map in vertical columns. These are also described in more detail in a later section.

Within this grid of perspectives and Strategic Themes are ovals that represent Strategic Objectives. Executing these objectives is what drives the success of the Strategic Theme. The causal links between objectives, where one objective drives another, are shown as arrows.

The Strategy Map is your executive team's hypothesis of how to drive success.

The Strategy Map is a one-page description that shows every employee how the organization will reach its Strategic Destination.

Strategy Maps are not static. Like a chemistry experiment from school, you form a hypothesis, or educated guess, about what drives success. Some parts of this chain of causal links may succeed, and others may fail. When a hypothesis is wrong, you modify that part of your strategy and the map to try to get it right. Over time a learning organization will modify its Strategy Map, Balanced Scorecard, and Implementation Plan until it has a map showing the objectives and drivers that accurately reflect the business. How well you execute that strategy is the subject of Chapters 5, 6, and 7.

Leveraging Your Strategy Map

Earlier in this chapter, I listed four reasons why Strategy Maps are fundamental to strategic success. First, a Strategy Map makes it easier to identify the "critical few" metrics that drive your model. These are measures of driving force or success on the causal links. It is a cause-and-effect model of how your organization expects to succeed.

Second, communicating a strategy to everyone in an organization helps get everyone aligned and onboard. The Strategy Map is a great "talking tool" that can be used in town hall meetings to discuss where the organization is placing its emphasis.

Third, monitoring the critical few metrics from your Strategy Map shows you how well you are reaching your Strategic Objectives. You learn what does or does not drive success. Instead of managing by instinct, you have data to back up decisions.

Finally, clients tell me that taking the Strategy Map through to the Implementation Plan phase makes their budgeting processes easier. Prioritizing and time-phasing initiatives and projects is visibly easier when you know what's necessary to support Strategic Objectives.

Perspectives: Monitoring Your Strategy from Different Points of View

Since the time of 4,000-year-old Sumerian records written on clay tablets, businesses have continued to rely on finance and accounting as their primary measurement tools. Financial measures are essential, but they show only the results of what happened in prior months. They are not predictive and cannot help you drive the business.

The Balanced Scorecard takes its name from the fact that it uses balanced perspectives of what drives business and strategy. Balanced Scorecards in for-profit businesses use the four perspectives described earlier in this chapter—financial, customer and marketplace, internal operations, and learning and growth. Learning and growth includes the people, culture, intellectual capital, and IT infrastructure within a company. You can see these four perspectives in Figure 4.1.

You can understand why the perspectives are in this order by asking a series of questions about for-profit businesses. Starting at the top, in the financial perspective, you ask, "What do our financial results have to be to satisfy our stakeholders?" In the customer and marketplace perspective you ask, "What must we achieve with our customers and marketplace to successfully reach our financial results?" In the internal operations you ask, "What must we achieve with our internal operations for success with our customers and marketplace?" Finally, in the learning and growth perspective you ask, "What must our people, culture, intellectual capital, and IT be to succeed with our internal operations?"

Even though these four perspectives appear in nearly every Strategy Map, they may not be in this specific order, and there may be an additional perspective. For example, most nonprofits put the mission perspective at the top instead of finance. Nonprofits or government bodies with fixed funding may move the finance perspective to the bottom. Other nonprofits, such as nonprofit hospitals earning revenue, don't want the appearance of aiming for higher revenue, so they put customer and finance perspectives on the second level, under the mission perspective.

RENAME AND REORDER PERSPECTIVES TO FIT YOUR CULTURE

The names for the four perspectives may not fit your culture, especially if you are a nonprofit with employees and volunteers who are not motivated by the for-profit business model. One of my clients, a nonprofit healthcare provider, was concerned about communicating the importance of sound finances to the employees, who were primarily motivated by service to others. The nonprofit renamed the financial perspective Financial Stewardship. The caregivers found this name and its intention easier to understand and accept.

Strategic Themes: Concentrating Resources and Momentum along Specific Themes

One major strategic lesson crosses all of human history and endeavors: Spreading your resources across too wide a front almost certainly spells defeat. Focus is the key to success.

Strategy Maps use Strategic Themes to focus strategy on specific points. Strategic Themes appear as columns of objectives in a Strategy Map. Most organizations have two or three and never more than five Strategic Themes. In fact, going beyond three themes significantly multiplies the number of initiatives, projects, and resources required exponentially, making success that much harder to achieve. Figure 4.1 shows three Strategic Themes: Total Solution, Customer Intimacy, and Operational Excellence. Notice in Figure 4.1 that the learning and growth perspective, at the bottom, spans all three Strategic Themes. It is not uncommon for the learning and growth perspective to span more than one theme.

Everyone is familiar with Strategic Themes; you just may not know them as such. When you think of most great companies, you probably are instantly aware of their predominant Strategic Themes. Table 4-1 shows some examples.

Table 4-1: Examples of Strategic Themes Used by Organizations

THEME	ORGANIZATION	DESCRIPTION
Operational Excellence	Toyota	Toyota uses Six Sigma and Lean to create a high-performance operation, eliminating variance and waste while satisfying customers' most important needs.
Total Solution	IBM	Selling against IBM is tough because IBM provides a total solution involving hardware, software, consulting, and support.
Leading-Edge Products/ Services	Apple	Apple has a cult-like following because of its delivery of products and services (such as iTunes) that are on the leading edge.
System Lock-In	Microsoft	Once you start using its software products, the cost of switching is too high to consider the competition.
Quality	Lexus	Employees have told me that they produce the highest-quality mass-produced cars in the United States.

Selecting Strategic Themes is a combination of art and science. My clients and I review their business environment by looking at the PESTEL, 5 Forces, and SWOT. Then we examine their Strategic Destination Statement. The gap between their current state and their future vision is what the Strategic Themes must fill.

After reviewing all of this, I guide my clients through a list of 18 Strategic Themes that recur throughout for-profit strategies. It is usually obvious at that point which Strategic Themes they must focus on.

TIPS ON SELECTING STRATEGIC THEMES

Here are a few tips on selecting strategic themes:

- Select two or three and never more than five Strategic Themes.
- Give them memorable and motivational names of three to five words beginning with a verb; select themes that complement each other.
- Avoid themes "owned" by a major competitor.
- Select themes that will bridge the strategic gap to your destination.
- Select themes you can defend with good execution.

It is important to select Strategic Themes that are complementary and that can be achieved within the organization's resources and time frame.

In some cases, Strategic Themes target an impending gap in the PESTEL analysis. For example, the aging worldwide population in Western industrialized countries presents many businesses with a serious problem: finding qualified, highly skilled people.

A frequent objective that supports many themes is "Developing Internal Talent" or "Acquiring Highly Skilled Talent." But two recent clients designated an entire Strategic Theme as "Acquiring, Developing, and Retaining High-Skill Employees." If they cannot succeed at this theme, their strategies may fail.

Objectives and Causal Links: Modeling What Drives Your Business Success

The vertical themes and horizontal perspectives create a grid on which to build your Strategy Map. It should have four (or more) perspectives down the left side and usually three Strategic Themes across the top.

The interior of this grid contains Strategic Objectives and the causal links between them. Strategic Objectives are what you need to execute if you are to accomplish your Strategic Theme. The causal links are the effects that one objective has on another. For example, succeeding at an internal operations objective may drive a result in a customer objective. The book *Strategy Maps*, by Robert

Kaplan and David Norton, has many examples of Strategy Maps in many different industries.[2] For more examples of Strategy Maps, go to my website at `http://www.criticaltosuccess.com`.

Developing a Strategy Map shouldn't be a long process, but it is something that most people, including executives, find difficult at first. This is where executives must have a big-picture vision they can clearly communicate. I've found that most managers find this difficult because they are too used to thinking from a project point of view, rather than from a high-level, strategic point of view. If you begin building your Strategy Map by focusing on projects or narrow goals, you will limit the scope of alternatives and solutions as you drill down to turn your strategy into action.

Success in the objectives, shown as ovals or rectangles within the Strategy Map, is what makes a Strategic Theme succeed. The causal links between objectives show your hypothesis of how success in one objective drives success in another. These causal links are important, because if you get them right, it's easy to select the critical few metrics for your Balanced Scorecard.

Selecting a Strategy Map Facilitator

A facilitator or consultant is important in leading the Strategy Map process. A facilitator who has developed successful Strategy Maps will know when to ask probing questions, when to point out that some Strategic Objectives are too tactical, and when to guide the discussion to conclusion.

It is difficult to use a member of the executive team as the facilitator. It is difficult, if not impossible, to switch between being a contributor and being an objective facilitator for any length of time. This is especially true when CEOs attempt to facilitate.

Even company employees who are experienced facilitators may find facilitating Strategy Map sessions difficult. They must be able to shake off the accepted "truths" in the organization and see an objective reality. They must be able to ask blunt questions about the "elephant in the room"—topics people are unwilling to acknowledge and discuss.

A good facilitator will know how and when to ask probing questions that spark deeper and animated discussion. An experienced facilitator will have a basket of business stories from other industries that can be interjected to illustrate different scenarios.

Finally, a good facilitator will have a broad knowledge of all business areas. This will help the facilitator ask probing questions about the relationships between objectives in finance, sales and marketing, operations, IT, and human capital.

USE A BALANCED SCORECARD CONSULTANT CERTIFIED BY KAPLAN AND NORTON

Your organization's strategy, performance, and possibly its ultimate success depend on how well you develop and implement your Balanced Scorecard. That is a lot of responsibility to put on a general or executive consultant who is inexperienced and untrained in the development of a Balanced Scorecard. Only a few independent consultants are certified each year by the Palladium Group, the consulting firm of Drs. Kaplan and Norton. Their certification process includes intensive training and examination. To learn more about finding a Balanced Scorecard consultant, refer to the Introduction. (The consultative and facilitative methods described in this book have not been certified or vetted by the Palladium Group.)

Step-by-Step to Creating Your Strategy Map

Two methods of developing Strategy Maps work effectively with executive leadership teams or their appointed strategic team. Each of these methods works in different situations.

The Straw Dog Approach

With the straw dog approach, you present the executive leadership team or their appointed strategic team with a Strategy Map you or a team of managers have built. This is used as a structure for discussion, to tear down, and to rebuild.

Here are some advantages of the straw dog approach:

- By reviewing the straw dog Strategy Map prior to the meeting, executives have time to do in-depth thinking about the objectives and causal links.

- Less executive time is required. This method can be quicker, requiring a single meeting of 3 to 4 hours.

Here are some of the disadvantages:

- If a lack of time for executives or their designated manager drives this method, the executive team may be too operational and may not have a strategic orientation. Lack of CEO commitment is a key cause of failure.

- There may be less buy-in from executives because they are just signing off on the Strategy Map rather than building it themselves.

- The team that builds the straw dog Strategy Map exposes their lack of knowledge if they don't have a thorough understanding of the business and its strategy.

Here are the steps for the straw dog approach:

1. Educate and motivate the executive leadership team on the Balanced Scorecard.

2. Interview executive leadership team members for themes and objectives (see discussions in earlier chapters).

3. Use a small team of three senior, cross-functional managers and the executive sponsor to build a straw dog Strategy Map. Focus on the following:

   ▪ What will get us to our Strategic Destination?

   ▪ What will fill the strategic gap we face?

   ▪ What are defensible Strategic Themes we can own?

4. Send out the straw dog Strategy Map and Destination Statement with the question, "Is this the best set of objectives and causal links to get us to our Strategic Destination?"

5. Convene a Strategy Map review with the executive leadership team.

6. Review the Destination Statement.

7. Walk through the straw dog Strategy Map. Use a whiteboard and large sticky notes to create an interactive Strategy Map you can present and rebuild.

8. Discuss and rebuild it on the fly. Plan at least 3 hours minimum.

9. Redraw the map and redistribute it, asking for comments.

10. Stay open to future revisions.

The Brainstorm and Intensive Discussion Approach

With this method the facilitator must be well schooled in the possible outcomes. The map begins with a blank wall. Intense brainstorming and discussion result in the generation of new ideas, cracking silo walls, and achieving greater buy-in.

Here are some advantages of these intense brainstorming sessions:

▪ This is a good but intense method.

▪ This method opens communication and begins to crack silo walls.

▪ There is greater opportunity for cross-functional and synergistic solutions.

▪ There is a better chance for breakthrough thinking.

▪ This method allows all voices to be heard.

▪ The ideas generated by brainstorming and affinity groupings produce excellent source notes to feed into the Initiatives and Projects steps that follow Strategy Maps.

CEOS SAY THE BRAINSTORM AND INTENSIVE DISCUSSION METHOD GENERATES GREAT DISCUSSION

This method, when done correctly, opens a lot of intense discussion on topics that are not faced in day-to-day meetings or that the leadership team normally does not discuss. It is an opportunity for operationally oriented executive teams to really immerse themselves in strategic thinking. CEOs have told me that the discussions resulting from this method have been some of the most valuable they have heard from their teams.

These are the disadvantages of taking the intense brainstorming approach:

- This method works best if the same executive team goes through the PESTEL and SWOT processes before building the Strategy Map. This gives them common background.
- This takes more executive time, usually two 3-hour meetings.
- This method requires a facilitator who is experienced with executives and who has strong business experience, a collection of "business stories" about alternative objectives and themes, and an understanding of the dynamics of "crucial conversations."

Here are the steps for this approach:

1. Educate and motivate the executive leadership team on the Balanced Scorecard and strategic themes.
2. Research the business, and interview executive leadership team members for themes and objectives.
3. Consider building a straw dog Strategy Map to understand possible outcomes and develop probing questions. This process helps the facilitator develop insight. It is not meant to distribute to the leadership team.
4. Send short whitepapers and industry-related Strategy Maps to bring the executive leadership team up to speed.
5. Convene Strategy Map building sessions with the executive leadership team.
6. Use brainstorming, affinity diagrams, and process mapping to build a Strategy Map on the fly with the executive leadership team. I do this using a process similar to the Post-it Note process described earlier and summarized here:
   a. Individually brainstorm what objectives are needed for each theme and perspective.
   b. Write each idea on a large 3M Post-it Note.

    c. Collect and place the Post-its into similar groups. For example, all notes related to "Highly Skilled Workforce" go together.

    d. Post as an objective just the title of each objective, such as "Hire, Develop, and Nurture a Skilled Workforce."

7. Discuss intensely whether this is how the organization will succeed.

8. Evaluate for causal links and missing objectives.

9. Redraw and redistribute the map.

10. Solicit comments and stay open to future modifications.

Examples of how to run this process are available in video courses at http:// www.criticaltosuccess.com.

CAPTURE INFORMATION WITH A HIGH RESOLUTION CAMERA

A lot of high-value thinking goes into a Strategy Map. Don't lose these great ideas. After the sticky notes are taken down from an affinity group exercise, they can easily be mistaken for trash and discarded or mixed up, and the causal links are lost.

I don't know if it's the Boy Scout in me or just knowing how much effort goes into a map, but I use a high-resolution digital camera to capture the map while it is on the board at different points in the process. At the end I also sketch a map. I upload the digital photos to my PC, and that evening in my hotel room or on the plane, I view the magnified pictures and convert them into a Strategy Map and affinity maps.

Conducting Strategy Map Sessions

Here are some tips on working with a team to build the Strategy Map:

- Use a team of executives who are familiar with strategic visions and thinking; otherwise, the process can become mired in tactics and operations.

- These processes usually take two or three 3-hour meetings after the PESTEL, 5 Forces, and SWOT are complete.

- The team should include six to 10 cross-functional members. Fewer than six members won't create enough dialog. More than 10 will create too much.

- Use large sticky notes to post repositionable notes on the wall. (Notes aggregated into related groups become an objective.) This beats any other method of interactive idea generation. I find that the 8-by-6-inch 3M Post-it Super Sticky Notes work best. Buy the unlined Post-its with adhesive along the long edge. This makes writing large words easier.

- Write the ideas and Strategic Objectives in large, bold block letters so that everyone can read them from a distance.
- Phrase objectives in three to seven words.
- When possible, use this syntax: verb, adjective, noun. For example:

     Manage Customer Expectations

     or

     Grow Legacy Sales

When you are finished with a draft Strategy Map, review it by starting at the top of each perspective and working your way down each theme. Ask these questions:

- Will the objective above be driven by the success of the objective below?
- Is this the best objective at this point?
- Is an objective missing?
- Is this a maintenance or operational objective that is done regardless of strategy?
- Will these objectives accomplish success for this Strategic Theme?

LIMIT A MAP TO 24 OR FEWER OBJECTIVES

Research on best practices by the Palladium Group and Kaplan and Norton's consultancy shows that the best success results from Strategy Maps that have fewer than 24 objectives. If you have too many objectives, it is difficult to form a clear and concise mental model of what drives your strategy. Some large multinational organizations use only 10 to 15 objectives in their Strategy Map.

Let the team know that the Strategy Map they have built will change. It is not static. Usually insights drive change in the first week or two as the map is reviewed and given more thought. After a map has been in use for 6 months to a year, it needs to change again as you learn what drives success or as the business environment changes. The Strategy Map is a living document that needs to be adjusted as the business environment changes and objectives are met.

Before you close the session, ask the following probing questions:

- Will this get us to the Strategic Destination?
- Can we identify the top two or three objectives that are the organization's defensible barrier against competitors?
- If successfully executed, will this strategy hold off competitors?

- Can competitors easily duplicate this strategy?
- Which of these objectives must be executed first? (This is important information as a first step in prioritizing initiatives.)
- Will everyone in the organization understand this map?
- How do you feel about this map and what it will do when executed?

Selecting Strategic Theme Sponsors

Strategic Theme Sponsors take executive responsibility for leading a Strategic Theme. Strategic Themes require cross-functional thinking and teamwork to execute successfully. Usually a Theme team of cross-functional directors or senior managers works to develop and manage the Strategic Theme. The Theme team reports to the Strategic Theme Sponsor monthly to ensure that they are on track.

During the Strategy Map process it usually becomes evident which executives have energy, enthusiasm, and knowledge regarding specific themes. Executive sponsors often self-select by the time the Strategy Map is built.

Summary

The Strategy Map is the foundation of your strategy. Done correctly it is a one-page strategic summary that clearly communicates to everyone in the organization how they can contribute to success. The objectives and causal links in the Strategy Map make it straightforward, although still not easy, to select the critical few metrics for the Balanced Scorecard.

After you have drafted the Strategy Map, it's time to complete an Action Plan and Implementation Plan. The Action Plan identifies the metrics that measure each theme and its initiatives. The Implementation Plan breaks down the projects in each initiative, describing which objectives are impacted and how projects should be phased in over time. These topics are covered in Chapters 5 and 7.

Notes

1. R. Kaplan and D. Norton, *The Execution Premium: Linking Strategy to Operations for Competitive Advantage* (Boston, Massachusetts: Harvard Business Press, 2008).
2. R. Kaplan and D. Norton, *Strategy Maps: Converting Intangible Assets into Tangible Outcomes* (Boston, Massachusetts: Harvard Business Press, 2004).

Step-by-Step from Strategy to Action

... the essence of strategy is in the activities—to perform activities differently or to perform different activities than rivals.

—Michael Porter

Your Strategy Map gives you a clear illustration of your strategy. Now you must translate that strategy into action, for only by executing your strategy do you win. Your Strategy Map has multiple perspectives into your organization— Strategic Themes that focus energy and resources, and objectives designed to close the gaps between your present and future. This chapter guides you through translating the Strategic Objectives on the Strategy Map into initiatives. In later chapters, these initiatives become the actions you use to execute your strategy.

Turning Your Strategy Map into Measurable Action

In Robert Kaplan and Peter Norton's *Harvard Business Review* article "Using the Balanced Scorecard as a Strategic Management System," they describe a simple table that makes the translation from Strategic Objectives into action a process that is straightforward, although not without effort.[1] Figure 5.1 shows an Action Plan that converts the objectives of one Strategic Theme into measures, metrics, targets, and initiatives.

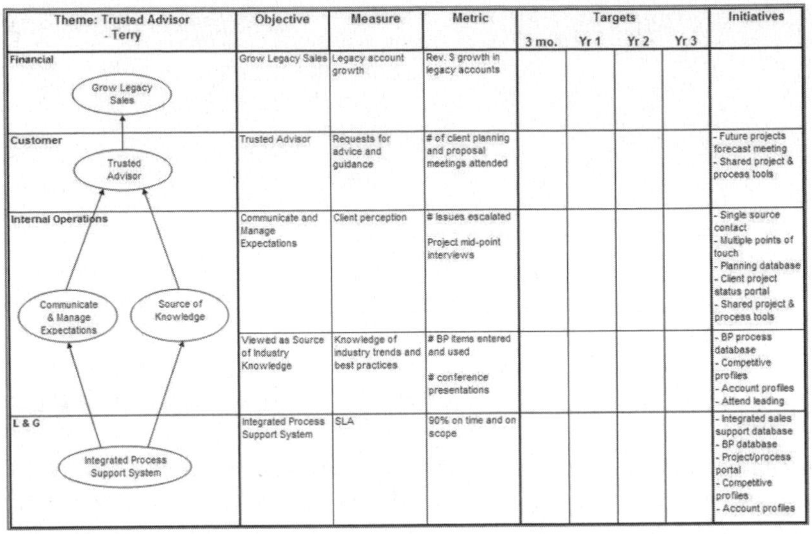

Theme: Trusted Advisor - Terry	Objective	Measure	Metric	Targets				Initiatives
				3 mo.	Yr 1	Yr 2	Yr 3	
Financial — Grow Legacy Sales	Grow Legacy Sales	Legacy account growth	Rev. $ growth in legacy accounts					
Customer — Trusted Advisor	Trusted Advisor	Requests for advice and guidance	# of client planning and proposal meetings attended					- Future projects forecast meeting - Shared project & process tools
Internal Operations — Communicate & Manage Expectations / Source of Knowledge	Communicate and Manage Expectations	Client perception	# issues escalated Project mid-point interviews					- Single source contact - Multiple points of touch - Planning database - Client project status portal - Shared project & process tools
	Viewed as Source of Industry Knowledge	Knowledge of industry trends and best practices	# BP items entered and used # conference presentations					- BP process database - Competitive profiles - Account profiles - Attend leading
L & G — Integrated Process Support System	Integrated Process Support System	SLA	90% on time and on scope					- Integrated sales support database - BP database - Project/process portal - Competitive profiles - Account profiles

Figure 5.1: Convert the objectives from each Strategic Theme in your Strategy Map into measures, targets, and initiatives.

The first column of the Action Plan is the Strategy Map for one Strategic Theme. The name under the Strategic Theme at the top of the first column is the executive sponsor for this theme.

Table 5-1 describes the other columns in the table.

Table 5-1: An Action Plan

COLUMN	DESCRIPTION
Strategic Theme Map	This segment from the Strategy Map shows the Strategic Objectives and causal links for one Strategic Theme.
Objectives	Listing the objectives as bulleted text makes it easier to align measurements and initiatives in the table.
Measure	This is the unit by which progress toward the objective is evaluated. An objective may have multiple measurements. The executive leadership team usually selects the measure during their Strategy Mapping workshop.
Metric	The metric is a quantifiable evaluation of the measure. A measure may have many different metrics. Metrics may be leading or lagging and are defined in detail by the Strategic Theme team.

COLUMN	DESCRIPTION
Target	Targets are the quantitative value at a given point in time needed to achieve the objectives.
Initiatives	Initiatives are collections of actions or projects designed to close the gap between targeted and actual performance and to achieve the Strategic Objective.

SELECTING MEASURES

The executive leadership team selects the measurements for each objective near the end of their Strategy Map workshop, as described in Chapter 4. Chapter 6 talks in detail about selecting and defining measurements, metrics, and targets. After the executive leadership team has defined what it wants as a measure for each objective, the Strategic Theme teams develop the metrics and their definitions.

Strategic Theme Teams

After the executive leadership team has developed a Strategy Map and selected measurements, it needs to select members for the Strategic Theme teams. The Strategic Theme teams will translate the Strategy Map into the Strategic Action Plan, similar to that shown in Figure 5.1, incorporating metrics, targets, and initiatives.

There is one Strategic Theme team per Strategic Theme. The Strategic Theme team reports to the Strategic Theme's executive sponsor, but each team has its own leader. Each Strategic Theme team is composed of four to six people. If there are three Strategic Themes, there will be a total of 12 to 18 people for all the Strategic Theme teams. The members of these teams:

- Are highly experienced managers or directors who may be on a development track as future executives.

- Have cross-functional knowledge and responsibilities supporting the Strategic Theme's objectives. Because Strategic Themes are cross-functional, it is critical that each team have experience in areas of operations, marketing, finance, human capital, and so on.

- Can dedicate time to analyzing and developing metrics and initiatives.

- Have the power and ability necessary to lead initiatives.
- Have experience in planning and executing initiatives and projects.

Motivating and Educating the Strategic Theme Teams

It is as important to educate and motivate the directors and managers who compose your Strategic Theme teams as it is to educate and motivate the executive leadership team. In preparation for the first meeting, which is focused on motivation and education, I usually send short articles that concisely describe the concepts of the Strategy Map and the Balanced Scorecard. It is important to also include articles and whitepapers about Balanced Scorecard successes by their competitors or within their industry. Keeping these articles short ensures that they will be read.

The first meeting with Strategic Theme team members has three parts. The meeting begins with the CEO, Strategic Theme sponsors, and the facilitator guiding the Theme team through the case for change. They must feel the need for change. Next, the facilitator explains the Balanced Scorecard process and its successful use in related businesses. The last hour-and-a-half is used to begin brainstorming about new initiatives and to develop commitment to specific themes.

I recommend that the CEO and each of the Strategic Theme team leaders be at this first meeting. The CEO should open the meeting with the case for change, explaining how the executive leadership team has developed a Strategy Map to articulate the organization's strategy. She should explain that the members of this meeting will be expected to translate the strategy and Strategy Map into initiatives that will drive the organization to its objectives.

After the CEO presents the case for change, the facilitator should illustrate how the Balanced Scorecard has worked successfully in the same or similar industries. At that point, each of the executive theme sponsors should explain the objectives and causal links in their Strategic Themes and the cross-functional responsibility they have in ensuring that the themes are successfully executed.

The facilitator and executive sponsor can then begin the education process to inform the Strategic Theme team members about the Balanced Scorecard and the duties of the Strategic Theme team members.

After the education and motivation process is complete, and before continuing, ensure that everyone understands the definitions of perspectives, Strategic Themes, objectives, and initiatives. People often confuse Strategic Initiatives with projects. Let them know that initiatives are collections of projects designed to reach a Strategic Objective. Your organization may have its own definition for these terms, so use terms everyone in your organization understands.

Brainstorming Initiatives

Before the meeting, you should have prepared sets of partially completed Strategic Action Plans. You should have copies of each Strategic Theme that have the Strategic Theme Map, Objectives, and Measurement columns completed. Team members will use these templates as guides for later work.

You should also have examples of completed Strategic Action Plans. People learn more easily from examples than from long-winded explanations. A variety of examples of Balanced Scorecards and Strategic Action Plans related to your industry can help team members see the syntax of initiative as well as how the Strategic Action Plan is completed.

CEOS AND SPONSORS SHOULD LEAVE DURING BRAINSTORMING

Executive sponsors should leave the room before brainstorming sessions, because their political and referential weight can limit new ideas.

There are many ways to brainstorm and develop ideas. Here is one way that allows you to capture the voice of quiet members as well as to get team members committed to specific Strategic Themes:

1. Tell the group that they will be brainstorming initiatives that will help the organization reach the Strategic Objectives. Let them know they will be working in groups focused on one Strategic Theme.

   It is important to let the Strategic Theme teams know from the beginning that they are developing ideas and proposals for initiatives, not developing the actual strategy. The Strategic Theme team's proposals must still be made consistent with existing initiatives and projects and must go to the executive leadership team for alignment, modification, and approval.

AN INEXPERIENCED FACILITATOR CAN CAUSE DISTRESS

In one situation, a city government staff nearly mutinied after they went through a process to develop initiatives. An inexperienced facilitator did not make it clear to the staff that the purpose of the meetings was to develop proposals for initiatives. The staff thought they were actually developing strategy. It wasn't until late in the action planning process that the facilitator and general manager finally clarified to the staff that they were brainstorming proposals that would then be rationalized, aligned, and approved. This shocking turn of events left the Strategy Theme teams feeling disempowered, and much ill will developed. Make sure that the teams understand that they are developing initiatives to make the Strategic Objectives happen.

2. Give the Strategy Theme teams a written set of rules for their brainstorming:

   - Any initiative can be proposed. These are proposals, not final initiatives.

   - Current initiatives and initiatives already in the general plan will be rationalized later with new proposed initiatives.

   - Brainstorming will be done individually and silently until everyone has finished. Repeat this process. Research has shown the best idea generation begins with silent brainstorming, followed later by group work.

   - Don't discuss ideas until everyone on the Strategic Theme team is finished with their individual ideas.

3. Give the Strategic Theme teams a written set of rules for writing their brainstorming notes:

   - Use the large-sized 8-by-6-inch 3M Post-it Super Sticky Notes to capture ideas.

   - Write one idea per note.

   - Write three to five words per note.

   - Write in bold letters.

   - Write initiatives using syntax such as this:

     - Cross-sell marketing

     - Single-source data system

     - High-value customer retention program

   A Strategic Theme team usually generates 30 to 40 initiative ideas.

4. Demonstrate to the entire group the affinity grouping process used to consolidate ideas into initiatives:

   - Post all notes on the wall. Discuss the meaning and intent of each note as it is posted.

   - Group notes with similar intent. Some groups may have a large number of notes; others may have just one or two.

   - Write a name for this group on a note, and post it over each group. These names will be the names of initiatives.

   - Keep all the notes. They can be used as ideas for projects to support the initiatives.

   - Select a Strategic Theme team leader to report back on the named initiatives that the Strategic Theme team develops.

5. Let the group know that they need to divide into Strategic Theme teams, with four to six people working on each Strategic Theme.

6. Dismiss the Strategic Theme teams to break-out rooms. Give them about one hour to work on brainstorming and initiative naming. Let them know that their ideas will be integrated with appropriate current initiatives. This is an opportunity for new ideas. Old projects and maintenance projects are not necessarily being eliminated.

7. While the Strategic Theme teams are in their breakout areas, create on the walls a large version of the Strategic Action Plan for each Strategic Theme. Use 3M Post-it Super Sticky Notes to create the map column of each theme. Leave room to the right of each theme's map for the initiatives developed by the Strategic Theme teams.

8. Go around to each group, and help them with their brainstorming processes.

9. Reconvene all the Strategic Theme teams.

10. Ask each team leader in turn to post and explain their initiatives next to each objective on the wall.

11. Ask the Strategic Theme teams for feedback on how they feel about their work and whether they think the initiatives will accomplish the objective.

12. Let the Strategic Theme teams know that prior to the next meeting, individual teamwork will further develop the initiatives. The work they have done here will be rationalized with existing organizational initiatives and projects and will be sent as a proposal to the executive leadership team.

This first meeting may or may not develop many new initiatives, depending on how much prior work has been done and whether these same team members were involved. I have found that if this is the organization's first attempt at a structured strategy and execution plan, many new ideas, excitement, and enthusiasm will be generated. However, if the organization has had multiple false starts or has failed previously with a strategic plan or Balanced Scorecard, people may exhibit more of a wait-and-see attitude. In the latter case, I can usually build enthusiasm by showing teams what happens next:

- Initiatives are rationalized and prioritized.
- Initiatives are divided into projects.
- Projects are phased in and funded over time.
- Progress is monitored using the Balanced Scorecard.

When people see that they have a structured way to reach these long-term goals, their optimism returns.

At the end of this first meeting, people usually have self-selected the Strategic Theme team they want to work on. This is a good point at which to ask Strategic Theme teams to enter the initiatives they have brainstormed into a Strategic Action Plan. They also need to enter all the brainstorming notes from their team. These notes may aid in developing ideas for projects within each initiative.

Developing a Robust List of Initiatives

After the initial brainstorming meeting, each Strategic Theme team usually needs one or two more meetings to fully develop a proposal of initiatives that support the Strategic Objectives. In the second meeting, Strategic Theme team members should look through current and planned initiatives and note those that support their team's Strategic Objectives. These current initiatives should then be added to the Strategic Action Plan.

A tool that helps at this point is a spreadsheet, like the one shown in Figure 5.2. This sheet has Strategic Objectives listed down the left side and current initiatives across the top. Dots within the cells indicate where a current initiative supports a Strategic Objective.

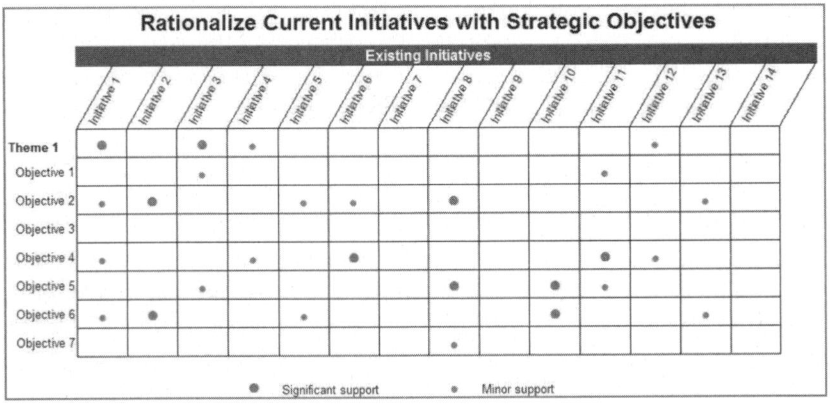

Figure 5.2: Check which of your existing initiatives support your Strategic Objectives.

Notice in this figure that Strategic Objective 3 is not supported by any current initiative. This is to be expected if the objective's performance is on target. Initiatives 7, 9, and 14 do not support any Strategic Objective. Unless these initiatives are needed for normal operation and maintenance, they might need to be eliminated.

A short description should be given of how any initiative with a dot supports its related Strategic Objective. Initiatives that do not support a Strategic Objective may be candidates to be phased out. The Strategic Theme teams should then sit down with their executive sponsors and review their initiatives and Strategic Action Plan, making any modifications necessary.

Prioritizing Initiatives

Organizations that face a crisis will find it easy to prioritize initiatives. Their selection of initiatives is driven by the need to surmount their crisis.

Complex organizations with a large number of initiatives need a structured approach to selecting and prioritizing them. One way to do this is to use a spreadsheet that prioritizes initiatives by weighting factors, as shown in Figure 5.3.

Initiative Prioritizing Matrix

	Strategic Value of Obj.	Impact on Obj. Success	Time to Implement	Resource Requirement	Current Alignment		Priority
	9 - High 3 - Mid 1 - Low	9 - High 3 - Mid 1 - Low	9 - Low 3 - Mid 1 - High	9 - Low 3 - Mid 1 - High	9 - High 3 - Mid 1 - Low		
Theme 1							
Initiative 1	9	9	1	3	1		243
Initiative 2	1	3	9	3	9		729
Initiative 3	9	3	9	9	3		6561
Initiative 4	3	3	1	3	9		243
Initiative 5	1	9	3	1	3		81
Initiative 6	9	3	1	9	3		729
Initiative 7	3	3	9	3	9		2187

Figure 5.3: Prioritize initiatives using a spreadsheet with exponential weighting.

Weighting values between 1 and 5 are often used. However, I find that this produces a narrow distribution between weighted initiatives. Using weights of 1, 3, and 9 gives a wider distribution:

- **1:** Lowest level
- **3:** Mid-level
- **9:** Highest level

In Figure 5.3, the weighting factors are

- Strategic value
- Initiative's impact on objective's success
- Time required for implementation
- Resources required for implementation
- Current alignment with initiative definition

The weighting factors you use depend on your business priorities. After developing a prioritized list of initiatives and completing the Action Plan for each Strategic Theme, you should present the result to the appropriate executive sponsor. In turn, these reviewed Action Plans, with their initiatives, as well as the metrics described in Chapter 6, should be proposed to the executive leadership team for revision and approval.

Summary

Your strategic success depends on selecting the right initiatives—ones you can execute well and ones that strongly affect the Strategic Objective. The processes in this chapter for developing, rationalizing, and prioritizing these initiatives may seem tedious, but the work involved is nothing compared to the wastefulness of selecting the wrong initiatives. In Chapter 6, you will complete the Action Plan.

Note

1. R. Kaplan and D. Norton, "Using the Balanced Scorecard as a Strategic Management System," *Harvard Business Review*, July 2007.

Step-by-Step to Selecting Metrics and Setting Targets

Get the data first! Then distort it with your judgment.
—Mark Twain
Satirist, author
1835–1910

There are two reasons for measures and targets. One is to drive change in behavior, and the other is to drive change in processes. It is that simple!

It is also that important! If you pick the wrong measure, you drive change in the wrong direction. If you pick a target that's too easy, you don't challenge people enough, which might result in unrealized gains. If you pick a target that's too difficult, you overwhelm people. You need to get the right metric with a target that is a stretch, but achievable.

Don't expect to get all your objectives and measures right the first time; few organizations do. Objectives and measures usually evolve as you test your model of what drives your organization.

Your Strategy Map is a map of where you want to go in the future. As you meet your strategic objective's performance targets, initiative will go into a maintenance mode; but it is important to still monitor the objectives performance to ensure it continues to meet its target. Otherwise, as your focus (and resources) shift to other objectives you risk losing the gains you have made. You can also shift resources to other objectives to keep up your momentum and direction toward the goal described in your Strategic Destination Statement.

Achieving Balance in Your Balanced Scorecard

Most Balanced Scorecards are not balanced when first developed. In fact, if they are developed in-house, they usually are heavily weighted toward the financial perspective. That's because the executive team is familiar with that perspective: Their minds are used to analyzing these numbers, and all the financial data are available. Finding the "critical few" measures for the financial perspective is usually quick and obvious.

It's important when you develop your Strategy Map that the team be cross-functional and know about all the parts of the organization. This will help you develop an even balance in your objectives and measures.

I find that what usually happens is that as soon as everyone lets go of financial objectives and starts working on a balanced viewpoint, there is a rush to operational objectives and measures—again because these are familiar.

When you have completed your initial Strategy Map, it is important that your facilitator guide you through each perspective from the top down. Test to ensure that the objectives and measures in one perspective actually drive the objective in the next-higher layer.

Some of the most difficult measures to develop are in learning and growth. The measures of culture, employee attitude, and employee engagement can be difficult to quantify. Some excellent books on this topic are available:

- *The ROI of Human Capital: Measuring the Economic Value of Employee Performance* by Jac Fitz-enz (New York, New York: AMACOM, 2000)

- *How to Measure Human Resources Management*, Third Edition by Jac Fitz-enz (New York, New York: McGraw-Hill, 2001)

- *The Workforce Scorecard: Managing Human Capital to Execute Strategy* by Richard Beatty, Brian Becker, and Mark Huselid (Boston, Massachusetts: Harvard Business School Press, 2005)

- *The HR Scorecard: Linking People, Strategy, and Performance* by Brian Becker, Mark Huselid, and David Ulrich (Boston, Massachusetts: Harvard Business School Press, 2001)

The Workforce Scorecard and *The HR Scorecard* have correlated a "critical few" human capital metrics to high-performing companies. Some of their findings are real eye-openers. Implementing a critical few human capital programs that are measured with a critical few metrics produces a magnitude of difference.

The Right Number of Measures

Well-developed, usable Balanced Scorecards seem to have 12 to 24 metrics, with the number being more on the lower side. Many global corporations have 10 to 15 metrics.

The more metrics you have, the harder it will be for you to form a clear picture of your Strategic Model's drivers and interactions. The Balanced Scorecards I've seen with more than 20 metrics usually have had operational metrics creep in. This happens when an executive leadership team is used to digging in and helping with operational issues. The executives feel a need to monitor those operational issues in the Balanced Scorecard. Remember, the Balanced Scorecard is for strategic alignment and focus. Operational Dashboards can be used to handle operational issues and troubleshoot operational concerns.

In an article titled "Swamped" in *CFO Europe* magazine (November 16, 2004), Janet Kersnar reported that the Hackett Group surveyed 2,400 European and U.S. companies. It found that 70 percent of the Balanced Scorecards were failing to help their companies as much as they should have. The conclusion was that these Balanced Scorecards were not providing "concise, predictive and action-able information about how a company is performing and may perform in the future." Notice the words "concise" and "actionable." One reason is that senior executives in the survey were inundated with 132 metrics, the large majority of them financial, which they reviewed every month. When Hackett compared the surveyed companies with best-practice companies in its extensive database, the researchers found that managers in best-practice companies used just 15 metrics instead of 132.

If You Have More Than the "Critical Few," You Lose

One of the leading reasons for failure in Balanced Scorecards is too many met-rics. The results are illustrated by a call I got from the quality control manager for a large telecom company. The company faced a difficult situation. The division vice president was reviewing about 100 metrics in a two-hour, death-by-PowerPoint meeting. The results were mind-numbing. No one knew which metrics were important. No one knew which metrics drove the business. No one knew which metrics signaled success. They needed help in identifying the "critical few" metrics.

We scheduled a meeting for two weeks out, but before we could get together, the organization was acquired by a larger telecom. I still wonder if the two-hour, all-hands PowerPoint meeting wasn't just one symptom of the larger problem that forced the company into being acquired. Clarity, alignment, and focusing on what was important might have prevented their problems.

Leading and Lagging Metrics: Drivers and Results

Metrics on a Balanced Scorecard can be divided into two main categories: leading and lagging. Leading measures drive an objective. They are the arrowhead on the causal link. Lagging measures are the results of an objective.

Well-built Balanced Scorecards have a good mixture of leading and lagging metrics. This helps the leadership team form a mental model of the most important drivers for each Strategic Theme and the most important results to be expected for a Strategic Theme.

It's obvious from the causal links on a Strategy Map that the lagging (result) metric from one objective will be the leading (driver) metric into another metric.

As shown in Table 6-1, all measures in the financial perspective will be lagging. A general rule of thumb in a for-profit Balanced Scorecard is that any measure in dollars is lagging. Conversely, almost all measures in the learning and growth perspective are leading. They drive change in internal operations and customer perspectives.

Internal operations and customer measures are a mixture of both leading and lagging metrics. These perspectives usually have multiple objectives in one perspective layer that feed each other.

Table 6-1: Each Perspective Has a Different Mixture of Leading and Lagging Measures

PERSPECTIVE	TYPE OF MEASURE
Financial	100% lagging (result)
Customer	Mixture of leading and lagging
Internal operations	Mixture of leading and lagging
Learning and growth	100% leading (driver)

Sample Objectives and Metrics

Many good books are available on defining new metrics, as well as lists of industry-standard metrics. Industry consultants, performance consultants, and Balanced Scorecard consultants have lists of metrics that are standard for your industry or similar business models.

MOTIVATING WITH METRICS

Being measured can be either intimidating or motivating. It depends on whether you feel the goal is achievable, your level of empowerment, and whether you have a way of learning the skills you will need to reach a higher level. The following is a personal, not business, story, but I think it illustrates my point.

My six-year old son entered first grade almost halfway through the year through no fault of his own. Through the work of two great teachers at his public school and his mom's mentoring, he finished the year slightly below average on reading tests. The principal sent a letter to all students saying that any student who read 800 pages over the summer would get to have an ice cream cone with her. Any student who read 1,200 pages would get to have a banana split with her.

The ice cream and the time with the principal were motivators, but the motivation lasted only a day for my son, because we walk to the ice cream store about every other week. I thought about what his motivators were and how to get him engaged. He and I talked through ideas and came up with the following plan:

- ■ **Visual indicator:** We put a thermometer chart on the kitchen door that showed how many pages he had read, with a picture of the reward at each major point.

- ■ **Awareness of progress:** It was up to my son to color the thermometer and write the name of the book (with some prodding) each time he finished a book.

- ■ **Personal empowerment and decision-making within a defined scope:** He got to pick about half the books to read from the Level 1 to Level 3 readers at the library.

- ■ **Modeling by mentors:** Either his mom, his GoGo (Zulu for grandma), or I read the book to him, with lots of emphasis and enunciation; then he read it himself sometime that day. This gave him good modeling.

- ■ **Short-term rewards:** Whenever my son achieved a jump in proficiency, we had an impromptu "parade" around the house to acknowledge how much he had improved.

- ■ **Rewards:** At 800 pages, he got the science kit he had been craving. At 1,200 pages, he and I went to lunch at the kids' fun center in town and played games.

The results were amazing. In the first five days, he read over 500 pages without prompting (he got his science kit shortly thereafter). After two weeks he slowed down a little, but he was still reading over 50 pages a day.

There has been a marked difference in his fluency and attitude. He got bored the other day while watching his hour of TV, picked up a book, and started reading to himself, ignoring the TV.

Our next steps will be to help him internalize his feelings of reward and power so that he doesn't need to depend on us.

Although a list may reduce your need for brainstorming, choosing the correct metric for your objective and situation is critical. Table 6-2 shows a sample of objective/measure pairs from a few of my clients. Many metrics may be possible for one objective. The one you select depends on your unique situation.

Table 6-2: Sample Pairs of Objectives and Measures

PERSPECTIVE	OBJECTIVE	MEASURE
Finance	Increase new-product sales	Percentage of revenue from products less than three years old
	Balanced revenue portfolio	Ratio of revenue by product line and segment
	Stabilize cash flow	Reduce variance from budget
	Increase account penetration	Percentage of the total contract
Customer	Customer delight	Percentage of survey respondents who said they would refer a friend
	On time, on budget, and within scope	Project time, budget, and scope variance
	Make it easy	Greater than 4 out of 5 on satisfaction surveys given at intermediate stage gates
	Trusted advisor relationship	Number of C-level meetings and client design meetings invited to
Internal operations	Be lean	Money saved due to top x Lean projects
	Hassle-free delivery of transactions	Percentage of claims paid in 30 days
	Close contact client engagement	Index of engagement scores
	Manufacturing performance	Cycle times, unit cost, waste
Learning and growth	Management/supervisor development	Percentage of management/supervisor training completed

PERSPECTIVE	OBJECTIVE	MEASURE
	Employee development	Percentage of employees with current 360 evaluation
	Managerial loyalty	Management positions filled through internal promotion
	Strategic readiness	Percentage of strategic employee positions with qualified successor

---

FINDING APPROPRIATE METRICS

There are many good books on metrics, measures, and key performance indicators (KPIs). Those books are in addition to all the internal experience you already have with measures in your organization. Here are some ways in which you can search for metrics that match your objectives:

- **Search Google using an industry and term, such as "hospital nosocomial infection metric" or "manufacturing HR metrics."**

- **Many good books are devoted to metrics in specific areas, such as manufacturing and operations, marketing, and human resources.**

- **Check with your industry association for industry benchmarks.**

- **Search for benchmark websites. These are usually membership websites where the members anonymously submit their metrics so that they have access to others' company results.**

- **Check with your banker and CPA for financial metrics. There are many lists of financial standard metrics for specific industries.**

Step-by-Step to Selecting Your Metrics

Developing measures and metrics seems to be either very easy or pretty tough. In some cases there are no clear answers about which is the best metric to use.

Compose your metrics teams of each Strategic Theme team and subject matter experts (SMEs) in the areas you need to measure. As much as possible, your team should have depth in the metric, but also have cross-functional knowledge.

I usually do this by having as many members of the Strategic Theme team as possible (usually three or four) meet and then augment them with SMEs for the specific metric being defined. You may also need to include someone from IT or human resources/human capital (HR/HC) when you talk about what data are available and who is responsible for them.

Here is a general outline for the steps to follow:

1. Quickly review the Strategy Map.

2. Review the objective you are focusing on.

3. Review the measure selected by the executive leadership team. You may need to redefine this if the SME has a constructive alternative.

4. Discuss the measure's "intent": What behavior, actions, or processes is it intended to change?

5. Brainstorm individually which quantitative metrics will work.

6. Reduce these to a single metric or two counterbalancing metrics:

   ∎ Does it measure the intent?

   ∎ Does it measure strategic or operational change?

   ∎ Is it "actionable"?

   ∎ Are the data available? If not, can they be captured cost/time-effectively?

7. While this information is fresh in everyone's mind, use a Metric Definition sheet, described in the next section, to capture a definition of the metric. One or two individuals can complete these later.

One of the things I observe in working with small- and midsized businesses on their Balanced Scorecards is the difference between strategic thinkers and operational doers. These two types have different ways of thinking, analyzing, and communicating. A good facilitator will help you smooth out these differences and keep the discussion moving at a strategic level while satisfying the SMEs' need for detail by capturing detailed ideas that may be valuable during implementation.

Defining the Metric with a Metric Definition

After you have selected a metric, the Strategic Theme team and its SMEs need to create a written description of that metric, the targets, and the alert values.

Many organizations create a Metric Definition table that includes the following items:

∎ Metric name

∎ Strategic Theme

∎ Objective measured

∎ Theme team leader and members

∎ Rationale for this metric

- What it drives or measures
- How it is calculated
- Data sources and where they are located
- Alert levels over time
- Target levels over time

In my experience it is difficult to get team members to complete the Metric Definition, so we usually do it interactively on a laptop as we are defining and selecting metrics. That leaves just cleanup work later.

Some of the items from the Metric Definition should be put in the Briefing Book of your Balanced Scorecard. The Briefing Book is a one-screen form linked to each Balanced Scorecard chart. The leadership team can see for which Strategic Theme and objective the metric is used, who the owner is, and what current actions are being taken. The Briefing Book is described in more detail in Chapter 28, "Finishing Touches."

Look Out! What You Measure Is What You Get!

The old saying "What you measure is what you get" has a corollary from the dark side: "If you measure the wrong thing, you'll get the wrong result." Be sure to select metrics that drive the behaviors and process changes you want.

In their book *The HR Scorecard: Linking People, Strategy, and Performance*, Huselid, Becker, and Ulrich reveal the results of their research into how HR/HC creates a high-performance work system (HPWS). Their findings for 429 firms in 1998 reveal a striking difference between corporations in the top and bottom 10 percent of financial performance. They found specific HR metrics that pinpoint the difference between top- and bottom-performing corporations. They said, "The most striking attribute of these comparisons is not any one HR management practice—it is not recruiting or training or compensation. Rather, the differences are much more comprehensive—and systemic." It wasn't one or two specific measures that made a difference. It was an entire system of specific metrics that seemed to make the difference between winners and losers. If you measure the right HR metrics, doing so can help make your organization a winner. If you measure the wrong HR metrics, at best you waste your time and money.

Another example showing the relationship between well-chosen metrics and strategic success is exemplified by the turnaround in Sears, Roebuck and Company in the 1990s. In a *Harvard Business Review* article written by Rucci, Kirn, and Quinn titled "The Employee-Customer-Profit Chain at Sears," Sears developed and communicated a set of metrics that saved the company. In one year, 1992–93, the merchandising group went from a loss of $3 billion to a net income of $752 million. They produced this dramatic change by building an *employee-customer-profit* model that defined the causal links that drove their business success. In one area they found that a 5 percent improvement in employee attitude drove a 1.3 percent improvement in customer satisfaction and resulted in a 0.5 percent improvement in revenue growth.

Of course, it isn't just the metric and measurement that made the difference for Sears. Sears had to align the organization around the model, foster a culture to reinforce the change, and then monitor and manage with the measures. Sears also had to develop a system of ownership and accountability through every level of the company. These are all parts of a fully implemented Balanced Scorecard.

Critical Questions to Ask about Your Measures and Metrics

Following are a few critical questions to ask as you evaluate any metric you select, whether it's new or a legacy:

- What do we need to change to reach this objective?
    - Does this metric drive the change in behavior we need?
    - Does this metric measure the change in processes we need?
    - Is this metric fair and understandable by all? Can it be "gamed" by a few to circumvent the intent of the Balanced Scorecard?
- Does this metric test our hypothesis?
    - Is this metric the best measure of success or a driver for this objective?
    - Will this metric help us prove how our business model works?
    - Will we be able to change our organization because of changes in this metric?
- Are the data available?
    - What is the data's source?
    - Are the data clean and usable?
    - If the data are unavailable, are there proxies or substitutes that act the same way?
    - Can the data be captured from an existing initiative?
    - Can a cost-effective and timely program capture these data?
- What action will we take?
    - What actions will we take if this metric changes?
    - Is someone responsible for those actions?

- What target and alert levels would signal the need to take action?
- If we don't intend to take action when an alert level is met, why are we using this metric?
  - How often do we measure?
    - How often are data available?
    - Is that frequency often enough for us to make an effective course correction?
    - How frequently do we need to make effective changes?

Some metrics, such as an annual employee satisfaction survey, are done only once a year because of the expense and volume. An annual measurement is not frequent enough to drive change with any insight; however, there may be a proxy metric you capture more frequently that can indicate change. For example, some proxies you can use for employee satisfaction are lost time from injuries, lost days from sickness, and productivity levels. Another alternative is to do a monthly mini-survey of a small random sample of employees to monitor change from the annual survey.

  - Is there a data owner?
    - Will someone be responsible for these data, their accuracy, and their entry into the Balanced Scorecard system?
    - Is there a data warehouse or portal where these data can be maintained?

Setting Targets

Executives and managers are used to setting targets, so I won't go into this topic in detail. But you might want to consider some nuances with respect to the Balanced Scorecard.

To begin, work from the top down. Start with the financial perspective, and consider what portion of the change here can be attributed to each Strategic Theme. For example, if the organization wants to increase from $80 million in revenue to $120 million in revenue in the next three years and has three Strategic Themes, the organization may need to apportion that growth across the three themes.

Now determine how much each Strategic Theme must contribute to reach the total target. As you work down the perspectives in each Strategic Theme, you need to ask yourself questions such as these:

- Revenue Increase Strategic Themes
  - What change will be necessary in market share, customer response, or repeat purchase?

- What increase in infrastructure will be needed?
- What new processes will need funding?
- Cost Reduction Strategic Themes
  - How much can we decrease production costs?
  - How much can we increase productivity?

Setting Target Values

If you use the preceding process, you will have defined the targets needed for the financial goals in each Strategic Theme. After you figure out how much each Strategic Theme contributes to the total financial goals, you can define how each perspective in that theme needs to change to make the financial goal happen. This is usually an iterative process that involves working up and down the theme as well as determining whether the math produces a realistic target. Here are some ideas for sources you can use to test whether the targets you've developed are realistic:

- Historical tracking and benchmarking of organizational data
- Horizontal comparison between similar business units in your organization
- Association benchmarks
- Best-practice surveys from private consulting firms
- Best estimates from a panel of experts
- Regulatory benchmarks set by legislative agencies

Setting Intermediate Targets

Your target for a three-year horizon may be a 100 percent improvement, but you'll never get your employees to believe that unless you do the following:

- Divide the amount of change into smaller increments over time.
- Tell a story that shows how each small, achievable step builds to the bigger goal.
- Celebrate when you reach intermediate goals.

When I work with my clients, we prioritize initiatives and projects and then schedule them over the three to five years of their strategic goal. As the next chapter explains, I help them spread initiatives across near-term and long-term schedules:

- First-year goals by quarter: Q1, Q2, Q3, Q4

- Second-year goals
- Third-year goals
- And so forth

You Will Not Move toward a Target at a Constant Rate

It's rare to approach an objective at the same rate over three or more years. You need to adjust your intermediary targets for different growth rates depending on the type of initiative you are measuring.

Productivity programs such as Six Sigma and Lean usually result in very rapid returns in the near term, with diminishing returns thereafter. Some marketing programs have this same diminishing-returns curve. The first year may see rapid growth, which then diminishes over the next few years as the market saturates and competitors enter the same market. For example, the growth rates in the following table build to an overall change of more than 200 percent in two years:

YEAR 1	YEAR 2	YEAR 3
50%	25%	10%

Entering a completely new and open market with high demand, a so-called greenfield, can produce sigmoid or S curve growth. The sigmoid curve has what looks like rapid exponential growth in the beginning, linear growth during market adoption, and then asymptotic or diminishing returns as the market becomes saturated. The first part of this curve is the infamous "hockey stick" that so many dot-com businesses bet on before failing.

Summary

The measures you choose will make all the difference to the results of your Balanced Scorecard. People will work hard to give you what you measure, so choose measures that reflect the causal links on your Strategy Map.

You can find many lists of measures on the Internet, through associations, and through your own experience. Choose a combination of leading or driver metrics and lagging or results metrics. Balanced Scorecards have almost all leading metrics in learning and growth, a mixture of leading and lagging in internal operations and customers, and all lagging measures in finance.

Be sure to document the metrics you select. People will forget, and accountability is important. Part of this documentation process is selecting an owner for the data and the formula.

Chapter 11 contains more information on operational metrics.

Step-by-Step to Developing Your Implementation Plan

No decision has been made unless carrying it out in specific steps has become someone's work assignment and responsibility.

—Peter Drucker
Management consultant
1909–2005

This is where strategy is translated into action. This is the point of translating objectives and initiatives into projects that go to budgeting, project management, and implementation.

To implement your strategy, you must have the buy-in, understanding, and creative problem solving of the managers and people who will make it work. The people on the front lines usually best understand how to improve their work. Without their motivation, understanding, and agreement, it is impossible to make strategic change permanent.

This chapter covers some methods of involving and motivating middle managers and subject matter experts (SMEs). They not only translate the strategic plan into action and carry it forward, but they also can add their own creative ideas.

Step-by-Step to Translating Initiatives into Projects

The following process works well to capture innovative ideas while building buy-in and personal commitment from mid-level managers and SMEs.

Your teams should have a diverse selection of people who are knowledgeable about existing projects and project management. Although these meetings usually involve eight to 16 people, they can sometimes involve as many as 40 people for a large, long-term project.

To follow the process described next, the teams should meet by Strategic Theme. If a Strategic Theme has many initiatives, you may want to limit each meeting to a few high-order initiatives. These large-group meetings can last from 3 hours to all day.

1. The Theme Team leaders guide the group through building its own case for change. This interactive process enables the group to build its own case for change that parallels the ideas and process used with the executive team. It's a good way for everyone to realize that "the iceberg is melting" (change is inevitable).

2. The Theme Team leader or, in small to midsized companies, the CEO or executive vice president explains how the executive team feels about the need for change and the time they've put into developing a Strategic Destination Statement, Strategy Map, and initiatives.

   In this case, the CEO or vice president says, "What we need from you today is your knowledge of and expertise in how we can convert these initiatives into projects that execute our strategy." At that point, the CEO or vice president can leave.

3. Members of the Theme Team explain the Strategic Initiatives and show how each contributes to success within the Strategic Theme. They explain the interdependence of initiatives and why projects are time-phased by dependence and strategic priority. This usually results in some good discussion about the initiatives, and sometimes it produces additional initiatives or barriers that haven't been discussed previously.

4. Individuals usually have some emotional or professional tie to an initiative, so break the team into groups of four to 12 people. Each group will work on a group of related initiatives.

5. Explain the brainstorming process you want to use, how to create a unified name for each project, and how to post the projects into a schedule. You are creating an environment for an interactive work-breakdown schedule.

   Each breakout group should then do the following:

   - Identify major projects needed to accomplish each Strategic Initiative.
   - Determine whether each project is already funded and scheduled.
   - Define project dependence and sequence.
   - Identify major resource requirements that might impact other initiatives.
   - Identify dependence on other initiatives.

6. In the main room, create a framework on the wall for a large Gantt chart. Initiative names should be on the left. Time frames such as Q1, Q2, Q3, Q4, Y2, and Y3 should be across the top.

7. Reconvene the groups.

8. The "natural leader" from each breakout group should explain the group's results while posting project names to the right of the initiative, under the approximate time frame.

9. After each group has posted its results, all the groups can see all the strategic projects for this theme over the strategic time frame. Encourage everyone to look at the big picture, and consider these issues:

   ■ Conflicts with current projects

   ■ Dependencies within the posted projects

   ■ Resource conflicts of key personnel, budget, and so forth

10. Involve everyone in moving sticky notes on the wall to schedule the highest-priority projects into achievable time frames.

Everyone should be aware that this is an interactive process that quickly creates a draft for Strategic Initiatives over the multiyear strategic time frame. When you are done with this workshop, considerable detail work still needs to be done to refine each project definition, build budget cases, and more.

One result of this process is buy-in to and development of innovative ideas for implementing your Strategic Initiatives. It also helps you identify the people who may be your best change agents. The people who exhibit the most enthusiasm will stand out. If they also have the knowledge, authority, and resources, they may be your best change agents. If they lack one of these attributes, team them with someone who complements them.

MEETING LOGISTICS

Meetings such as the implementation planning meeting can get bogged down because of poor logistics. Here's a list of items you might need:

- Ask everyone to bring current project schedules for the next year.

- Ensure that the meeting room is large enough and has adequate air conditioning.

- Supply attendees with food, snacks, and drinks. Intense thinking takes as many calories as walking. Keep them fed and happy.

- Set aside breakout rooms for large groups to break into smaller groups of four to 12 people dedicated to a specific project.

- Have sufficient supplies for all breakout groups: easels, 3M Blue Tape to tape findings on the wall, markers, and 3M Post-it Super Sticky Notes (large size).

Monitoring Initiatives in Progress

It is rare to begin a Balanced Scorecard having all the data you need for your metrics. One-third to one-half of the data may be missing or not readily available. Another reason for missing metrics is that some Strategic Initiatives won't start for 6 months to a year.

So what do you display on your Balanced Scorecard?

Some Balanced Scorecard developers use a grayed-out chart or metric where data are missing or an initiative is incomplete. If possible, you can give feedback on the progress of initiatives or data development.

Executives shouldn't be doing project management, but they should be aware of whether major strategic projects are ahead of or behind schedule. Figure 7.1 shows a simple chart created in Excel. It's like a Gantt chart, but it displays only the difference between target and actual delivery for initiatives and projects. Creating this chart is explained in Chapter 25. You can use the techniques you'll learn in Chapter 24 to color each horizontal bar according to the size of its variance.

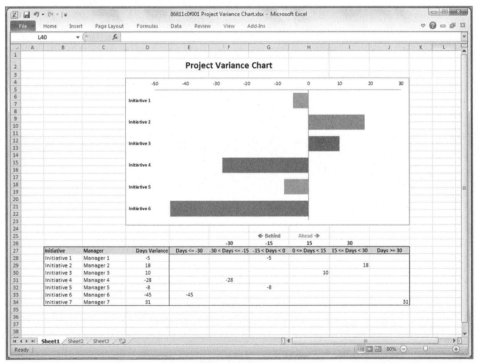

Figure 7.1: A project variance displays the difference between target and actual delivery data for initiatives and major projects.

MICROSOFT EXCEL AS A PROJECT-MANAGEMENT TOOL

I put some effort into using Microsoft Project to manage projects, but I found it too burdensome to use for many projects. It took at least a part-time worker to enter and maintain all the data.

Finally, I developed a fairly robust project-management system in Excel, which I used successfully for years. With Excel I've managed software and publishing projects that involved a dozen people on three continents and met every final deadline. I've since found that many of my small to midsize clients have the same problem with their project management. A couple of nice project-management systems built into Excel work well for small projects. To learn more about project management with Microsoft Excel, go to my website: http://www.criticaltosuccess.com.

Summary

All the best plans are worthless if you can't execute them. And motivating your people and getting them dedicated to making strategy happen is critical. The process described here has been used many times to quickly develop an implementation plan, draft schedules, develop new project ideas, and build agreement on and motivation for the new direction. It works.

CHAPTER 8

Step-by-Step to Rollout and Strategic Reviews

I sure wish I'd done a better job of communicating with GM people. I'd do that differently a second time around and make sure they understood and shared my vision for the company. Then they would know why I was tearing the place up, taking out whole divisions, changing our whole production structure... I never got this across.

—Roger Smith
CEO of General Motors
Strategic Choices **by Kenneth Primozic, Edward Primozic, and Joe Leben**

The Balanced Scorecard is a tool for change. It is not just for reporting metrics. It is not just for managing performance. It is definitely not just a one-time performance project. The Balanced Scorecard is a tool for creating a strategy-focused organization. To become a strategy-focused organization, you must communicate your strategy so that everyone knows how they can and will contribute.

This chapter examines a few of the processes involved in communicating and rolling out the Balanced Scorecard. It's the beginning of your journey toward building a strategy-focused organization.

Creating a Culture Focused on Strategy

I occasionally use laser pointers during presentations. Each is powered by a single AAA battery. My kids sometimes play "light tag" at night by shining two laser pointers across the fairway of the golf course beyond our backyard. That single AAA battery gives this 2-inch-long laser enough power to light a spot on a tree 100 yards away.

I also keep a small flashlight in my travel kit that also is powered by a single AAA battery. However, its light barely shines across a hotel room.

The input power to both lights is the same, but the difference in output is immense. The difference is focus and alignment. The laser light comes out as coherent light. All the frequencies are the same, and they all travel in the same direction, so there is no need for extra effort to focus the light. On the other hand, the flashlight wastes most of its energy in heat, shines a broad spectrum, and scatters the light in all directions. A small mirror and lens attempt to focus the beam, but most of the power is wasted, and the output is dispersed. Does this sound like organizations you've worked in?

The organizations I've worked with seem to have a common profile. They usually have one or more of these characteristics:

- New CEO
- New CFO
- High growth rate and the need to build the infrastructure before it gets away from them
- Merger or acquisition and a need to merge cultures and processes
- Changing workforce demographics
- Changing customer buying patterns
- Significant increase in direct or functional competition
- Current or expected changes in government regulation

All of these characteristics involve change or preparation for significant change. The Balanced Scorecard enables organizations to manage the change, as well as to align and focus on strategy while simultaneously increasing performance. For long-lasting cultural change, you need a process to make change part of your culture.

Strategy Review Meeting

In the Strategy Review Meeting the executive leadership team uses the Balanced Scorecard as a pivot point for strategic conversations. These conversations should dig into the strategy's effectiveness, the organization's forward-looking performance, and the lessons and best practices that can be shared throughout the organization.

It is important to get the format and attitude correct at the first strategy review meeting. In the first few meetings you need to set a model for the meeting's focus, attitudes, and outcomes.

It is important to keep the momentum rolling when implementing the Balanced Scorecard. You should have your first strategy review meeting that incorporates the Balanced Scorecard within a month or two of the scorecard's completion.

CREATING LASTING CHANGE IN YOUR ORGANIZATION

The last few decades have seen the introduction of many tools for organizational change and performance improvement: TQM (total quality management), reengineering, learning organization (Senge), Six Sigma, Lean. All of these attempt to change the culture and improve performance. For all of these methods the Balanced Scorecard acts as a management envelope to track the change and evaluate what works. But you also need a proven process of organizational change to make the change a lasting part of the culture.

One of the best processes I have seen for guiding an organization through change and making it stick comes from professor John Kotter of the Harvard Business School. In 2001, *Businessweek* surveyed 504 enterprises and concluded that Kotter was the top "leadership guru" in the U.S. His books remain in the top 1 percent of books sold on Amazon.com. I believe in Kotter's eight-step action plan for creating lasting change in organizations:

1. **Make a case for change:** Point to a "burning platform" that will drive an urgent need for change.

2. **Leadership:** Create a "guiding collaboration"—a powerful, high-level team that can make change happen.

3. **Vision:** Create a clear picture of the objectives and the steps each person can take to reach them.

4. **Communicate:** Create stories and images that capture every audience, through every medium, all the time.

5. **Empower:** Give people the power to make change happen at their jobs.

6. **Celebrate:** Plan for and create short-term wins, because lasting change takes time and wears down motivation.

7. **Adapt:** Learn what works, and continue to change and grow. Don't let naysayers slow down the change by viewing short-term wins as the finish line.

8. **Institutionalize:** Cement changes into the fabric of the culture, people, and processes.

When you look through Kotter's eight-step action plan, it becomes pretty clear how it works as a perfect companion for the Balanced Scorecard.

When the executive sponsor, your change agents, and your Balanced Scorecard facilitator develop your plan to roll out the Balanced Scorecard, you need to be familiar with and incorporate these eight steps.

Attendees at the strategy review meeting should include leaders who have a broad vision of the organization's objectives as well as responsibility for the strategic themes. I recommend that your meetings include the following people:

- CEO
- Executive leadership team

- Senior strategic business unit leaders responsible for implementing strategy
- Strategic Theme sponsors
- Subject matter experts (SMEs) appropriate to the topics being discussed in that meeting. SMEs may be on standby and called when needed.
- A Balanced Scorecard facilitator to guide the meeting
- Data managers and the Balanced Scorecard editor, who should be on standby in case questions arise about data freshness or validity

Because many of these functions are duplicated in the same person, a meeting can have from 8 to 12 people, not including the facilitator and people who are on standby for questions.

Two meeting agendas are used frequently:

- Monthly meetings focused on the Strategic Theme that the CEO feels is the most important to discuss. The theme sponsor for that Strategic Theme should facilitate that meeting.
- Quarterly meetings that cover the entire Balanced Scorecard. Begin with a brief status report on each theme and its objectives, and then spend the majority of time on the issues of concern.

WARNING Very few organizations can hold operational and strategic review meetings on the same day. Because everyone's mind is on the "alligators in the swamp," it is difficult to get into and maintain the long-term view needed for a strategy review meeting. It is far better to have the strategy review meeting on a different day. If an operational issue comes up during the strategy meeting, save it for discussion after the strategy review meeting.

Most organizations hold their strategic review meetings monthly or quarterly. Meetings held monthly usually spend the majority of the time on one Strategic Theme. At a quarterly meeting all Strategic Themes, the Strategy Map, and its objectives can be reviewed. A strategy review meeting with good, intense discussion can take from 3 hours to all day.

If you use a meeting format that focuses each meeting on one specific Strategic Theme, the facilitator for that meeting should be the strategic sponsor for the theme being discussed. Keeping the meeting on track and focused on strategic issues can be an issue for organizations that are used to holding only operational meetings.

Some of the first meetings may devolve into discussions about the following:

- Operational issues
- Data analysis
- Balanced Scorecard charts

This can occur because the organization isn't accustomed to sharing internal issues across silos or because participants are used to operational rather than strategic meetings. Your facilitator needs to return the meeting to its purpose: improving the organization's strategic performance and validating the model represented by the Balanced Scorecard.

Preparing for the Strategy Review Meeting

Ready your data, analysis, and Balanced Scorecard a few days before the meeting. If you are focusing on one Strategic Theme, you will want that theme's sponsor to write up an analysis and comments so that these can be distributed before the meeting. Attendees must have a chance to review data, the Balanced Scorecard, and the analysis ahead of time. If they can't review and analyze these first, the meeting may turn into a data presentation rather than remaining a discussion of strategy.

Prepare the attendees for the fact that the meeting will focus on issues and actions and not on presentations and data so that little time will be taken up by presenting the available data. This allows you to jump right into discussing strategic issues.

I recommend meeting separately with the CEO and the theme sponsor before each of the first meetings to reiterate the purposes:

- The meeting should discuss strategic issues.

- Operational issues need to be set aside to maintain a strategic mindset.

- The purpose is intense, strategic discussion that usually doesn't occur during the overload of operational issues. (Have I said this before?)

- It is good to have a mixture of red, yellow, and green alerts. An absence of red lights would mean you achieved your objectives; or that people are afraid to reveal their true performance. (Another way of saying this is "Don't shoot the messenger for a red light.")

- Fear suppresses the information about aspects you need to improve. If people fear reporting all the information, you get only good news.

- The meeting needs to include the sharing of best practices.

- The focus of the meeting needs to be looking forward.

- Expected results include identifying which actions are needed, the time frame, and the person accountable.

- Expected results also include identifying what information from the meeting should be communicated to the organization.

Facilitating the First Meeting

At the beginning of the first few meetings, the facilitator needs to set the tone of the meeting by reviewing its purpose—the same points that were reviewed in private with the CEO.

Remind everyone that it can take up to a year to get all the data for metrics on the Balanced Scorecard. You can gray out the missing data and charts or present a miniature Gantt chart showing the progress of key initiatives in that objective.

Communication, Training, and Rollout

Viewing the Balanced Scorecard as a tool for creating a strategy-focused organization makes it obvious that you need programs to help your organization adapt, change, and learn new behaviors. This takes an ongoing commitment to communication, training, and motivation.

Communication

Research published in the *Journal of Strategic Communication* shows how critical communicating strategy is to everyone in your organization. In high-performing organizations, 67 percent of employees had a "good understanding of the overall organizational goals." In poorly performing organizations, that level was 38 percent.

The communication program you set up should be run like any other program. It must have a project manager who is experienced with communication. Before developing your communication calendar, you need to define the basics needed in any communication program:

- **Audience:** Your communication plan must stretch from the board of directors to the individual contributor and all levels in between. Each level will have its own WIIFM—"What's in it for me?"—as well as thoughts such as "How painful will it be for me?"

- **Media:** What media works best for your culture, industry, resources, and geographic distribution? Some large corporations have created multimedia and video productions embracing the Balanced Scorecard. Smaller organizations have used recurring articles from the president in their newsletter as well as "town hall" meetings.

- **Message:** Define how this will affect your organization. Does everyone need to know the case for change? How many will need direct training on the Balanced Scorecard? Will you cascade the scorecard to business units and personal levels?

One thing is necessary: The CEO or senior executive needs to continuously endorse developing a strategy-focused organization through the Balanced Scorecard.

When I interview executives and mid-level managers, they frequently ask, "How interested is the CEO in this?" or "How do I know this isn't just another management fad?" The only way to dispel this attitude is with a consistent message and actions from senior executives that continuously reinforce the commitment to the Balanced Scorecard.

Communication Media

Your organization is unique. You have your own culture, communication channels, resources, and distribution. You need to create and manage your own ongoing communications program.

Here are some ways to communicate the Balanced Scorecard:

- Regular messages from the CEO in the organization's newsletter.
- The CEO personally presents the new vision and Balanced Scorecard with the Strategy Map to all employees in a program and webinar.
- Recognition programs.
- Share best practices discovered through the Balanced Scorecard.
- Train all managers to align with objectives.
- Use the Balanced Scorecard as the agenda for meetings: Are we on track? What needs to change?
- Town hall meetings.
- Videos with the CEO speaking on the importance of the Balanced Scorecard.
- Visual metaphors for the Strategy Map and the new culture posted in communal gathering locations.
- Web-based presentations and webinars.
- Company portal front page.
- Balanced Scorecard, Strategy Map, and operational metrics posted in high-traffic hallways or gathering areas.
- E-mail postings and reminders about the Balanced Scorecard when it has been updated (everyone likes to see how they're doing).
- Include Balanced Scorecard objectives and initiatives as a core for operational change presentations.
- Focus on the Balanced Scorecard in the annual report.
- Focus on the Balanced Scorecard in the message to shareholders.

With all of these strategies, you must use multiple media with multiple messages to multiple audiences. It is imperative that senior leaders continually be seen endorsing the move to a strategy-focused organization.

Training

Using the Balanced Scorecard as a way to manage and develop a culture of high performance requires new skills and understanding. You need to plan for motivation and training at all levels. Training doesn't need to happen all at once. You can roll it out over 6 months or more as different levels of the organization are touched by the Balanced Scorecard.

The training that I have delivered to clients to help in the transition to using a Balanced Scorecard includes these workshops clients have asked me to deliver:

- Executive level
  - Building the case for change
  - Successes in similar industries and the reasons for failure
  - Understanding the Strategy Map and Balanced Scorecard
  - Conducting the strategy review meeting with the Balanced Scorecard
- Strategic Theme teams
  - Building the case for change
  - Understanding the Strategy Map and Balanced Scorecard
  - Developing initiatives and projects
- Facilitators (you need to train multiple facilitators if you are cascading the Balanced Scorecard to multiple department or division levels)
  - Facilitating Strategy Map development
  - Facilitating metric development meetings
  - Facilitating initiative and project implementation development
- Mid-level managers
  - Building the case for change and motivating the workforce
  - How to present the Balanced Scorecard and capture feedback
- Human resources, change agents, and managers
  - Developing a communication plan
- Scorecard and Dashboard programmers and developers
  - Developing operational dashboards and the Balanced Scorecard with Excel
  - Best practices in Excel development
  - Integrating and automating your dashboards and Balanced Scorecard

Once the Balanced Scorecard is in use, operational managers often want to incorporate data-driven decision-making and operational dashboards in their operations. This drives increased demand for operational dashboards (discussed in Part II). This in turn pushes a need for facilitators to help with process mapping and metrics definition for operations. And you need to train people on how to efficiently create dashboards in Excel.

Summary

For the Balanced Scorecard to be effective, senior management must have strategy review meetings that use it as the agenda. These strategy review meetings must focus on strategic, not operational, issues.

The Balanced Scorecard is a major force in creating a culture of high performance aligned with strategy. But organizations don't change easily. You must continually restate the case for change, develop teams that support the change, and communicate, communicate, communicate.

Operational Performance with Dashboards

In This Part

Developing Executive and Operational Dashboards

Strategy without tactics is the slowest route to victory. Tactics without strategy is the noise before defeat.

—Sun Tzu

Dashboards are not "the next new thing." I remember developing what were probably the first executive information systems (EISs) that used Microsoft Excel in the late 1980s for an international division of a major pharmaceutical company. It saved their analysts weeks of Lotus 1-2-3 and manual work. And then there were the myriad decision support systems (DSSs) that everyone hoped would help business decision-makers. But EIS and DSS never reached the level of impact that their proponents hoped for.

So what has changed between now and then? Many of the original EISs and DSSs were built as a way of putting the same information online that was previously collected in printed reports or documents.

NOTE Scorecards and dashboards should be the lever that changes culture in an organization.

If dashboards are to succeed in improving performance, they must

- Be based on the causal links that drive success for organizational objectives
- Derive their metrics using a scientific process
- Increase the speed, ease, and accuracy of decision-making
- Drive discussion on what is causing the results

- Cause decision-makers to take action
- Use "right time" data that enables timely decisions to keep objectives on track
- Communicate desired behavior in the culture

Why Are Dashboards Used with Increasing Frequency?

Dashboards are becoming ubiquitous. Forrester Research estimates that 40 percent of the top 2,000 corporations use dashboards with their Business Intelligence initiatives. Managers are using dashboards to keep strategy and operations on track and to detect hot spots in the organization.

An article titled "Giving the Boss the Big Picture: A 'dashboard' pulls up everything the CEO needs to run the show" in the February 13, 2006 issue of *BusinessWeek* quoted Ivan Seidenberg, CEO of Verizon Communications, as saying:

> *The dashboard puts me and more and more of our executives in real-time touch with the business. The more eyes that see the results we're obtaining every day, the higher the quality of the decisions we can make.*

Later in the same article, Jeff Raikes, president of Microsoft's Office division, explains that CEO Mike Ballmer uses dashboards to set the agenda for meetings with the seven heads of Microsoft divisions:

> *Every time I go to see Ballmer, it's an expectation that I bring my dashboard with me.*

Executives, managers, and supervisors are using dashboards to track strategy, operations, and tactics. Smart organizations such as Verizon and Microsoft use dashboards to set the agenda for meetings because the metrics in the dashboard measure the drivers for their business objectives. Searching for the term "business dashboards" returns over eight million results and a full display of banner ads promoting software for business dashboards. Small-business programs such as QuickBooks come with built-in dashboards, and large enterprises spend more than $250 million just to get started with business intelligence dashboards. With all these offerings, Microsoft Excel is still the most widely used software for creating custom operational dashboards.

Well-designed dashboards enable better and faster decision-making. In fact, surveys have shown that two of the key benefits of implementing dashboards are faster decision-making and reduced administrative work in research and analysis.

Dashboards are least effective when they are developed as "the next new thing," or when management misuses them. Jeffrey Immelt, CEO of General Electric, has stated that even though he uses dashboards, executives should focus on broad strategy and deal-making. These areas can't be captured in an operational dashboard, but they can be monitored with a Balanced Scorecard.

Another area that causes concern is the use of dashboards by managers and supervisors as a way to micromanage subordinates. The scorecards and dashboards must be rolled out and cascaded through an organization in a culture where everyone at all levels understands that the organization is looking for best practices and the fine-tuning of business models, not the daily grading of individual performance.

Balanced Scorecards and operational dashboards are highly effective tools of culture change. Bad managers who use them incorrectly to micromanage employees end up hurting the organization. But when Balanced Scorecards and operational dashboards are used as tools to build a high-performance learning organization, they monitor performance, culture, and the business model.

The Differences between Dashboards and Scorecards

If you have listened to many discussions or web seminars on the topics of performance management, Business Intelligence, or Balanced Scorecards, you've probably heard the terms "dashboard" and "scorecard" used interchangeably—but there is a difference between the two.

Executives use scorecards to monitor strategic alignment and success with strategic objectives, and the Balanced Scorecard is undoubtedly the best-known corporate strategy scorecard, used to help organizations align with strategy. Other forms of executive scorecards can show multiple dashboards that give an executive-level view into operational or functional performance.

Dashboards are used at the tactical and operational levels. Managers use dashboards to monitor the success of tactical initiatives, such as marketing campaigns or sales performance during the introduction of a specific new product. Managers and supervisors use dashboards to monitor operational performance on a weekly, daily, and even hourly frequency. Operational uses include areas such as monitoring manufacturing quality or budget variance on projects.

Table 9-1 compares operational and tactical dashboards and strategic scorecards.

Table 9-1: A Comparison of Operational and Tactical Dashboards and Strategic Scorecards

	OPERATIONAL	TACTICAL	STRATEGIC
TYPE	Dashboard	Dashboard	Balanced Scorecard
USERS	Managers, supervisors, and operators	Managers	Executives
INFORMATION	Detailed	Detailed/ Summary	Summary
USAGE	Monitor daily production and operation	Monitor progress on an initiative	Monitor alignment and success of strategic objectives
ORGANIZATIONAL LEVEL	Work unit	Department	Enterprise or strategic business unit
HOW OFTEN IT'S UPDATED	During the day	Daily or weekly	Monthly or Quarterly

Challenges in Developing Dashboards

Early predecessors to current dashboards and scorecards were in the area of DSSs and EISs. Overall, these systems failed to produce the hoped-for results—largely because they were usually implemented as IT exercises, ways to move information from paper onto computer screens. Data was often missing or spread across numerous computer systems that were difficult to integrate. They were not part of a culture change designed to align the organization around strategic objectives and focus on strong performance. Often, little science was involved in the selection of metrics or performance indicators; thus, these methods didn't aid managers in their daily decisions.

Successful operational dashboards often are part of a larger culture change. They are just one tool in an organization's shift to high performance levels. To succeed with dashboards, you need to do the following:

- Develop a model of your business process.
- Define the causal links in that process.
- Define key performance indicators using management science methods, such as those of Lean Six Sigma.
- Be willing to change your business model and causal links if changes to a driver do not create change in the objective.
- Collect the data for "right-time" decisions. Surveys have shown that the average enterprise-level dashboard system uses six to seven data sources.

- Tailor dashboards to the needs, data sources, and decision factors facing individuals.

- Build a scalable system that can expand to meet the organization's needs.

- Absorb fact-based management and the use of dashboards into daily operations.

Developing Your Dashboard

Strategic business units of large corporations or small to midsized businesses can use a winning approach to develop operational dashboards in Microsoft Excel:

1. Start small, with winnable systems.

   Introduce operational dashboards to your organization by selecting a manageable problem. Choose a problem that you are likely to solve and that will have a visible effect. This will reduce your risk, prove the concept, and increase general interest in doing other dashboard projects.

   Start with a small problem and a solution you can grasp. The Business Intelligence industry is rife with stories of organizations that have purchased $250,000 systems before proving the concept or correctly defining their needs.

2. The business manager, not IT, should own the dashboard.

   Business needs to lead the project, with IT as an enabler. Start small, with existing reporting and query systems that can feed Microsoft Excel dashboards and test business needs. As soon as you have winning solutions and understand your needs, look for buy-ins from other groups, and work with IT to create an integrated strategy.

3. Select metrics using a scientific management method.

   The metrics your dashboard measures should align with corporate strategy and operational objectives for the greatest impact and visibility. To select these metrics, you must build a model of your operational processes and understand the drivers. The next chapter touches on this with a discussion of operational mapping. Lean Six Sigma processes are a good way to pinpoint where you can create the greatest impact.

4. Limit dashboards to the "critical few" key performance indicators (KPIs).

   Use only the "critical few" metrics or KPIs on your dashboard. More than seven per operational process or dashboard is too many. Having too many metrics can be as bad as having the wrong metrics, making it difficult or even impossible for you to understand what drives success.

   You can have more dashboards that aid with diagnostics or troubleshooting, but your "critical few" that you monitor frequently should be limited.

5. Get results quickly.

   Produce a working system in 30 days, before momentum and interest are lost. Work as quickly as possible while still following good processes. Know how you will roll out the dashboard and apply its use in daily work. Explain to users of the dashboard the business model that was used and how KPIs were identified. Doing so will help them believe in the dashboard's capabilities.

6. Work constantly at making dashboards part of your culture.

   Dashboards are not a one-time project that, once completed, the company can put a checkmark in a box and move on. To make changes in performance, dashboards need to become part of the company culture. It's a step that continues and is included in meetings and decisions.

   Remember that dashboards are just indicators of performance. Some people will view them as a threat to their personal performance or as a sign that management is becoming overbearing. You must develop a culture of high performance that understands that dashboards are just tools to help the organization learn and grow.

   Good executives and managers are like good pilots. They spend the majority of their time looking around, using their senses and experience. Only 20 percent or less of their time is spent looking inside, scanning the dashboard instruments. In my eight years as a military pilot, I had two near misses while flying low-altitude missions. I would have been unable to avoid those small civilian planes flying in restricted areas if I'd had my "head in the cockpit." Running a business is much the same. Managers must constantly scan back and forth, comparing what they sense as they walk around with what they see on their dashboards. It is the comparison and balance between the two that will give you good performance.

Summary

Dashboards, whether operational or tactical, are essential if good managers are to stay on top of their business. Well-designed dashboards must use the business or operations model to select the "critical few" metrics or KPIs that drive operational performance. Even if you are designing a quick operational dashboard, follow the development process described in this chapter. Use a scientific process such as Lean Six Sigma to identify the "critical few" metrics that should be on your dashboard. The next chapter describes some of the tools you can use to identify the metrics that drive your operations.

CHAPTER 10

Mapping Your Operational Processes

*If you cry "Forward" you must be sure to make clear the direction in which to go.
Don't you see that if you fail to do that and simply call out the word to a monk and
a revolutionary, they will go in precisely opposite directions?*

—Anton Chekov
Short-story writer, playwright
1860–1904

Mapping operational processes creates a foundation for your improvement efforts. It creates a common language and understanding for team members and workers, and it helps identify the tasks needing improvement as well as the critical few metrics.

A process map is a visual representation of how a product is built or a service delivered. The map shows the work flow involved as a series of activities. Some process maps show additional information at each action, such as the time and resources required or the customer value added. Process maps may have multiple levels of detail. A "30,000-foot map" can show a process at such a high level that people unfamiliar with the process details can understand it. Detailed process maps show minute specifics to point out ways to improve the process.

With Excel you can combine the clarity that comes with a process map and the monitoring and control that come with metrics and dashboards. When you build your process map in Excel, you can include formulas that recalculate time and resources as they cascade through the map. Adding sliders and spinners enables you to test different scenarios easily by changing inputs and then seeing the resulting changes in outputs.

Many types of process maps are used in operations. But they all help create a common language, bring clarity to diverse ideas, create a shared vision, and identify where the organization can best focus its resources. Using a diverse group to create process maps can increase agreement and consensus, align resources, create a unifying purpose, and communicate why specific metrics are monitored.

Before You Map, Know Why

Before you begin work on any operational or process improvement project, you must know how and why these changes will benefit your organization. Stories abound of Six Sigma and Lean proponents searching for any project and any sponsor. Failure to identify targets of greatest impact, or failure to prove the impact, can result in performance improvement projects being placed low on the organization's priority scale. The consequence is low return on investment and lack of sustainability.

If your organization uses a Balanced Scorecard, the areas of highest priority for long-term improvement identified through process maps should align with the Strategic Initiatives defined by the Balanced Scorecard. Aligning process improvement programs with Strategic Initiatives makes it easier to build the case and receive funding. Your long-term process improvement initiatives and process maps should align with the Balanced Scorecard themes, objectives, and initiatives.

Operational and process improvement projects face the same organizational change barriers as the Balanced Scorecard. They have the same failure points and must have an effective implementation team. You must build a case for change, get commitment from senior management, get buy-in from managers, and develop a process for communicating and sustaining the change.

Dashboards and Six Sigma

Six Sigma is the science of identifying and removing defects and variation from products and services so that the quality to the customer improves while costs of production decrease. One of the key principles of Six Sigma is DMAIC. This acronym stands for

- **D**efine
- **M**easure
- **A**nalyze
- **I**mprove
- **C**ontrol

Dashboards are critical to many of the DMAIC stages. The measure and analyze stages can use dashboards to monitor data that track a process. With Excel's statistical functions, it's straightforward to plot control charts and have Excel automate the statistical analysis. Examples of this are given in Chapter 25.

The completion of many Six Sigma projects should include a dashboard for the control phase. By using some of the mapping methods described in this chapter, as well as normal Six Sigma statistical process control methods, you can create dashboards that will help you "control" the process you have improved so that it doesn't revert to its previous form. Your dashboard can act as an alert for process variation, a diagnostic tool to analyze relationships in the system, and a modeling tool for performance improvement.

Types of Process Mapping

Many process maps are used in business. The concept of using process maps to identify inputs, outputs, leverage points, choke points, and risk points is the same for all process maps. These are leverage points where you can identify metrics and then use a dashboard to monitor performance and change. If you create your map directly in Excel, you can create an interactive simulation that enables you to monitor current status and see how changes will affect output.

Table 10-1 describes a few of the many types of process maps you can draw and model in Excel. You can find more information on these maps by searching the Internet. Two of the types of maps used in performance improvement, SIPOC and value stream mapping, are described in the following sections.

Table 10-1: A Sampling of the Many Process Maps You Can Draw in Excel

PROCESS MAP TYPE	DESCRIPTION
Supplier, Input, Process, Output, Customer (SIPOC)	SIPOC is one of the first steps taken in a Six Sigma improvement project. SIPOC takes a 30,000-foot view of the work flow, from a triggering event, such as a request, to the customer receiving the finished product or service. SIPOC is described in more depth in the following section.
Value Stream Map (VSM)	Value stream maps are used in Lean projects to map the chain of activities in producing a product or service. Through the use of the map, Lean practitioners look for ways to reduce the seven causes of waste. VSM is described in more depth later in this chapter.
Supply Chain Operations Reference Model (SCOR®)	SCOR® is a model developed by the Supply Chain Council to visualize, evaluate, analyze, and improve supply chain performance both inside and outside the organization. SCOR incorporates five hierarchical levels and five major process work flows. To learn more about SCOR, go to http://www.supply-chain.org.

Continued

Table 10-1 *(continued)*

PROCESS MAP TYPE	DESCRIPTION
Program/Project Evaluation and Review Technique (PERT)	PERT is a visual model used to represent and analyze the relationships and timing between tasks in a project. One use of PERT is to identify which paths in a project can be changed to reduce the total time for project completion.
	Dashboards are useful to quickly monitor the risks, resources, and variance from schedule at critical points in a PERT chart.
Program Logic Model (PLM)	Program logic models are more frequently used in nonprofit, social, and organizational change situations. PLMs produce a graphical map showing the relationship between input, outputs, and outcomes or impact. Outputs are segmented into activities, products, and participation. Outcomes are the changes in knowledge, awareness, and behavior, among others. Outcomes are segmented into short term, medium term, and long term.
	Dashboards are useful with PLM to monitor the variance from estimates of the input (people and money) and output (activities, products, and participation) against the hoped-for outcome, or change in behaviors.
	Search the web for "program logic model Wisconsin" for more information.

Six Sigma SIPOC Mapping

SIPOC is an acronym for supplier, input, process, output, and customer. The SIPOC map shows high-level activities in a process, from the initial request from the customer all the way to the product or service delivery:

- **Supplier** is the major internal or external supplier to the process.
- **Input** is the major materials and resources used in the process.
- **Process** is the map showing the high-level activities.
- **Output** is the major outputs of product or service to the internal or external customer.
- **Customer** is the major recipient of the product or service.

For example, consider a biorefinery producing ethanol through the use of genetically modified enzymes acting on biomass that is the by-product of agriculture (noncorn) or yard waste. Its SIPOC might look like this:

Suppliers	Agricultural suppliers
Input	Plant stock, enzymes
Process	Refining
Output	Fuel-grade ethanol
Customer	Distributors

A SIPOC map, like the one shown in Figure 10.1, is used at the beginning of Six Sigma quality and performance improvement projects to explain the process. Building a SIPOC map is a quick way to identify your customer's needs, map the process at a high level, identify metrics, build a cohesive team with common language and understanding, identify potential areas of improvement, and build rapport with people in the process.

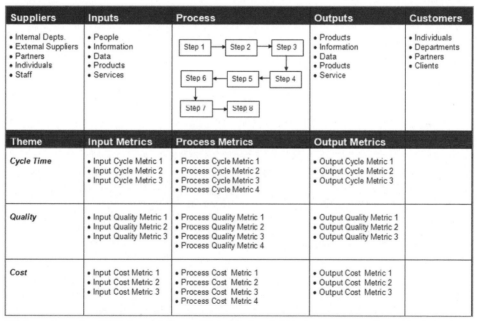

Figure 10.1: The SIPOC map shows high-level activities in a process, from the initial request from the customer all the way through the product or service delivery.

The following questions will help you identify the parts of a SIPOC map:

- **Suppliers:** Who or what supplies the inputs?
- **Input:** What information, data, resources, and people are needed for this process?

▪ **Output:** What is the end result of this process that the customer will use? It could be products, services, data, or something else.

▪ **Customer:** Who or what is the recipient and user of the output?

Value Stream Mapping

Lean practitioners use value stream mapping to create a drawing with a set of standard symbols representing all the activities and information used to produce a product or service. Maps are then used to find areas of waste or areas of little or no value to the customer, which then can be reduced or removed. The "seven wastes" that Lean works to reduce are

▪ Defects

▪ Inventory

▪ Processing

▪ Waiting

▪ Motion

▪ Transportation

▪ Overproduction

Value stream maps are produced by "walking the floor." This involves watching people do their work; following the flow of paper, products, or information; interviewing workers; and watching the work as it is performed. In many cases, an independent observer and interviewer identify activities and inputs that individuals in the process are unaware of.

A standard set of symbols is used to draw value stream maps. (You can even create flowchart and value stream maps in Excel, as described in Chapter 13.) Start your value stream map at the customer, or the request for product or service, and then define the processes with data boxes. Next, draw the material flow and the push and pull of material, and follow that with the flow of information—the triggers.

Figure 10.2 shows a sample value stream map created by the Environmental Protection Agency. Notice the metrics in the tags below the map. These tags can include metrics such as

▪ Number of operators

▪ Cycle time

▪ Changeover time

- Batch size
- Performance
- Uptime (percentage)
- Yield (percentage)

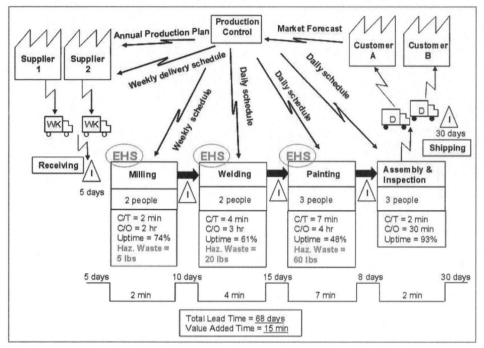

Figure 10.2: This value stream map from the EPA shows time and environmental data throughout the value stream.

You can build your own Lean and value stream mapping in Excel or purchase flowchart and mapping software that runs directly within Excel. An advantage of creating your flowcharts in Excel is that you can include formulas and database links that automatically update the diagrams and flowcharts.

Figure 10.3 shows a value stream map built in Systems2Win, a robust add-in with many Lean templates.

Figure 10.4 shows a value stream map built with Flowchart from FlowBreeze. Flowchart works well for simpler flowcharts, swim lane diagrams, and value stream maps. Both of these Excel add-ins enable you to create flowchart, value stream, and process maps from within Excel.

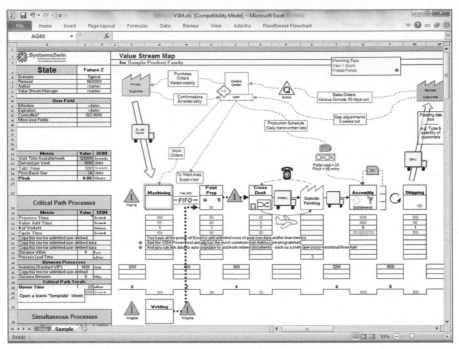

Figure 10.3: Systems2Win can create Lean and value stream mapping in Excel.

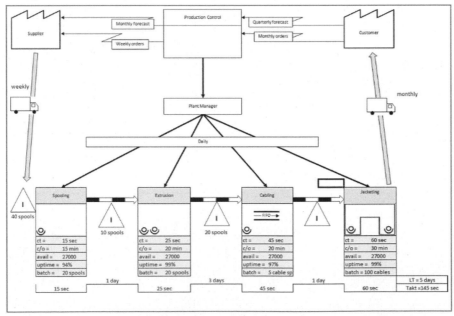

Figure 10.4: Flowchart is another Excel add-in that enables you to create flowchart, Lean, and value stream mapping in Excel.

These and other process improvement tools that run in Excel are described in Chapter 27. My website, http://www.criticaltosuccess.com, contains additional listings and reviews of Excel add-ins.

Value stream maps are created for two states: current and future. The current state map shows the activities, information, times, and resources currently being used. The future state map shows the activities, information, times, and resources for the ideal state after Lean principles have been applied.

Dashboards are valuable in monitoring key metrics that measure the gap between current and future states. Dashboards can help you monitor the change between current and future states and help ensure that the improved future state is sustained.

Some of the tools used for value stream mapping are Microsoft Visio, iGrafx, Systems2Win, FlowBreeze, and SmartDraw. You also can use Microsoft Excel to draw value stream maps with the Shapes available in the Illustration group on the Insert tab. Although Excel doesn't come with value stream symbols, you can create your own. Excel gives you the added ability to develop a value stream simulation so that you can see the impact of changes.

PROCESS MAPPING IN EXCEL

Process mapping in Excel requires some extra work, such as creating custom symbols, but it also gives you significant advantages in that you can create simulations of your process using Excel functions and formulas. For example, clicking a slider like those described in Chapter 20 adjusts process times that cascade throughout the process model. Of course, you can also use all the Excel capabilities described throughout this book to add dashboards with trends, alerts, and statistical control charts to show the status of your process.

To see examples of process maps in Excel and for referrals for process mapping software that works with Excel, go to my website at

http://www.criticaltosuccess.

Step-by-Step to Building a Map

After you have aligned the goal for your process improvement with your organization's goals, the next step is to do a first-pass map. The purpose of a first-pass map, no matter which type of map you are creating, is to capture the big picture of the process by documenting the large processes and the metrics and their relationships.

One of the best ways to do this is to start at the customer/recipient's end of the process and walk through the process to the trigger, or where the customer initiated the first request. In many cases this literally means walking through the process, going to each person involved and each work area. For example, to track customer shipments, you would start at the shipping dock and walk until you reached the phone or e-commerce system where the customer first placed the order. Often you will find that the way processes are really completed is not the way they are documented.

A high-level first pass may take a day for one person to complete. A knowledgeable person can walk through the process, interviewing participants and recording process steps, metrics, choke points, and waste. It is easiest to simply draw the process by hand and record important metrics at each stage. Good interviewing skills come in handy: The individuals doing the work usually know best how it can be improved.

This first-pass map should give you a high-level picture of the processes, times, metrics, choke points, and areas of waste. At this point, you can clean up your hand-drawn map, and you may want to create a map using just the drawing tools in Excel or PowerPoint.

After you have cleaned up your first-pass map, review it with people familiar with the process. They can identify and normalize any areas or metrics you may have missed. The first-pass map gives you a framework on which to add more details about where you can make performance improvements.

Creating a second-level map gives you the additional details for subprocesses, detailed metrics, target values and ranges, additional areas of waste, and the workforce's ideas about where improvements can have the greatest impact. You should involve a large group of knowledgeable and influential people in creating these maps. Having their contribution can help influence their buy-in and your subsequent success.

Follow these steps to create your second-level map:

1. Use 3M Post-it Super Sticky Notes (the large 8-by-6-inch unlined type) to create a large version of your first-pass map on the wall. These high-level notes should be at the highest level on the wall, and each major process should have its own color and heading. (Some color duplication will occur, because this kind of Post-it Notes has a limited color range.)

2. Gather a cross-functional group of subject matter experts (SMEs) for the process you are mapping. The room needs to be large, with enough space in front of the wall to allow for people to crowd around.

3. Distribute stacks of the notes, along with large-tip markers. Recommend that people use the note color that matches the heading for the process they work in.

4. Ask people to write on their notes a five-to-seven-word description of the most important tasks under each heading. To focus their notes on the most important tasks and because of limited wall space, I usually limit notes to no more than 40 for a map.

5. When everyone is ready, have people post the notes themselves under the appropriate headings.

6. Rewrite any notes that are difficult to read. If any note is difficult for the group to understand, have the SME who wrote the note briefly explain it.

7. Hand out 1.5-by-2-inch Post-it Notes. Ask the SMEs to write on them the amount of time or another resource needed for each task, and then post these on the task note.

8. Have the SMEs do a verbal walk-through for the group so that everyone understands the entire map.

9. Use "dot voting" to discover which tasks the group thinks can have the greatest impact on improvement. Hand out sheets of colored sticky dots. Each person gets three dots, one of each color. Green dots indicate that the product or service was transformed by adding value for the customer. Red dots indicate that the product or service was not transformed. White dots indicate the task had to be completed whether or not it added value (for example, to comply with safety or government regulations). Ask all members of the group to vote for any task they feel strongly about by sticking the appropriate color of dot next to the task.

10. When everyone is seated again, it is usually obvious where the greatest impact can be gained. At this point, good discussion often occurs about what changes can be made. You need to have pads and easels ready to capture this information so that it isn't lost.

11. Now that you have an idea which tasks have the highest priorities for improvement, take a look at Chapter 11.

ANY PROCESS IMPROVEMENT PROGRAM IS ALSO AN ORGANIZATIONAL CHANGE PROGRAM

If you want your process improvement effort to be a success, you should also view it as an organizational change process. Process improvement changes have all the people and cultural issues that any other organizational change has. A consultant or experienced change agent can help you manage and sustain the culture change needed to support your performance improvement efforts.

Summary

Mapping processes is important to improving and maintaining those processes. To improve or maintain them, you must identify which tasks are most critical, where the greatest return will be, where choke points are, and where risks are greatest. You can identify these using a number of different mapping methods, some of which have been covered here briefly. After you have mapped your processes, you can use the methods described in Chapter 11 to identify which metrics are critical and should appear in your dashboards.

Identifying Critical Metrics and Key Performance Indicators

The dashboard is the CEO's killer app, making the gritty details of a business that are often buried deep within a large organization accessible at a glance to senior executives.

"Giving the Boss the Big Picture"
BusinessWeek
February 13, 2006

Mapping processes is a big aid in identifying critical business activities and the causes and effects you need to monitor. This chapter teaches you methods that can help you identify and select metrics for use on an executive or operational dashboard.

I have seen departments where the only public statistic was a chart hung in the hallway. I've also seen the overload caused by an overdeveloped Business Intelligence system that produced so many metrics that no one knew which metrics were the "critical few." This chapter describes a couple of methods that can help you select those critical few out of the hundreds of metrics that may exist in a process.

General Rules for Metrics in Operational Dashboards

You should follow a few general rules for the use of metrics in operational dashboards:

- **Identify and select metrics using a scientific approach.** Heed the maxim that some attribute to Einstein: "The definition of insanity is doing the same thing over and over and expecting different results." Don't just take the metrics you've always used and slam them into a dashboard. No matter how pretty your dashboard is, and how many dials and gauges it has, you won't achieve any better results. Select your metrics by using a scientific method. First create a model of the process you want to control, and then develop a hypothesis of what will control that process, and finally test the hypothesis.

- **Test your metrics for validity.** If the metrics you are using to control a process don't help you make the change you expect, your hypothesis is wrong. Try different metrics.

- **Limit your dashboard to three to eight metrics per process.** Your dashboard should show only the first-order metrics—those that have the greatest impact. Almost every process has only a few first-order metrics. Another consideration is the human mind's ability to manage only a limited number of relationships. Experiments have shown that professional jugglers can juggle three or four balls for long periods. However, when the number of balls reaches seven, accidents start to occur, and the juggler begins losing control. With just a few more balls in the air, even the best jugglers lose control quickly. The same is true for juggling metrics and business models in your head. Keep it simple.

- **You've got most of what you need already, but new data may be necessary.** As a general rule, 50 percent of the data for strategic and operational dashboards is already accessible from accounting systems, enterprise resource planning (ERP), customer relationship management (CRM), and human resources information systems (HRIS). But some data—usually customer and employee data—always will require new data collection methods.

- **Capturing data is often more work than defining and creating a dashboard.** Most of the small and midsized businesses I've worked with have good financial and operational data. They are building their customer relationship data, but they often lack data on employees and customers. Gathering this information requires setting up new data collection and validation channels.

- **Build what you can of your dashboard, and let the missing data follow later.** It's rare that all the data is available to start with. If a metric that has been identified as critical is unavailable, show it as a gray chart on the dashboard, or display a differential Gantt chart that shows the progress of the initiative to collect the missing data. The project variance or differential Gantt chart is described in Chapter 25.

- **Create a metric definition.** Over time, people forget the how and why of metrics. Create a table for each metric with definitions that explain why it was selected, what effect it will have, what formula was used and why, where the data comes from, and who owns the data.

- **Create a data map.** Surveys have shown that most Business Intelligence systems use 6 to 11 data sources. Balanced Scorecards in midsized companies where data is kept in Excel or Access files can have even more data sources. To keep your data sources straight, create a data map showing the data use, data source, file type, and so forth.

- **Display all the information necessary for decision-making on one screen.** By interviewing the people who use the dashboard, you can learn what decisions they need to make and what information they need to do so. Often it is a relationship between two or more pieces of data that is important. Make sure you put all the related information for a decision on one screen. If you can't do that, at least make the secondary data single-click accessible.

WARNING You won't find long lists of metrics in this book. It would be fairly easy to fill over half this book with metrics and their descriptions, related objectives, and formulas. However, what is most important is having the critical few metrics, not having lots of metrics.

If what you measure is what you get, you don't want to measure the wrong things. Also, if you measure too many things, and no one knows what is important, confusion will result.

If you need examples of metrics, check with your trade association or industry consultants, or search online using the keyword "metric" and the topic you are measuring. There are many lists of metrics; the important thing is to choose the right metric.

For a list of metrics and related objectives, check my website.

http://www.criticaltosuccess.com

Interview the Decision-Makers

Long before setting your hands on the keyboard and gathering a team to map a process, you should interview the people who will be using the dashboard for decision-making. Interviewing them will help you understand the purpose of the dashboard/improvement project, the alignment with corporate strategy, and the mental model they currently use to understand the system.

Here are some of the questions you should ask in the interview:

- Who is responsible for the outcomes of this process?
- Who controls or monitors the process?
- Is the person who controls or monitors the process the same person who will monitor a dashboard?
- What business decisions do you need to make routinely?
- What business decisions are most critical?

- What data or information do you use to make each decision?
- Do you monitor families or categories of data or information?
- What triggers your decisions?
  - Control limits or boundary limits?
  - Trends?
  - Alert levels?
  - Indexes?
- What behavior or actions do you want to affect?
- Which measure or metric will have the greatest effect on those behaviors and actions?
- How do you know whether your business decision was correct?
- Do you have reports containing these data?
- May I speak with whomever owns the data?

Identify Metrics Using Your Map

Process maps, whether high-level or detail-level, help you select the critical few metrics most important to monitoring status and control. Maps help you visually identify and prioritize these items:

- Choke points
- High-risk activities
- Leverage points of greatest impact
- Activities that add or do not add customer value
- Change between the current state and future state
- Degradation of processes back to old, low-performance states
- Diagnostic and troubleshooting solutions

If you have many years of experience with a process, you probably know the metrics that drive its results. However, you need a scientific process for selecting metrics if you want to gain new insights, test causes and effects, or communicate your experience to others.

The maps discussed in Chapter 10 are a basis for making sound decisions when selecting metrics. By mapping a process, you identify major inputs and outputs, risk points, choke points, high-waste areas, key stage gates, and much more. All of these areas are up for nomination for membership in the critical few metrics that need to be on a dashboard.

A MEASURE IS NOT A METRIC

For the purposes of this chapter, a "measure" is what you want to evaluate. A "metric" is a quantitative value or statistical unit of that measure. Sound confusing? Some examples might help. Measures common to all organizations include customer satisfaction, employee engagement, and employee retention. These aren't the rock-hard numbers that, for example, financials are. Usually one measure has many metrics. However, for each organizational process, only a few of these metrics best describe the measure. You can use the following metrics to imply future employee retention:

■ Total number of employees approaching full retirement benefits

■ Employee engagement index

■ Number of sick days taken

■ Number of accidents on the line

Step-by-Step to Identifying Critical Metrics

Based on the interview questions listed earlier or on the dot voting techniques described in the section "Selecting a Metric," you should be able to identify the areas on your map that most critically need measuring.

Here's a step-by-step method that's useful for identifying measures and metrics:

1. Identify the critical areas on the map. (Chapter 10 describes dot voting as one method of identifying critical areas.)

2. Brainstorm the measures you need to control each critical area. Measures can be leading (drivers of the process) or lagging (success measures).

3. Research metrics for each measure. If the process you are measuring is common in your industry, first try using an industry-standard measure.

4. Reduce the possible metrics to a short list by using either a dot voting technique or a weighted table.

The following sections describe these steps in more detail.

Brainstorming and Identifying Metrics Using an Ishikawa or Fishbone Diagram

The fishbone diagram, so named because it resembles a fish skeleton, was the brainchild of Kaoru Ishikawa, a pioneer in quality management. The fishbone diagram, also known as an Ishikawa or cause-and-effect diagram, is used as a structure for brainstorming the causes and effects in a process. It works just as well for brainstorming metrics.

Figure 11.1 shows a fishbone diagram for a chemical process. The major branches in the diagram can be labeled with the names of critical areas in your process. Chapter 10 describes how to identify the areas you want to measure.

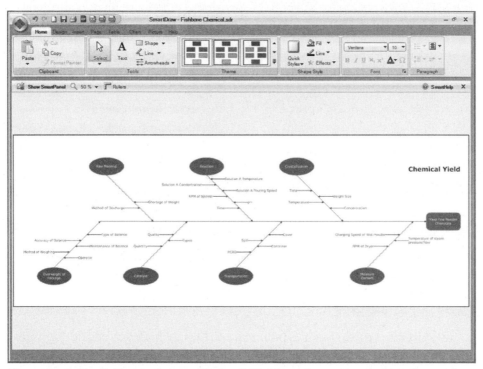

Figure 11.1: The fishbone shows critical activities from the process as branches and metrics as minor branches.

USING THE SIX M'S (AND TWO P'S) WITH METRICS BRAINSTORMING

For small processes, or if time is limited, you may want to skip mapping. Instead, gather a team experienced in the process. Post a fishbone diagram on the wall, but instead of labeling branches with the names of critical process areas, label them with the six M's: man, machine, Mother Nature, materials, method, and measurement. Figure 11.2 shows a fishbone diagram with the six M's. If the process is affected by regulatory or social structures, also include the two P's: policies and procedures. Using the fishbone with the six M's and two P's, brainstorm about the most important metrics for each branch. Use dot voting to decide which metrics the team wants to include in the critical few.

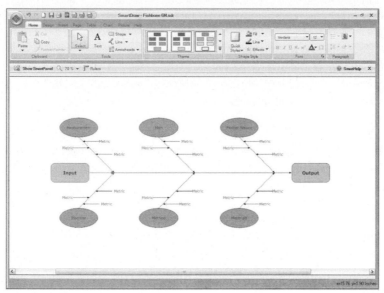

Figure 11.2: A fishbone with the Six M's can be used to quickly brainstorm metrics for a process.

Selecting a Metric

As soon as you have identified possible metrics, you need to select the critical few that you want to track, or that feed your dashboard. Limit your critical few to three to eight metrics.

Two methods are frequently used to select the critical few from all the brainstormed metrics. One method is dot voting, a quick, subjective method. The other uses a prioritization table.

To conduct dot voting, follow these steps:

1. Discuss the metrics you've brainstormed until everyone understands the advantages and disadvantages of each one.

2. Distribute sticky dots to the group. Divide the number of metrics on the fishbone diagram by three. Each member gets that many dots. For example, if the fishbone diagram has 15 metrics, each team member gets five sticky dots.

3. Team members place their dots on the metrics they think need to be in the critical few. Team members can put as many or as few dots as they want to on metrics.

4. The metrics that end up marked with the highest number of dots become the critical few.

If you have more time and want a more analytical selection method, use a prioritization table with weighted values to prioritize your metrics. Again, you need to do this with a team experienced with the process.

When building a prioritization table with a group, you can project an Excel worksheet onto the wall. Complete the Excel matrix as you work so that when you are done you have complete documentation.

1. List the metrics that you are considering down the left side of a worksheet.

2. Across the top, enter headings for what is important to the metric's purpose. For example, is the process's change in value twice as important as the change in speed?

   Here are a few weighting factors; yours may differ:

   ▪ **Value:** If this process changes, what affect will it have on output value?

   ▪ **Speed:** If this process changes, what affect will it have on output speed?

   ▪ **Quality:** If this process changes, what affect will it have on quality?

   ▪ **Cost of measurement:** Will this metric's data have a high cost to capture?

3. Under the headings, enter a value from 1 to 10 for each weighting factor. The numbers aren't as important as their relative weights. In Figure 11.3, for example, the "value" of change is twice as important as "speed" to the metric's purpose.

	Value	Speed	
Weight	*6*	*3*	**Total**
Metric 1	9	3	63
Metric 2	9	1	57
Metric 3	3	1	21
Metric 4	9	3	63
Metric 5	3	3	27
Metric 6	9	9	81
Metric 7	3	1	21
Metric 8	1	3	15
Metric 9	3	9	45

Weights of 1, 3, 9 in the cells are estimates of how that metric affects the column heading.

The column heading is the measure of what is important to the purpose of the dashboard.

Figure 11.3: Use a weighted table for a more rigorous selection process.

4. Poll team members for a value of 1, 3, or 9 in each table cell. Using 1, 3, or 9 rather than 1 to 10 gives greater differentiation between top and bottom choices. For example, Metric 1 has a great effect (9) on value but less effect (3) on speed.

   The total weighting column on the right is the total of cell weights times the column heading.

5. Sort the table in descending order by the total weight column using Excel's Data Sort command.

Cross-Check Your Metric

Test your critical few metrics by asking the following questions about them:

- What action will I take if I see significant change in this metric?

  If you are unclear about what action you would take, either you don't need the metric, your model of what you are trying to control is inaccurate, or you haven't selected the correct metric.

- Will the action I take control the process in the way needed?

  Metrics exist to drive changes to behavior and actions. A metric may have unintended consequences. For example, using machine use time as a measure of success could have the unintended consequence of building unneeded inventory. In that case, you may need a counterbalancing measure to watch for that unintended consequence.

- Will measuring this metric change the behavior and action as I want?

  Your purpose should be to change a behavior or action. If you don't see behaviors or actions changing to create the output you need, change the metric. It might take months to determine whether you have a metric that affects behavior and actions the way you want. But if it doesn't work, change the metric. Don't be tied to it.

- Will people try to "game" or manipulate this metric?

  Will your metrics work in the real world with real people? We all know people who "game the system," lying or manipulating numbers rather than stepping up to a culture of performance. I've seen a division of a Fortune 1000 company go bankrupt and end up sold because upper management and the sales management team allowed gaming in the posting of sales numbers. I've seen contractors manipulate their project management numbers to make bonuses even though they must have known they would be caught in the end. Gaming happens when the organization's culture, executives, and management tolerate it. As long as gaming is allowed, no performance management system will work effectively.

What's Simple Can Be Difficult, and What's Difficult Can Be Simple

Large lists of metrics are available through associations and web searches. But having large lists of metrics can be overwhelming. What is important is selecting one of the critical few that will leverage your business and understanding the ramifications behind the metric.

Some measures, such as employee contribution to a company, might seem simple, but they actually can be complex. Others that seem difficult, such as customer satisfaction or employee engagement, can be easy. Here are two examples.

First, let's examine a measure that looks easy but is actually complex. If you want to measure how employees contribute to stakeholders, you might use the often-published *revenue per full-time employee equivalent* (FTE).

When you begin to examine this metric, you realize it presents some problems. The revenue depends on sales effectiveness, competitiveness in the marketplace, and the economy. And how can margin and the cost of capital be factored in?

Using FTEs in the divisor doesn't really make sense, because different business models derive different value from employees at different levels. Perhaps a better metric would be *economic value added per strategic employee*, where economic value added could be defined as follows:

$$\text{net operating profit} - (\text{capital} \times \text{cost of capital})$$

This metric uses the economic value added divided by the number of strategic employees. Strategic employees are those who have been defined through the Balanced Scorecard to have a direct impact on strategic themes and objectives.

One final adjustment might be needed for this formula. Some industries go through cyclical variations, or perhaps the organization is in a growth industry. In such cases, evaluating contribution per strategic employee requires adjustment for cyclicality or for the industry growth rate. Luckily, Excel can easily handle these calculations.

Some measures can seem impossible to quantify, but study can make them easy. For example, user satisfaction and employee engagement seem pretty inscrutable. But recent research has found that one question, "Would you refer us to a friend?," has a higher correlation with user satisfaction than do long, expensive surveys that are difficult to administer.

Another important measure, employee engagement, also seems difficult to measure. But Gallup, after studying the issue, came up with 12 short questions that do an excellent job of determining how engaged employees are with their work. Instead of trying to evaluate employee attitudes once per year with a large, expensive survey, a quick, e-mail-based "flash" survey can be administered monthly to a statistically valid sample using a variation of these questions. Quickly and easily, you have a metric to measure your workforce's engagement.

Again, what is of value to your business is not having a lot of data and metrics, but knowing how to select the critical few metrics that drive significant impact.

Summary

Use a scientific method to select your metrics. Don't just reuse the same metrics on a new dashboard. Know why you are selecting your critical few.

You should have a clear understanding of what behavior or action will change when you begin capturing and displaying your metrics. Metrics drive change. If you've done your job correctly, they will drive the change you want.

Building Maps, Scorecards, and Dashboards

In This Part

Creating Dashboards for Decision-Making

Entia non sunt multiplicanda praeter necessitatem.
(Entities should not be multiplied more than necessary.)

—"Occam's Razor"
William of Ockham
1285–1349

A dashboard's purpose is to aid decision-making. It should not be a display of data, but rather a display of information that has had a template of knowledge applied to it. If your dashboard does not accelerate and improve decision-making, you might as well be displaying streams of raw data onscreen.

You could satisfy the need for business decision tools with Excel charts and tables just as Excel creates them. However, rules have evolved over the hundreds of years of graphical display of data and the tens of years of visual information display on computers. Some of these are process rules that help you identify how to aid in making the business decision. Some rules have evolved to help people understand information and make decisions from it. This chapter covers a few of these important rules and lists numerous resources to help you learn more.

Step-by-Step: Creating Dashboards That Aid Decision-Making

You can certainly create a dashboard just by giving a client exactly what it asks for. Often this results in a dashboard that is either used for a point solution or used only a few times and then never again. To create a dashboard that affects the business, you need to spend the time and energy up front to interview users, investigate business needs, and learn how a dashboard can help them improve their decision-making. Two or three hours of upfront work can save you a lot of downstream time and produce a more valuable dashboard.

Here is a big-picture view of the steps required to create a dashboard that will aid decision-making:

1. **Learn the dashboard's purpose.** Interview the dashboard users. Learn what decisions they want to make using the dashboard.

2. **Learn how dashboard users expect the dashboard to help them.** What can the dashboard do to help them make decisions? What relationships are they looking for? What trends? What targets and alert limits? What analytics are they not using now that could be done in a dashboard?

3. **Learn what they think the dashboard might look like.** Often the request for a dashboard comes from one executive or manager who has seen another's dashboard. Users may have charts or tables they've created themselves in Excel to work with. Learn what ideas they have for their tool.

4. **Ask for business or decision rules.** Learn what can be automated in the dashboard. What logic rules can be programmed in? What about limits, boundaries, and alerts?

5. **Walk through the decision process if it is complex.** Experts are so familiar with making decisions that they may not actually know the steps they take and the rules they use. Getting them to walk you through their decision-making process can reveal what has been left unsaid. If you are building a process-oriented dashboard—for example, to monitor a value stream or supply chain—you *must* use a process map like those described in Chapters 10 and 11.

6. **Learn the parameters.** What time frames and granularity of data (detail level) are needed? What naming conventions are used for products, regions, and departments?

7. **Gather the Excel workbooks and printed reports used to make decisions.** Ask which data in the reports is actually used. What totals and calculations are necessary?

8. **Check the data sources.** Make sure the data is accessible. Will it be released by IT for use in a dashboard? Who owns the data? What files are used, and how often do they refresh?

9. **Use a sketch pad to work up ideas on your own.** In the idea phase, I find that nothing beats pencil and paper. It's still faster than drawing objects on a screen.

10. **Get feedback.** Once you have some ideas, gather two or three of the main users in a room and present your ideas for the dashboard, user interface,

results, and data flow on a whiteboard. Although you can create a prettier proposal in PowerPoint, doing so doesn't allow user participation. Using a whiteboard lets people step up and draw their ideas.

11. **Create a limited-functionality dummy dashboard.** Present a sample dashboard with limited functionality and dummy data.

    Sometimes I create a "wireframe" in Excel or PowerPoint that is just a shell containing fixed numbers, headings, and inactive menus. You can even apply hyperlinks in Excel or PowerPoint so that clicking a fake menu or table takes you to new data or another page.

    Talk through how it works. Fill the drop-down lists or interactive portions with the actual lists used in the final dashboard. Walk through the use of the dummy dashboard.

12. **Build the dashboard.** Use an Excel architecture to separate the chart and user controls from analytics and data. This is described further in Chapter 30.

13. **Release a beta version to a few users.** Clearly label it as a beta version, and get their feedback.

14. **Make corrections to the dashboard, and then release it.**

15. **Don't expect the dashboard to be perfect on the first release.** After people use it for a while, they will have suggestions and improvements.

Make Your Dashboards Actionable

Don't just report data. Great dashboards are designed to aid decision-making, and your dashboards will do just that if you follow a few guidelines:

- **Group information visually by decision criteria.** Group information needed for one type of decision into a visually identifiable "chunk."

- **Display analyzed information, not raw data.** Dashboards for decision-making should display information that has already been filtered and analyzed using human knowledge, business rules, or Excel functions such as top n, bottom n, Pareto, and others described in this book.

- **Automate alerts and business rules.** Automate business rules to identify problems and make decisions. For example, the alert charts described in Chapter 24 automatically show the viewer where an issue arises. The Pareto chart described in Chapter 25 automatically identifies the 20 percent of issues that cause 80 percent of the problems. For example, one client needed to reduce client dissatisfaction with its software service. While continuing its program to build in quality, it wanted a dashboard that would take the data logs from its telephone support calls and provide some actionable items. The end result was an Excel worksheet that used support call logs to create a Pareto chart that identified the most frequent and highest-level support issues each week. From a parent dashboard that showed summary issues, the client could drill down to identify critical areas by product line or issue.

▪ **Show context, judgments, and comments.** Routine decisions that fit well-defined business rules, such as alerts, trends, and limits, can be programmed into your Excel dashboards, but the context of issues, opinions of analysts, unforeseen consequences, and so forth aren't displayed on a chart or in a table. Create a linked or scrolling text box that helps analysts post comments on your dashboard.

▪ **Give access to source data.** Although automated alerts and business rules help identify issues, a manager with many years of experience may want to see the actual data so that he can look for nuances. To allow for this while maintaining an uncluttered appearance, include a button on the dashboard that links to a scrolling table of source data or replication of a printed report. Scrolling tables are described in Chapter 18.

▪ **Suggest "next steps."** Include the information that makes it easy to take the next step, such as knowing what action has already been taken and contacting the issue owner. A briefing book page includes this information and can be updated by the data owner. Include a pop-up e-mail button, as described in Chapters 26 and 28. Such a button pops up when a condition is met, and clicking the button opens an e-mail message to the owner of this activity.

Rules of Design

Entire books have been written on the science and art of visually crafting a dashboard. Among the cognoscenti, it's known as "data visualization," a term you might want to search for on the Internet. Certain psychological and mathematical rules also dictate what type of chart should be used to represent each type of data. But rather than try to compress all that into a few pages, I've tried to distill a few overarching principles.

BUY THE BIBLES OF DASHBOARD VISUALIZATION

Stephen Few's books are the bibles of dashboard visualization:

▪ *Information Dashboard Design: The Effective Visual Communication of Data* (O'Reilly Media, 2006)

▪ *Now You See It: Simple Visualization Techniques for Quantitative Analysis* (Analytics Press, 2009)

▪ *Show Me the Numbers: Designing Tables and Graphs to Enlighten* (Analytics Press, 2012)

Author, statistician, and former professor Edward Tufte is famous for his books on the visual display of information. They combine graphics, art, history, and cognitive psychology. Although his books are beautiful and fascinating to read, Few's books focus on the practical issues of crafting dashboards that communicate with and aid decision-makers. Both Few and Tufte have informative websites. (URLs to these websites are listed near the end of this chapter.)

▪ **Keep things simple and uncluttered.** This has been said several times in this chapter, and you will see it mentioned a lot in the websites described near the end of this chapter: Keep your dashboards and charts simple. Keep the focus on the information needed for decision-making.

▪ **Kill cute dashboards.** Cute dashboards, like those with lots of airplane or car dashboard gauges, look cute, but when they are used frequently to make important business decisions, they become annoying. Cute doesn't last; useful does.

The space used by one cute gauge to represent one metric could display five or more bullet charts showing related information. When you need to present executives with a lot of information that they use frequently, stay away from cute.

I've made a few cute dashboards in my time, especially in Xcelsius, but I'll plead that they were either meant to attract attention or demanded by the client.

▪ **Command the viewer's eye.** Magicians use a technique called "forcing" to focus their subjects' minds on a limited set of responses. For example, they mention elephants early in a conversation and then later ask people to visualize a gray animal. When the magician then guesses what someone is thinking, it looks like magic. In the same way, your dashboards should "force" a focus.

Your interviews should have made you aware of the information most important to decision-making. Command the viewer's eye by grouping that information at the top left of the dashboard. Put the dominant colors on the critical information, and mute or eliminate other distractions.

▪ **Limit feature creep.** I've had more than one user want to keep adding feature after feature to a dashboard (and I frequently find myself wanting to add extra features the user didn't ask for or need). The rule of thumb I've come up with is that users are usually correct for the first two or three changes. They know what they want, and they know how they use it. But some clients have a strange glint come into their eyes, a little like Mr. Toad in *Wind in the Willows*. Suddenly, they lose control and begin asking for lots of little gadgets that are rarely used and that fog the brain.

It's up to you to know when to draw the line. Sit down with the user and discuss how much value she will get from the extra feature and how much work it will cause you now, and cause later in future maintenance.

▪ **Use a clean, consistent visual layout.** Dashboard viewers in the Western world are trained to look from left to right, top to bottom. Nearly all computer programs put their menus across the top and control items, such as drop-down lists, down the left side.

Organize information into meaningful groups. For example, a chart or table with the main information should be at the top center; supporting or detail charts should be smaller and at the bottom.

▪ **Put one decision on each page.** I briefly lived in Texas. While there, I came across a wonderful story that illustrates competency, force, and focus. In the late 1800s, Texas was still a wild frontier. A contingency of 80 Texas Rangers represented the only law and order for the large territory. When the first prize fights were scheduled in Dallas, the good citizens feared that riots would engulf the city. The mayor telegraphed the governor to send a company of Texas Rangers.

When only a single Texas Ranger, Captain W. J. McDonald, stepped off the train, the mayor was taken aback. Albert Paine, a historical author, wrote that the mayor blurted out, "Where are the others?"

To this Captain McDonald responded, "Hell, ain't I enough? There's only one prize fight!" His words have been immortalized as "One riot, one ranger."

Give your dashboards competency, force, and focus. Don't cheat by including every possible piece of data and type of chart just because you are unsure what is needed.

Using competency, force, and focus should help you build the dashboard that puts the critical information on one concise screen.

- **Make dashboards accessible to color-blind and aging eyes.** Design your chart elements so that they are accessible to those with less-than-perfect vision. Dashboards are for business decision-making. I've seen dashboards created by Business Intelligence software companies that obviously gave their artists too much license. The dashboards look pretty and artistically elegant, but they contain little decision-making data and are unusable.

Approximately 8 percent of men and 2 percent of women are color-blind. One of my clients, a CEO, is color-blind. Would Excel's standard conditional colors of red, yellow, and green work for his Balanced Scorecard? Yes, but only if the following modifications were used.

Instead of using only conditional colors as alerts, include a conditional icon, such as an arrowhead, and adjust the color saturation. Chapter 15 describes how to combine conditional icons with conditional colors in all versions of Excel. For example, when a condition is poor, a heavily saturated red background displays behind a downward-pointing arrowhead. When a poor but improving condition occurs, a medium-saturation yellow background displays with a left-pointing arrowhead. When the condition is good, an arrowhead points up with no background. No background is needed for good conditions, because we want to draw attention only to areas that need attention. (This is yet another area where Excel is flexible. Numerous expensive Business Intelligence software systems have no way to compensate for color blindness.)

When you adapt colors for color blindness, in alerts and chart elements, consider how a color will translate into black, shades of gray, and white. You can still use red, yellow, and green, but change the color saturation so that each prints (or displays to a color-blind person) with a strikingly different level of gray. Color saturation is controlled in the Custom Colors dialog box with the vertical bar to the right of the color box in the custom color window.

Tips on Graphical Elements

Here are just a few big-picture concepts to consider when designing the graphical layout, look, and feel of your dashboards:

- **Use your client's branding.** Your organization or client has probably paid a lot of money and spent a lot of time developing a "corporate identity." The corporate identity is the brand imaging for printed and web materials. It includes fonts and color palettes and probably layouts.

Contact the marketing department and get the officially sanctioned corporate identity. (A corporate identity is a corporation's official colors with RGB for video and CMYK for print colors, its formats for addresses, stationary layouts, and so on.) Midsized and large corporations usually have this information in a compressed file ready to send to you.

▪ **Use conservative color palettes and intensities.** Nearly everyone agrees that Excel has a superb chart engine, but its standard color palette for charting is garish. Create a custom color palette as described in Chapter 16. Use the color palette from the corporate identity, and make sure you compensate for color blindness and aging eyes.

Never put light colors on dark backgrounds, such as white or yellow on dark blue or black. This might work in PowerPoint, but never do it in a dashboard. Don't put red on black. It's a verified medical fact that 17.3 percent of viewers will find their eyes beginning to oscillate uncontrollably when viewing this color combination, causing them extreme frustration and nausea. (Just kidding. But don't do it anyway.)

▪ **Get rid of chart junk.** Chart junk includes all the unnecessary elements in a chart that detract from decision-making. For example, why does a legend need a box around it? It doesn't, so remove it. Charts are used for trends and relationships, not for reading precise data values, so why include gridlines? Remove them.

Edward Tufte, professor emeritus of statistics at Yale, was called the "da Vinci of data" in the *New York Times* As an adamant opponent of chart junk, he rails against it on his website, http://www.edwardtufte.com. Tufte may have summed up his philosophy of data visualization when he said, "Good displays of data help to reveal knowledge relevant to understanding mechanism, process and dynamics, cause and effect." Get rid of everything else that detracts.

▪ **Mute the less important.** Excel chart elements, like axis lines, are inserted at full-intensity black. These are unimportant to the chart. In fact, a large majority of the chart junk that Excel automatically puts in is unimportant. Remove it, or use a muted color. The only things you want to stand out with intensity are the pieces of information being used for decision-making.

▪ **Use the correct chart type.** Some chart types should rarely, if ever, be used. My votes for the "never" category are stacked bar charts and radar charts. In the "only under special circumstances" category are pie charts.

Use pie charts to show how three to five pieces of data relate to the total. The pie chart must include all the data elements that comprise 100 percent of the data set. In general, I use pie charts when the client makes a special request and it meets the rules just stated; otherwise, a column chart works better.

I'd like to see some examples where a stacked column chart was the best choice. I haven't seen any yet. Some people attempt to use stacked column charts to show the relative change in segments over time. But this change is nearly impossible to see. Only the bottom segment of each column has a baseline. The baseline for all other segments moves up and down, making comparison difficult. Instead of using a stacked column chart, use a normal column chart with multiple columns. If there are too many data series, give your viewer check boxes or a selection list allowing her to select and display the data series desired. The Excel techniques to do this are described in Chapter 20.

- **Limit the use of shadow bands in tables.** It can be difficult for the eye to track across wide tables of numbers. If a table becomes so wide that it is hard to visually track a row, use alternating bands of shading behind the lines. But there is a proviso. Keep the shading as light as possible. Even the light colors that come with Excel's standard palette are too dark. Create your own custom palette.

- **Use legends.** Legends give references for a chart or table. Because they aren't a main topic of interest, keep them small and out of the way. Reduce clutter by decreasing their font size, removing their boxes and background shading, and moving them out of the visual focus.

- **Watch your text orientation.** Try not to use vertical text; it's too difficult to read. If text doesn't fit, use a smaller font. If that doesn't work, abbreviate the text. And if that doesn't work, reposition the text by putting it in a floating text box and moving it out of the chart area.

Some Important Sources on the Art and Science of Visualizing Data

Much good information on data visualization can be found in a few websites and books. The following sections describe some that will help you.

Excel Charting Techniques

- **Ron Person** (http://www.criticaltosuccess.com): Ron is the author of this book. He has spent more than 25 years helping organizations improve their performance. He is an expert at developing and implementing Balanced

Scorecards and operational dashboards. Ron has more than a million copies of Excel books in print and was one of Microsoft's first consulting partners.

■ **John Walkenbach** (`http://www.j-walk.com`): I've been using Excel since 1985, before its public release. One invaluable book I keep on my bookshelf is Walkenbach's *Excel Formulas*. When a solution doesn't immediately come to mind, I reach for one of his books, and I often find the answer.

■ **Jon Peltier** (`http://www.peltiertech.com`): Peltier's Technical Services, Inc., has many examples of Excel charting techniques on its website, which is a great source of all-around Excel knowledge.

The Art of Visualizing Data

■ **Stephen Few** (`http://www.perceptualedge.com`): Few has written the bible on the visual aspects of designing dashboards: *Information Dashboard Design: The Effective Communication of Data.* He contributes to blogs on data visualization and hosts his own website filled with tips.

■ **Edward Tufte** (`http://www.edwardtufte.com`): *Nature*, one of the leading magazines of science, described Tufte as "the world's leading analyst of graphic information." His books on representing data through visual images, not just dashboards, are beautiful and intriguing. Tufte is the originator of Sparklines, the miniature minimalist charts described in Chapter 19.

■ **Charles Kyd** (`http://www.exceluser.com`): Kyd's work in magazine-quality charting with Excel is described in detail in Chapter 19. Be sure to sign up for his Excel Users newsletter, which contains lots of great tips.

■ **Junk Charts** (`http://junkcharts.typepad.com`): Junk Charts has critiques on some intriguing charts. In addition to seeing some of the bleeding edge of chartdom, you will learn about statistics and about how *not* to present data. The site also reviews some cool tools.

■ **TED, inspired talks by the world's greatest thinkers and doers** (`http://www.ted.com`): TED is one of my favorite websites on any topic. TED is a conference held each spring in Monterey, California, that brings together thousands of the world's most creative doers. Topics cover design, business, religion, medicine, music, and more. TED streams free videos of all its presentations. (Most are less than 15 minutes.) To see an impressive example of how to analyze data for insights into world problems, watch any of the TED videos by Hans Rosling. For an artistic representation of the "graphics of excess," search for Chris Jordan.

Summary

The purpose of any dashboard you create should be to aid decision-making. By interviewing users and understanding their reasons for requesting a dashboard, as well as how they make decisions, you can create a tool that will help them make better decisions faster.

Most of the rules for visualizing data can be condensed to just a few:

- Eliminate chart junk.
- Keep the focus on the information required for decision-making.
- Help the user make better decisions faster.

CHAPTER 13

Drawing Process and Strategy Maps

As I grow older, I pay less attention to what people say. I just watch what they do.
—Andrew Carnegie
Industrialist
1835–1919

Strategy Maps, value stream maps, and process maps of all types provide visual clarity. They make complex processes understandable and memorable. They also make it significantly easier to identify the points in a strategy or process where you can get leverage to create the greatest impact. As soon as you have identified these points of impact, you can identify the metrics to measure.

This chapter shows you how to draw Strategy Maps and simple business process maps using the tools built into Microsoft Office. Additional drawing and mapping tools are described in Chapter 27.

Which Drawing Tool Should You Use?

Strategy Maps and process maps range from simple maps you create once, which only need to be "good enough," to maps that dynamically link to databases that update continuously and are critical to operations. Figure 13.1 shows a Strategy Map drawn in Microsoft PowerPoint 2010. A range of software exists that can satisfy your needs across the spectrum.

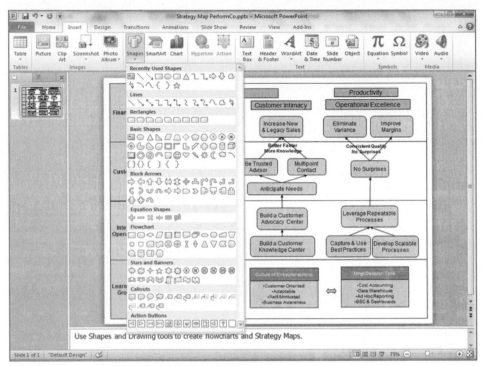

Figure 13.1: Microsoft Office has drawing tools that can create Strategy Maps and simple business process maps.

This chapter describes different software solutions with different levels of user knowledge and different levels of output. Of course, these have different pricing levels.

If your needs are minimal and you need to create only one or two Strategy Maps or simple process maps, the Shapes and Drawing tools in Excel or PowerPoint may be all you require. If you want to build flowcharts and Lean or Six Sigma process improvement charts, you should consider FlowBreeze and Systems2Win, described in Chapter 27. If you need unlimited flexibility, manual control, and the ability to link data tables or databases to the map's display, you might want to use Microsoft Visio.

Drawing with Microsoft Office Drawing Tools

Office 2007 and Office 2010 have Shapes, and Office 2003 has the Drawing toolbar. These all give Microsoft Word, PowerPoint, and Excel drawing tools that do a good job of creating simple Strategy Maps, process maps, and flowcharts.

They give you basic shapes, lines, and arrows that stay connected, and enough formatting capability to make your work look pretty good.

PowerPoint and its Drawing tools work well for drawing Strategy Maps. This is because the maps usually will be displayed in PowerPoint. Also, PowerPoint can print large output using a banner or custom page setup.

If you are creating process maps or flowcharts, you may want to draw directly in an Excel worksheet. This enables you to link the labels in shapes, and process tables to formulas in the worksheets. As data changes, the flowcharts change. If you are drawing process maps or flowcharts, you may want to consider the add-ins described in Chapter 27.

This chapter describes basic guidelines for drawing maps in PowerPoint. Figure 13.1 shows a Strategy Map drawn in PowerPoint 2010. You can draw this same Strategy Map in Office 2003, Office 2007 and Office 2010 applications such as PowerPoint, Word or Excel. I prefer drawing these maps in PowerPoint as it allows presentation and printing in large formats. In PowerPoint 2007 and PowerPoint 2010, choose the Insert tab, the Illustrations group, and Shapes. In PowerPoint 2003, display the Drawing toolbar, click AutoShapes and then select the drawing tool you need. In PowerPoint 2003 you can "tear off" the Basic Shapes toolbar and position it onscreen, a handy feature. This is not possible in Office 2007 and Office 2010. Use Connector lines and arrows when possible to draw lines and arrows that stay connected as you reposition shapes.

Displaying the Drawing Toolbar in Versions of Office Prior to 2007 and 2010

A Drawing toolbar was used to hold drawing tools in versions of Office prior to Office 2007 and Office 2010. If you are using an earlier version and the Drawing toolbar is not visible, you can make it appear:

1. Right-click a toolbar and choose Drawing, or select View ➢ Toolbars ➢ Drawing.

2. Move the toolbar to the location you want by dragging the title bar or dotted "handle" at an end of the toolbar.

Drawing Objects and Connectors

In PowerPoint 2007 and PowerPoint 2010, on the Insert tab, in the Illustrations group, click Shapes. Click the shape you want, and then click in the document where you want the shape; drag to size it. Holding down the Shift key as you drag constrains rectangles so that they become squares and constrains ellipses to become circles. Additional tabs for applying formatting and effects to drawing objects appear on the ruler when a drawing object is selected.

In earlier versions of PowerPoint, the drawing objects you will use most frequently are the Basic Shapes, Flowchart, and Connector tools. These steps show you how to put a shape on the PowerPoint slide:

1. Click AutoShapes.

2. Point to Basic Shapes or Flowchart, and then click the shape you want to draw.

3. Move the crosshair pointer to one corner of where you want the shape, drag it to the opposite corner, and release it.

Connector lines or arrows stay connected between objects you draw, even when you move the objects. Figure 13.2 shows a connector arrow being drawn from its starting point to its end point. As the pointer moves over an object, connector sites—small dots or squares—appear on the edges of the object. These connector sites are locations where you can anchor the end of the connector. Lines and arrows stay attached to an anchor, even when objects are moved.

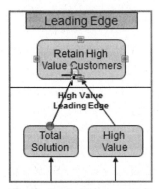

Figure 13.2: Connector sites appear on the edges of objects where connector lines or arrows can be attached.

Do the following to draw and connect a connector between two objects:

1. Display the palette of Shapes or AutoShapes.

2. In Office 2007 and Office 2010, select the line or arrow you want to draw. In Office 2003, point to Connectors, a special class of line, and then click the type of connector you want. You can later modify a connector by double-clicking it to change the style of its line or arrowhead.

3. Move the pointer over the first object, and click the connector site where you want to anchor the tail.

4. Move the pointer over the second object, and click the connector site where you want to anchor the head.

Adding Text to Objects or Connectors

Add text inside objects by clicking in the center of the object and typing. To format the text in an object, select the text, right-click, and choose the formatting command you want. In Office 2007 and Office 2010, you can adjust the positioning or layout of text. Right-click the object containing text and select Format Text Effects. In the Format Text Effects dialog box, select Text Box. In Office 2003, adjust the positioning or layout of text in an object by right-clicking the object and selecting options you want in the Text Box tab. Change the layouts and margin as you want.

Lines, arrows, and connectors do not have text associated with them, but you can create a text box next to the line or arrow and then enter text in it.

Moving Objects or Connectors

Move objects by dragging them to new locations. The easiest way to select them to drag is to click the object and then hover the mouse pointer over its top edge. When the mouse pointer changes to a four-headed arrow, you can drag the object. If connectors are attached to an object, the connector moves and realigns itself with the object in its new location.

Formatting Objects or Connectors

You can format the size, line style, and color of all objects, lines, and connectors. Right-click the object or connector you want to format, choose Format Shape, and make the formatting changes you need.

Grouping Objects So That They Act as One

Some objects need to stay together and act as a unit. Grouping objects is easy:

1. Select all the objects you want to group by clicking the first object, and then hold down the Ctrl key as you click the edge of other objects.

2. Right-click the edge of one of the objects and choose Group (Grouping in Office 2003) ➢ Group.

   To ungroup a group of objects, right-click the group and choose Group (Grouping) ➢ Ungroup.

Using Grid and Nudge for Accurate Positioning

Move objects in large increments by selecting them and then using the arrow keys. To move objects in small increments, hold down the Ctrl key as you press the arrow keys.

In Office 2007 and Office 2010, you can quickly display gridlines and guides by selecting the Gridlines or Guides check boxes on the View tab in the Show group. For greater control, you can display the Grid and Guides dialog box, shown in Figure 13.3, by clicking the small down arrow at the lower-right corner of the Show group. In Office 2003, select View ➤ Grid and Guides.

Figure 13.3: The Grid and Guides dialog box makes it easier to align and position objects when you are working on finishing touches.

If you are having trouble getting objects to align, zoom the magnification to expand the map to 200 percent or 400 percent. This magnified view makes it easier to make minor adjustments and to see corners and alignment.

Controlling Objects That Overlap

Objects appear in layers. Layers are like virtual sheets of glass, each holding one object. Visually, the objects can cover each other. Moving the order of the layers enables you to make different objects appear on top of others, allowing you to overlap objects.

However, you will find that sometimes you want to change an object's layer. In Office 2007 and Office 2010, change an object's layer by right-clicking the object's edge and then choosing Bring to Front or Send to Back, or one of their submenu options. To change an object's layer in Office 2003, right-click the object and choose Order; then select one of the four commands to shift the layer.

Saving Time When You Draw

Figure 13.4 shows how you can save considerable time when drawing a map in PowerPoint or Excel. As you begin your project, decide which objects you will need and what their format should be. Create and format one of each object, and drag them off the PowerPoint slide to the side. In Excel you can create an out-of-view area or put them on a different sheet. These objects are your library.

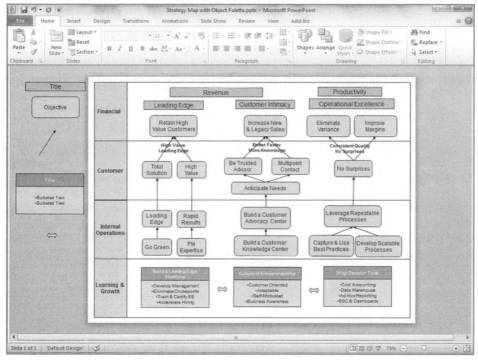

Figure 13.4: Save time by creating a library of frequently used objects outside the viewing area of your slide or worksheet.

Whenever you need one of your preformatted objects or connectors, select it from the side area, and hold down the Ctrl key as you drag a duplicate onto the slide. This ensures that all your objects have the same formatting and size.

You may find it easier to work by starting at the macro or global view and working toward the micro or detail view. Begin with a 66 percent view or one that enables you to see the entire slide as well as your library of objects on the side. Create and format a library of objects to the side of your slide, and then drag them to their general location. Now, zoom to a closer view and begin entering text, aligning objects, and attaching connectors.

Drawing with Microsoft Visio

Microsoft Visio is the drawing tool for heavyweight production. It can lift any load, but you need to be able to spend time with it. If you want to create a quick Strategy Map or process map, Visio may take more time to learn than you want to spend. It also is expensive. But if you have many models to draw, or you need to link process maps to databases so that text and numbers update dynamically, Visio is your tool.

As an alternative to Microsoft Visio you should first review the free trials of the Excel-based flowcharting tools described in Chapter 27.

Microsoft Visio gives you a blank sheet on start-up, so you need to know what type of map you want, rather than looking through a library. A few templates are available at the Microsoft Office download website. Figure 13.5 shows one of the examples available online.

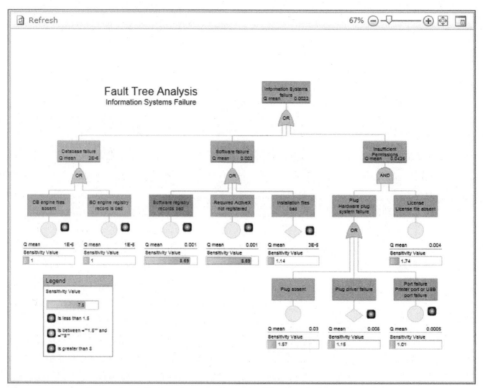

Figure 13.5: Microsoft Visio is a heavy-duty workhorse that can handle any type of business process mapping. As shown in this Fault Tree Analysis, you can even hook datasources to the drawing.

After selecting a symbol from one of Visio's many symbol libraries, position and connect the symbol on the map using the same methods you would use with the Drawing tool. When you need to apply formatting and color, you can use Visio's predefined color themes.

Microsoft Visio excels in the areas of data connectivity and analysis. Maps and charts you draw can be linked to data in Excel workbooks or databases. This enables displayed data in symbols to automatically update when the data changes. You can even assign alert levels to connected data so that areas out of tolerance are flagged with a warning color.

Summary

At in-house workshops or after presentations, someone often remarks how Strategy Maps and operational flowcharts have clarified a problem. Don't lose that clarity.

When you need to capture the Strategy Map or process it and communicate it to your organization, use a drawing tool that is up to the task. If you are creating a single Strategy Map, the Microsoft Office shapes and drawing tools are sufficient. If you plan to create many flowcharts or do a lot of Lean work, but you can't afford to spend much, check out the Excel add-ins described in Chapter 27. And if you need maps that have no limits on their robustness and that can work dynamically with data, choose Microsoft Visio.

CHAPTER 14

Using Microsoft Excel for Balanced Scorecards and Dashboards

Once we accept our limits, we go beyond them.
—Albert Einstein
Theoretical physicist
1879–1955

I'll come right out and say it: IT departments don't like Excel. I'll admit that they do have some justifiable issues with using Excel for complex business systems, or as a Business Intelligence engine in some environments.

But the truth is, Excel is ubiquitous. According to my highly unscientific and impromptu polls over the last few years, Excel is the most-used software for Balanced Scorecards. And I would bet that Excel has far more operational dashboards than enterprise-level Business Intelligence systems.

So how do you handle this disparity between business users' needs for fast, personally controlled analysis and IT needs for management, security, and control? Perhaps there is a middle ground.

Excel Is the Most Widely Used Balanced Scorecard Software

At a meeting of fellow Six Sigma Black Belts, I asked how many of the 32 Black Belts present were using Balanced Scorecards and operational dashboards created in Excel. Everyone raised their hand. Only one, working for a large corporation, had access to an IT-governed Business Intelligence system.

The night before I started writing this chapter, at a meeting of the Association of Strategic Planning, someone asked, "What software is everyone using for

Balanced Scorecards?" Everyone in the room acknowledged using Excel. The Balanced Scorecard sponsor for a major bank told how the bank had attempted to build its scorecard using an enterprise software package. After six months, the bank realized that doing so had been a serious mismatch. It rebuilt its Balanced Scorecard using Excel and went on to have a successful Balanced Scorecard implementation. It was so successful, in fact, that the parent bank will be using Excel for subsequent Balanced Scorecard implementations in its other holdings.

Sometimes a Balanced Scorecard is used to roll up or integrate more than two levels, or a hybrid scorecard is needed that integrates data from multiple business units. In that case I recommend using Excel for the Balanced Scorecards in a nonintegrated environment for the first year or two. After you have acquired and cleaned data and the culture has adapted, begin the process of building a multilevel integrated Balanced Scorecard or Business Intelligence system. This method of testing, learning, and evolving could save you hundreds of thousands of dollars.

Excel's ubiquitous nature isn't just in Balanced Scorecards. I always keep an eye out for dashboards when walking through my clients' financial or manufacturing facilities. Perhaps it is selective perception, but it seems that every other corridor has a posted collection of Excel charts showing targets versus actuals. I'm coming to the conclusion that the Western world is being measured using Excel scorecards and dashboards.

Consider the Trade-Offs between Excel and Large BI Systems

It is pretty easy to claim that Microsoft Excel is the most widely used numeric analysis and financial software in the world. It has made business and financial analysis available to millions of business people. In the context of this book, Excel is used for the following:

- Ad hoc queries to databases
- Analyzing business data
- Business modeling
- Planning and budgeting
- Presentations of charts and tables
- Reporting
- Scenario testing

With all its use, Excel is still held in low esteem by IT. Whenever Excel is discussed with IT departments, three issues arise:

- **Excel isn't scalable.** It is difficult to distribute, manage, and control Excel applications—for example, scaling an Excel dashboard for use by 1,000 users.

- **Excel produces multiple versions of the "truth."** When users get personal copies of data, it spawns different versions that, although they have the same title, may have different source data and origination dates and may have been manipulated using user-defined formulas.

- **Excel lacks referential integrity.** There is no way to track where the data in an Excel spreadsheet came from, when changes were made (and by whom), and what business rules lie behind the formulas.

Business users, however, are less concerned with a manageable IT environment and data integrity. They are more concerned about managing the alligators in the swamp. Here are some of the alligators that keep users on Excel and away from Business Intelligence systems:

- **Business changes quickly.** Analysis is needed rapidly. It can't wait for IT that is short-staffed or unresponsive.

- **Users know their own assumptions and rules.** In Excel, users can modify variables and formulas quickly as the environment changes.

- **Low-cost solutions are needed.** Some situations require simple, low-cost solutions that would never stand up to the rigor and resources required of a system sent through the entire IT process.

- **Users know Excel.** Business users don't have the time to learn a new Business Intelligence system when they already know Excel.

- **Users have existing solutions in Excel.** Implementing a Business Intelligence system would also force users to re-create all their existing tools and solutions that they use to manage daily crises. Without their existing tools, they would fall even further behind.

Disadvantages of Excel

The IT department raises valid objections to Excel. You need to understand IT's concerns before assuming that Excel can always replace a Business Intelligence system.

Many Versions of One Truth

A fairly common scene in corporate America is the business user with a special need who puts in a request to IT. IT can't build the analysis or report quickly, so the user asks, "Can you just export the data for me?"

The user then sucks the static data into Excel, manipulates the data to fit his needs, uses unaudited formulas to add or forecast more data points, and then prints the report or sends the resulting data to other users. Nowhere is there documentation or version control. Two people doing this to similar data sets the stage for a fight about whose data is correct.

A solution to this common problem is to follow these rules:

- Data stays in the database and is retrieved to the worksheet for calculation and reporting.
- All reports show the date of data retrieval and its source in the footer.

It is not difficult with IT's help to connect your worksheet to a SQL or OLAP database. As soon as you have a connection, you can retrieve and update data using a PivotTable or PowerPivot. Chapters 21 and 22, which cover PivotTables and PowerPivots, show you how to format this data into any type of report or chart.

Technical Scalability versus User Scalability

A common IT refrain is that Excel is not scalable. This depends on the type of scalability needed. In the area of multidimensional work, Excel doesn't scale well. Excel is great for building a budget and forecast for a single department, but it doesn't work well for rolling up the budget and forecast for dozens of departments and divisions. If you want to build a Balanced Scorecard that rolls up through more than two levels of your organization, Excel is probably not what you want.

Many Excel systems, like those for Balanced Scorecards and operational dashboards, work well without needing to be scaled to large levels.

One area of scalability where Excel wins is cost and time. The cost of licensing Business Intelligence seats for each user quickly increases. With Excel, that cost is already paid.

Another cost in large-scale production is training and support. Although most Excel users can use more job-specific training, the cost is minimal. Training on enterprise Business Intelligence systems usually costs thousands of dollars per user. And then the users must return and use the new system while facing the pressure of daily work. Such a solution usually takes a long time to work. The cost to the business is huge.

In one case, a large northern California bank implemented an enterprise-wide Business Intelligence system from one of the largest Business Intelligence vendors. After three days of training, business and account managers returned to their desks unable to use the new, very expensive BI system to do the simple analysis for which they all had existing Excel worksheets. They understood how their Excel analyses worked, and they knew how to correct them. By the end of the week, everyone had returned to using Excel just so they could get their work done. Within weeks, the minimal skills they had learned on the new system were forgotten.

Hidden Errors

Spreadsheets contain errors. Poorly constructed spreadsheets make it worse by mixing formulas and data, so it is easy for users to type over formulas. The users are never taught how to structure their spreadsheets or how to audit the results, so spreadsheets go out to the world containing errors.

Excel contains some marvelous troubleshooting tools to help you find errors in your worksheets. For example, it can pinpoint where someone has probably typed a number over a formula. It can trace the formulas that feed into a cell and the formulas that depend on a cell.

Spreadsheets Spawn Spreadsheets

Spreadsheets spawn spreadsheets, and that spawns trouble. When one department or user sees a useful application or data set, it asks for it. Even if the original application was well maintained, the spawned spreadsheet gets changed, spawns again, mutates, and soon spreads throughout the organization with neither version control nor documentation.

KNOW SPREADSHEET BEST PRACTICES

In one Excel system I audited for a major pharmaceutical company, the spreadsheets had numeric values typed over where critical formulas should have been. The result was that decisions had been made using incorrect sales reports and forecasts.

IT would say it was Excel's fault. However, I've also found SQL statements that were incorrect and data warehouses with incorrectly defined data. In all these cases, good training and time spent testing and auditing would have found the errors.

In Excel, you can significantly reduce errors by following a few best practices:

■ Use a spreadsheet architecture that separates data, formula, and chart and reporting areas.

Continued

(continued)

- Link Excel spreadsheets to shared data that refreshes on a recurrent basis.
- Keep the data in a database, and connect and extract it for calculations, models, reports, and charts.
- Use range names in formulas.
- Include a documentation sheet that lists critical formulas, assumptions, and range names.
- Use the Formula Auditing Group on the Formula menu to check for values in formula areas, track formulas, trace circular formulas, and more.
- Evaluate segments of nested formulas by selecting a valid segment and pressing F9 to see what that segment evaluates to. Press Esc to return to the original formula.
- Include the date and data source on all dashboards and reports.
- Subscribe to the Excel newsletter at `http://www.criticaltosuccess.com` to get tips on worksheet layout and troubleshooting.

These are all simple disciplines that are easy to learn and monitor. Make sure your developers know them. I teach them to my clients.

The Ineluctable Modality of User-Built Conundrums

Excel's popularity with business people causes problems. It puts power in the hands of users. Business users love Excel for its capability to quickly analyze data. But the majority of business users have not had even rudimentary training in spreadsheet design, security, and auditing. They were shown how to enter formulas, create charts, and perhaps build a PivotTable, and then they were let loose without the discipline or structure of trained or experienced programmers.

Spreadsheet applications may work fine, but when the original developer leaves, maintaining and documenting a proprietary system can create problems. Again, this is really an issue with user training. What is needed is a professional system of documentation and development.

Advantages of Using Excel

In business users' minds, the advantages of Excel clearly outweigh those of other analysis software. And in most cases, there are no alternatives to Excel. Furthermore, the advantages of using Excel are many. Knowledgeable users and consultants are everywhere. Excel is basically free, because it is a part of Microsoft Office. And it has the add-ons and calculating power necessary to solve most business analysis problems that the average user faces.

Get It Done Now!

One of the biggest advantages of using Excel is that the analysis can be done *now*, by the person who needs it. Excel's 300+ functions and hundreds of add-ons allow users to solve almost any business analytic and reporting problem, so long as they can get the data. Of course, this is also one of Excel's biggest problems. Jamming out quick solutions usually means that the spreadsheet application wasn't constructed with a good architecture and certainly wasn't documented.

Prove the Business Intelligence and Dashboard Concept

Excel is an excellent, low-cost way of proving the need and value of a Balanced Scorecard or operational dashboard. It makes sense for management to want to see a working system to test the concepts before they allocate money for the year of development and hundreds of thousands of dollars that a full Business Intelligence system can cost.

Experienced Users

Excel knowledge is pervasive. And most organizations have one person they turn to as the Excel guru who understands most of the features, and perhaps a little Visual Basic for Applications. The web has numerous excellent sites with databases full of tips and examples. This means that the support load is low. Users can help each other.

Total Costs for Scalability

IT departments talk about the technical limits of scalability for Excel. But another area needs to be discussed—the true cost of scaling or expanding a Business Intelligence, Balanced Scorecard, or dashboard effort.

License fees and the definition of a user are making Business Intelligence systems from large vendors increasingly expensive. On the other hand, Excel is a sunk cost because it is included in Microsoft Office.

Another, even larger cost that is rarely discussed is the total cost of retraining and redeveloping existing business systems. Converting users to a large Business Intelligence system requires a couple days of training at a thousand dollars or more per day. Then, when users return to work, they are expected to leave behind their existing spreadsheets and use the new system for their analysis. The reality is that this doesn't happen. People return to their desks with high hopes, fail to get the results they need (the examples in class are always dumbed down), and, under the pressure of deadlines, go back to their old Excel spreadsheets.

If users are forced to use a BI system, they must take time from being productive to create new solutions that replace the Excel solutions that have taken them years to create. That time away from production damages the bottom line.

Excel Is Flexible and Extensible

I've been using Excel since 1985, before its first public release. Back then it came on a stack of diskettes about six inches high and ran on a runtime version of Windows. Since that time, Excel has polished out the glitches and has developed a warehouse full of analytical add-ons you can use to extend its analytical capabilities. Also, the Excel format has become a *lingua franca* for data interchange between computer systems, almost like CSV files.

Excel's Chart Engine Is a Powerful Standard

One of the best chart engines available is in Microsoft Excel. You can customize almost any part of a chart you want. A common request I hear when doing Business Intelligence work is to make the chart look as good as it does in Excel while having the same analytic capability.

When to Use Excel

Excel works well for Balanced Scorecards and operational dashboards that have one or two levels of organization. If your data is stored in a well-designed data warehouse or OLAP cube, you can create dashboards that span dozens of geographic regions and hundreds of products. But it is still difficult to make them user-friendly when drilling down more than one or two levels into data. For that reason, and because of its excellent charting and math capabilities and its common use in business, Excel is the preferred choice for initial development of Balanced Scorecards.

Using Excel for the first year gives organizations a chance to evaluate their objectives and causal links, to refine their metrics, and to gather their data without spending a lot of time and resources on a large IT project. Stories abound of companies that have bypassed the "functioning prototype" Excel stage and then have failed to deliver with their too-large BI system. Only upon restarting the Balanced Scorecard process and rebuilding with Excel did they succeed.

Excel also works well for operational dashboards that are point solutions working with narrow sets of data and that aren't shared between large numbers of users. Excel doesn't work well for dashboard systems that give users ad hoc query capability. You can build dashboards that allow queries, but these usually are used against narrowly scoped data sets.

If you are a small to midsized business or a department within a large corporation, using Excel within these limits, and when linked to a good database, may be all you need. Excel may fit your BI needs, your budget, and your time constraints far better than a large, resource-intensive BI system.

WHEN NOT TO USE EXCEL

You don't want to use Excel if you are considering large-scale Business Intelligence solutions. For example, some government agencies have Balanced Scorecards that cascade and roll up through 14 layers of the organization. I wouldn't recommend using Excel by itself to cascade through more than two layers in an organization.

Excel can drill into data when it has the appropriate relational database or OLAP cube back end. In most Balanced Scorecard systems, however, Excel uses static data imported into an Excel worksheet. This makes drilling into more than one or two layers difficult. If you need extensive ad hoc queries and drill-down capability, you may need a Business Intelligence system.

If you plan to cascade your Balanced Scorecard and dashboards through multiple levels of the organization and through hundreds of users, I recommend prototyping in Excel to determine users' needs before developing the Business Intelligence system.

Solutions

Although there are IT reasons for not using Excel for Business Intelligence, Excel works well for Balanced Scorecards and point solution operational dashboards.

Excel also helps small and midsized businesses (SMBs) or departments within large organizations that need agile systems that are easy to support, that cost little to develop and maintain, and that can handle flexible analysis. Balanced Scorecards and dashboards developed in Excel have certain advantages:

- Less time to development
- Low or nonexistent licensing fees
- Accessible developers
- An established, knowledgeable user base
- Easily accessible user training
- Quick and inexpensive testing of user requirements
- Excellent analytical capability with over 300 functions
- Extensibility that allows additional features, such as Monte Carlo techniques, for nominal cost
- Arguably one of the best charting engines around

What about scalability and data integrity? The solution might be using Excel as the analysis and presentation layer and storing all data in a relational database or OLAP cube and then linking in the Excel scorecards or dashboards. This enables you to share common data, maintain backups, maintain standard metric definitions, have secure access, and scale to a large number of users. Increase the integrity and professionalism of your spreadsheets by giving your power users a one- or two-day course that specifically targets the rules described earlier for professional spreadsheets.

Summary

Excel is the world standard for financial and business modeling. Combine this with its powerful charting engine and broad user base, and it's easy to see why it continues to be the most widely used platform for Balanced Scorecards and operational dashboards. But there are caveats. You must be aware of Excel's limits, and the systems you build must subscribe to spreadsheet best practices, or you may develop systems that are difficult to maintain.

CHAPTER 15

Text-Based Dashboards

This report, by its very length, defends itself against the risk of being read.
—Sir Winston Churchill
Statesman
1874–1965

Knowing that Excel has one of the best graphical engines available in business software, why would you consider creating text-based dashboards? There are numerous reasons.

The text-based dashboards described in this chapter use text elements that fit within worksheet cells. They take up little room in a printed report yet give the reader a quick comparison between relative values. And text-based dashboards are compatible across earlier versions of Excel.

This chapter also describes conditional formatting used in Excel 2007 and Excel 2010 that can alert users with colors, icons, and bars. Chapter 19 describes how to insert miniature charts into cells in Excel 2007 and Excel 2010.

With the addition of conditional colors and conditional icons, we can create information-rich screens or printed reports that contain a great deal of data and also convey a great deal of information. The text-based dashboard techniques in this chapter enable you to do the following:

- Create information-rich printed reports to complement dynamic and chart-oriented dashboards.

- Match the information-rich format used in some Business Intelligence software.

- Create color alerts and icon alerts that draw attention to text data.

- Create report elements that make alerts more readable for those who are color-blind.
- Create text elements compatible with any version of Excel.

NOTE   Chapters 19 contains more examples of in-cell and text-based dashboards. It describes in detail how to create miniature charts and cool charts that fit within a worksheet's cells.

Alerting with Conditional Formats

Conditional formats change text and cell formatting depending on a condition you prescribe. They are an excellent way to highlight data that exceed alert levels you have set. In some simple Balanced Scorecards, conditional formatting is used on a single page of metrics to highlight whether values are within green, amber, or red limits.

Figure 15.1 shows how a color created with conditional formatting in combination with a text icon arrowhead draws attention to a miniature chart in a Balanced Scorecard. On the right, the text icon arrowhead and its background color have changed to show that an alert limit has been exceeded. This type of alert system can be done in any version of Excel with conditional formatting.

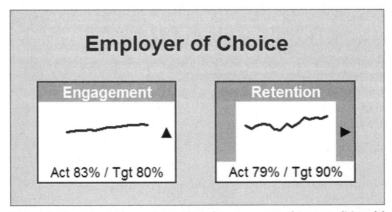

Figure15.1: Using any version of Excel, you can combine conditional formatting with a conditional icon to create an alert system for Balanced Scorecards.

Conditional Formatting with Earlier Versions of Excel

Microsoft Excel 2003 had conditional formatting that allowed for four formats—the original cell format and three formats that depended on a cell's content. The cell's content can be tested against a value or tested against a complex formula. Figure 15.2 shows a simple list where the format of the numbers in the Sales column depends on the numeric value in the cell.

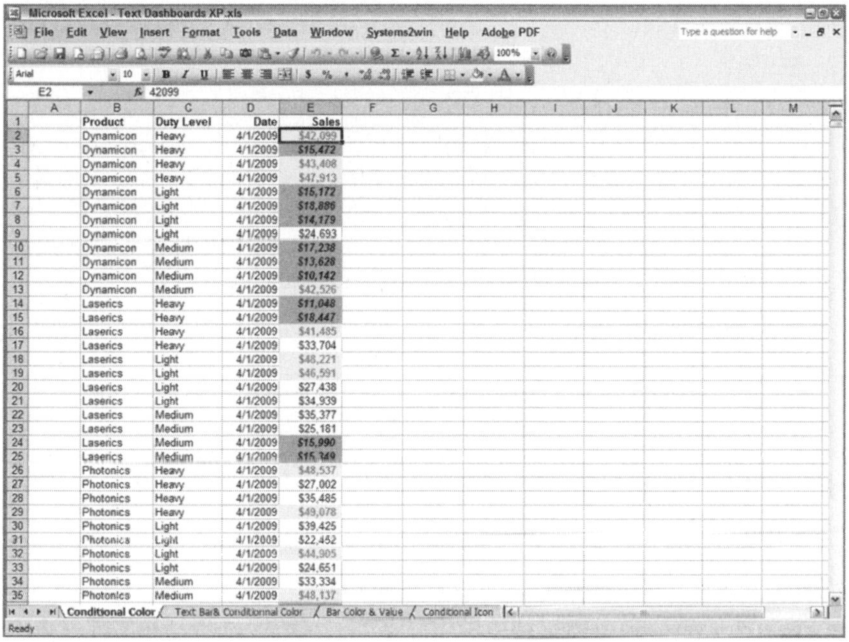

Figure 15.2: Conditional formatting helps you quickly identify numbers and dates that exceed limits.

The following steps for Excel 2003 set a conditional format that changes the appearance of sales values if they are greater than or equal to the 75th percentile or less than or equal to the 25th percentile:

1. Select all cells down the column that will have the conditional formatting.

2. Choose Format ➢ Conditional Format to display the Conditional Formatting dialog box.

3. For Condition 1, select Formula Is and enter this formula:

```
=E2>=PERCENTILE($E$2:$E$625,0.75)
```

This formula is TRUE when the contents of E2 are greater than or equal to the 75th percentile of values in E2:E625.

4. Click the Format button, and format the cells that meet this condition with a bold, dark green font and light green background. This formatting enables color-blind readers to see the bold difference.

5. Click Add to add another condition.

6. For Condition 2, select Formula Is and enter this formula:

```
=E2<=PERCENTILE($E$2:$E$625,0.25)
```

This formula is TRUE when the contents of E2 are less than or equal to the 25th percentile of values in E2:E625.

7. Click the Format button and format the cells that meet this condition with bold, italic black font and a light pink background. This formatting enables color-blind readers to see the bold italic difference. The Conditional Formatting dialog box looks like Figure 15.3.

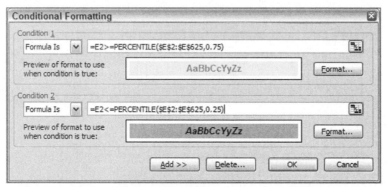

Figure 15.3: Apply up to three conditional formats in older versions of Excel to help identify four different alert ranges—the original color and three conditional colors.

8. Click OK.

TIP Excel versions prior to Excel 2007 allowed three conditional formats. However, this actually means that each cell has four conditional formats. The normal worksheet format is a separate color, so if you write your conditional format correctly, you can have four distinct conditions.

Conditional Color Formatting with Excel 2007 and Excel 2010

Excel 2007 and Excel 2010 take conditional formatting even further with the ability to show data bars, color scales, and icons, depending on a cell's contents. You aren't limited to three conditions, as in previous Excel versions. Many built-in rules and conditions, such as Top *n* and Bottom *n*, identify the top or bottom number of cells.

Conditional formatting with the newer versions of Excel does more than just change cell formatting. In addition, each cell meeting a condition can display one of these conditional formats:

- **Data bars**: shaded horizontal bar charts
- **Color scales**: color backgrounds
- **Icons**: colored graphical icons

In Excel 2007 and Excel 2010, conditional formatting has limited backward compatibility with earlier versions of Excel. Saving to earlier versions keeps the first three conditional formats for cell formatting, but you lose other Excel 2007 and Excel 2010 features such as data bars and icons.

To apply simple cell formatting based on a condition, follow these steps:

1. Select the cells that will have a conditional format.

2. On the Home tab, in the Styles group, select Conditional Formatting to display a list of different types of conditional formatting.

3. From the list, select Highlight Cells Rules ➢ More Rules to display the New Formatting Rule dialog box, shown in Figure 15.4.

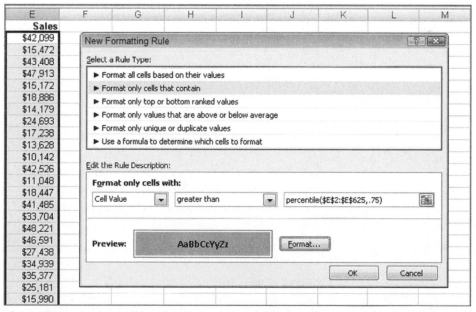

Figure 15.4: Many conditional options are predefined in Excel 2007 and Excel 2010.

4. In the Select a Rule Type list, select Format only cells that contain.
5. In the Edit the Rule Description group, select Format only cells with Cell Value greater than.
6. In the reference box, type this function:

   =PERCENTILE($E$2:$E$625,.75)
7. Click the Format button, and select a format for cells containing values greater than 75 percent of the range.
8. Click OK. Then click OK again.

TIP **To edit, delete, or set priorities in Excel 2007 and Excel 2010 conditional formats, open the Home tab. In the Styles group, select Conditional Formatting, and then select Manage Rules.**

Creating In-Cell Charts with Text

Creating charts with text characters sounds like returning to the 1970s and drawing text charts using printers connected to mainframe computers. But even with all of Excel's great charting capabilities, there is still a place for in-cell charts made with text.

Text charts, like the one shown in Figure 15.5, work well to identify relative differences in reports with long columns of data. Text charts like this can also be combined with conditional formatting so that the characters change color to indicate an alert condition as well as show their relative size. Although Excel 2010 has more advanced in-cell charting, this technique works in all versions of Excel.

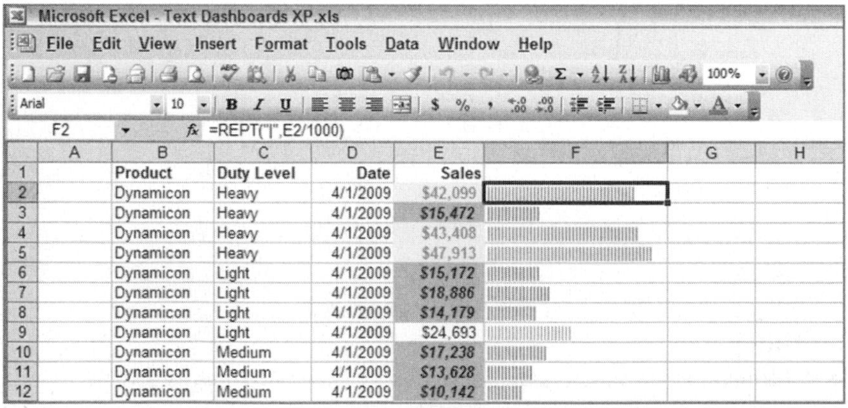

	A	B	C	D	E	F	G	H
1		Product	Duty Level	Date	Sales			
2		Dynamicon	Heavy	4/1/2009	$42,099	||||||||||||||||||||||||||||||||||||||||||		
3		Dynamicon	Heavy	4/1/2009	$15,472	|||||||||||||||		
4		Dynamicon	Heavy	4/1/2009	$43,408	|||||||||||||||||||||||||||||||||||||||||||		
5		Dynamicon	Heavy	4/1/2009	$47,913	|||||||||||||||||||||||||||||||||||||||||||||||		
6		Dynamicon	Light	4/1/2009	$15,172	|||||||||||||||		
7		Dynamicon	Light	4/1/2009	$18,886	||||||||||||||||||		
8		Dynamicon	Light	4/1/2009	$14,179	||||||||||||||		
9		Dynamicon	Light	4/1/2009	$24,693	||||||||||||||||||||||||		
10		Dynamicon	Medium	4/1/2009	$17,238	|||||||||||||||||		
11		Dynamicon	Medium	4/1/2009	$13,628	|||||||||||||		
12		Dynamicon	Medium	4/1/2009	$10,142	||||||||||		

Figure 15.5: Text charts work well to identify relative differences in data. This figure shows text bars combined with conditional colors. This works in any version of Excel.

Creating Text Charts with Earlier Versions of Excel

The REPT function is used in Excel to create text charts. The syntax is

```
REPT(text,number_times)
```

The text is repeated the number of times indicated by *number_times*. The *text* character to be repeated must be enclosed in quotes, such as "|". A vertical bar, co-located on the \ key, is often used for simple bar charts.

You can use other nonkeyboard characters as repeated characters. To do that, use the CHAR function to convert an ASCII number into a character. The cell's font format must also match the font set containing the nonkeyboard character. You can see the font and the ASCII numeric codes for available symbols by choosing Insert ➢ Symbol. Look for the symbol you want, its numeric code, and its font.

Figure 15.6 shows text bars adjacent to the Sales values.

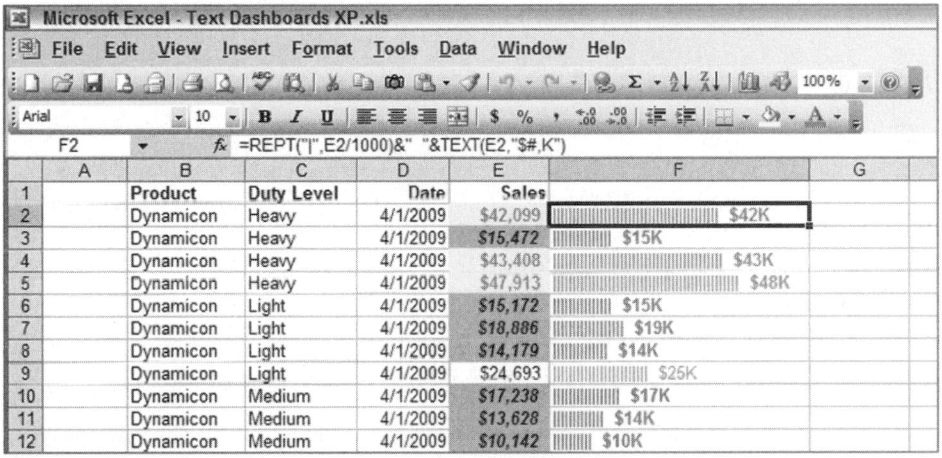

Figure 15.6: Combine the REPT function with a text bar, a concatenated value, and conditional formatting to create conditionally colored bar charts that show a value in any version of Excel.

Start the formula in F2 with the portion that draws the bars:

```
=REPT("|",E2/1000)
```

The cell is formatted with the Arial font so that the bar character, co-located on the backslash key, appears as a vertical bar in the cell. The value in E2 is divided by 1,000 to scale the number of bars to an appropriate width.

Another technique is to apply conditional formatting on the text charts. This enables you to color the bar charts depending on the values in adjacent cells.

You may also want to show the numeric value or a scaled value next to a bar chart. To do this, concatenate the REPT function with a TEXT function that specifies the value. In this example, the value following the bar is scaled down by 1,000 and has a K following it for thousands. F2 contains this:

```
=REPT("|",E2/1000)&"   "&TEXT(E2,"$#,K")
```

You can employ many tricks to create more informative bars. For example, this formula:

```
=REPT("-",E2/1000)&"   "&"o"
```

creates a line the length of the scaled number and then ends with an o.

Another text chart that is useful for variances has two columns. The left is for negative values, and the right is for positive values. The left column is formatted with right justification. The formula in cell F2 is

```
=IF(E2<0, REPT("|",E2/1000),"")
```

The right column is formatted with left justification, and the formula in G2 is

```
=IF(E2>0, REPT("|",E2/1000),"")
```

By formatting the left column with a red font and the right with a green font and then copying these formulas down columns F and G, you can make positive and negative variances stand out.

Now copy this formula down column F.

Creating Data Bars with Excel 2007 and Excel 2010

Excel 2007 and Excel 2010 include data bars, a conditional display that seems to replicate the function of the in-cell bar charts just described. As shown in Figure 15.7, the new data bars are more attractive. You can choose to use subtle gradient colors, but gradients are not very effective for visualizing data. They are not distinct and precise enough to give an accurate representation of data. Subtle color variations make it difficult for people to tell differences in value. When possible, choose the Solid Fill option.

WARNING Excel 2007 and Excel 2010 data bars are not backward-compatible. If you want a backward-compatible "data bar," use the conditional text charts described in the preceding section. You can combine conditional text charts with conditional formatting so that the in-cell chart appears with special color formats and fonts.

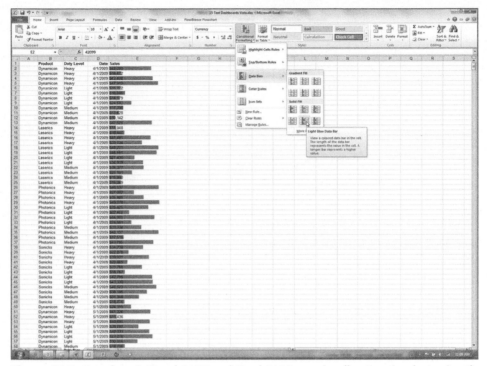

Figure 15.7: Data bars in Excel 2007 and Excel 2010 are visually attractive, but using the gradient fill is not distinct or precise enough for good data visualization.

To create data bars in Excel 2007 and Excel 2010, follow these steps:

1. Select the cells that will have a conditional format.

2. On the Home tab, in the Styles group, select Conditional Formatting to display a list.

3. Roll the mouse over Data Bars.

4. Select the type of Data Bars you want to use.

Excel immediately inserts data bars with a color gradient. Each bar's width is proportional to the value in the adjacent cell.

Alerting with Conditional Text Icons

Text icons help draw attention to specific conditions. They are helpful in augmenting colors for color-blind readers and indicating trends within the small area of one cell.

You can create conditional text icons in Excel 2007, Excel 2010, and earlier versions. To create conditional text icons in earlier versions of Excel, use text symbols. As shown in Figure 15.8, they work with any version of Excel.

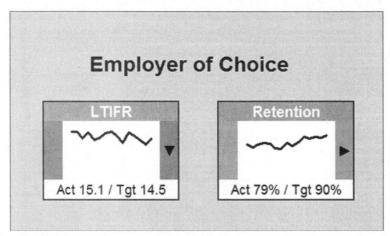

Figure 15.8: These conditional arrowheads in a magnified view of an Excel 2003 Balanced Scorecard change colors and directions depending on alert conditions. They are compatible with any version of Excel.

Excel 2007 and Excel 2010 have additional capabilities for conditional icons and have many unique icons. However, Excel 2007 and Excel 2010 conditional icons are not backward-compatible, so they cannot be used with older versions.

Creating Conditional Icons with Earlier Versions of Excel

With Excel versions prior to Excel 2007 and Excel 2010, you can create conditional icons that appear in a space as narrow as one character. You can combine these conditional icons with conditional formatting to create icons and color schemes that identify complex conditions and alerts. Figure 15.8 shows a magnified view of two miniature charts in the Learning and Growth section of a Balanced Scorecard created in Excel 2003. The miniature trend chart created with the techniques outlined in Chapter 19 shows the trend. A conditional icon and conditional formatting enable the executive to see at a glance whether that metric is yellow or red. The arrowhead icon reinforces the color by showing whether the alert status is poor or marginal.

Conditional text icons are just text symbols that appear depending on the conditions in a conditional statement such as IF or CHOOSE. The symbols you can choose from are the symbols you see when you choose Insert ➤ Symbol and scroll through the symbols in the Symbol dialog box of Excel versions prior to 2007. This is shown in Figure 15.9. In Excel 2007 and Excel 2010, from the Insert tab, choose Symbols from the Symbol group.

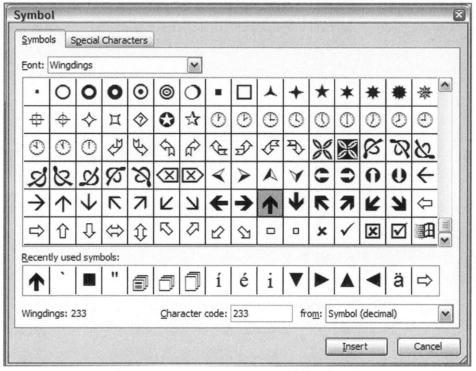

Figure 15.9: Select the symbol you want as an icon from the Symbol dialog box.

To select an icon, select a font from the Font list, and then scroll through until you see the symbol you want. Click it and note the font name, character code, and decimal ASCII code (seen in the Character code field). The Wingdings fonts have many symbols that are available on printers. For example, if the cell is formatted with the Wingdings font, CHAR(233) creates an upward-pointing arrow.

WHICH SYMBOL? WHICH FONT?

The symbol you select must be from a font set that you know your scorecard or dashboard users have. If they do not have the font set, the symbol appears on their displays as a different symbol than what you want. You are usually safe if you use a character or symbol from Arial, Times New Roman, Wingdings, Wingdings 2, or Wingdings 3.

You must format the cell containing the CHAR function with the same font you saw in the Symbol dialog box, such as Wingdings. If you don't, you see the character with that decimal ASCII code from a different font set.

Figure 15.10 shows the example we have used previously in Excel 2003. However, a column has been inserted at column F, and the formula in cell F2:

```
=IF(E2>=PERCENTILE($E$2:$E$625,0.75),CHAR(236),
IF(E2<=PERCENTILE($E$2:$E$625,0.25),CHAR(238),""))
```

has been copied down. If E2 is in the 75th percentile of the column, an arrow pointing up at a 45-degree angle (CHAR(236)) is displayed. If E2 is in the 25th percentile of the column, an arrow pointing down at a 45-degree angle (CHAR(238)) is displayed. If E2 is in between, nothing appears. In this example, the arrows do not point directly up or down because perfectly vertical arrows are too difficult to tell apart.

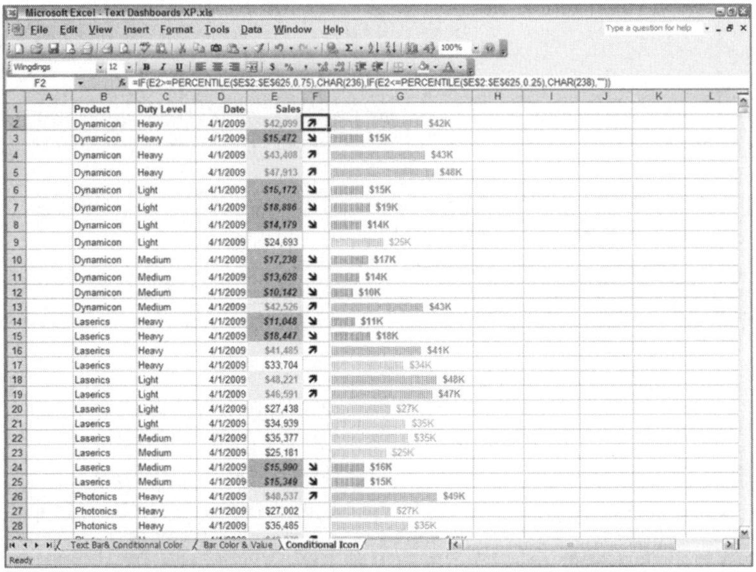

Figure 15.10: Conditional icons can be used in any version of Excel to help readers identify trends or alert limits.

The Wingdings fonts have many useful symbols. The ASCII codes from 219 to 248 in the first Wingdings font set are all arrows. Table 15-1 shows some examples.

> **TIP** In printed reports or on Balanced Scorecard home pages, you can indicate trends by showing conditional arrows. Use a conditional IF or CHOOSE function with the SLOPE function to display one of five different arrows, depending on the value and sign returned by SLOPE.

Table 15-1: Sample Wingdings Symbols with Corresponding ASCII Codes

WINGDINGS	ASCII
←	231
→	232
↑	233
↓	234
↖	235
↗	236
↙	237
↘	238

Creating Conditional Icons with Excel 2007 and Excel 2010

Excel 2007 and Excel 2010 present a wide choice of icons for use with conditional formatting. The Excel 2007 and Excel 2010 conditional icons appear in the cell with the data being examined. Figure 15.11 shows up, down and sideways arrows that appear depending on the value in column F. Conditional icons are an excellent way to identify trends or data that have exceeded alert limits.

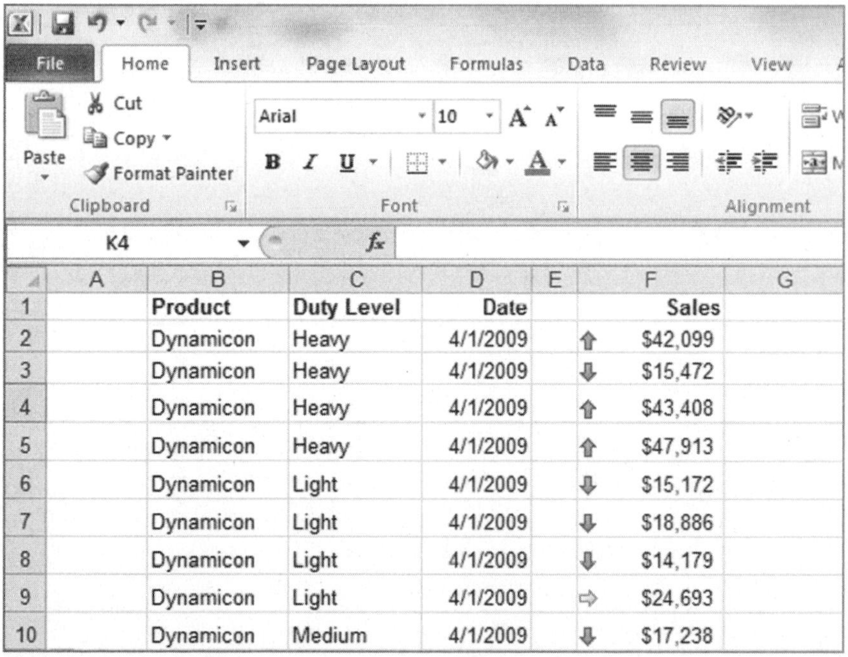

Figure 15.11: Conditional icons identify alerts or conditional levels with a set of variable icons.

WARNING If you want to ensure that the conditional icons in your dashboard or report work with earlier versions of Excel, use the conditional text icons described earlier. You can combine conditional text icons with conditional formatting so that they appear with special color formats and fonts.

To add conditional icons to data with Excel 2007 and Excel 2010, do the following:

1. Select the cells that will have a conditional format.

2. On the Home tab, in the Styles group, select Conditional Formatting then choose Icon Sets. Then select the icon set you want, or select More Rules. If you select More Rules, continue with the following steps.

3. In the New Formatting Rule dialog box, shown for Excel 2010 in Figure 15.12, at the top of the dialog box, in Select a Rule Type, select Format all cells based on their values.

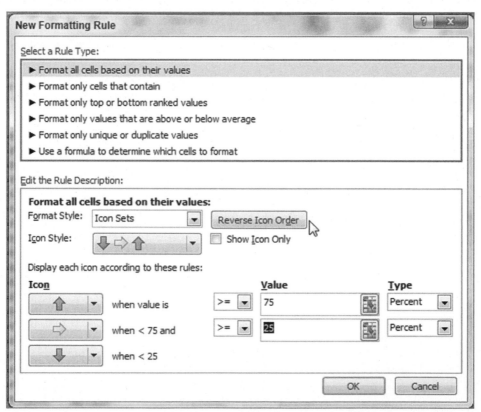

Figure 15.12: Excel 2010 presents a wide choice of icons and many types of rules for their display.

4. In the Format Style drop-down select Icon Sets.

5. Select the Icon Style you want. In this example, select the three colored arrows.

6. Specify the icons as follows:

   Up arrow for >= 75 Percent

   Sideways arrow for >= 25 Percent

   The down arrow defaults to values less than 25 Percent.

7. Click OK.

Summary

Text charts and conditional formatting are powerful additions that make dense reports more informative. When used correctly, they can show more information in a smaller area than any other format. If you use conditional formatting to focus a user's attention, also consider using a text icon to assist color-blind users or to give additional information such as trends. Don't forget to look at Chapter 19 for more information about and examples of using small or in-cell graphics.

CHAPTER 16

Custom Labels and Formatting

To conquer the enemy without resorting to war is the most desirable. The highest form of generalship is to conquer the enemy by strategy.

—Sun Tzu
The Art of War

Balanced Scorecards and dashboards always seem to need custom titles, custom dates, custom formatting, and custom data labels. These requirements usually can be addressed with a few special techniques.

The need for custom date formats often appears when you must have a label with a specific format, or you need a database query constructed a certain way. Organizations also often need calculated dates for the beginning or end of a financial quarter or the first or last day of a workweek.

Most organizations have a unique "corporate identity." It includes the font, color palette, layout, and logo used on the organization's website, letterhead, and forms. If you want your executives and managers to identify your scorecard as one of their own, use your organization's color palette, layout, and logo. Using your organization's "official" colors adds credibility and a feel of professionalism to the Balanced Scorecard and dashboard you produce.

Knowing how to combine text, numbers, and dates allows you to create dynamic custom titles for your scorecards, dashboards, and reports. You aren't limited by the automatic chart titles that Excel creates. You can combine calculated text, numbers, and dates for any title you need.

Combining Numbers, Text, and Dates to Create Custom Labels

Some labels and titles need a combination of numbers, text, and dates. These titles often need to recalculate as data changes. This is easy to do with two functions: & (concatenation) and TEXT().

The & (ampersand) function joins text strings. Text must be enclosed in double quotes:

```
="Balanced "&"Scorecard"
```

Of course, the real power comes when you combine text with the result of a numeric or text formula. In that case, if the formula in cell C5 results in 542, this formula:

```
="Number of Units Sold is "&$C$5
```

produces this result:

```
Number of Units Sold is 542
```

Concatenation and calculation give you the power to create dynamic titles. Fixed text in quotes can be joined with text, numbers, and dates generated by formulas that change dynamically. You get even more power when you use a conditional formula, such as an IF condition, or when you look up data and titles from lists using VLOOKUP, HLOOKUP, or INDEX.

Joining Text with Custom-Formatted Numbers

Although a concatenation formula like those just described joins text and a date or number, it probably won't produce the formatted appearance you want. For example, suppose cell B4 contains the number 2,400. Cell B4 is formatted to show Currency formatting with no decimal values. A concatenation formula like this:

```
="The dollar value is "&$B$4&"."
```

will look like this in the display:

```
The dollar value is 2400.
```

The Currency formatting on the cell does not appear in the concatenation formula's result. To format numbers or dates when they are displayed as text, use the TEXT() function, which has this syntax:

```
=TEXT(value, format_text)
```

value is the cell reference containing the number or date. *format_text* is the same formatting syntax used to create custom numeric and date formats in the Format Cells dialog box. For example, if cell B4 contains 2,400, as in the previous example, you would want to use this:

```
="The dollar value is "&TEXT($B$4,"$#,##0")&"."
```

to create a display that looks like this:

```
The dollar value is $2,400.
```

NOTE In early versions of Excel you could see examples of these custom formats usable in TEXT by choosing Format ➤ Cells, selecting the Number tab, and then selecting Custom from the Category list.

In Excel 2007 and Excel 2010, on the Home tab, in the Cells group, choose Format and click Format Cells. On the Number tab of the Format Cells dialog box, select Custom to see examples of custom numeric and date formats you can use.

USE THE TEXT FUNCTION TO FIT WIDE NUMERIC RESULTS

When a calculated numeric result won't fit in the cell width because the column is not wide enough, the cell fills with ####. Work around this by using the TEXT function to format the result of the formula. The textual result that appears as a number appears and flows outside the column width as long as the adjacent cell is empty.

Formatting numbers and dates for inclusion in titles or creating custom formats for use in your worksheets is easy; you just have to know a few rules. Custom formats are defined by a format entered in as many as four segments. Each segment is separated by a semicolon (;). You can create a different format for the positive, negative, zero, and text-only portion of a numeric or date format. The syntax for custom formats is as follows:

```
positive_format;negative_format;zero_format;text_format
```

To continue with the previous example, you could create a custom format for both positive and negative currency. It might look like this:

```
="The dollar value is "&TEXT($B$4,"$#,##0_);($#,##0)")
```

This produces a negative dollar value enclosed in parentheses. The positive format ends with _) so that a space is left at the trailing end of positive numbers that is the same width as the trailing parenthesis behind negative numbers. This enables positive and negative numbers to align in columns.

Table 16-1 shows some of the symbols you can use for formatting numbers.

Table 16-1: Symbols for Formatting Numbers

SYMBOL	RESULT
#	A placeholder. 0 is not displayed if a trailing digit is absent, so use a trailing 0, as in the preceding example. Fractions round up.
0	A placeholder. Displays a 0 when there is no number. Fractions round up.
,	Marks the place of the first thousands separator.
.	Marks the location of the decimal point.
_	Leaves a space that is the width of the character following the underscore (_). You can use this to allow space for the formatting difference between positive and negative numbers when the negative number is enclosed in parentheses. Using the appropriate trailing space enables numbers to right-align.

Joining Text with Custom-Formatted Dates and Times

Dates and text can also be joined with concatenation. This is frequently done for titles or notations to show the date of the dashboard's data. Here's a frequently used combination:

```
="Data as of "&TEXT(NOW(),"mmm d, yyyy h:mm AM/PM")
```

A formula like this enables you to put a date/time stamp on a dashboard. When the dashboard is printed, you can see the date of the data. This reduces the questions people have when their data doesn't match the dashboard because data was acquired at different times. The result of the preceding concatenation produces this:

```
Data as of Mar 9, 2013 9:52 PM
```

ALWAYS SHOW A DATE/TIME STAMP ON DASHBOARDS

Put a date/time stamp in a consistent location on dashboards to show the date and time of printing. This prevents confusion when printouts of the same dashboard show different data.

You can create your own date and time formats within TEXT(). Look at the custom date formats in the Custom Category of the Cell Formats dialog box for examples. Table 16-2 shows some of the symbols you can use to format dates and times.

Table 16-2: Symbols for Formatting Dates and Times

DATE/TIME	FORMAT CODE	DISPLAY EXAMPLE
Month	m	9
	mm	09
	mmm	Sep
	mmmm	September
Day	d	8
	dd	08
	ddd	Tue
	dddd	Tuesday
Year	y	9 or 12 (includes two digits if not a leading 0)
	yy	12
	yyyy	2012
12-hour clock	H:mm AM/PM	7:45 PM
	H:mm:ss AM/PM	7:45:33 PM
24-hour clock	hh:mm	19:45
minutes:seconds	mm:ss	45:33

Time and Data Calculations

Although most Excel users are familiar with often-used time and date functions such as NOW(), TODAY(), DATE(), DAY(), HOUR(), MONTH(), and YEAR(), sometimes you want to do more. Usually, you need these additional time and date functions for an information label on a dashboard or for a limiter in a SQL query to the database feeding your worksheets with data. The following sections describe a few date/time functions you may find useful.

The x-axis on charts and headings on tables usually require a series of dates. For example, the workdays of each week in a month, the first day of each month in a quarter, or the first days of each month in a year might be required. When you create these date series with formulas, they update automatically when data changes. Later in this book, you will learn how to use a calculated date series to create animated charts that show how data changes over time.

WARNING The Analysis ToolPak has some helpful date conversion functions. However, whenever possible, avoid using functions that are found only in Excel's Analysis ToolPak. Not all users of your scoreboards and dashboards will have the Analysis ToolPak installed. Some of the date functions in the earlier versions of the Analysis ToolPak are included as normal worksheet functions in Excel 2007 and Excel 2010. Here are the date functions that are in the Excel 2003 Analysis ToolPakand that are available natively in Excel 2007 and Excel 2010:

- NETWORKDAYS() is thenumber of whole workdays between two dates.
- WORKDAY() finds the start or end date of a project given the number of workdays.
- WEEKNUM() isthe week number in the year.

Unless a version of Excel 2003 or earlier has the Analysis Toolpak installed, these functions will appear as an error.

Calculating the Beginning and End of Any Month

It's easy to calculate the beginning of a month, because they all start with day 1. The formula for the first day of any month is

```
=DATE(YEAR(ref),MONTH(ref),1)
```

In this formula, *ref* is a reference to a cell containing a date.

If you assume that a "seed" date for the first date in a series of months is in cell B5, the first day of the next month in the cell to the right is

```
=DATE(YEAR(B5),MONTH(B5)+1,1)
```

Copying this formula to the right creates a series of months with the same day as the original. Excel automatically skips to the next year when appropriate.

To find the last date of any month, you need to know a trick with Excel. The DATE function calculates the last day of a month as day 0 of the following month. For example, if the "seed" date is in cell B5, the last day of the month prior to B5 is as follows:

```
=DATE(YEAR(B5),MONTH(B5),0)
```

Creating a Month Series

The most common type of date series used in dashboards is a month series. Monthly financial data is most frequently viewed over a 12-month or 15-month span. Showing data over a 15-month span allows month-by-month, month over prior year, and prior-quarter comparisons.

It is rare to create a fixed monthly series in dashboards. Instead, you want a date series that updates when the start or end date changes. To create a monthly series based on a single "seed" date in cell B5, follow these steps:

1. Enter a starting date in cell B5.

2. Enter this formula in cell C5:

```
=DATE(YEAR(B5),MONTH(B5)+1,DAY(B5))
```

3. Copy this formula to the right to fill cells you want to contain sequential months.

This formula works by calculating a new date from the year and day of the date in the cell to the left. The month that is used for the calculated date is one more than the month to the left. Each new copy across row 5 looks to the formula to its left and adds one month. When the calculated date gets to month 13, a new year is automatically started. Using this formula makes it easy to create a date series that updates when the "seed" date changes. If this date series is used to look up the data from a historical list of data, you can animate a data series so that it scrolls through time. Chapter 20 describes how to scroll charts through time with a scroll bar.

Calculating the Beginning and End of a Quarter

Financial reports frequently report data in quarters. You may find that you have to summarize monthly data and report it in charts or tables using the appropriate quarterly headings. The upper portion of Figure 16.1 shows the formulas used to calculate and format a quarterly heading when given a date.

You can calculate the financial quarter for a date entered in cell C4 using the following formula:

```
=ROUNDUP(MONTH($C$4)/3,0)
```

To display a more finished expression such as "Qtr 1," as shown in cell C6, use a concatenation formula:

```
="Qtr "&ROUNDUP(MONTH($C$4)/3,0)
```

A longer concatenation formula such as the one in cell C7 produces "1Q '13." Note that this formula has an apostrophe within the set of double quotes. It creates the apostrophe for the year abbreviation:

```
=ROUNDUP(MONTH($C$4)/3,0)&"Q"&" '"&TEXT($C$4,"yy")
```

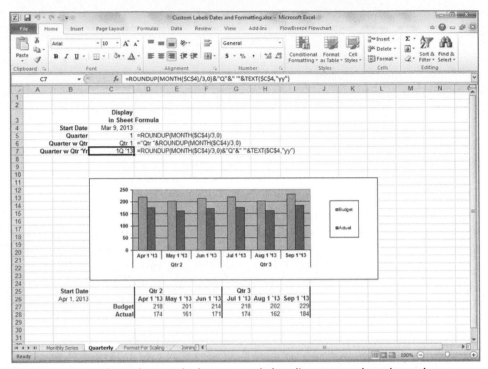

Figure 16.1: Use formulas to calculate quarterly headings even when dates change.

Automatically Updating Quarterly Titles on the Category (x) Axis

The lower portion of Figure 16.1 shows how these calculated quarterly titles can be used effectively in a dashboard chart. This example is simple and uses a manually entered start date to update the quarterly titles. A better way to do this is to select the start date. You can also use these formulas to automatically reformat and retitle with data retrieved from a database.

In Figure 16.1, a starting date has been entered in cell B26. This date must be in the first month of any quarter. Cells D26 to I26 contain a calculated series of months that begin with the start date. The formula in cell D25 is

```
="Qtr "&ROUNDUP(MONTH($F$26)/3,0)
```

This formula examines the third date from the start in F26 and calculates the quarter. The quarterly text formula in G25 examines the last date in I26. As long as the starting date is the first month in a quarter, the text quarter labels update automatically.

The chart uses a dual row of Category (x) axis titles. The chart was created using the Chart Wizard and selecting C25:I28. Selecting contiguous rows for the Category (x) axis creates dual or triple-row Category (x) axis titles.

Scaling Numbers with Formatting

Financial and production data usually involves large numbers. You will probably want to adjust the appearance of these large numbers for two reasons. First, executives and managers who monitor Balanced Scorecards and management dashboards should be concerned with the big picture, not minute details. If financial results are in the millions, they shouldn't be looking at numbers with hundreds or thousands. Second, without scaling, the numbers might not fit in the cells or chart.

An obvious way to scale data is to divide it by a scaling factor. For example, if you are working with numbers in the hundreds of thousands, you can divide by 1,000 and use ROUND() to round to the precision you want.

A better way to handle this is to leave the original data intact and use custom formatting to scale the data. You can use custom formatting to scale numeric displays in cells and charts. Figure 16.2 shows the use of custom formatting in cells to change the display. A comma is used after the 0 to indicate the hundreds or thousands separator in the custom format.

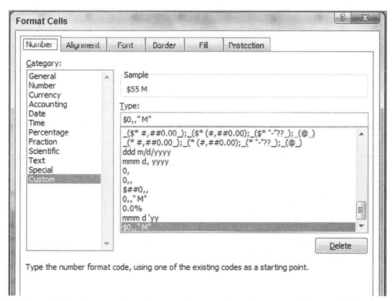

Figure 16.2: Use custom formatting on numbers to retain precision but change the display in tables and charts.

A text character can be included in custom formats to indicate millions (M) or thousands (K). For example, as shown in Figure 16.2, in the Number tab of the Format Cells dialog box, select the Custom category and enter a format like this:

```
$##0,," M"
```

This formats the number 54678639 as

`$55 M`

Creating a chart from custom-formatted data produces a chart that shows the data with the custom format.

Scaling Charts and Sheets Separately

You can keep high precision in the data on your sheet while charting with scaled data. Excel 2000 and later enable you to do this by formatting the chart's y-axis scale.

To format the y-axis scale so that it shows shortened values, follow these steps:

1. Right-click the y-axis to display the Format Axis dialog box, shown in Figure 16.3. Select the Axis Options.

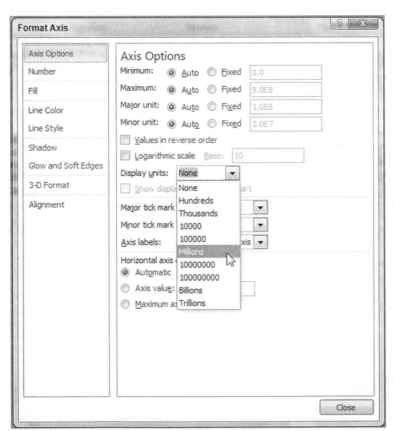

Figure 16.3: Use the Format Axis dialog box to scale y-axis values and display a units label showing the scaling factor.

2. Select the scaling factor you want to use from the Display Units list. For example, select Millions if you want to round displayed values to millions.

3. Select the Show display units on chart check box if you want the scaling factor—Millions, Thousands, and so on—to appear at the top left of the y-axis.

4. Click OK.

Creating Custom Titles and Floating Text

Excel has arguably the best chart generation engine available. But just because you can create complex charts with fancy formatting, colors, textures, and patterns doesn't mean you should.

Your purpose should be to create Balanced Scorecards and dashboards that communicate information and allow clear decision-making. The addition of nonessential colors, patterns, and text may make your charts look prettier, but the extra "noise" is distracting and can lead to misinformed decisions. I hope some of the tips in the following sections will help you communicate more clearly with your charts and keep embellishments to a minimum.

Keep it clean and simple.

Creating Dynamic Chart Titles

When you first create an Excel chart, the main title, x-axis title, and y-axis title are static. However, it is easy to link any of these titles to cell contents. If the cell contains a formula that calculates a title, like those shown earlier in this chapter, the titles update when the cell content recalculates. This is useful for displaying dates or product information in a title.

Follow these steps to create chart titles that display cell contents:

1. Create your calculated title in a cell. For example, a formula for a main title or x-axis title might look like this:

```
="Chart Data as of "&TEXT($D$6,"mmm d, yyyy")
```

If cell D6 contains the formula =NOW(), which calculates the current date and time, the text for the subtitle looks something like this:

```
Chart data as of Mar 30, 2013
```

2. Create the chart.

3. Click the main title, Value (y) axis label, or Category (x) axis label you want linked to the cell.

4. Type an equals sign (=) in the formula bar, and then select the cell containing the calculated title. You can also type the cell reference if you include the worksheet tab's name within single quotes followed by an exclamation mark. For example:

```
='Joining Text, Dates and Numbers'!$D$8
```

5. Press Enter.

If the chart does not have a title for you to choose, select the chart. On the Chart Tools Layout tab, in the Labels group, choose Chart Title and make a selection. In versions prior to Excel 2007, choose Chart ≻ Chart Options. Then select the Titles tab and type a title in the Chart title entry box.

CREATE TWO-LINE TITLES

Create static subtitles with two lines by creating a long title that contains the title and subtitle as one long title. When these appear in the chart, click the title to select it, move the insertion point to where you want the line break, and press Shift+Enter. The title and subtitle break into two lines. Select and format each line separately with size, color, and attributes.

Creating Floating Titles in Charts

Excel charts automatically create a main title, Value (y) axis label, and Category (x) axis labels if you choose that layout from the Chart Layouts. You might find that you want to add a subtitle or comment in the chart for additional information. These "floating titles" can be dragged anywhere on the chart. You can link these floating titles to cell contents so that they display a calculated title like the concatenated text described earlier in this chapter.

To create a floating title in versions prior to Excel 2007 and Excel 2010, do the following:

1. Enter a formula or text in a cell.
2. Click a clear area of the chart.
3. Type = in the formula bar.
4. Click a cell or type the cell reference, and press Enter.

A floating text box contains the cell's results. You can drag this text box anywhere on the chart, including over other chart elements. Format the floating text box by double-clicking it and selecting from the Format Text Box dialog box. You can format the font, alignment, colors, lines, size, protection, properties, and margins.

If you want line breaks and paragraphs of text to appear in your floating text box, use Alt+Enter to create line breaks in the cell containing the text box contents. Or format the cell contents with the Alignment tab to allow word wrap.

Floating text boxes that do not have borders can be difficult to select. Don't click directly on the text. Click where you think the border of the floating text box is.

Creating Dynamic Titles That Float in Worksheets

You can create floating text or titles in worksheets that reflect the results of calculations. Floating titles in a worksheet enable you to create titles that are larger than the cell size allows or to show text boxes that contain comments without distorting the size and position of nearby cells.

To create floating text on a worksheet, do the following:

1. Enter the text or formula in a cell on the worksheet.

2. In Excel 2007 and Excel 2010, on the Insert tab, in the Illustrations group, select Shapes. In Excel 2003, display the Drawing toolbar if it is not displayed by choosing View ➤ Toolbars and selecting Drawing.

3. Select a shape to contain the floating text. An AutoShape, text box, rectangle, or circle will work.

4. With the shape selected, type = in the formula bar and click the cell containing the text or formula you want displayed.

5. Press Enter.

You may want the text in the floating shape to have a different orientation, such as a Category (x) axis title and subtitle. To change the orientation of the text in the shape, select the shape, right-click its edge, and choose Format AutoShape. Select the Alignment tab in the Format AutoShape dialog box, and then select the text orientation from the Orientation box.

In most cases, you will want the text in your shape to be in the center of the shape. To format the shape so that the text is where you want it, select the shape, right-click its edge, and choose Format AutoShape. Select Text Box or the Alignment tab, and then select the text positioning from the Horizontal and Vertical alignment lists.

Rotating Text, Shapes, and Charts in Any Direction by Using a Picture of Cells

The text inside shapes you draw can be formatted, aligned, and positioned. In Excel 2007 and Excel 2010 you can even select a shape with text inside, grab the green handle, and rotate the shape and text within it. In Excel 2003 you can't rotate the text. However, as with many things in Excel, a trick will get you past this.

Create the shape you want, and link the text with a formula as described previously. Notice that if you select the shape and drag the green selection handle, you can rotate the shape in Excel 2007 and Excel 2010, but the text does not rotate in Excel 2003.

To rotate the text to any position, you need to use Excel's Camera tool to create a picture of the shape, and then rotate that picture and text. Chapter 19 has multiple sections on using Excel's camera tool and adding the camera tool to a toolbar or ribbon.

Shapes with links to text appear at the top of Figure 16.4. The lower half of Figure 16.4 shows rotated camera pictures of these same shapes. The text inside the AutoShape rotates to any angle with the camera picture.

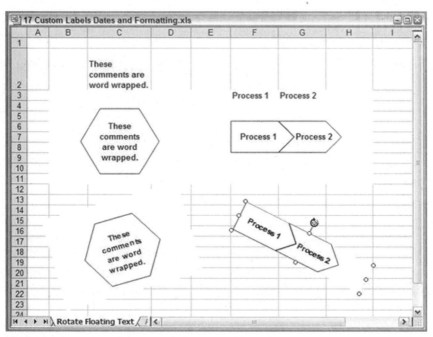

Figure 16.4: Rotate shapes and the text in them by using the Camera tool in Excel 2003.

To create text, shapes, and charts that can be rotated in any direction in Excel 2003, take a picture of the shape and then rotate the picture following these steps:

1. Create the text, shape, or chart.

2. Remove the cell edges by selecting all the cells in the background and choosing Format ➢ Cells.

3. Select the Patterns tab and select the background you want. In most cases, this will be white. Click OK.

4. Select the cells containing the text, shape, or chart you want to rotate.

5. Hold down the Shift key as you choose Edit ➣ Copy Picture. The Copy Picture and Paste Picture commands appear on the Edit menu only when you hold down Shift.

6. In the Copy Picture dialog box that appears, select Appearance as Shown on Screen and Format Picture, and click OK.

7. Move in the workbook to where you want the picture. This can even be in another worksheet or over a chart.

8. Hold down Shift as you choose Edit ➣ Paste Picture.

This picture is linked to the original area. The picture also changes when the original text, shape, or chart changes. You can resize this picture of text, shape, or chart while maintaining proportions by dragging one corner.

Rotate the picture of text, shape, or chart to any angle by selecting the picture and then dragging the green handle.

Creating Custom Data Labels

Data labels appear adjacent to a data point, as shown by the numbers above the column chart in Figure 16.5.

Figure 16.5: Data labels show the numeric value for a chart element. You can also create custom data labels.

In Excel 2007 and Excel 2010, select the chart area to add data labels to all charts, or select a single chart element. With the chart selected, in the Chart Layout tab, in the Labels group, select Data Labels, and choose the position at which you want the data label to appear.

In Excel 2003, when you create an Excel chart using the Chart Wizard, you can display data labels in the third step of the Chart Wizard. You can show the Series Name, Category Name, and Value for each data point. If you have already created a chart, double-click an element in the chart series, such as a column. From the Format Data Series dialog box, select the Data Labels tab.

Data labels may not show the content you want, or they may be positioned so that they cover chart elements. If you have lots of data, you may not want to show it all, or you may want to show data labels for only points that are of special interest.

To select an individual data label, click any data label to select all of them. When you see the entire series of labels selected, click the individual data label you want.

If an automatically created or custom data label does not appear where you want, you can select it and drag it to a new position. After you have manually repositioned a data label, it no longer moves as a chart element moves.

If you want to create custom data labels, start by entering into the worksheet the text, number, or formula you want as a custom label. Select a data label on the chart. Type = in the formula bar, click the cell containing the custom content, and press Enter. If you want to create a custom label for each data point, you need to link each data point individually.

Data points can clutter a chart. Instead of displaying data points, an alternative is to use a data table below a chart. Chapter 19 describes how to create custom data tables that are easy to position and format.

Creating Pop-Up and Alert Data Labels

A great way to use data labels is as alerts that appear only over data points of special interest. You can specify alert limits so that if a data value is outside a specific range or criterion, that individual data label appears.

Using the techniques described earlier in this chapter, you can create data labels that appear or hide depending on whether a check box is selected. This enables executives or managers to turn the labels on or off, removing them when they aren't needed.

The Variance chart shown in Figure 16.6 shows data labels that appear only when the budget variance is outside 10 percent. The appearance of a data label acts as an alert to help identify a data point that exceeds limits. The formula in cell H9 of the Alert data label row is

```
=IF(ABS(H8)>0.1,H8,"")
```

This formula displays the variance in cell H0 if the positive or negative variance is greater than 10 percent. Copying this across row 9 creates formulas that show the variance percentages only when they are outside the 10 percent alert limit.

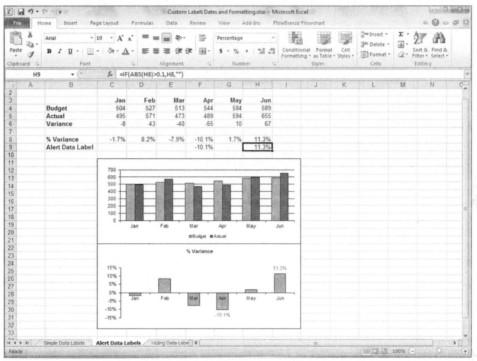

Figure 16.6: Use conditional formulas and linked data labels to create labels that appear as alerts when a limit has been exceeded.

Each data label in the chart is then linked to its corresponding cell in row 9. The data labels have all been selected and formatted with no background pattern and a red font.

Figure 16.7 shows how you can use a check box control to turn data labels on and off. The check box control puts TRUE or FALSE into cell B10, depending on whether the check box is selected. The formula in cell C10 then checks this TRUE/FALSE status to see whether data values should appear. The formula has been copied across row 10 to show or display all data values. The formula in cell C10 is

```
=IF($B$10,C6,"")
```

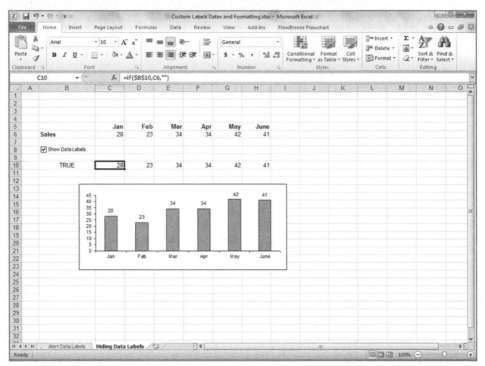

Figure 16.7: Using a check box to turn data labels on and off displays a cleaner chart until more detail is needed.

If you now link each individual data label for each chart element to its appropriate cell content in row 10, the data labels will appear only when the check box is selected. Chapter 20 describes how to use check boxes in more detail.

Creating New Color Palettes

Business people used to seeing the stark colors in earlier versions of Excel's default palette are surprised to see the improved palette in Excel 2007 and Excel 2010. If you are using Excel 2003, don't give up. You can still create custom color palettes with just the colors you need.

The ability to place any color in your palette lets you create a much more professional appearance than is normally seen in Excel worksheets. Customizing Excel's color palette to match your organization's branding will make your Balanced Scorecard or dashboard seem more professional and give it a sense of integrity. Being able to select your own palette also enables you to make the information in your dashboards more understandable. I frequently find that I need different alert colors than what are available and that I need more muted shades of tan, cream, or yellow as backgrounds for text, titles, and notes.

Creating a Custom Color Palette in Excel 2003

To create a custom color palette in Excel versions prior to Excel 2007, do the following:

1. Open the Excel workbook you want to contain the custom palette.

2. Choose Tools ➢ Options to display the Options dialog box with the Standard color palette, as shown in Figure 16.8.

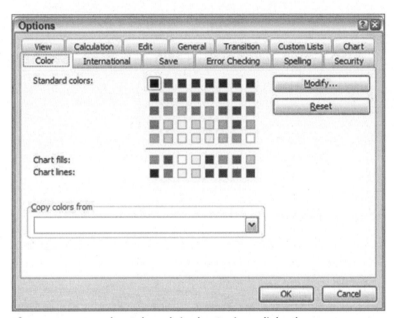

Figure 16.8: Use the Color tab in the Options dialog box to create your custom color palette.

3. Choose the Color tab.

4. Select the color you want to change, and then click the Modify button.

5. To change your selected color to a Standard color, select the Standard tab and click a color.

   Or, to modify the existing color or create a new color, select the Custom tab.

6. Click OK.

7. Modify another color or click OK if you are finished.

To reset colors to the original palette of Standard colors, click the Reset button in the Options dialog box.

Excel 2007 and Excel 2010 use a different system for controlling available color selections. You can select a color for a cell that is independent of other colors, or you can select colors from a color theme. You can use the color themes built into the more recent versions of Excel or create your own color theme. When you modify a color in a color theme, that color changes throughout the workbook wherever it has been used.

Follow these steps to create your own color theme:

1. On the Page Layout tab, in the Themes group, select Colors.

2. If you want to use a different color theme, you can select one of the themes displayed. If you want to create a new color theme, choose Create New Theme Colors. This opens the Create New Theme Colors dialog box.

3. Select the color in the theme you want to change. A Theme Colors dialog box opens, enabling you to select from predefined colors for that theme. Or you can click More Colors and define your own color.

4. Enter a name for your theme in the Create New Theme Colors dialog box, and click Save.

You can select your custom theme when you need it by choosing it from the Colors drop-down in the Themes group. To delete a custom theme, right-click it in the Colors drop-down and click Delete.

Matching Your Dashboard to the Corporate Identity

Most organizations, especially large corporations, have a well-defined "corporate identity" that consists of the corporation's colors, fonts, logo, signature, signage, and all the elements that visually represent its brand. As you begin developing your Balanced Scorecard or dashboard, check with the marketing department, and get a copy of its corporate identity package. It should contain the colors as RGB (red, green, blue) values, fonts, correct spellings of business entities and products, files of logo images, and usage of the copyright (©), trademark (™), and registered trademark (®) symbols.

Transferring Color Palettes between Workbooks

If you have a color palette you want to use in a different workbook, you can transfer the palette between workbooks. Follow these steps to transfer palettes between Excel 2003 workbooks:

1. Open both workbooks.

2. Activate the workbook to which you want to transfer the new palette.

3. Choose Tools ➢ Options and select the Color tab.

4. From the Copy colors from list, select the workbook containing the palette you want to transfer.

5. Click OK.

CREATE A TEMPLATE FOR FREQUENTLY USED COLOR PALETTES

If you will frequently use the same color palette, create a workbook with the palette you want, and then save it as a template. When you open that template, the new workbook will include your custom palette.

Creating Aesthetically Pleasing Color Palettes

If you're color impaired and couldn't create an aesthetically pleasing color palette if your job depended on it—which it might—there are excellent ways to "grab" well-coordinated color palettes. Some tools can help you select colors from websites or images.

Selecting Predesigned Color Palettes

Thank heavens artists are willing to share their color aesthetics. On numerous websites, artists have posted, for free, thousands of color palette combinations of every imaginable type and energy level. Three of these websites are listed here.

The Kuler website, `http://kuler.adobe.com`, has beautiful color palettes to select from, as well as tools to create new palettes that are automatically color coordinated. You also can capture a color palette from an image you upload.

Figure 16.9 shows Kuler's Create tool being used with a Custom rule. Dragging the spokes of the color wheel at the top of the screen creates color combinations in the color swatches below. Color RGB codes are listed below each swatch.

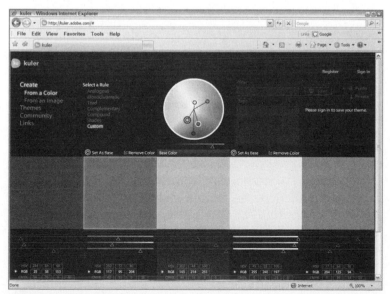

Figure 16.9: Kuler enables you to create color palettes that are coordinated by different rules such as Complementary and Monochromatic.

On the Kuler website, you can use rules that recommend a palette when given a main color:

- **Analogous** matches colors with adjacent hues.
- **Monochromatic** has one color with varied levels of intensity.
- **Triad** shows colors spaced around the wheel for a contrasting palette.
- **Complementary** uses two opposite colors and their hues.
- **Compound** uses interesting color combinations.
- **Shade** shows variations on the base color.
- **Custom** lets you drag the color spokes to any position.

In addition to creating your own palettes in Kuler, you can select Create ➤ From an Image and then upload an image and create a palette from the colors in the image. To see collections of palettes that have been shared by a community of color-adepts, select Themes. Figure 16.10 shows a few of the most popular themes. You can also view different color themes, or palettes, by selecting Themes and then Newest, Most Popular, Highest Rated, or Random. You can also use the Search box to search for key words.

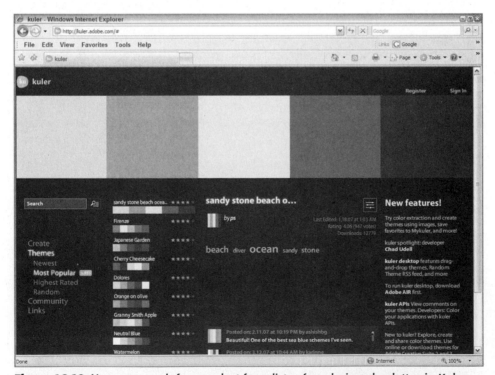

Figure 16.10: You can search for or select from lists of predesigned palettes in Kuler.

Two other websites can help you with your color palettes. Colorcombos.com is located at `http://www.colorcombos.com`. The ComboLibrary tab displays hundreds of color palettes. The codes for these colors are hexadecimal HTML codes, but you can use ColorPic, described later in this chapter, to pick up the RGB colors for use in Excel.

The website COLOURlovers, at `http://www.colourlovers.com`, has thousands of free color palettes. Use ColorPic, described in the next section, to select RGB colors from the screen.

Capturing Colors from the Screen

ColorPic is a free time-saving tool from Iconico, located at `http://www.iconico.com`. With it, you can read the color code from any area of the screen. Figure 16.11 shows ColorPic displaying the color code of bright red next to "Masters of Excel" on my website, `http://www.criticaltosuccess.com`. Use the RGB code or the Hue, Saturation, Value code to create the same colors you pick up with ColorPic in Excel. ColorPic also enables you to store the color codes you capture and group them as palettes.

Figure 16.11: ColorPic is a free utility you can use to select colors from anywhere onscreen and see the corresponding RGB codes.

Summary

This chapter didn't cover the decision-making part of a dashboard. Nevertheless, the custom labels, dates, and color formatting make a significant difference in how pleasing your dashboard is and whether it ties in with the corporate portal and culture. Custom labels can make your dashboard titles update automatically to reflect the data. Custom dates and numbers can help you format dates and numbers to match the format your organization expects. They can also help you fit in data when there isn't enough space for a long format. Of course, custom colors or themes are important for creating a look and feel that matches your organization's identity.

CHAPTER 17

Working with Data That Changes Size

What business strategy is all about, what distinguishes it from all other kinds of business planning, is, in a word, competitive advantage. Without competitors there would be no need for strategy, for the sole purpose of strategic planning is to enable the company to gain, as effectively as possible, a sustainable edge over its competitors.

Kenichi Ohnae
"One of the top five management gurus in the world"
—The Economist

A useful skill when creating Balanced Scorecards and dashboards is being able to handle data that changes size or location. This is useful if you want to import new data and the size of the data source changes, and it is also useful with charts. For example, you might have one chart, but you might want to allow the user to choose from among four different data sources. In another situation, you may have one chart, and you want it to use different starting dates or different periods of time.

The ability to work with data that changes size or shape also comes in handy with source data that changes size or shape. You will find this useful whether your dashboards work from manually entered data or from data retrieved through a dynamic link to a database.

This chapter begins by describing tables, a feature that was introduced in Excel 2003 as a List.

Tables are great for storing data that will expand or contract. Tables can be used for lists, databases, and charts. In earlier versions of Excel, complex OFFSET formulas were needed to create named ranges holding data that changed size. In Excel 2007 and Excel 2010, tables handle most of these issues for you.

Even though Excel 2007 and Excel 2010 have the power of tables to accommodate data that changes size, you still may need dynamic range names. In general, I find that range names are critically important to creating worksheets that are self-documenting, easier to understand, and semiautomated. These same capabilities are available in Excel 2003, but they are known as Lists.

Even with the newer versions of Excel, sometimes dynamic range names are important, as described later. Range names are a useful Excel feature that every intermediate to advanced user should understand. They are the foundation for solving the problems that arise when you have data of varying sizes and shapes.

Using Tables for Data That Changes Size

In versions of Excel prior to Excel 2003, charts and formulas that referenced data that changed size or shape presented a problem. The charts or formulas didn't automatically adjust as the area of data changed. Excel 2007 and Excel 2010 have a feature called tables that eliminates most of this issue. In Excel 2003 this feature is called a List.

To create an Excel table in Excel 2007 and Excel 2010, create your data, with or without headings and labels, and select it, as shown in Figure 17.1. Then, on the Insert tab, in the Table group, select Table. In the Create Table dialog box, ensure that the correct cell range is selected, and select the check box if your table has titles as headers. Click OK. The range of cells you selected is reformatted and becomes an Excel table, as shown in Figure 17.2.

In Excel 2003, select the data, with or without headings and labels; then choose the Data, List, Create List.

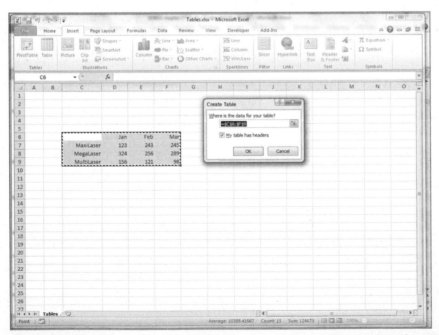

Figure 17.1: Create a table in Excel 2007 and Excel 2010 with or without headings.

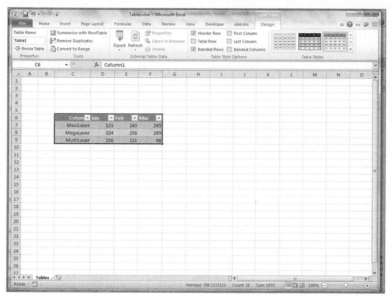

Figure 17.2: The table you create automatically has a format applied, which can easily be changed.

The table automatically expands to include headers or data entered in adjacent cells. For example, Figure 17.3 shows how the table has expanded to include a column with the heading Apr and a row for MiniLaser. The chart, which initially included only the original table, has now expanded to include the additional header and row.

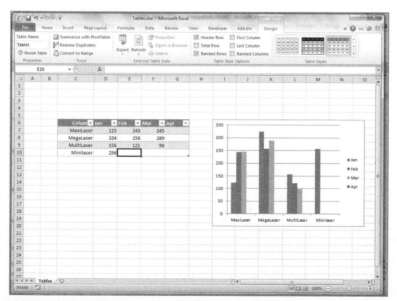

Figure 17.3: A chart created using this same table automatically adjusts to include new data or headers you add to the table.

To create a dynamic chart that expands and contracts as you add rows of data or new columns with headers, select the table and then create a chart using any of your usual chart-creation techniques.

Formatting Tables

Formatting tables is about as easy as anything you can do in Excel. To format a table, select a cell in the table. Then, on the Table Tools Design tab, in the Table Styles group, click the down arrow to see predefined formats, as shown in Figure 17.4. You can select one of these predefined styles or create your own custom style.

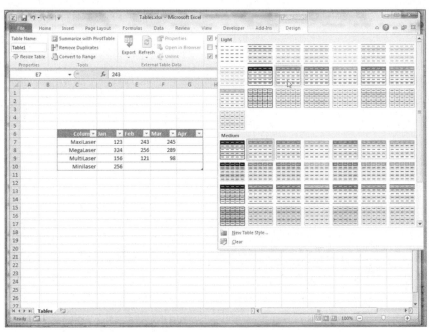

Figure 17.4: Formatting a table is easy using the predefined styles.

You can make even more custom format changes to a table by selecting a cell inside the table and then selecting from the variety of options on the Table Tools Design tab in the Table Styles group.

Attaching a Dynamic Range Name to a Table

One of the cool things about tables is that you can assign a range name to a table and the name will expand or contract as the table changes size.

What's so cool about that? You can refer to this dynamic table using a single name, such as tblRevenueSources.

USE THE DYNAMIC NAME THAT EXCEL AUTOMATICALLY CREATES

If you create a table in Excel 2007 or Excel 2010, or you create a list in Excel 2003, Excel automatically assigns a dynamic name to that list. The dynamic name Excel creates will automatically adjust as your list changes size. A later section in this chapter gives the trade-offs between using the automatically assigned name and creating your own dynamic range name.

By having a range name on the table, you can apply many different Excel functions and macros on that range and know that you are working with all the data, because the table takes care of the changing size.

For example, if you want to reference data by the labels on the left or top side of the table, you can look up the content of any cell using VLOOKUP or HLOOKUP and the range name. For example, in Figure 17.3, if the table is named tblLaserProducts, you can find the contents on the MegaLaser row in the second column with this formula:

```
=VLOOKUP("MegaLaser",tblLaserProducts,2)
```

You can gain even more lookup power with the use of INDEX and MATCH, as described in the Chapter 18.

Tables Use English-Like Formula References

When you create a formula that uses rows or columns in a table, the rows and columns are referenced with English-language names, rather than cell references. For example, in Figure 17.5 the SUM formula in cell D3 looks like this:

```
=SUM(Table1[[#All],[Jan]])
```

This totals all rows in the Jan column.

Naming Ranges for Ease of Use and Functionality

Range names are English-language names used in place of range references such as B5:G26. Range names can be used in formulas and in a chart's data series just like cell references but are much more readable than cell references. For example, using the word Revenue as a reference in a formula is easier to understand than using $B$5:$I$20.

Range names also make it easier to navigate in a worksheet. In any version you can go to a named location by pressing Ctrl+G or F5 and then choosing a name from the Go To dialog box. You can go to a named reference in Excel 2007 and Excel 2010 by choosing the Home tab. In the Editing Group, click Find &

Select, and then choose Go To. In Excel 2003, choose Edit ➤ Go To. Excel moves to that named range and selects it.

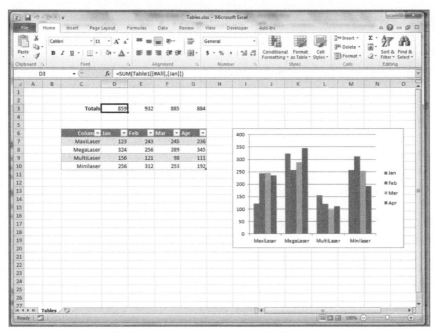

Figure 17.5: Formulas involving tables use English-like references for the rows and columns.

When you insert or delete rows or columns through a range name's reference, the range name expands or contracts like a normal cell reference.

Range names should describe what they are referencing, as a name like Revenue does. This helps you when you return to a worksheet you haven't seen in a long time. It also helps others understand your worksheet and makes diagnostics easier. Furthermore, as you will soon discover, you can use range names to name powerful formulas.

Creating Named Ranges

Follow these steps to manually create a named range:

1. Select the cell or range of cells you want to name. You can select nonadjacent cells or ranges by holding down the Ctrl key as you make your selections.

2. Type the range name inside the Name box, as shown in Figure 17.6. The Name box is to the left of the formula bar and normally shows the currently active cell.

3. Press Enter.

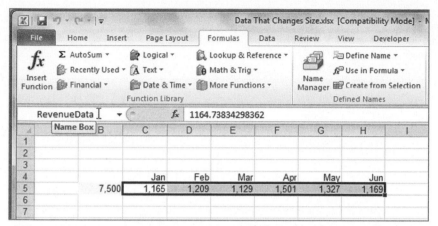

Figure 17.6: Type a name for a new named range in the Name box to the left of the formula bar.

You can use another method instead of typing a range name in the Name box. Select the cell or range and then, in Excel 2007 and Excel 2010, on the Formulas tab in the Defined Names group, select Define Name. In Excel 2003, choose Insert ➢ Name ➢ Define, type a name in the Name in Workbook box, and click Add to add the name.

Keep in mind the following conventions when naming ranges:

- Excel does not allow names with spaces.

- Never use a hyphen (-) to separate words in a name. You or Excel may misinterpret this as a minus sign in a formula. If you want to separate words, use an underscore (_).

- Use a leading capital letter at the beginning of each word in a name, such as RevenueNewProduct. This helps you prevent errors. Get in the habit of always typing range names in lowercase in formulas. When you press Enter, they will be converted into leading caps if Excel recognizes them as a valid range name. If they do not automatically convert, this means that either you mistyped, or the name does not exist.

- If a workbook contains many names, they are easier to find if you use a naming convention that puts the category first, such as RevenueNewProduct instead of NewProductRevenue.

- Names for special types of ranges are easier to understand if you use a prefix convention. You can make up your own prefixes; just be consistent. Table 17-1 shows a few examples of prefixes you can use.

- Never use names that look like cell references, such as D250.

- If you use a name that has not been defined, Excel returns the value #NAME?.

Table 17-1: Sample Prefixes for Range Names

TYPE OF RANGE	PREFIX	EXAMPLE
Form list (such as a drop-down box)	fl	flStates
Database	db	dbMfgProduction
Report	rpt	rptDailyQuality
Chart range	ch	chBudgetVariance

TIP Large systems may have many range names, and the spellings can be hard to remember. Rather than typing range names, you can paste them into formulas. Move the insertion point in the formula to where you need the range name, and then press F5 to display the Go To dialog box with the list of names. This saves you from possible typing errors and is definitely easier than trying to remember possibly hundreds of names in one workbook.

If you know in advance that you will be using names for cells adjacent to lists of labels, you can create multiple range names at one time. To create range names from labels on the worksheet, do the following:

1. Select the cells containing the labels and adjacent cell or range to be named with the label. Figure 17.7 shows multiple cells selected and about to be named.

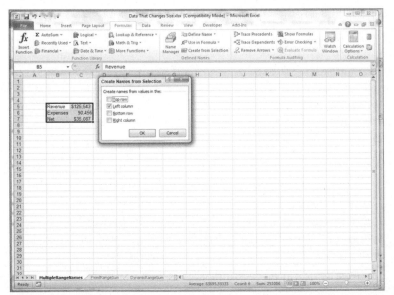

Figure 17.7: Name multiple cells from adjacent labels using the Create Names dialog box.

2. In Excel 2007 and Excel 2010, on the Formulas tab, in the Defined Names group, select Create from Selection. In Excel 2003, select Insert ➢ Name ➢ Create.

3. Select the check boxes that describe where the labels are that can be used as names. Name rows and columns at the same time by simultaneously selecting row and column check boxes.

4. Click OK.

WORKING WITH GLOBAL AND LOCAL NAMES

The two different types of range names are global and local. Global names apply across multiple sheets. Local names apply to a specific sheet. To learn more, refer to a book on the fundamentals of Excel, such as the *Excel 2003 Bible*, by John Walkenbach (Wiley, 2003). If you are using Excel 2007 or Excel 2010, you can look at *Excel 2007 Bible* or *Excel 2010 Bible*, also by John Walkenbach (Wiley, 2007/2010).

TIP **Even with the use of range names, the logic behind some formulas can be obscure. It is a good idea to document complex formulas. In addition to inserting comments to add documentation on a cell, you can add a comment directly inside the formula in a cell. To do this, use the** N **function:**

```
=CHOOSE($F$3,rptQuality,rptProduction)+N("Option button value F3
 selects the report range")
```

The N **function returns 0 for text, so you must enclose your comment in quotes.**

When to Use Tables or Dynamic Range Names

Tables are a feature in Excel 2007 and Excel 2010. They first appeared as Lists in Excel 2003. Dynamic range names do the same thing and can be customized for special behavior, but they are more work to create. So when should you use one or the other?

Here are a few situations where you might want to use dynamic range names rather than Excel tables:

- Use dynamic range names to maintain backward compatibility with earlier versions of Excel. Charts referencing the dynamic ranges work in newer and older versions of Excel.

- Use dynamic range names when you want a chart to expand or adjust under your control. For example, you might want to change the start date under user control or change between a 12-month or 15-month view.

- Use a dynamic range when retrieving data from an external source into a blank worksheet. You can create a dynamic range that starts at A1, even though the sheet is initially blank, and then calculates exactly the width and depth of the retrieved data.

■ Excel tables must be surrounded by a moat of empty cells. If you need dual rows of headers, adjacent columns of data, or some other content that touches, you may need to use a dynamic range.

■ You may need a dynamic range that has a layout other than the shape of a table.

Creating Dynamic Range Names That Adjust Automatically When the Size of Data Changes

Although range names are great for reducing errors and making formulas easier to decipher, their real power comes when they are used to name formulas. Named formulas recalculate just like formulas in cells do. You can use them within other formulas or within chart series, just as you would use a reference or result. The formula used by a named formula does not appear in a cell. It appears in the range definitions.

Figure 17.8 shows cell G7, containing this simple SUM formula:

```
=SUM(RevenueData)
```

where RevenueData is the range name for B5:G5. Although the range name makes this formula more readable, it doesn't help you if you want to add the data in cells H5 and I5 and automatically include that new data in the SUM.

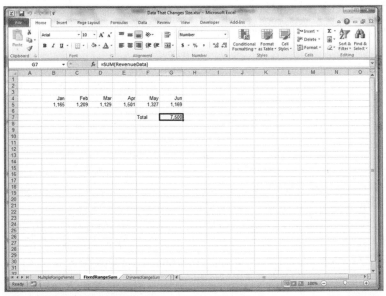

Figure 17.8: A simple SUM formula totaling the range named Revenue.

The following section shows you how to make a dynamic range name that expands or contracts so that it continues to function as the size or shape of the data range changes. The principle used in this simple example will be used next to create a dynamic range for chart data.

The OFFSET function can be used to calculate a range that changes shape. The OFFSET function returns a reference, cell, or range based on a single reference cell. Its syntax is

```
OFFSET(reference,rows,cols,height,width)
```

where

- *reference* is the origin point or upper-left corner of the calculated range.
- *rows* is the number of rows by which the calculated range is offset from *reference*.
- *cols* is the number of columns by which the calculated range is offset from *reference*.
- *height* is the height of the calculated range.
- *width* is the width of the calculated range.

You need one other function to create a range that automatically updates itself. As you add data to the right of existing data, you need to know the new width that encompasses the new data. To do this, use COUNTA to count the number of filled cells in the range B5:M5. This enables you to add data from left to right in the range B5:M5. The SUM function automatically includes filled cells to the right, because the dynamic range name drRevenueData dynamically expands.

Here's the OFFSET formula you need:

```
=OFFSET(DynamicRangeSum!$B$5,0,0,1,COUNTA(DynamicRangeSum!$B$5:$M$5))
```

OFFSET begins the calculated range at B5 in sheet DynamicRangeSum. There is no offset from B5, because the range starts at B5, so the offset row is 0 and the offset column is 0. The height of the calculated range is 1 row, the height of the data. The width of the calculated range is the number of filled cells in B5:M5. The name of the worksheet, the name on the tab, is included with the cell references so that this range name applies only on this worksheet. If the worksheet/tab name had spaces in it, you must enclose the worksheet/tab name in single quotes (').

To make a dynamic range name formula, you must create the formula in the New Name or Define Name dialog box. In Excel 2007 or Excel 2010, on the Formulas tab, in the Defined Names group, select Define Name. In Excel 2003, choose Insert ➤ Name ➤ Define and type **drRevenueData** in the Name in

Workbook box. (The dr prefix indicates to users that this is a dynamic range.) Type or select the formula in the Refers To box. Click Add, and then click OK.

In Figure 17.9, the drRevenueData formula is

```
=OFFSET(DynamicRangeSum!$B$5,0,0,1,COUNTA(DynamicRangeSum!$B$5:$M$5))
```

This OFFSET formula is now stored in the range name drRevenueData. Whenever new data is entered in the range B5:M5, the OFFSET formula recalculates, which updates the value for drRevenueData.

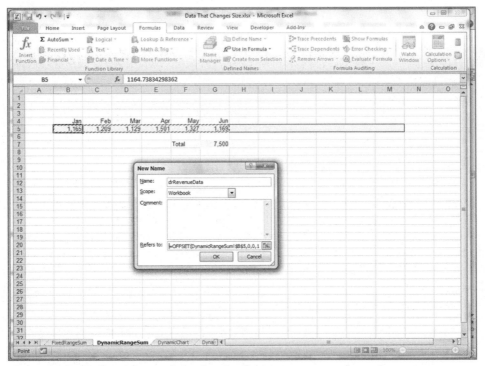

Figure 17.9: The New Name dialog box is where you create a dynamic range name formula.

Now, in any cell in the worksheet you can enter this formula:

```
=SUM(RevenueData)
```

and see the result.

As you type data in the range B5:M5, it is included in the SUM. There is one caveat with using COUNTA to calculate a new width or height. Data you enter must be from left to right or top to bottom, without blank cells.

You can see how the range drRevenueData expands as you add more data by selecting the drRevenueData range. Named formulas do not appear in the Go To dialog box. To select a dynamic range name, do the following:

1. Press F5 to display the Go To dialog box. Notice that drRevenueData does not appear in the Go To dialog box. Named formulas are not visible.

2. Type the name **drRevenueData** in the Reference box and click OK.

Excel selects the new range associated with drRevenueData. As you add new data to adjacent cells to the right, the range of drRevenueData expands to include them.

VIEWING OR EDITING NAMED FORMULAS

Named formulas do not appear in the Go To dialog box, but you can always see them and edit them. In Excel 2007 or Excel 2010 in the Formulas tab, in the Defined Names group, click Name Manager. In Excel 2003, select Insert ➤ Name ➤ Define and select the named formula.

Creating Charts That Expand to Include New Data

Adding data to the right edge of existing chart data does not expand the chart. Without the following technique, you would need to re-create charts as data expands. However, you can use a named formula in a chart's series to automatically expand the chart's data range. This can save you a lot of work because you don't have to rebuild charts.

WARNING All dynamic range names used for dynamic charts in Excel 2007 and Excel 2010 must be fully expressed. This means that you must include the name of the workbook and tab when typing the range name. For example, the range name must be typed as

```
DataSize.xlsx!NPMonths
```

It cannot be typed as NPMonths, as in earlier versions of Excel.

To create charts that automatically adjust as new data is added, you must go through this process:

1. Create a dynamic range name, as described previously, that will include the chart's data range as it expands.

2. Manually create a chart using existing data in the range.

3. Enter the dynamic range name into the reference for the chart's data series. (Substitute the range name for the unchanging cell references the manual chart uses.)

In Figure 17.10 the chart's data series, defining the columns, is selected so that you can see the series formula in the formula bar. By knowing what the parts of this data series formula are, you can make substitutions and make the chart do what you want (see Table 17-2). The formula with dynamic range names substituted into it looks like this:

```
=SERIES(DynamicChart!$B$7,DataSize.xlsx!NPMonths,DataSize.xlsx!NPSales,1)
```

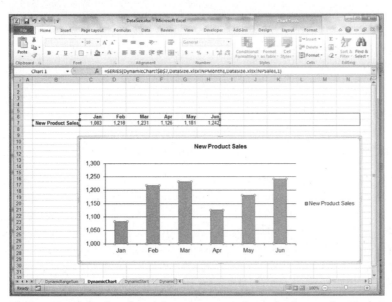

Figure 17.10: Typing dynamic range name formulas into a chart's data series creates charts that automatically adapt as the size of their data changes.

Table 17-2: Parts of a Chart Data Series, Including Dynamic Range Names

CHART ELEMENT	SERIES FORMULA	DEFINITION
Data heading	DynamicChart!$B$7	Defines the heading
Date range for chart series	DataSize.xlsx!NPMonths	Dynamic range calculating date range
Data range for chart series	DataSize.xlsx!NPSales	Dynamic range calculating data range
Series number	1	Identifies the chart series if there are multiple series

In any version of Excel, you can manually edit the chart series formula by typing or pasting in the dynamic range names. However, you may find it easier to use the Chart Series editor.

In Excel 2007 and Excel 2010, enter the dynamic range for the chart's data series by clicking a chart series so that all elements (bars or dots and so on) are selected. On the Chart Tools Design tab, in the Data group, click Select Data. In the Select Data Source dialog box, shown in Figure 17.11, select the Legend Entry (Series) and click Edit so that you can enter the dynamic range for the data. Then select the Horizontal (Category) Axis Labels and click Edit to enter the dynamic range for the date series.

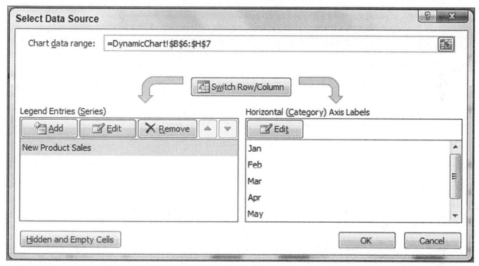

Figure 17.11: Typing dynamic range name formulas into a chart's data series creates charts that automatically adapt as the size of their data changes. In Excel 2007 and Excel 2010 you must include the worksheet name and tab with the dynamic range name.

In Excel 2003, enter the dynamic range name in a chart's series formula by clicking the chart and then choosing Chart ➢ Source Data. In the Source Data dialog box, shown in Figure 17.12, select the Series tab. The figure shows the dynamic range names, NPSales and NPMonths, used in the chart's data series. The dynamic formula for NPMonths, the chart's date range, is

```
=OFFSET(DynamicChart!$C$6,0,0,1,COUNTA(DynamicChart!$C$6:$N$6))
```

The chart's date range can include a changeable range of dates from C6 to N6. The dynamic formula for NPSales, the chart's data range, is

```
=OFFSET(DynamicChart!$C$7,0,0,1,COUNTA(DynamicChart!$C$7:$N$7))
```

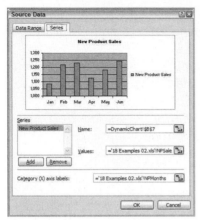

Figure 17.12: Typing dynamic range name formulas into an Excel 2003 chart's data series creates charts that automatically adapt as the size of their data changes.

Dynamically Changing a Chart's Start Date

When the dashboard user needs to record and review large amounts of historical data, you can give the user the ability to change the chart's start date. The user can select any starting date. By combining what you learn here with what you learn in Chapter 20, you give your dashboard users the ability to select start dates from a menu or scroll through historical data by moving a slider bar.

DOWNLOAD ALL THE EXAMPLES FOR THIS BOOK

Refer to the Introduction for information about how to download the examples in this book.

Figure 17.13 shows a chart displaying 6 months of data in the range C7:N7. Changing the start month in C3 changes the starting and subsequent months in the chart. By linking a slider bar to cell C3, your dashboard's users can scroll through the data a month at a time.

Two dynamic range names are needed to create this dynamic chart. The dynamic range formula to calculate the months on the Category (x) axis series is

```
NPMonthsStart=OFFSET(DynamicStart!$C$6,0,DynamicStart!$C$3-1,1,6)
```

The dynamic range name NPMonthsStart uses C6 as the starting reference point. The row offset for the start is 0, because there is only one row, so there is no offset. The height and width for the range are 1 and 6, so the chart always shows 6 months. The animation occurs in this formula:

```
DynamicStart!$C$3-1
```

This is the column offset for the range's starting point. When the value in C3 is 1, the first month, the offset is 0. Increasing the value in C3 moves the range's starting point farther to the right.

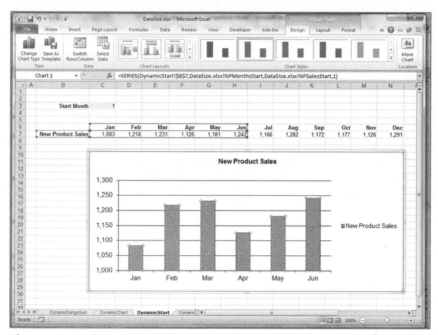

Figure 17.13: The Category (x) axis and data range for the New Product Sales chart use dynamic ranges so that the chart can animate across time periods.

The data series is almost the same formula as the axis, but the data series references the row containing formula data:

```
aNPSalesStart
=OFFSET(DynamicStart!$C$7,0,DynamicStart!$C$3-1,1,6)
```

Enter the NPSalesMonth and NPSalesStart names by selecting the chart and then substituting the dynamic range names directly in the series formula, as described earlier, or using the chart Data Manager.

To display the chart's Data Manager in Excel 2007 and Excel 2010, select the chart series. On the Chart Tools Design tab, in the Data group, click the Select Data icon.

In Excel 2003, choose Chart ➤ Source Data, and select the Series tab. Do not forget to enter the worksheet/tab name when you enter the formula. For example, in the Values box you will enter

```
='DynamicStart'!NPSalesStart
```

because the name of the tab containing the dynamic range name is DynamicStart.

Dynamically Changing a Chart's Start Date and Width

With a small modification you can make the dynamic chart adjust so that it displays variable amounts of data. This makes charts extremely flexible for tasks such as switching views from one year of financial data to multiple years or switching from a week of manufacturing data to months of data. Figure 17.14 shows the chart and data entry fields for a chart that allows users to adjust its start date and the number of months it displays.

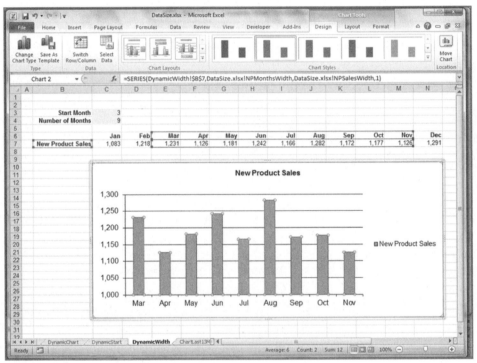

Figure 17.14: Allowing your dashboard users to change the start date and amount of data plotted gives them the power to display what they want.

In this example, the DynamicStart worksheet from the previous example has been copied and the tab renamed DynamicWidth. This preserves the two dynamic range names, so you need to make only two small modifications. First, type a number from 1 to 12 in cell C4, which will contain the width of data plotted.

Second, you need to modify the width of OFFSET in each dynamic range formula so that it references cell C4. When the contents of C4 change, the amount of data in the chart changes.

The dynamic range names have changed from referencing the DynamicStart to the DynamicWidth sheet, and the width has changed too, so they now look like this:

```
NPMonthsWidth=OFFSET(DynamicWidth!$C$6,0,DynamicWidth!
$C$3-1,1,DynamicWidth!$C$4)
NPSalesWidth=OFFSET(DynamicWidth!$C$7,0,DynamicWidth!
$C$3-1,1,DynamicWidth!$C$4)
```

Dynamically Charting the Last 13 Months of Data

Executives and managers usually want to see the most current data series. For financial data, this is usually the last 12, 13, or 15 months of data. Displaying 13 months of data lets you compare the current month and the same month in the prior year. Displaying 15 months of data lets you compare the months in the current quarter against the same months in the prior year.

When static charts display this type of information, you usually can choose one of three approaches, none of which is good. First, you can waste time by re-creating the charts over the range of the new data. Second, you can waste time by reentering data on top of the previous data. Third, you can create aesthetically offensive charts by making the chart so wide it leaves blank spaces on the right in anticipation of forthcoming data. (Another and the best alternative is to use dynamic retrieval from PivotTables or PowerPivots, as described in Chapters 21 and 22.)

Using a range name formula to calculate the range to be plotted produces a much better solution. It creates a clean-looking chart with no gaps, and data can be added at the end of the existing data. The chart automatically determines the most current data needed. In Figure 17.15, for example, the dynamic range names have calculated the most current 13 months of data in E6:Q7.

```
NPMonths13Mo=OFFSET(ChartLast13Mo!$C$6,0,COUNTA(ChartLast13Mo!$C$7:$Z$7)
-13,1,13)
NPSales13Mo=OFFSET(ChartLast13Mo!$C$7,0,COUNTA(ChartLast13Mo!$C$7:$Z$7)
-13,1,13)
```

The magic here is done by this formula:

```
COUNTA(ChartLast13Mo!$C$7:$Z$7)-13,1,13)
```

This formula calculates how many data cells are filled in the row and subtracts 13 to find the starting place for data. For example, if 20 cells are filled with data, 13-7 specifies that the new series will start in the sixth cell. The 1 says that the data series is one row high. The last 13 indicates that the series is 13 columns wide.

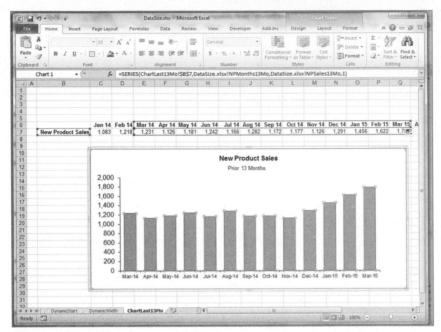

Figure 17.15: Use dynamic range names to automatically chart the most current data from a larger range.

Creating Dynamic Range Names for Lists

Dashboards and scorecards in Excel use a lot of lists (Excel's name for a flat database). Lists are used to hold data for analysis, data for charting, menu contents, lookup table ranges, and so forth. Over time, and with changing requirements, these lists change in height and width. More data may be added manually, data retrieved from an external database may be larger or smaller than expected, or user requirements may change.

In Excel 2007 and Excel 2010, the need to accommodate lists of changing size is taken care of with Excel tables. In Excel 2003 use the feature known as Lists. These features are described at the beginning of this chapter. If you are using Excel 2003 or meet one of the cases described earlier where tables cannot be used, you need to use dynamic range names.

> **TIP** Excel recognizes a list as a rectangular block of filled cells. The block may contain unfilled cells, but all filled cells must touch each other at one edge. The list must be surrounded by unfilled cells and may or may not have a row of headers. To quickly select a list, click one cell in the list, and then press Shift+Ctrl+*. You can go "around the clock," seeing all corners of a selected list, by pressing Ctrl+. (period). Each press of Ctrl+. displays the next corner.

Creating range names that update dynamically for lists is much like creating dynamic range names for charts. You assign a formula to a range name, and that formula calculates the list's height and width. The difference with charts is that lists may expand downward, as well as to the right.

In the following example, a dynamic range is created for the list:

```
MedianHouseHoldIncome1996_2006_US_State_CAcounty.xls
```

This and many other large data files are available for download at my website, http://www.criticaltosuccess.com. These large data files are great for experimenting and learning.

You expect that additional U.S. Census data will extend the list each year, and you want the list's range to expand to account for years up to 2012, or column S. Also, additional counties from a few other states may be added, so the last row may go from its current 111 entries to as many as 300. Figure 17.16 shows the list.

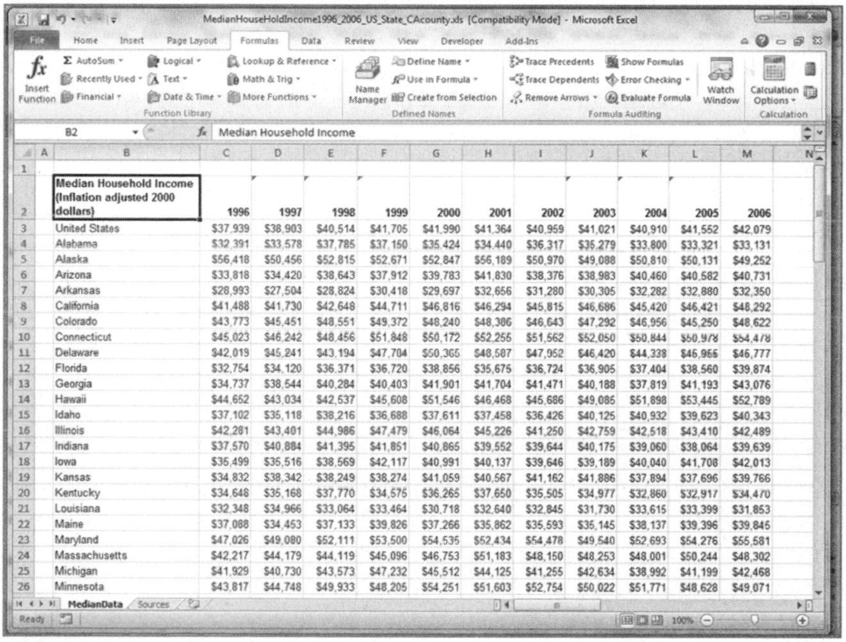

Figure 17.16: Dynamic range names can automatically adjust as the height and width of the list change.

To reference this range, even if it grows to 3,000 rows and column XX, you need to use a dynamic range name that expands vertically and horizontally. You can do this with two COUNTA functions inside an OFFSET function.

To create a dynamic named range for this list, follow these steps:

1. Display the New Name or Define Name dialog box.

2. Type the range name **dbMdnHseInc** in the Names field.

3. Type or enter the formula that calculates the range in the Refers To box:

```
=OFFSET(Data!$B$2,0,0,COUNTA(MedianData!$B$2:$B$3000),
COUNTA(MedianData!$B$2:$XX$2))
```

Notice that MedianData is the name of the tab.

4. Click OK.

`MedianData!$B$2` is the base reference at the top-left corner of the list. The `0,0` indicates that the base reference is not moved from B2. `COUNTA(MedianData!$B$2:$B$3000)` calculates the range's height by counting the number of filled cells between the base reference and row 3000. `COUNTA(MedianData!$B$2:$XX$2)` calculates the range's width by counting the number of column headers between the base reference and column XX.

> **TIP** The Define Name dialog box can be frustrating to edit or type in until you realize that it works like the formula bar. Press F2 to go into edit mode before attempting to use arrow keys to move the insertion point or select portions of the formula with the mouse. When you are in edit mode, you can move the insertion point in the formula and then click or drag in the worksheet to enter a reference.

Now, test to see whether you created the dynamic range name dbMdnHseInc correctly. Press F5 to display the Go To dialog box. You cannot see named formulas, so type the name **dbMdnHseInc** into the Reference box and click OK. The range of cells should be selected.

The reason you went through all this work is to create a named range that expands automatically. Check to make sure your dynamic range expands downward and to the right. Type **2007** to the right of 2006 in the headers. Type the name of your county in the last cell of column B, below the California counties. Press F5, type in **dbMdnHseInc**, and see whether the range expands to include the new column and row. If it does, you'll be ready to start creating dashboards that automatically update themselves.

Summary

With the minor amount of work required to create a dynamic range name, you will save yourself from the repetitive work of updating your scorecard or dashboard. As you become more comfortable creating dynamic range names, you will find that they have uses beyond databases and charts. You also can use them to create scrolling lists that automatically expand, combo boxes that expand, or combo boxes that change contents.

CHAPTER 18

Retrieving Data from Lists and Tables of Data

Information is a source of learning. But unless it is organized, processed, and available to the right people in a format for decision-making, it is a burden, not a benefit.

—William Pollard
Historian

Although charts are what people usually look at first in Balanced Scorecards and dashboards, it is tables and lists that are the source of the information. They contain the data from which Excel builds charts, displays tables, fills menus, and builds printed reports. They are also what managers and executives refer to when they want more detail. Being able to manage your lists and tables dynamically will save you a significant amount of time, give your dashboard users more capabilities, and reduce chances for error.

Other techniques you will learn in this chapter include sorting lists using a function rather than a command. This enables you to retrieve or import data from any data source, sorting it multiple ways according to your user needs.

More Powerful Than VLOOKUP: INDEX and MATCH

One of the first powerful Excel features people learn as they move from novice to intermediate level is the use of the vertical and horizontal lookup functions, VLOOKUP and HLOOKUP. The VLOOKUP function searches the first column in a list for a term and then returns the value in the row of the item found, but in a column you specify. HLOOKUP accomplishes the same function on horizontal lists. These functions are usually used to retrieve items, such as purchase amounts, when given a search item, such as a transaction code.

Although the VLOOKUP and HLOOKUP functions are powerful, they can get you in trouble. They are easy to use incorrectly. If used incorrectly, they return the wrong values.

VLOOKUP and HLOOKUP use this syntax:

```
VLOOKUP(lookup_value,table_array,col_index_num,[range_lookup])
HLOOKUP(lookup_value,table_array,row_index_num,[range_lookup])
```

Errors most frequently occur with VLOOKUP and HLOOKUP when someone is looking for exact matches and fails to use FALSE for range_lookup. If range_lookup is TRUE or omitted, VLOOKUP and HLOOKUP expect the list to be in sorted order. When they cannot find an exact match, they return an approximate match, which is usually worse than returning an error.

Another failing of VLOOKUP is that the column being searched must be the left column. The row being searched with HLOOKUP must be the top row. When you create dashboards that use multiple drop-down lists to search on different search fields, you will want to be able to search on the columns or rows of your choice.

A more flexible and powerful approach to finding data in a list is with the combination of INDEX and MATCH. INDEX has this syntax:

```
INDEX(array,row_num,[column_num])
```

In an array or table of data, INDEX returns the value at the intersection of the row and column number specified. MATCH finds the row or column containing the header or date you want. By combining MATCH and INDEX, you can find exactly the cell you want in a table or list.

The syntax for MATCH is

```
MATCH(lookup_value,lookup_array,[match_type])
```

In MATCH, lookup_value is the value being searched for—the value used to identify the information, such as a part name, transaction code, or invoice number. lookup_array is the column or row being searched. match_type specifies how close you want the match to be. Table 18-1 shows the values for match_type.

Table 18-1: Values for match_type

IF MATCH_TYPE IS	THE RETURNED VALUE IS
−1	The smallest value that is greater than or equal to lookup_value. lookup_array must be in descending order
0	The first value that is exactly equal to lookup_value. lookup_array can be in any order
1	The largest value that is less than or equal to lookup_value. lookup_array must be in ascending order

The MATCH syntax you will almost always use for Balanced Scorecards and dashboards uses a *match_type* of 0 to find exact matches in unsorted lists. If MATCH does not find an exact match, it returns the #N/A error value. You can trap for this error with the ISNA function.

For example, in the following formula, INDEX returns the value in the second column (2) of the array C4:D17. The row is determined by the MATCH function. The MATCH function finds the row in C4:C17 that matches the search term in F2:

```
=INDEX($C$4:$D$17,MATCH($F$2,$C$4:$C$17,0),2)
```

But what happens if someone enters a term in F2 that is not in the array C4:C17? MATCH returns an error and causes the entire INDEX function to return #N/A. You don't want your dashboard returning incorrect data, and you don't want your users to receive errors. Here's how to handle it.

Use the ISNA function to determine whether MATCH will cause an error. Then handle that error by returning a message to the user that the item was not found in the list. This formula either finds and returns a valid item or returns the message "Value not found in list:"

```
=IF(ISNA(MATCH($F$2,$C$4:$C$17,0)),"Value not found in list.",
INDEX($C$4:$D$17,MATCH($F$2,$C$4:$C$17,0),2))
```

The condition in the IF function is ISNA(MATCH()). If the MATCH is not found, ISNA returns TRUE, so the text appears in the cell. If MATCH does find a value, the INDEX function calculates and returns the value found in the array.

TIP Earlier versions of Excel used ISNA or other error detection combined with an IF function to trap for errors. This required entering the error-prone formula twice: once in the IS... function and again for the result. In Excel 2007 and Excel 2010 you can use the IFERROR function. With IFERROR you need to enter the error-prone formula only once.

If you use Excel 2003, you can combine IF and ISNA to trap for many errors so that your scorecard and dashboard users aren't left perplexed.

Another way of preventing lookup or INDEX(MATCH()) errors is by using combo boxes or lists from which users select the item they are searching for. By only giving users valid choices from a combo box or list, you eliminate the chance for data entry errors. Chapter 20 describes how to add these interactive controls to your dashboards.

The Key to Retrieving Data and Creating Interactive Dashboards

This section describes how to combine INDEX and MATCH to find and retrieve a value from a list. You can search for and retrieve data from any row or column, whether it is sorted or not.

The first example shows you how to select median family income for a state from a list and then chart the retrieved data. This process is fundamental to creating most interactive dashboards. In a following section, you will learn how to add a drop-down list so that you won't have to type the state's name. After that, you will see how to retrieve and chart data using multiple keywords.

> **WARNING** F9 is a wonderful key for an Excel user of any proficiency level to know. Pressing F9 enables you to see the result of a portion of a formula. For example, if the formula
>
> ```
> =INDEX(dbMedianIncome,$E$21,MATCH(C$17,$B$25:$M$25))
> ```
>
> does not return the results you expect, you may want to see the results of the MATCH function to check whether it is correct. To do that, in the formula bar, select the portion of the function that can calculate on its own. For example:
>
> ```
> MATCH(C$17,$B$25:$M$25)
> ```
>
> When you press F9, you see the result of the MATCH. Do not press Enter, or you will replace MATCH with its results. Press Esc to return to the original formula. If you make a mistake, press Ctrl+Z to undo.

Using a Keyword to Retrieve and Chart Data

Figure 18.1 shows a chart plotting a state's median family income. The charted data in row 18 was retrieved from the named range dbMedianIncome, B25:M75.

> **DOWNLOAD SAMPLE DATA FILES**
>
> See the Introduction for information on downloading the sample files and data used in this book, as well as for additional valuable information.

The INDEX and MATCH functions are used to retrieve data to chart from the list. When you type a valid state name in C21, the MATCH formula in E21 finds the row in the list containing that name and returns the row number within the list. The INDEX formulas in row 18 then use that row number to retrieve the appropriate data for charting.

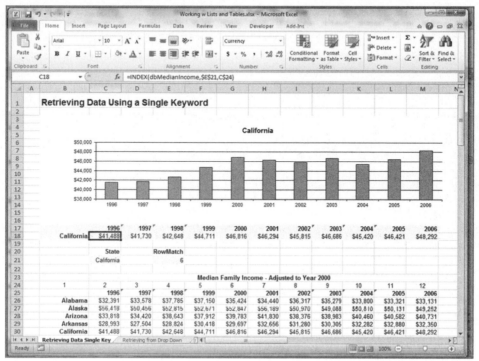

Figure 18.1: Use INDEX and MATCH to find data in a list and retrieve it for charting.

Cell E21 contains this formula:

```
=MATCH($C$21,$B$25:$B$75,0)
```

The MATCH function finds which row in B25:B75 contains an exact match for the state in cell C21. The MATCH function looks through the range B25:B75 to find the state name the user entered in C21. The 0 in the MATCH function forces MATCH to look for only exact matches, no matter how the contents of B25:B75 are sorted. This is one advantage over VLOOKUP and HLOOKUP. MATCH returns the row number that matches within the range B25:B75. This row number is the row containing California's data in the list range dbMedianIncome.

Cells B17:M18 feed data to the chart. The data in B18:M18 changes depending on the state entered in C21. Each cell in B18:M18 uses INDEX to retrieve from the list the row calculated by MATCH.

Cell C18, for example, contains this formula:

```
=INDEX(dbMedianIncome,$E$21,C$24)
```

This INDEX function looks at the list with the range name dbMedianIncome, B25:M75, and retrieves the row specified by $E$21. The column number for the data to be retrieved is in C$24.

Column numbers for each column of data were entered in row 24 to make this example easy to understand. Later in this chapter, you will see how rows and columns can be selected by formula, no matter what their order is.

Using the relative reference C$24 enables you to copy the first INDEX formula from B18 to M18. The formula continues to reference the correct column number in row 24. For example, the formula in cell B18 to retrieve the state's name is

```
=INDEX(dbMedianIncome,$E$21,B$24)
```

LEARN HOW TO USE DYNAMIC RANGE NAMES FOR TABLES

To get the full capability of extracting data from lists and tables, you need to understand dynamic range names. These are range names that automatically update themselves as the list or table changes, as described in Chapter 17.

Adding a Drop-Down Selection List to Make Retrieval Easier

When your keywords are long or complex, you will want to give users a drop-down list instead of forcing them to type an entry. Typing requires memorizing often-complex names or numbers and is error-prone. It is very easy to create a simple drop-down list from which you can select, rather than type, what you are looking for. Chapter 20 shows many more examples of how to use drop-down lists, buttons, and menus.

Figure 18.2 shows a drop-down list that has been added to the previous example by using data validation.

To add this drop-down list, do the following:

1. Select the cell where you want the list to appear. In this case, the cell is C21.

2. In Excel 2007 and Excel 2010, on the Data tab, in the Data Tools group, select Data Validation. In Excel 2003, choose Data ➢ Validation. The Data Validation dialog box appears, as shown in Figure 18.3. Select the Settings tab.

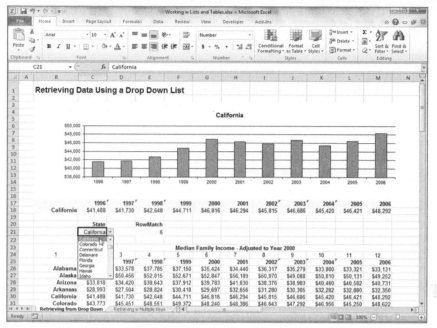

Figure 18.2: Using a drop-down list to select data is easier and less error-prone.

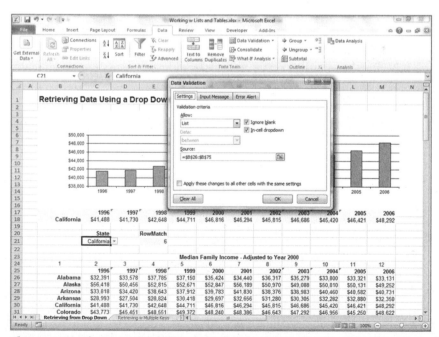

Figure 18.3: The Data Validation dialog box makes it easy to create drop-down lists for data entry.

3. In the Allow box, select List.

4. Select the Ignore blank and In-cell dropdown check boxes.

5. In the Source box, select the range containing the list of entries. In this case, it is B26:B75. If you specify this range with a named range, the named range must be on the same sheet as the drop-down list.

6. Click OK.

Retrieving Data Given Multiple Keywords

When you need to access large amounts of data on your dashboard, you will probably have to use multiple keywords to select the data to chart. For example, you might select a product line and then select a product within the product line, or you might select a division and then a department within the division.

Retrieving data using multiple keywords is very similar to using a single keyword. The difference is that you will use the concatenation function, &, to join multiple keywords to form a single key on which you can search. In Figure 18.4, for example, the Product Line and Region fields in columns C and D of the list have been concatenated to create a new key found in column B—labeled, not surprisingly, Key. This key is unique for each row, so when you search with MATCH, only one possible row matches the selected Product Line and Region.

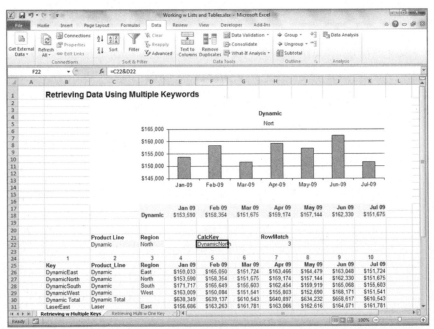

Figure 18.4: Retrieve data using multiple keys by creating a new key using concatenation.

You create the Key column by entering this formula:

```
=C26&D26
```

in cell B26 and copying it down the column. The concatenated values from B26 down are used as the search array for MATCH.

Now, when you enter a Product Line name in cell C22 and a Region in cell D22, the formula in cell F22:

```
=C22&D22
```

creates the term used to search down the Key column. If you enter Dynamic and North, cell F22 contains DynamicNorth.

The MATCH function in cell H22:

```
=MATCH($F$22,$B$25:$B$46)
```

calculates the row number that matches DynamicNorth. The INDEX functions in row 18 then use that row number to retrieve the row of data that matches Dynamic and North. Cell E18, the first data cell, contains this formula:

```
=INDEX($B$25:$K$46,$H$22,E$24)
```

TIP Your list of data may contain more content than you need for searching. For example, suppose a column contains the combined text LastName, FirstName in a cell, but you want to search only by LastName. You would use the text functions LEFT, RIGHT, FIND, LEN, MID, &, and TEXT to extract the piece of text you need. Many examples of how to do this are available on the Internet.

Retrieving Multiple Rows Using a Single Keyword

A common need is to retrieve multiple rows of data when given a single keyword. For example, for a hospital you might select a clinical value, such as whether aspirin was administered for a heart attack on arrival. Then you would retrieve and chart three associated rows of data: the actual data, a benchmark derived from similar hospitals, and the level of aspirin on arrival recommended by an association. As in the previous example, this is done by concatenating multiple words, but the additional search terms, such as Actual, Benchmark, and Recommended, are hidden from the user.

Figure 18.5 shows a list of hospital clinical quality data. The list is in the range dbClinical and contains Actual, Benchmark, and Recommended data for each of 17 clinical measures. What is needed is a dashboard where the user can enter the desired measure so that the chart shows the associated data for Actual, Benchmark, and Recommended for the measure entered.

Figure 18.5: Retrieve multiple rows of data associated with an entered key by using fixed keys hidden from the user.

Each measure in dbClinical has three entries, one each for Actual, Benchmark, and Recommended data. The measure's name is in column D or column 2 of dbClinical. Whether the data is Actual, Benchmark, or Recommended is entered in column E or column 3 of dbClinical.

The key used to identify each unique row of data is in column C and is created by concatenating D and E. For example, C28 contains

```
=E29&D28
```

and produces

```
ActualAspirin on Arrival
```

a unique key in the list.

To examine how this works, consider row 18. Table 18-2 shows what specific cells should contain if you enter Aspirin on Arrival in D23.

Cell C18 creates the lookup term for actual data by concatenating the fixed text Actual with the entered term Aspirin on Arrival to create the term ActualAspirin on Arrival, which can be found in column C. This is used to retrieve Actual data.

The MATCH function in D18 then uses ActualAspirin on Arrival to find the row that contains that term, row 3.

Cell E18 contains a text title, Actual, that the chart uses to create the legend.

Cell F18 retrieves the data from dbClinical for row 3 and column 4, Jan 09, in dbClinical. This formula is written with relative references so that it can be copied across to the right.

Table 18-2: Formulas Used to Retrieve Data and the Returned Value

CELL ADDRESS	CELL TITLE	FORMULA	RESULT
B18	Fixed Hidden Key	`Actual`	Actual
C18	Concatenated Key	`=B18&$D$23`	ActualAspirin on Arrival
D18	Matching Row	`=MATCH($C18,$C$26:$C$92,0)`	3
E18	Legend Titles	`Actual`	Actual
F18	Jan 09	`=INDEX(dbClinical, $D18,F$25)`	92.0%

Rows 19 and 20 use the same process to create a unique lookup term for Benchmark and Recommended data that matches Aspirin on Arrival.

The data series in the line chart are formatted so that only the Actual data shows a line. The other two series hide the line and show only the data markers. To do this, right-click a line and choose Format Data Series. The Format Data Series dialog box, shown in Figure 18.6, appears. Set Line Color as No line; this makes the line invisible and the markers visible. Select Marker Options, and select a marker size of approximately 10.

Figure 18.6: Create benchmark or target points by hiding the line and increasing the size of the data marker.

Retrieving Data with a Two-Way Lookup

Data may not always import with the structure or orientation you expect, and you don't want to develop a dashboard that requires manual intervention whenever it updates. You want a dashboard that can adjust for data where rows or columns are in the wrong order or where there are additional unexpected rows or columns.

The previous examples have shown how to calculate the row containing the data you want. In the following example, you will see how to calculate which column contains the correct data. Usually this technique is used to find the column containing a specific date header.

The example shown in Figure 18.7 uses MATCH to look across the list's column headings to find the appropriate column, just as MATCH was used to look down to find the appropriate row.

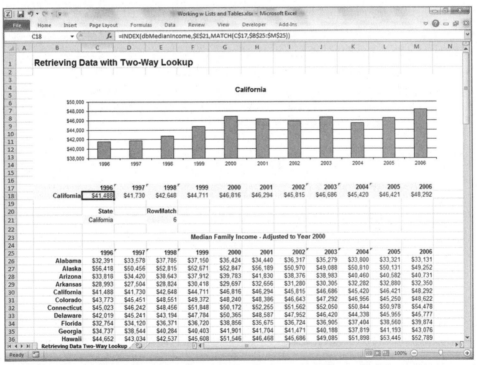

Figure 18.7: A dashboard that accepts data with rows and headings in any order uses MATCH to find the data row and header column.

Consider the INDEX function in C18:

```
=INDEX(dbMedianIncome,$E$21,MATCH(C$17,$B$25:$M$25))
```

It looks in the array dbMedianIncome across row 3, which is found in E21, as shown earlier.

The column for the data in C18 should match the heading 1996 in C17. So MATCH looks for a match to C17 in the row of date headings in B25:M25. The match is column 2 of dbMedianIncome, with the heading 1996.

Summary

A critical part of developing interactive dashboards is being able to retrieve only the data that interests you, in a layout that makes sense. Using the methods described in this chapter, you can have a workbook that contains hundreds or thousands of rows of data imported from or linked to a database. If you use the INDEX and MATCH functions, you can give your dashboard users the power to extract just the data they want or sort on just the column they want.

Initially the INDEX and MATCH functions seem as if they are more work than a simple VLOOKUP, but they actually are more flexible, allow greater functionality, and are less prone to errors. After you've used them a few times, you will find them as easy to understand as VLOOKUP, and well worth learning.

Excel's most powerful analytic features are the PivotTable and PowerPivot. Using a PivotTable's GETPIVOTDATA function or PowerPivot's Data Analysis Expressions (DAX), you can combine analytic power and the ability to select and lay out data as you want. You'll learn more about these topics in Chapters 21 and 22.

CHAPTER 19

Creating Miniature Charts and Tables

Good business leaders create a vision, articulate the vision, passionately own the vision, and relentlessly drive it to completion.

—Jack Welch, 1935
Chairman and CEO of GE

When possible, business dashboards should have the information necessary for a business decision on a single information-rich dashboard. Most often you need dashboards that show just the critical few metrics, but for some dashboards and for highly experienced decision-makers, you want to create information-rich dashboards. To do so, you can't use glitzy gauges or large charts; what you need are sets of miniature charts that fit in a single display.

Balanced Scorecards show a collection of information related to the drivers and success of an organization's strategy. If you want to see all of these metrics at one time, and any related trends and alerts as well, you need to use miniature charts arrayed on a larger scorecard. As illustrated in Chapter 30, clicking the titles of these miniature charts drills down to detailed charts and data.

Miniature charts are not used for a detailed examination of data values. Rather, by putting numerous miniature charts in one display, you can see many trends, relationships between many metrics, and proximities to target values.

Using Miniature Charts, Tables, and Sparklines for Greater Information Density and Improved Layout

When you try to put multiple Excel charts on a dashboard, you find that you can put about four charts on a dashboard just by reducing the size of a normal chart. However, when you need more than four charts on a screen, the chart's content becomes so crowded that it is difficult to read. Figure 19.1 shows 17 miniature charts used to give a summary overview for a Balanced Scorecard or executive dashboard. As other chapters explain, each of these miniature charts is live. You also can add a hyperlink to drill down to more detailed charts.

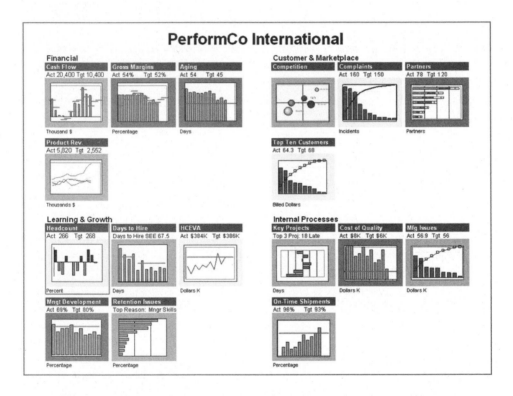

Figure 19.1: One use for miniature charts is to show a summary overview in Balanced Scorecards or executive dashboards.

Another situation where you need miniature charts is when you have tables of data and you want a chart adjacent to them to show relationships and trends. Miniature charts can fit perfectly next to tables. Figures 19.2 and 19.3 show pages from printed reports using miniature charts next to supporting data.

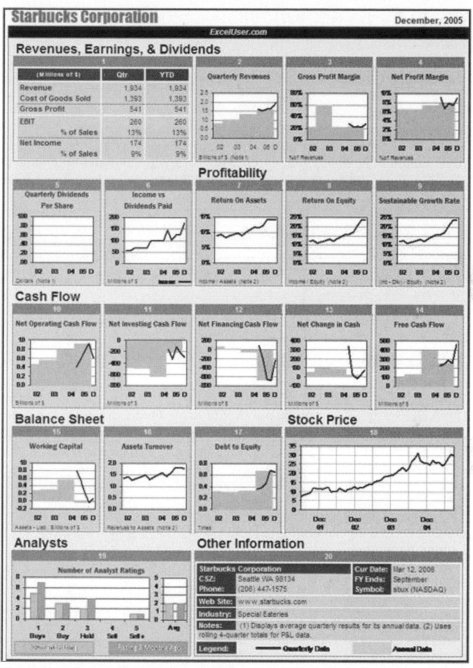

Figure 19.2: Seeing relationships and trends across related metrics enables you to form a mental model for different aspects of your business.

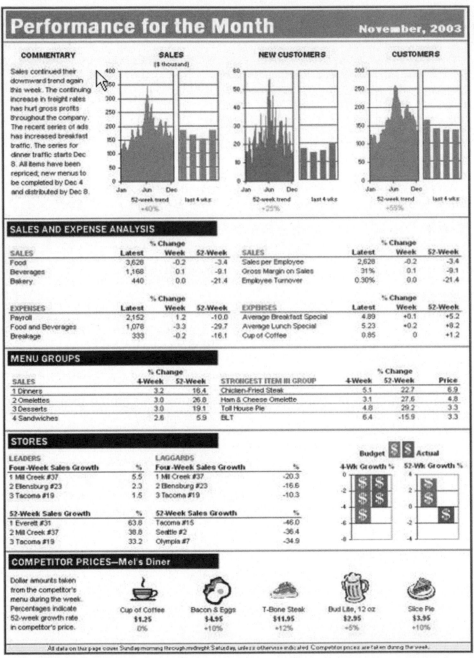

Figure 19.3: Miniature charts enable you to create dashboards and reports with near-magazine layout quality.

LEARN MORE ABOUT MINIATURE CHARTS AND MAGAZINE-QUALITY REPORTS

Charles Kyd is a master at using Excel to convey a maximum amount of information in a minimum amount of printed space. He has perfected the art of creating, in his words, "magazine-quality" reports. Figures 19.2 and 19.3 are examples of his work.

Charley's website, http://www.exceluser.com, contains lots of tips on using Excel to create concise, high-quality reports. It also includes numerous articles about how to represent unique financial problems with Excel charts. You can sign up for his free ExcelUser newsletter at http://www.exceluser.com.

Charley has written e-books that contain additional tips on miniature charts and creating dashboards and that cover these topics:

- How to set up common y-axis scaling for multiple charts

- How to use the Camera tool to create stoplights

- Multiple methods of integrating data into Excel

- How to lay out magazine-quality reports

If you do a lot of financial reporting, you might also be interested in his Plug-N-Play Dashboard Kit. This kit contains preformatted tables, miniature charts, and multiple color schemes; all you add is data.

Please let Charley know I sent you. We started together as the first Microsoft consultants.

Creating Miniature Charts from Standard Excel Charts

Creating miniature charts from standard Excel charts is pretty straightforward. You just get rid of all the "chart junk" that doesn't add any communication value and then reduce the size. Although the process isn't complicated, a few tricks are helpful. Figure 19.4 shows a typical chart created (in Excel prior to Excel 2007) by selecting the data to be charted and pressing F11, the create chart key. Figure 19.5 shows a chart with the "chart junk" removed, prior to being reduced in size.

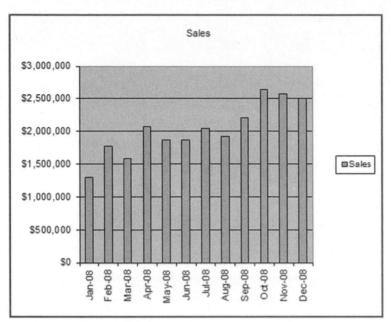

Figure 19.4: When charts are created with the default settings, they contain unnecessary "chart junk."

Figure 19.5: Miniature charts should show just the information they want to communicate. Remove all the clutter.

Removing Titles, Grid Lines, and Legends

Prior to its 2007 release, Excel created its default charts (like the one shown in Figure 19.4) with an unnecessary gray background that made them difficult to read. To remove the gray background, click the background and press Delete.

Now make the chart even more readable by removing the titles, grid lines, and legend. Miniature charts are often used adjacent to the data they represent; data represents only one or two data series, so the chart title and legend may be unnecessary. Deleting the title and legend helps reduce the size, because the fonts and legend do not adjust well when reduced and may require a lot of manipulation.

Grid lines also can be removed, because they do not convey information necessary for decision-making. If actual numeric values are needed, the chart should be accompanied by a table with numbers. To delete grid lines, click them and press Delete.

Legends also are unnecessary in miniature charts and Sparklines. Remove the legend by clicking it and pressing Delete.

At this point, your chart should look like the chart on the right in Figure 19.6.

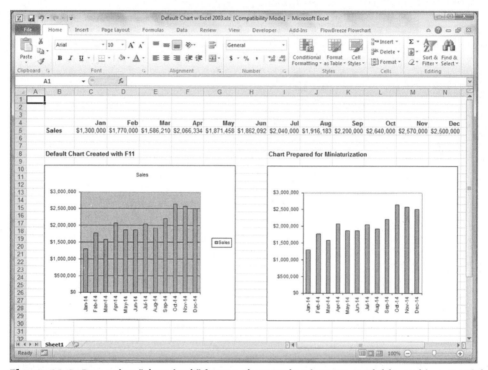

Figure 19.6: Removing "chart junk" from a chart makes it more readable and is essential before reducing its size.

Formatting the Y-Axis to Remove Unnecessary Scales and Width

At this point, you need to decide what you want to retain on the y-axis. Values along the edge of the y-axis on a full-sized chart are helpful when reading approximate values for data points. In miniature charts, values usually are unneeded; miniature charts are used primarily to see general trends, relationships with other trends, and proximity to target values.

Tick marks on the y-axis are the small dashes that appear on the axis. Like grid lines, tick marks are unnecessary, because users are looking at miniature charts for trends and relations, not to read data values.

To remove the values and tick marks, right-click the vertical or y-axis and choose Format Axis to display the Format Axis dialog box. If you do not want values to show, select the option for no tick marks on the major or minor axis. Figure 19.7 shows what the default chart looks like at this point, with y-axis values still displayed.

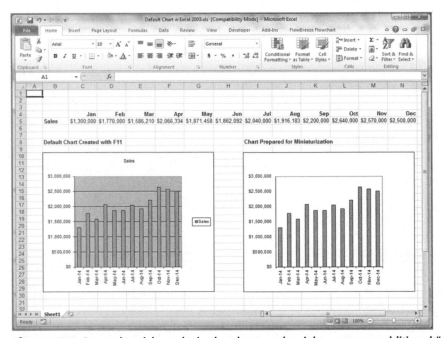

Figure 19.7: Removing tick marks in the chart on the right removes additional "chart junk," but you still need to manage the y-axis values.

Reducing the Size and Width of Y-Axis Numeric Values

You may want to keep y-axis values, but if you do, you need to reduce their size and width so that they don't take up unnecessary width and push the y-axis out of position. Here is how to reformat numbers on the y-axis so that they are narrower.

To make y-axis values like $1,500,000 appear shorter, such as $1,500, you can use a custom numeric format command. Right-click numbers on the y-axis to display the Format Axis dialog box, shown in Figure 19.8. Select the Number tab, and then select Custom from the Category list. In the Type box, type in the custom numeric format you want to appear on the y-axis. Click OK. Table 19-1 gives examples of custom formats. Notice that you can even create a custom format that automatically adds text to show your scaling value, such as K for thousands or M for millions.

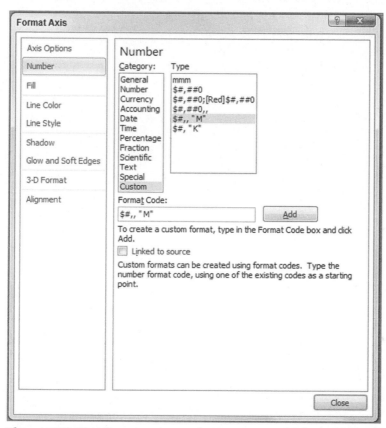

Figure 19.8: Use the same custom formats you use in the worksheet to modify displays on the x- and y-axes.

Table 19-1: Use Custom Numeric Formats to Scale Y-Axis Values

	ORIGINAL FORMAT AND Y-AXIS APPEARANCE	CUSTOM FORMAT AND Y-AXIS APPEARANCE
Currency shortened by thousands	$#,##0$2,000,000	$#,##0,$2,000
Currency shortened by millions	$#,##0$2,000,000	$#,,$2
Currency shortened and text added	$#,##0$2,000,000	$#,," M"$2 M

In Table 19-1, notice that custom formats have one or more trailing commas. The trailing comma tells Excel to drop a trailing three zeros. One trailing comma drops three zeros, and two trailing commas drops six zeros. You can add quoted text at the end of a custom format for text to appear after the number. In this example the M indicates millions. You can further reduce y-axis width by not adding a text label of K or M to every number, as shown in the last custom format, but instead creating a floating label with $M that appears at the top of the y-axis.

At this point the chart is using a $#,, custom format, as shown in Figure 19.9.

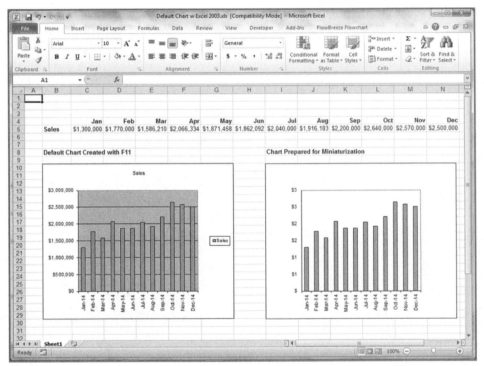

Figure 19.9: Reduce the width of values on the y-axis by using custom labels.

The chart on the right in Figure 19.9 contains repeated y-axis values. You need to eliminate ones that are showing for the half-scale values. Also, a small chart doesn't need all the values along the y-axis. Often just a top and bottom value are needed to give a sense of proportion. You can take care of either of these using the Scale tab in the Format Axis dialog box.

To adjust which numbers appear on the y-axis, display the Format Axis dialog box again by right-clicking the y-axis. In Excel 2007 and Excel 2010, select Axis Options. In Excel 2003, select the Scale tab, shown in Figure 19.10. In all of the versions, select Fixed for the Maximum, Major unit, and Minor unit boxes, and clear their values. These boxes tell Excel to automatically format the scales. For the example shown in Figure 19.10, a maximum value at the top of the y-axis is set to 3,000,000. To use a minimum number of extra numbers on the scale, show the value at every 1,000,000 point. Enter **1000000** in the Major unit box, as shown in Figure 19.10. Click OK to see a chart that looks like the one shown in Figure 19.11.

Figure 19.10: Clear the check boxes and use large major unit values on the Scale tab to remove unnecessary numbers along the y-axis.

Formatting the X-Axis

As you can see in Figure 19.11, the x-axis is crowded. Reducing the chart's size would make the x-axis look even worse. Luckily, there are a couple of ways to handle this. One of the easiest methods is to reformat the numeric values on the x-axis to a display format with a smaller size.

To reformat the x-axis so that it displays every other month on the x-axis, as shown in Figure 19.12, right-click the x-axis to display the Format Axis dialog box. In Excel 2007 and Excel 2010, select Axis Options. In Excel 2003, select the Scale tab. Clear the Major unit and Minor unit boxes. Enter **2** in the Major unit box. Click OK.

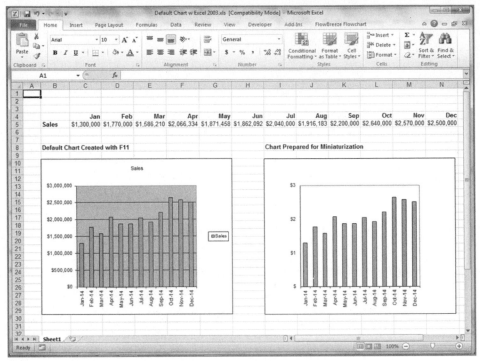

Figure 19.11: The chart on the right is almost ready to be reduced in size.

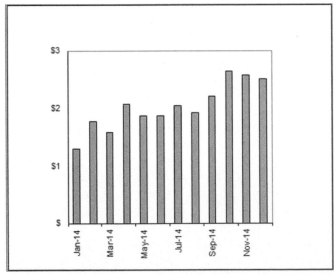

Figure 19.12: Display every other month to create more space on the x-axis.

Displaying only every other month gives more space on the x-axis, but you can improve it more. Return to the Format Axis dialog box for the x-axis and select the Number tab. By entering a custom format, as you did for the y-axis, you can make the date displays appear in almost any format you want.

Select Custom from the Category list. In the Type box, enter **mmm** as the custom format. This displays a three-letter abbreviation for each month. For example, Mar-14 will now appear as Mar. Click OK.

Once there is room on the axis, you can change the dates to a horizontal orientation so that they are easier to read. Right-click the x-axis and choose Format Axis. Then choose the Alignment tab in the Format Axis dialog box and change the Text direction to Horizontal.

The x-axis should now look like the simplified version shown on the right in Figure 19.13.

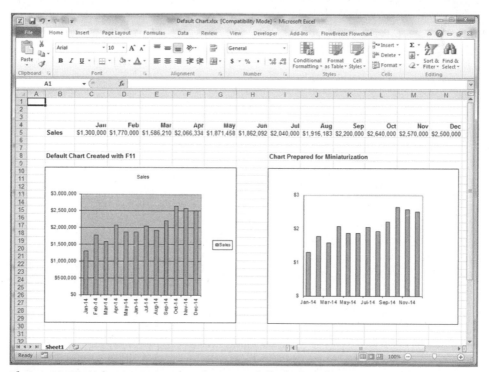

Figure 19.13: Using a custom date format and displaying alternating months makes the x-axis easier to read.

Make sure that the plot area of your chart completely fills the chart area. Click inside the plot area, and drag the corner handles as far to the corners as possible. This reduces the white space around the edges of the chart.

Finally, adjust the font sizes of the x- and y-axes so that they are legible. Usually an 8- or 9-point font will work.

You can now reduce the chart to miniature by dragging a corner of the chart. Hold down the Alt key as you drag to make the chart's corners align with cell corners. Figure 19.14 shows this example reduced in size. If you want to make the chart even smaller, eliminate the x- and y-axis fonts, or follow the steps described later in this chapter for creating a Sparkline.

TIP Some items in a chart are hard to select by clicking. They may be small or hidden. You can still select them. Click anything in the chart so that the selection handles (small black squares) show. Now slowly press any direction arrow key to move through all the selectable items in the chart until the one you want is selected.

In Excel 2007 and Excel 2010 there is an alternate method of selecting elements. Click on your chart, then select the Layout tab. At the far left on the ribbon is a drop-down selector. Open the drop-down selector to see and select any chart element.

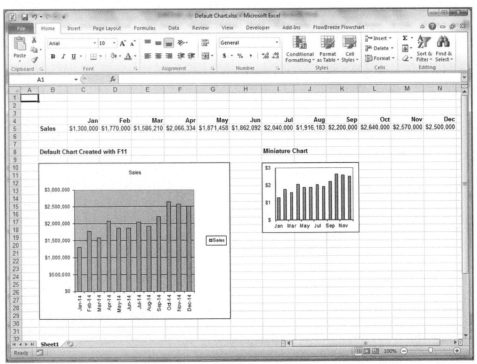

Figure 19.14: Use the Alt key while dragging to align miniature charts with cell corners.

Formatting Multiple Miniature Charts

It takes a lot of work to remove chart junk so that you can reduce a chart in size. Luckily, there is an easy way to duplicate this process for other charts.

Format multiple charts with your miniature formatting by first formatting one chart the way you want it. Select that chart and choose a copy command. Now select the other charts and in Excel 2007 or Excel 2010 in the Home tab, in the Clipboard group, choose Paste Special. In Excel 2003 choose Edit ➢ Paste Special. From the Paste Special dialog box, select Formats and then click OK. The charts you have selected change to match your master copy.

Creating Sparklines

Edward Tufte is an acknowledged thought leader in the visual display of information. One of his many innovations is the Sparkline. In Microsoft's interpretation of Sparklines, each miniature chart fits within a cell. This makes it easy to show a pleasing trend or win/loss chart adjacent to the data it represents.

Tufte's premise is that many charts are used to show trends or relative changes. Sparklines are line charts reduced to show just that trend or relationship. Sparklines are usually presented in the context of textual discussion or tables so that specifics are available if needed. Figure 19.15 shows the previous example reduced to a Sparkline chart.

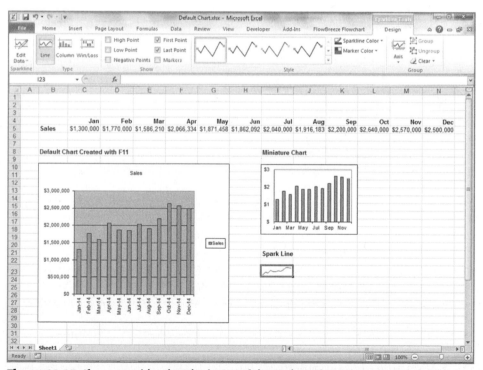

Figure 19.15: If you consider that the intent of these charts is to convey a trend, it becomes obvious that a Sparkline serves your purpose well without taking up a lot of space.

So when should you use Sparklines and when should you use miniature charts? Sparklines are excellent for displaying a trend or win/lose in a cell next to the data it represents. You can fit many Sparklines on a screen or printed page. Figure 19.16 shows a sales chart that enables a sales manager to quickly see who is meeting sales goals, their trend, and their win/loss.

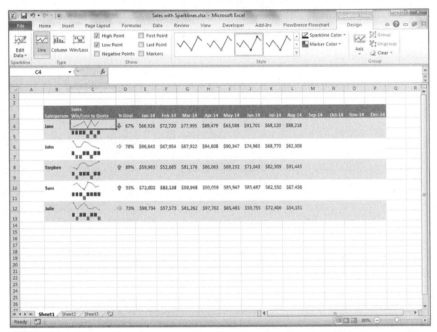

Figure 19.16: Sparklines are great for showing trends or win/loss in a small amount of space.

Consider using miniature charts instead of Sparklines when you need a small chart showing multiple sets of data and when your chart requires legends or titles.

LEARN MORE ABOUT EDWARD TUFTE

You can learn more about Edward Tufte, Sparklines, and the visual display of information at `http://www.edwardtufte.com`. It is an intriguing site with lots of content about the visual display of information. For information specific to Sparklines, search for the article titled "Sparklines: theory and practice."

If you use Sparklines, take pity on people over 40 and those who wear glasses. Colored lines may be visible in large charts, but colored lines, especially red hues, can be difficult to differentiate in miniature charts. Color your lines with darker hues such as black and blue.

Sparklines are easy to create in Excel 2007 and Excel 2010. To create them in Excel 2010, select the cells containing the data. On the Insert tab, in the Sparklines group, click the type of chart you want. Your choices are line, column, or win/loss. In the Create Sparklines dialog box, shown in Figure 19.17, the data range appears in the Data Range box. Select the Location Range box, click the cell where you want the Sparkline, and click OK.

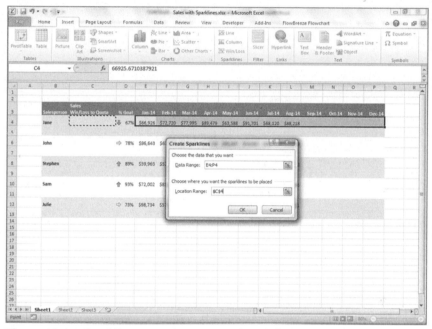

Figure 19.17: Sparklines are easy to create in Excel 2010.

Win/loss charts are used to give an overall impression of winning or losing. They show a positive or negative bar relative to positive or negative data, but all bar lengths are the same.

SPARKLINES FOR EXCEL 2007 AND EARLIER

Sparklines are only built in to Excel 2010. They are not a standard feature of Excel 2007 and earlier versions. However, a couple of add-in packages for earlier versions of Excel are equivalent to Excel 2010 and more. To see reviews of these latest packages, check my website, http://www.criticaltosuccess.com.

Sparklines created in Excel 2007 and Excel 2010 will not show up in earlier versions of Excel. They do not even show as a picture, but show instead as a blank. If you need to create Sparklines that are compatible in all versions of Excel use either the text-based charts described in Chapter 15, miniature charts as described in this chapter, or one of the add-in packages that create Sparklines compatible with all Excel versions.

Modifying or Deleting Sparklines

Sparklines intentionally do not have a lot of elements. Their purpose is to show a clean and clear representation of a trend. However, you can add design elements to Sparklines to highlight important data points.

You can change between Sparkline types by selecting the cell containing the Sparkline. On the Sparkline Tools Design tab, in the Type group, select the new chart type.

If you need to change the size of the data series or where the chart is located, select the cell containing the chart. Then, in the Sparkline group on the left, select Edit Data.

Add markers to indicate high, low, and other data points by selecting from the check boxes in the Show group.

After you have selected markers, you can choose the line, bar, or marker colors from the Style list. Create your own custom color combinations using the Sparkline Color and Marker Color lists.

To delete a Sparkline, select the cell containing the Sparkline. Then, on the Design tab, in the Group group, click Clear.

Sparkline Tricks

If you have a series of Sparklines that all have the same data configuration and format, you don't have to re-create each Sparkline. You can copy and paste to create additional Sparklines if the data is in the same relative location.

When you want to copy and paste a Sparkline into another application, such as Microsoft PowerPoint, copy the Sparkline by clicking the arrow next to the Copy icon on the Home ribbon. Select Copy as Picture. Then Paste into the other application.

If you want to create a group of Sparklines that are adjacent and act in the same manner, select all the cells where the Sparklines will appear. On the Insert tab, in the Sparkline group, choose the Sparkline you want. When the Create Sparklines dialog box appears, select the range containing all the data cells for all the Sparklines, as shown in Figure 19.18. Click OK.

You can control the x-axis and y-axis appearance of Sparklines that are created in a group. This enables you to show the same vertical and horizontal scales for all Sparklines. This is important because normally the scale for each Sparkline is unique to that Sparkline. When each Sparkline uses its own scale, more detail is shown. However, when each scale is different, it's impossible to compare relative change between Sparklines. For example, two charts that each use unique scales may look the same but be very different. One may have a y-axis scale from 0 to 500, and the other a scale from 0 to 2,000. If you want to compare them, they should have the same vertical scale.

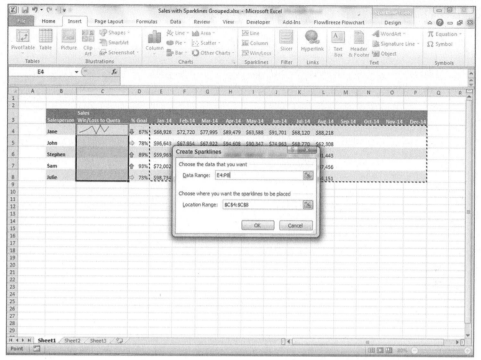

Figure 19.18: Create and format adjacent groups of Sparklines.

To control the behavior of scales in a group, select the group of Sparklines. Then, on the Sparkline Tools Design tab, in the Group group, click Axis. Select from the options shown in Figure 19.19 to control the behavior of the Sparklines in the group.

Figure 19.19: Control the behavior of axis in a group of Sparklines using the Axis options.

Excel's Amazing Camera Tool

Hidden deep within Excel is the Camera tool. Once you learn the pathway to the Camera tool, you can access its powers. The Camera tool enables you to escape the positioning limits of Excel's dashboard and report layouts. It acts like a television camera that lets you see and reposition views into other parts of your workbook. As shown in Figure 19.20, the Camera tool enables you to create dashboard layouts using tools normally reserved for photos. And when you update the worksheet cells or dashboard, the Camera object updates as well.

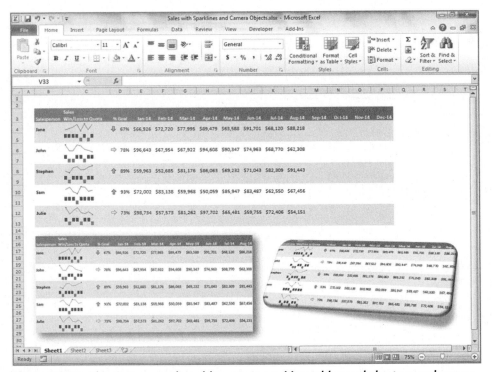

Figure 19.20: The Camera tool enables you to position tables and charts anywhere as well as apply picture formats and cropping.

With the Camera tool, you can do the following:

- Create pictures that are live windows to another worksheet.
- Arrange live pictures of charts and tables unhampered by row height or column width.
- Shrink or magnify charts and tables.
- Rotate sections of a worksheet or chart.

TIP Dashboards and reports look more professional when all the elements are aligned horizontally and vertically. To make sure you align chart or picture corners, and therefore the edges, hold down the Alt key while dragging the corner handle of a chart or picture. Holding down the Alt key forces an object's corners to align with the nearest cell corner.

If you want to align objects manually and the edge is not at a cell corner, use the Zoom button or View Zoom to magnify the worksheet to 200% or 300% and then position the elements you want to align. Select the object and then use the arrow keys to move it, rather than the mouse. The magnified view enables you to see smaller imperfections in alignment.

Camera objects can be resized and cropped like any picture. This makes them handy for positioning adjacent charts and tables that would be impossible to align using a normal sheet layout.

Taking Pictures with the Camera Tool

The Camera tool is easy to use. You select a portion of a worksheet, take a picture with the Camera, and then paste the live picture in another location.

It is like having a video camera trained on the area you took a picture of. Anything that changes in the original area is shown in the picture. Everything in the range you select appears in the picture, and when any change occurs, it is reflected in the Camera's picture.

You can move the Camera's picture after you have pasted it by dragging it as you would any drawn object.

You can capture a picture using keystrokes:

1. Select the range you want pictured.

2. Right-click on it and choose Copy.

3. Select a cell where you want the Camera picture.

4. In Excel 2007 and Excel 2010, on the Home tab, in the Clipboard group, click the down arrow on the Paste button. In the Other Paste Options, select Linked Picture. In Excel 2003, hold down the Shift key as you choose Edit ➢ Paste Picture Link.

You can also add a Camera tool to your toolbars. The Camera tool is accessible in two ways: either through the menu, while holding down the Shift key, or via a button you can add to a toolbar.

To add the Camera button to a toolbar in Excel prior to Excel 2007, follow these steps:

1. Choose Tools ➢ Customize.

2. Select the Commands tab, and then select Tools from the Categories list.

3. Scroll through the Commands list until you see the Camera.

4. Click and drag the Camera onto a toolbar, and drop it between two existing buttons.

5. Click Close.

Follow these simple steps to capture a picture:

1. Select the range you want pictured.

2. Click the Camera tool.

3. Click in the same workbook where you want the upper-left corner of the picture.

4. When the picture appears, you can drag it to a new location like any drawing object. You can resize it by dragging a handle on the edge of the object. You can rotate it by dragging the rotate handle.

USING THE CAMERA TOOL IN EXCEL 2010 AND EXCEL 2007

The Camera tool is also available in Excel 2010 and Excel 2007 to move onto a ribbon. In Excel 2010, in the File tab (the Office button in Excel 2007), select Options. Select the Customize ribbon or the Quick Access Toolbar. In the Excel Options dialog box, in Choose commands from, select the Camera tool and add it to the ribbon on which you want it to appear.

TIP If you captured too large or too small a range with the Camera tool, you can increase the "view" of the picture you have already taken without reshooting it. Display the Picture toolbar, click the crop tool, and then use the crop tool to drag the picture's edge or corner. The view of the source worksheet shown in the picture expands correspondingly.

Using Camera Pictures of Charts, Tables, and Miniature Charts

With the Camera tool, you can take a picture of anything in or over a range of cells. Your picture can include cell contents, a chart, multiple charts, or charts and tables.

TIP The Camera tool does an excellent job of maintaining fonts and proportions when shrinking charts, but don't expect it to make a readable miniature chart from a large chart containing titles, legends, and backgrounds. When you make a miniature chart, it is best if the large chart being captured has its elements reduced to a minimum using the methods described at the beginning of this chapter.

The Camera tool takes a picture of everything over a range of cells. For example, to take a picture of a chart, do not select the chart itself; select the cells behind the chart. Take the picture using one of the methods described earlier, and then paste the picture on a worksheet, where you can move it as needed.

You can position a Camera picture without regard to rows or columns. Change the size of a Camera picture by dragging a corner. This enables you to create miniature "detail" boxes alongside data in a report, as you might see in a magazine layout.

Treat Camera pictures as you would any picture pasted into Excel. When you select the Camera picture, the Picture Tools Format tab becomes available, and you can format the Camera picture with shading, 3D perspective, picture frames, and more. You can even crop it.

Simultaneously Formatting the Size of Multiple Charts or Camera Pictures

In most arrangements of charts and miniature charts, you want all of them to be the same size. There are two ways to do this quickly. The first way is useful if you have a few charts and you want to arrange them in free form, with no alignment to rows and columns. To do this, select all the charts using Ctrl+click. Right-click one of the selected charts and choose Format Object. Select the Size tab and then set the Height and Width in either the Size and Rotate or Scale groups. All selected charts change size. To make further changes, you must repeat the process.

The second method works well when you have many mini-charts you want to arrange and keep aligned with rows and columns. This method also enables you to easily experiment with different heights and widths by changing all the charts' heights and widths at the same time.

In this method, you "embed" mini-charts in the cells of a row or column and then adjust their sizes by changing row height or column width. For example, if you have multiple mini-charts you want aligned vertically, put them in the same column. Drag the mini-charts over each cell in the column where you want a mini-chart. Align the corners of each chart with the cell under it by holding down the Alt key and dragging the chart corner to snap to the cell corner. Each mini-chart should now exactly cover the cell. Don't worry about chart height—that will be adjusted later.

Now change the mini-chart's properties so that they stay the same size as the cells they cover. To do this, select all the mini-charts using Ctrl+click. Right-click a selected mini-chart and choose Format Object. Select the Properties tab, select Move and Size with Cells, and click OK. All mini-charts now keep the size of the cells they cover.

Now format the heights of all the mini-charts by selecting all the rows containing mini-charts and dragging the row header to a new height. All mini-charts in a row keep the same height as you change the row height, and all mini-charts in a column keep the same width as you change the column width.

The Dark Side of Excel's Camera Tool

Even though the Camera tool is an instrument of power, it has a dark side. The Camera tool has two nasty personality problems you should be aware of before using it.

In every Excel version since Excel 2000, linked pictures created with the Camera tool have acted quirky for some computer and printer combinations. If you have a certain combination of computer and printer and you print a page containing a picture linked to a worksheet area or chart, the linked picture may resize or disappear. This doesn't happen for all computer and printer combinations. On some of my computers it works fine, and on others it doesn't.

Microsoft doesn't seem to know how to fix this problem, because it has had a warning about the problem in its knowledge base since Excel 2000. This problem occurs only with linked Camera objects, which are the most useful type. To learn more about this problem, go to the Microsoft Support Developers Network at http://msdn.microsoft.com and search for the knowledge base article ID 211633 or the title "XL 2000: Linked Picture of Cells Changes Size with Print Quality."

Another issue with the Camera tool is that putting a large number of Camera pictures on a page slows recalculation. This is a hindrance, but you can turn off worksheet calculation. In Excel 2007 and Excel 2010 on the Formulas tab, in the Calculation group, select Calculation Options. Select Automatic for calculations to automatically refresh. Choose Manual to stop automatic calculation. In Excel 2003, choose Tools ➢ Options and select Manual on the Calculation tab. Pressing F9 forces a recalculation.

The Camera tool in Excel 2010 is less quirky than previous versions. Search the Internet for "Excel 2010 camera bug" to find issues and workarounds as we learn more.

Summary

Miniature charts, Sparklines, and camera pictures are essential to creating an information-rich display. You want a display where all information that is vital to decision-making can be grasped quickly.

An important lesson to take from this chapter is that you should eliminate nonessential information from your charts. Doing so enables you to present critical information for decision-making.

Controlling Charts with Menus, Combo Boxes, and Buttons

The vision is really about empowering workers, giving them all the information about what's going on so they can do a lot more than they've done in the past.

—Bill Gates
Founder of Microsoft

Microsoft Excel allows you to create a user interface for your scorecards and dashboards that looks and operates like any Windows application. You can add several kinds of controls to your scorecards and dashboards: lists, combo boxes (also called drop-down lists), scroll bars, and option buttons. As shown in Figure 20.1, with the addition of combo boxes, check boxes, and option buttons, you can make your dashboards more interactive and easier to use and prevent many errors. In Chapter 20 you will learn how to add these user controls to your dashboards. They will make your dashboards easier to use and reduce the mistakes users make.

Chapter 18 describes how to select data from a database and manipulate it by using INDEX and MATCH. Now, by combining INDEX and MATCH with controls, you can create interactive charts, data selectors, scrolling charts, and more that any level of user can operate.

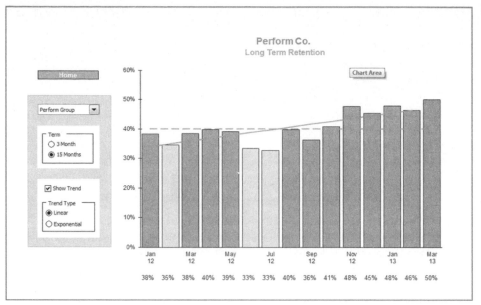

Figure 20.1: By combining combo boxes, option buttons, and check boxes, you help your users easily interact with the scorecards and dashboards you create.

Adding Combo Boxes, Lists, Check Boxes, and More to Your Dashboards

As shown in Figure 20.1, you can add many controls to your dashboards: menu buttons, check boxes, option buttons, list boxes, combo boxes, scroll bars, and spinners. There are many form controls, and they all work in a similar way.

Form controls are not automatically available in Excel 2007 and Excel 2010. To use them in Excel 2007 and Excel 2010, you must enable the Developer tab.

In Excel 2010, select File ➢ Options. Under Customize the Ribbon, select Main Tabs or All Tabs, and then select the Developer tab check box. Click OK.

In Excel 2007, click the Microsoft Office button, and then click the Excel Options button. On the Popular tab, select the Show Developer tab in the ribbon check box. Click OK.

To insert a form control when using Excel 2007 or Excel 2010, on the Developer tab, in the Controls group, click the Insert button, and then select the form control you want. Click and drag in the worksheet where you want the control.

To format a control in Excel 2007 or Excel 2010, right-click the control and then select Format Control to display the Format Control dialog box. This chapter's instructions on formatting controls apply to Excel 2007 and earlier versions of Excel.

BE CAREFUL WHEN SELECTING FORM CONTROLS

There are two sets of similar looking icons, Form Controls and ActiveX Controls. These icons appear next to each other when you are inserting a form in Excel 2007 or Excel 2010. Unless you are programming in Excel VBA you will want to use Form Controls. ActiveX Controls are more customizable, but they are more complicated to use.

In Excel 2003, you must display the Forms toolbar, shown in Figure 20.2. To do so, choose View ➢ Toolbars ➢ Forms. Table 20.1 describes each of the form controls displayed on the toolbar.

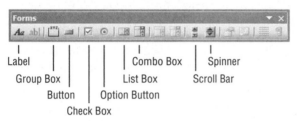

Figure 20.2: The Forms toolbar enables you to drag and drop controls onto your worksheets.

To draw a form control, display the Forms toolbar, click the toolbar icon you need, and then click the worksheet where you want your form control.

Table 20.1: Controls Available in Forms

FORM	DESCRIPTION
Label	Adds a floating text box.
Group box	Draws a box with an editable title. Use this tool to enclose multiple option buttons so that only one option button in the box can be selected at a time.
Button	Draws a button that runs a macro.
Check box	Draws a single check box with an editable title. When selected, it enters TRUE in the linked cell; when deselected, it enters FALSE. Check boxes are independent of each other.
Option button	Draws a single option button (radio button). Place multiple option buttons within a group box so that only one option button can be selected from within the group. The selected button inserts its rank order into the linked cell. (Selecting the third button, for example, puts 3 in the linked cell.) Option buttons normally are used in place of a combo box or lists when there are three or fewer items.

Continued

Table 20.1 (continued)

FORM	DESCRIPTION
List box	Contains a list within a cell range on the worksheet. Selecting an item from the list inserts that item's numeric position in the list into the linked cell.
Combo box	These drop-down lists have the functionality of a list box but require little screen space when they are not in use.
Scroll bar	These are like the scroll bars on the side or bottom of the Excel worksheet. Use a scroll bar to quickly "drag" from one end of a numeric range to another. Scroll bars are good when someone wants to test numerous approximate numeric entries. Once the range is found from dragging the slider, the exact number can be entered manually if needed. The "thumb" is the small movable box within a scroll bar. Dragging the thumb within the scroll bar inserts a number into a cell. You can control the number's range. When you create a scroll bar, the direction in which you initially drag to create the shape determines whether it is vertical or horizontal.
Spinner	These vertical up and down arrows enable you to quickly "spin" through numbers. Unlike the scroll bar, which allows large jumps between numbers, the spinner increments through every number in its range. The numeric result from the spinner is inserted into a linked cell.

To move, resize, or format a form control, you must first select it. This may cause you some confusion at first, because clicking some controls checks or unchecks the check box, selects an option button, or selects an item from a list. To select a form control so that you can move or format it, hold down the Ctrl key and click the form control.

Drag a form control after it is selected by dragging the hatched outside border. To format a form control, right-click the edge of the control and select Format Control. To delete a control, select it and press Delete.

TIP You can align form controls with cell corners so that multiple controls are in vertical and horizontal alignment. To align controls, select them, and then, as you drag a selection handle, hold down the Alt key. This forces that selection handle to align with cell boundaries.

To modify a form control, right-click the edge of the form control and choose Format Control from the context menu. In the Format Control dialog box, all form controls contain the same four tabs: Size, Protection, Properties, and Web. These are fairly self-explanatory. Most of the form controls also contain a tab named Control. The Control tab is where you specify such things as the list that will appear in a combo box and which cell will contain the output from a selection on the form control.

Each Control tab displays properties unique to each form control. Figure 20.3 shows the Control tab for the combo box. On this tab, specify the range containing the contents of the drop-down list, the output cell that will contain the result of a selection, and the number of items shown in the drop-down list when it is displayed.

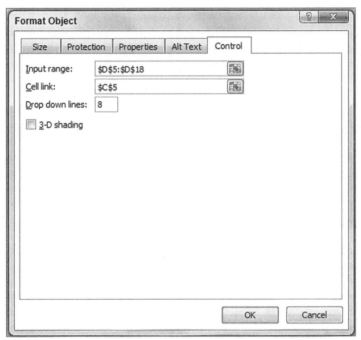

Figure 20.3: On the Control tab, you specify the input and output locations for a form control.

Selecting Data with a Combo Box or List

Using scrolling lists and combo boxes is an excellent way to let users select one item from a long list. Selecting from a list reduces data entry errors and enables users to see all alternatives instead of just what they remember. With scrolling lists you can create a short object onscreen that offers a long list of possible selections. Combo boxes are only one word high, but when selected they open to show a scrolling list. This saves considerable screen real estate.

> **TIP** If you would like to work with the examples in this book, check the Introduction for information on how to download the sample data and sample worksheets. These book files, additional resources, and more examples are available on my website, http://www.criticaltosuccess.com.

Figure 20.4 shows a combo box on a simple dashboard that enables users to select a U.S. state, retrieve that state's median family income from 1996 to 2006, and display that income on a chart.

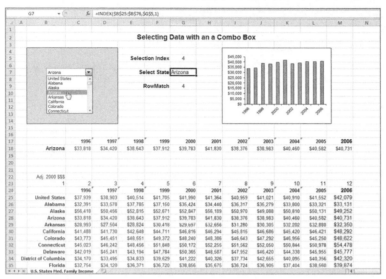

Figure 20.4: The row selected from the combo box identifies the row retrieved from the database.

To add the combo box and formulas that identify the selection, follow these steps:

1. Depending on your version of Excel, select the combo box from the Forms toolbar or Developers tab, and then choose the Controls group. The combo box shows a gray text entry area above a blank square that represents the list.

2. Drag in the worksheet where you want the combo box. Dragging creates the width and height of the combo box. If you click, you see just a large arrow. You can drag a corner of this arrow so that the combo box appears correctly.

3. Right-click the combo box and select Format Control to display the Format Control dialog box.

4. In the Input Range box, enter the range containing the items you want to appear in the drop-down list. In this case the items are the names of the states and the phrase United States in the range B25:B76.

5. In the Cell Link box, enter the cell where you want the number of the item selected from the list to appear. This is cell G5.

6. In the Drop Down Lines box, enter the number of lines you want displayed when the list drops down.

7. Click OK.

When you click the combo box after you create it, the drop-down list appears. Selecting an item from the list puts the number of that item's position in the list into cell G5. In some cases, you can use that position number directly to retrieve data; however, more often you will need to convert it into text so that it can be used with VLOOKUP or MATCH, as described in Chapter 18.

Here are the other formulas in the example that convert the selection, in G5, into the row of the database containing the selected state:

NAME	CELL	FORMULA	DESCRIPTION
Select State	G7	=INDEX($B$25:$B$76,$G$5,1)	INDEX finds the state name by looking down B25:B76 to the row returned in G5 by the combo box. Column 1 is specified in INDEX so that the first and only column will be looked at. An advantage of using INDEX instead of VLOOKUP is that you can look down any column in the table. It need not be just the first column.
Matching Row	G9	=MATCH($G$7,$B$25:$B$76,0)	MATCH uses the state's name in G7 to search down the first column of the database to find that state's corresponding row.

This example unnecessarily finds the row for the selected state using MATCH. You already know the row, because it is the same as G5. If you are performing a simple database retrieval task like this one, you can use G5 directly to retrieve data.

You need to use this system of matching with MATCH and INDEX if you are dealing with more complex situations in which the following conditions hold true:

- You need multiple drop-down lists to specify multiple criteria, as described in the section "Retrieving Data Given Multiple Keywords" in Chapter 18. (This is also explained in the following section.)

- You need one set of names displayed in the combo list, but the database contains another set of longer or more technical names. For example, a combo box might show English-language product names but the database contains products listed by a product identifier code.

Now that the row in the database is calculated—either from G5 for a simple situation, or by looking it up with MATCH, as in G9—you can retrieve the data from the database. The section in Chapter 18 titled "Adding a Drop-Down Selection List to Make Retrieval Easier" describes how to build this database and the retrieval formulas.

Basically, an INDEX function uses the row from G9 to retrieve a row of data from the database into the range B18:M18, where it is displayed in a chart. The following functions do this:

NAME	CELL	FORMULA	DESCRIPTION
Range Name	B24:M76	Db_MedianIncome	Range name containing the data.
Name of state retrieved from database	B18	=INDEX(db_ MedianIncome,$G$9+1,B$23)	INDEX retrieves the contents from the database at the intersection of the row G9+1 (plus one for the date header) and the column number in B23.
1996 data	C18	=INDEX(db_ MedianIncome,$G$9+1,C$23)	INDEX retrieves the contents from the database at the intersection of the row G9+1 (plus one for the date header) and the column number in C23.
Other data	D18:M18	Copy C18 across.	

Note that the row found in G9 must have 1 added to it to correspond to the database rows, because the database range, B24:M76, has an additional row at the top for the date headers. Row 23, above the database, has numbers entered for each column in the database. This makes it easy to copy the formula in C18 across to D18:M18. C$23 in the INDEX formula makes a relative reference adjustment as it is copied, so each copy refers to the correct column in the database.

LIST AND COMBO BOXES ARE SIMILAR BUT DIFFERENT

The list box is like a combo box, but a list box is always open. Users can scroll down the list to select the item they want. The Control tab for the list box has two additional options, Multi and Extend. These are available for use only through Visual Basic for Applications.

Selecting Data with Multiple Criteria Using Multiple Combo Boxes

You can select from a database using multiple criteria by using multiple combo boxes, lists, or other controls and then matching against a key column in your database created by concatenating keywords. This technique is often needed when your user must retrieve data from an Excel-based file that has hundreds or thousands of rows of information separated into categories.

In Figure 20.5, two combo boxes are used to retrieve a specific row from a database of 48 rows. Although this sample database is small, I've used the same technique to retrieve data from Excel-based lists with thousands of rows and several combo boxes.

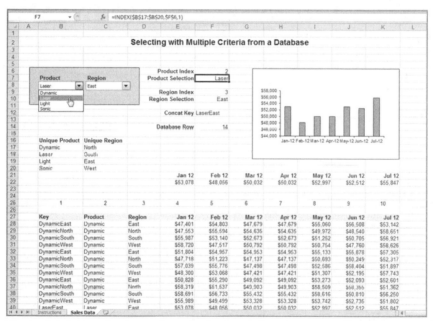

Figure 20.5: By using several combo boxes and a concatenated key, you can select data using multiple criteria.

In Figure 20.5, the Product combo box receives its list from B17:B20. The number of the product selected goes to cell F6. Cell F7 then converts this to text using this formula:

```
=INDEX($B$17:$B$20,$F$6,1)
```

The Region combo box receives its list from C17:C20. The number of the region selected goes to cell F9. Cell F10 then converts this to text using this formula:

```
=INDEX($C$17:$C$20,$F$9,1)
```

Cell F12 then concatenates, or joins, these two words to create a new keyword that will be matched against the contents in column 1 of the database. The concatenation formula in cell F12 is

```
=$F$7&$F$10
```

As explained in Chapter 18, you can use the concatenation function, &, to join words in the database so that each row has a unique identifier or key. In this case, the formula in B28:

```
=C28&D28
```

has been copied down column B to create a unique key for each row in the database. The MATCH function in cell F14:

```
=MATCH($F$12,$B$27:$B$75,0)
```

can then be used to find the unique row in the database by matching the concatenation of your combo box selections against the concatenation in column B of the database.

When to Use a Data Validation List or Combo Box

The data validation list, described in Chapter 18, allows you to create a cell that displays a list of choices when clicked. You also can type into the cell. In a data entry worksheet, I might use a data validation list, but in scorecards and dashboards I use a list or combo list.

These are the advantages of data validation:

- The user can type if desired, instead of selecting from a drop-down list.
- You can create an error message that warns if an entry is invalid.
- The result is text rather than an index number. (Depending on what you want to do, this can be an advantage or disadvantage.)

These are the disadvantages of data validation:

- Unless you give it special formatting, the data validation cell looks like a normal cell. Dashboard users may not know to click in the cell.
- Because the data entry box is a cell, it must be aligned with other cells.
- Data validation does not prevent Excel from accepting some instances of pasted data that are invalid.

These are the advantages of the combo box:

- It is obviously a drop-down list, and the user knows to click the down arrow.
- The user is forced to select items from a drop-down list, thus preventing errors.
- You can position it anywhere, regardless of cell alignment.
- You can attach a macro that triggers when the combo box is used.

These are the disadvantages of the combo box:

- If you are just looking for the text of the selection, a combo box requires a VLOOKUP or INDEX.
- No pop-up instructions or error messages appear unless you write a function to display them when a match is not found.

Creating Dynamic Cascading Combo Boxes or Lists

Cascading combo boxes or lists are useful when you have a very large list. Breaking this list into categories and items, with categories in one list and items in the other, results in a more usable system. In Figure 20.6, for example, a long list of hospital quality indicators has been separated into categories that appear in the Category list in the combo box at B6. Selecting from this Category combo box changes the contents of the Quality Metric combo box at F6. This is easier for users than scrolling through long lists.

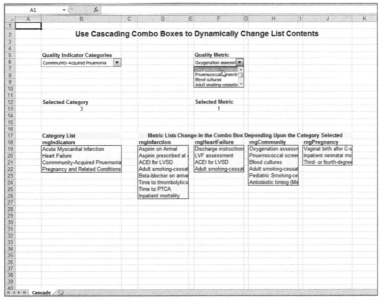

Figure 20.6: Cascading combo boxes allow you to present long lists by category and item within a category.

To create up to 29 cascading lists, use range names to name the lists that will appear in the combo box containing the list of items, not the Category combo box. In this example, four ranges are used: rngInfarction, rngHeartFailure, rng-Community, and rngPregnancy. An invisible dynamic range name is used to switch between these four range names depending on the number in cell B13. You change the number in B13 by selecting a category from the left category list in B6.

To create the invisible dynamic range name, do the following:

1. Create range names for each list that will appear in the combo box whose contents will change.

2. In Excel 2007, on the Formulas tab in the Defined Names group, click the Define Name button to display the Define Name dialog box. In Excel 2003, choose Insert ➢ Name ➢ Define Name. Figure 20.7 shows the completed dialog box.

3. Enter a name such as **rngComboList** in the Names in workbook entry box. This will be the name of a named formula. The contents of that named formula change depending on the value in cell B13.

Figure 20.7: Use the Define Name dialog box to create a new dynamic range name that changes lists depending on the category selection.

4. In the Refers to entry box, enter a CHOOSE formula that selects between the range names you have assigned to the lists. Here's the formula in the example:

```
=CHOOSE(Cascade!$B$13,rngInfarction,rngHeartFailure,rngCommunity,
rngPregnancy)
```

5. Click Add, and then click OK.

Within the input range for the combo box or list, you enter the dynamic range instead of a cell reference. In this example, you would enter **rngComboList** in the Input Range for the Quality Metric Combo Box.

The CHOOSE function uses the value in B13 from the Quality Indicator Categories combo box to select from a list of choices which range to display in the Quality Metric combo box. CHOOSE can handle up to 29 choices.

Using Option Buttons

Option buttons, also known as radio buttons, are the round buttons that appear in groups. Option buttons are no different from combo boxes or list boxes in that you can make only one selection at a time. Use option buttons when there are only two or three choices, and use combo boxes or lists when there are more than three choices.

You can select only one option button from a group at a time. If you put two or more sets of option buttons on a worksheet, they interfere with each other. To prevent groups from conflicting, put option buttons in groups by drawing a group box around each group of option buttons that you want to act as a single entity. The group box looks like a small box with an XYZ title. Drag the outline of the box so that it encloses all the option buttons in a group.

> **MAKE SURE ALL BUTTONS AND TITLES ARE INSIDE THE GROUP BOX**
>
> Make sure that option buttons and their text outline are completely enclosed inside the group box. This keeps the groups distinct so that only one option in a group can be selected. If even one pixel from an option button title is outside the group the option buttons will not operate correctly.

Title a group box by clicking in its title area and typing. You may need to add a few blank spaces after the title to ensure that the entire title appears.

Displaying or Hiding Data with a Check Box

It is easy to overwhelm a dashboard user with too much data. Initial requests for a dashboard sometimes include four data lines, a forecast line, and a target or benchmark all on the same chart. Of course, presenting that much information on one chart makes for a confusing presentation. Instead, you should design your charts so that they show just the information needed for decision-making. When additional data such as trend lines, forecasts, or comparative data is needed, design your dashboards so that additional data series can be displayed on demand. Here's how to do that.

Figure 20.8 revisits the chart of median family income by state. This time, a straight-line trend line is calculated in D19:M19. The FORECAST function in these cells references the data in D18:M18 so that the trend reflects the currently selected state.

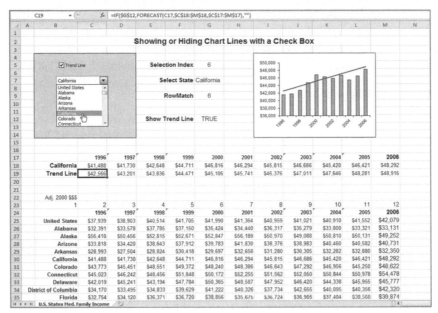

Figure 20.8: Selecting the Trend Line check box displays the trend line data in the chart.

The check box above the combo box returns TRUE or FALSE to cell G12, depending on whether the check box is selected or cleared. G12 is specified as the cell link in the Control tab for the check box.

An IF function in cells B19:M19 controls whether the contents of row 19 appear. The formula in cell C19 is

```
=IF($G$12,FORECAST(C17,$C$18:$M$18,$C$17:$M$17),"")
```

If G12 contains TRUE, the FORECAST function displays its results. If G12 is FALSE, nothing is displayed. If you want to make individual data points disappear in a line, use the NA function instead of "".

Scrolling Charts through Time with a Slider Bar

Data series spanning many years may have your dashboard users wishing they could scroll through time so that they can compare prior quarters and years. There is a way to do that—and to make it easy for users at the same time. Figure 20.9 again shows the median family income dashboard. A horizontal scroll bar has been drawn below the chart. Dragging the "thumb" in the scroll bar animates the chart so that it scrolls through the time span from 1996 to 2006. For demonstration purposes, this example has a short time frame, but the method is handy when you have many years or months of data.

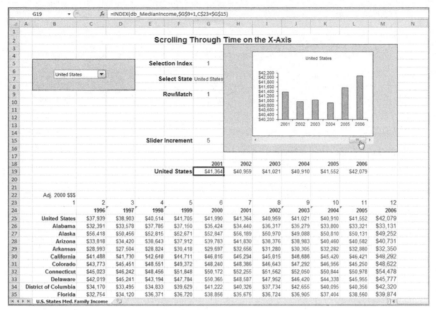

Figure 20.9: Use a horizontal scroll bar to scroll through a time series.

To draw a scroll bar in either the horizontal or vertical direction, click the scroll bar icon on the Forms toolbar. Then click and drag on the worksheet in the direction you want the scroll bar to appear.

The scroll bar shown in Figure 20.9 has the following values on its Control tab:

Minimum Value	0
Maximum Value	5
Incremental Change	1
Page Change	5

Dragging the slider's thumb changes the value in cell G15. The dates in G18:M18 and the data in G19:M19 change as the value in G15 changes. The first year's formula in cell G18 is

```
=INDEX($C$24:$M$24,1,$G$15+1)
```

The first data's formula in cell G19 is

```
=INDEX(db_MedianIncome,$G$9+1,C$23+$G$15)
```

In the INDEX formula, G15, which is the slider value, is in the column parameter of INDEX. A change to G15 increments the column referenced by INDEX.

Scroll bars can be used in other ways. The vertical scroll bar shown in Figure 20.10 produces the effect of scrolling through a financial statement.

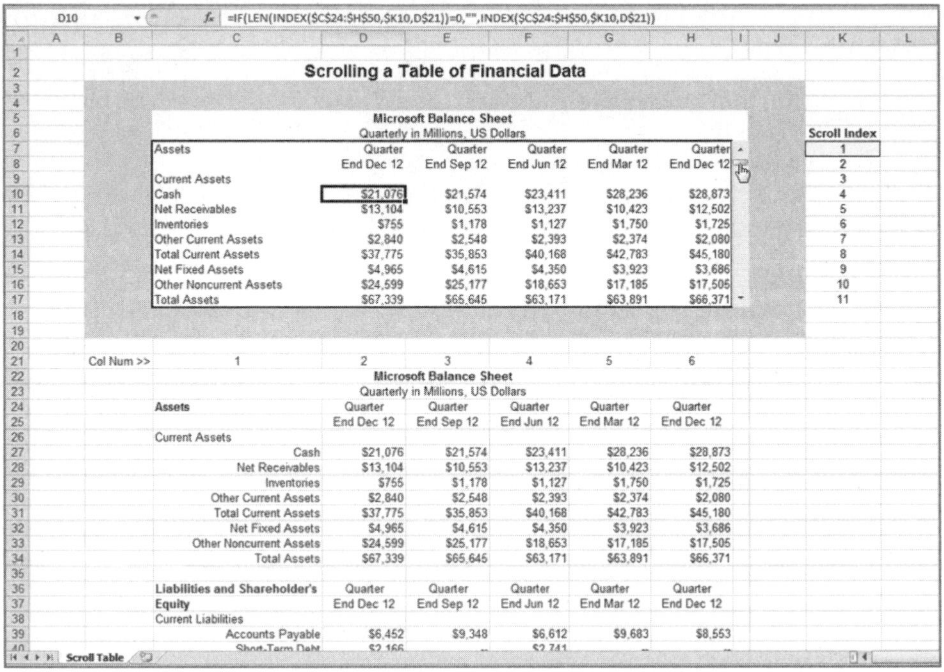

Figure 20.10: Here a vertical scroll bar enables users to scroll through a financial statement that is too large to appear in one screen.

For more tips on creating dashboards and scorecards in Excel, as well as for information on Balanced Scorecards and process mapping, go to http://www.criticaltosuccess.com.

Summary

With the use of form controls and good formatting, you can create dashboards and scorecards that look good, are easy to use, and help you make business decisions. The form controls are an excellent way to make your work professional-looking and easy to use.

CHAPTER 21

Working with PivotTables

What we see depends mainly on what we look for.
—John Lubbock
Biologist and politician
1834–1913

It's not hard to argue that PivotTables are the most powerful feature in Excel. What is amazing is that they are also one of the least-used features. Most Excel users have heard of them but have never used them.

If you have ever needed to analyze large amounts of data, such as building a summary table of sales by month, or doing statistical analysis on large lists, or finding the top 10 in a list, you would have benefited from knowing how to use PivotTables. All Excel users beyond novice level should at least learn the concept of a PivotTable so that they know when to use this powerful tool.

The power of PivotTables can have a big impact on accounting and finance people. I used to teach a course at Sonoma State University on computers and spreadsheets for finance and accounting. About a week after going through an exercise on PivotTables, I got a call from a small company's internal accountant, who sounded close to tears. She told me how she used to spend a day and a half at the end of each month building and rebuilding tables in Excel so that she could categorize revenue and expenses in different ways, "slice and dice," and do some auditing. With what she had recently learned about PivotTables, she had reduced that day and a half to less than an hour of work. She could use the rest of that time in more productive ways for her company. She was ecstatic!

The data that a PivotTable analyzes can be stored in a list on a worksheet, in a small Access database, or in a large SQL server. The end result is that with a few minutes' work, your worksheets can import data and summarize (and then display) it the way you want.

Basic Concepts of PivotTables

PivotTables take lists and databases, analyze the data, and then return it into an Excel worksheet summarized in the layout you specify. Figure 21.1 is a simple Excel list used in the examples in this chapter. It contains one header row and 624 rows of data covering product unit and dollar sales by region and date. To build a summary table from this, you would need to write complex SUMIF, COUNTIF, or any number of other statistical or financial formulas. And then, when you wanted a different view into the data, you would need to rewrite the formulas or conditions.

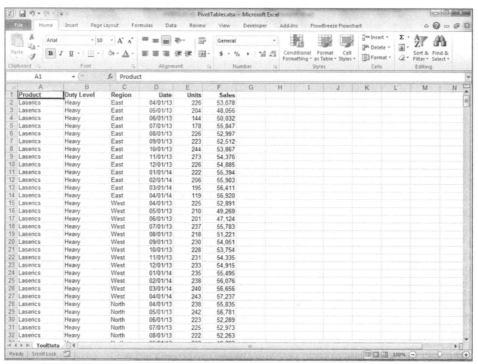

Figure 21.1: PivotTables are a powerful tool that can be used on Excel lists, such as the one shown, or on external databases.

With a PivotTable you can easily create a formatted table like the one shown in Figure 21.2 from the data shown in Figure 21.1. Building this table took no typing or formulas. It required a few clicks and drags for basic construction and layout. Another couple of clicks added the color and border formats and formatted the dates. What makes this even more powerful than using conditional consolidation formulas such as SUMIF and COUNTIF is that you can reorganize the table and solve for different analyses with just a few clicks.

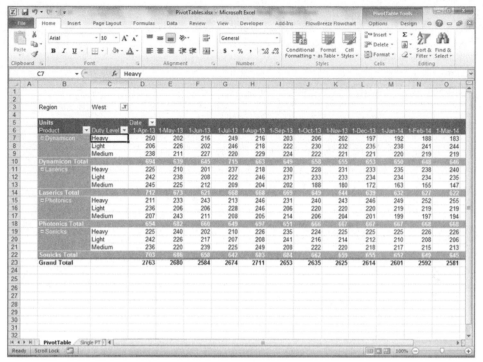

Figure 21.2: With a few clicks and drags, you can convert a list like the one shown in Figure 21.1 into a dynamic table like this.

PivotTables can access data from lists within an Excel worksheet or from relational databases. To connect to a relational database, you need to create an Office Data Connection to the database.

If you need to create a PivotTable that uses data from multiple databases you should explore using PowerPivot for Excel 2010. PowerPivot is described in Chapter 22. With PowerPivot you can connect to and join tables from multiple databases. PowerPivot is also extremely fast; it can analyze millions of rows of data in the same time it takes to recalculate a normal PivotTable. There are some trade-offs, however, so be sure to read the front section of Chapter 22 that describes the advantages and disadvantages of PowerPivot.

USING PIVOTTABLES WITH OLAP

If you want or need to use PivotTables with OLAP, check the Microsoft website for support and whitepapers.

WHERE TO LEARN ABOUT BUILDING PIVOTTABLES

This chapter is not an introduction to creating PivotTables. PivotTables are covered in most introductory Excel books, and many free resources are available on the web.

To learn more about PivotTables online, go to these sources:

- ▪ `http://www.ozgrid.com`: **Search for PivotTables.**

- ▪ `http://www.contextures.com` **is the website of Debra Dalgleish, author of multiple books on PivotTables.**

Creating an Auto-Expanding Database or List Name

If you are entering, retrieving, or storing data in Excel worksheets, before you create a PivotTable, you should create an automatically expanding name for the database (list) referenced by the PivotTable. (You don't have to do this, but it will save you work and potential errors when your database or list changes size.) Using an auto-expanding name allows you to add rows or columns of data, confident that they will be included in the PivotTable the next time it updates. There are two ways to do this. If you plan to use the list for only data entry and database reporting, you can change the list to an Excel table. This process is described briefly in this chapter and in more detail in Chapter 18. If you plan to use the database for PivotTables, reports, and dynamic charts, use an auto-expanding range name.

DOWNLOAD THE SAMPLE DATA AND SAMPLE FILES

Check the Introduction of this book for instructions on how to download the sample data and sample files to work along with the instructions in this book. The Introduction also contains links to additional resources for developing Balanced Scorecards and operational dashboards.

To change your database or list into an Excel table in Excel 2007 or Excel 2010, do the following:

1. Select a cell in the list or database.

2. On the Insert tab, in the Tables group, select Table.

3. Click OK in the Create Table dialog box.

4. Assign a name to the table. On the Table Tools Design tab, in the Properties group, in the Table Name field, enter a descriptive name for this list that you will recognize, such as tblProducts.

Follow these steps to create an auto-expanding range name for your data:

1. Enter your data on a new worksheet starting at cell A1. Enter headings in row 1. Enter only the database on this worksheet.

2. In Excel 2007 and Excel 2010, on the Formulas tab, in the Defined Names group, select Define Name. In Excel 2003, choose Insert ➤ Name➤ Define. This opens the New Name or Define Name dialog box.

3. Define a calculated range name. Figure 21.3 shows the new range name of dbToolData. The db prefix is a naming convention for identifying a database. The formula that calculates the range for this name is in the Refers to: entry box. The OFFSET formula syntax is

   =OFFSET(*reference*,*rows*,*cols*,[*height*],[*width*])

An explanation of the OFFSET formula follows these steps.

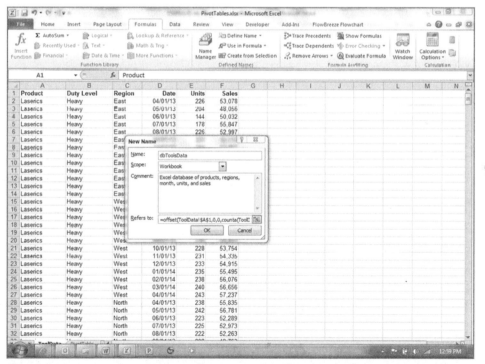

Figure 21.3: Create an auto-expanding range name for your database to ensure that new data is included in your PivotTable.

4. Click Add, and then click OK.

reference is A1, the top-left corner of the data. There is no offset for rows or columns because the top-left reference for the defined name is the same as the top left of the database.

The height of the named database range is calculated by counting all filled cells in column A. The width of the database range is calculated by counting all filled cells in row 1:

```
COUNTA(sheetname!A:A)
COUNTA(sheetname!1:1)
```

The complete formula is

```
=OFFSET(ToolData!$A$1,0,0,COUNTA(ToolData!$A:$A),COUNTA(ToolData!$1:$1))
```

where ToolData is the name of the worksheet tab.

> **WARNING** This formula works correctly only if all data is entered without leaving blank rows or columns. Calculations for the size of the database depend on counting the filled cells in column A and row 1 so that one filled cell equals one row or column in the database. If column A or row 1 has blank cells, the size of the database will calculate incorrectly. It is best to choose row 1 for the width count, because this row contains headers and no blanks inside the database. For the height, choose a column—in this case, A—that will always be filled.

In this example, you cannot use the range name dbToolData in a function on the same worksheet where dbToolData resides. The OFFSET formula in this case covers all cells in the worksheet, and this will cause a circular reference.

To use OFFSET on a database that is on a sheet with other calculations, you could restrict the range across which COUNTA counts. For example, instead of counting down all of column A with COUNTA(ToolData!A:A), the formula could be written as COUNTA(ToolData!A1:A200), which would work as long as the database did not exceed row 200. Likewise, the width of COUNTA could be limited. An OFFSET for a database that had its upper-left corner at $B$25 and that never grew to more than 500 rows and beyond column G would use an OFFSET like this:

```
=OFFSET(ToolData!$B$25,0,0,COUNTA(ToolData!$B$25:$B$525),
COUNTA(ToolData!$B:$G))
```

There are two ways to check the range name you have created (dbToolData in this example). Press F5, type **dbToolData** in the Reference field, and press Enter. The range of entered data should be selected. You can move to each corner of the selected range by pressing Ctrl+. (period).

Another way to test the name dbToolData is to see if the correct data is returned using the INDEX function. Enter an INDEX formula to retrieve the contents at the limits of the database. For example, the third row and fourth column would be

```
=INDEX(dbToolData,3,5)
```

This returns 204, the third row from the top of the database, including headers, in the Units column.

To reference this auto-expanding database name for your PivotTable, enter the range name as your database reference when you create a PivotTable, as shown in Figure 21.4.

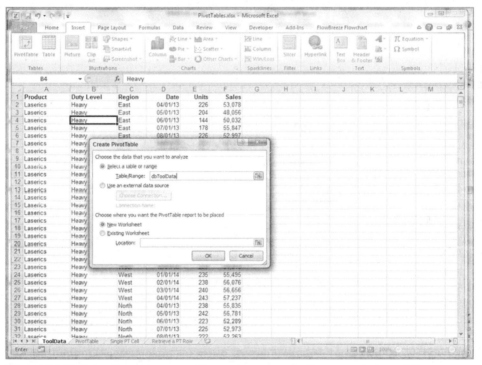

Figure 21.4: Enter the auto-expanding range name in the second step of the PivotTable Wizard.

Using PivotTable Results in Dashboards

In nearly all cases, you will want to keep the actual PivotTable as well as the data hidden from the Balanced Scorecard or dashboard users. PivotTables are one of those things that are easy once you understand their concept. But when multiple users share a dashboard, it takes only one untrained user to change the PivotTable layout so that it is unusable by the scorecard or dashboard. PivotTables are so powerful that you should still use them, but you should incorporate them safely into scorecards and dashboards.

I recommend that you keep your PivotTable in a hidden worksheet and then extract and manipulate from it the data you want. With the following techniques, your users will have a lot of power with little danger—and you won't have to write any VBA macros.

Retrieving a Single Cell of Data from a PivotTable

One worksheet function works with PivotTables:

```
GETPIVOTDATA(data_field,pivot_table,[field1],[item1],[field2],
[item2],...)
```

data_field is the explicit text name in quotes of the data you want to retrieve. In most cases, these text names appear in the PivotTable titles to identify a result, such as "Sum of Sales." This is the field being calculated within the table. *pivot_table* is the name of the PivotTable, a cell within the PivotTable, or a named range in the PivotTable. This is used to identify the PivotTable from which data will be extracted. You can see and change the name of the PivotTable at the top of the PivotTable options box.

The associated pairs of [*field1*] and [*item1*] are the field names and an item within that field. [*field*] and [*item*] enable you to identify which cell of data within the table you want. In Figure 21.2 (the finished table previously shown), an example would be a field named Product with an item of Dynamicon. You can have up to 14 sets of [*field*] and [*item*], and they do not need to match the order in the data or PivotTable.

Figure 21.5 shows a GETPIVOTDATA function retrieving a single cell's content from the PivotTable shown in Figure 21.2. The function in the figure is

```
=GETPIVOTDATA("Units",PivotTable!$B$5,"Product","Dynamicon",
"Duty Level","Heavy","Date",DATE(2013,4,1))
```

This function retrieves the result 250 from cell D7 in the West region in the PivotTable shown in Figure 21.2. Another way to look at this function is as a series of query requests:

```
Data = Units
Product = Dynamicon
Duty Level = Heavy
Date = April 1, 2013
```

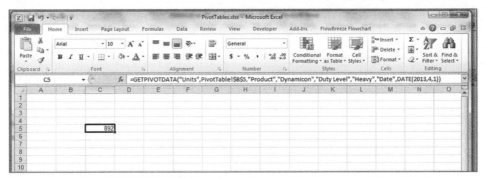

Figure 21.5: The GETPIVOTDATA function retrieves data from a specific cell in the PivotTable.

Note that the current region selected in the PivotTable in Figure 21.2 is West. The result of 250 is for the West region only. Selecting a different Region in the PivotTable would change the value that GETPIVOTDATA returns. Later in this section, you will see how to control this.

You can retrieve the total for all Dynamicon products of any Duty Level for April 1, 2014 by removing the "Duty Level" Field and Item like this:

```
=GETPIVOTDATA("Units",PivotTable!$B$5,"Product","Dynamicon","Date",
DATE(2014,4,1))
```

AN EASY WAY TO CREATE COMPLEX GETPIVOTDATA FUNCTIONS

Entering GETPIVOTDATA functions would be tedious and error-prone if you had to do so manually. But you can enter functions easily by typing = in the worksheet where you want the PivotTable result and then clicking the appropriate cell within the data area of the PivotTable. Excel writes the full GETPIVOTDATA function for you.

Dynamically Retrieving Data from a PivotTable

The quoted text within the GETPIVOTDATA function might give you the idea that it can be replaced by text results from other worksheet functions. By following up on that idea, we will see how to extract data from a PivotTable using combo boxes or text entry fields.

Figure 21.6 shows a row of data retrieved from the PivotTable based on the Duty Level selected from the combo box. Selecting a Duty Level from the combo box in cell D4 changes the entire row of data in row 11 retrieved from the PivotTable in Figure 21.2.

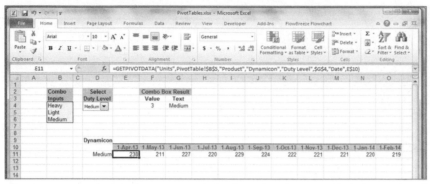

Figure 21.6: Replacing the parameters in the GETPIVOTDATA function with cell contents allows you to selectively retrieve whatever data you want from a PivotTable.

The combo box in D4 uses the list of names in B4:B6. Selecting the Duty Level from the combo box in D4 enters the item number selected in F4. Cell G4 then uses this number in an INDEX function to retrieve the text value of the selection from the range B4:B6. This may seem convoluted. Why not just type in the Duty Level name in G4? This would be fine for short lists with simple names, but if you have long lists, you will want your dashboard users to select from a combo box to prevent errors and to give them all possible choices. Using a combo box is explained in detail in Chapter 20.

The following GETPIVOTDATA function is in cell E11. It shows how the Item2 that matches "Duty Level" is the content of cell G4, the result of the combo box.

The date used in the function is the date directly above the cell containing the GETPIVOTDATA function. When the function in E11 is copied across, it refers to the date in each column, but the same Duty Level.

```
=GETPIVOTDATA("Units",PivotTable!$B$5,"Product","Dynamicon",
"Duty Level",$G$4,"Date",E$10)
```

Again, the data retrieved changes depending on the Region selected in the PivotTable's Page control. The following section shows you how to control all fields.

Once you understand how this works, you can use what you learned in Chapter 20 to build tables that retrieve data from PivotTables based on selections from option buttons, combo boxes, and lists. It allows your users to query the results of PivotTables, and it gives you control of the format while limiting potential mishaps.

Building a Safe User-Controlled PivotTable Display

Most dashboard users have a limited set of questions they need answered. Managers usually aren't out to probe every conceivable query using the PivotTable, and if a business analyst needs that capability, you should teach her PivotTables.

However, if you have done your homework and you know the types of queries and analytics your users need, you can build sets of PivotTables that will answer most of their questions, and you can safely control the user interface.

To build a dashboard that gives users the answers they need, you need to know what fields they want to query, such as Product, Regions, and Dates. You also need to know which data they want analyzed (such as Units and Sales) and how they want it analyzed. In the sample PivotTable shown in Figure 21.7, the Layout has been constructed to allow data retrieval by region, product, duty level, and date. (Note that in this example, the region is included on the left side and is not in the page field, as in the previous example.) The data being analyzed is the sum of units and the sum of sales, as shown in Figure 21.7.

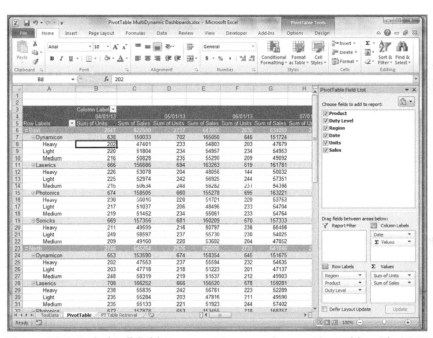

Figure 21.7: Include all fields you want to access in your PivotTable with GETPIVOTDATA.

PUT FIELDS IN A ROW OR COLUMN IF YOU WANT THEM ACCESSIBLE TO GETPIVOTDATA FUNCTIONS

The GETPIVOTDATA **function retrieves data using the PivotTable's row and column field names. You cannot retrieve data based on selections from the Page Field, the drop-down menu(s) at the top left of a PivotTable. So, any data you want to retrieve with** GETPIVOTDATA **should have a row and column heading in the PivotTable.**

Figure 21.8 shows how data can be retrieved from the PivotTable through the use of combo boxes. In this figure, cell C18 contains the following:

```
=GETPIVOTDATA("Sum of Units",PivotTable!$B$5,"Product",$G$10,
"Duty Level",$B18,"Region",$G$4,"Date",C$17)
```

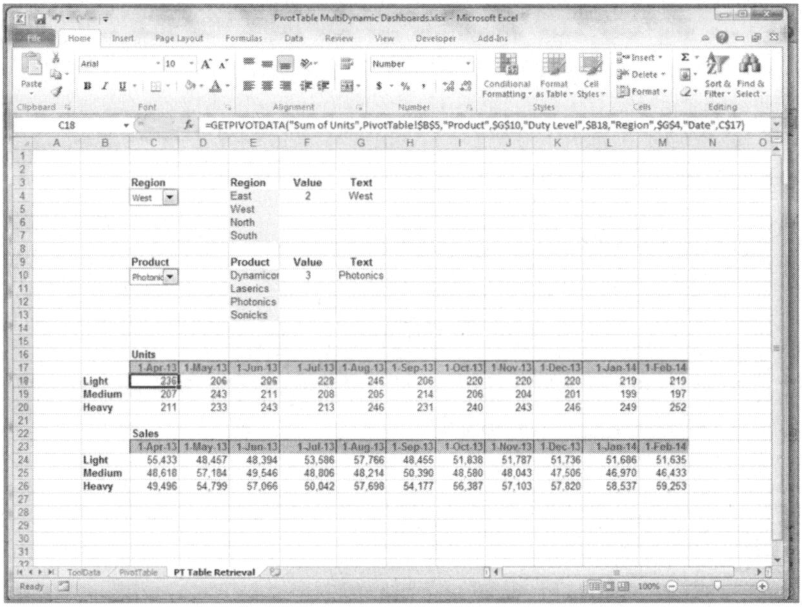

Figure 21.8: Combining a robust PivotTable with combo boxes lets users extract the data they need from a PivotTable into any report format.

The Product field refers to the contents of G10, the result of the combo box in C10. Region is specified in G4, the result of another combo box. Duty Level comes from the headings to the left in B18.

TIP Figure 21.8 shows two separate worksheet tables to display the Sum of Units or Sum of Sales. You can allow your users to choose between Sum of Units and Sum of Sales by using an IF or CHOOSE function to select which quoted text will be used as the *data_field* in GETPIVOTDATA. The following formula changes the GETPIVOTDATA results between Sum of Units or Sum of Sales, depending on the value in C13 (not shown in Figure 21.8). If C13 is 1, Sum of Units is displayed. If C13 is 2, Sum of Sales is displayed. The CHOOSE function chooses between Sum of Units and Sum of Sales, depending on the value in C13. Two option buttons that output to C13 would be a good way to give your users a choice of results:

```
=GETPIVOTDATA(CHOOSE($C$13,"Sum of Units","Sum of Sales"),
PivotTable!$B$5,"Product",$G$10,"Duty Level",$B18,"Region",
$G$4,"Date",C$17)
```

It is important to note that the term "Sum of Units" is specified uniquely as quoted text in the function. It does not reference a cell.

Drilling Down to Detail with PivotTables

PivotTables include another powerful feature to aid in analysis. Double-clicking a data cell within a PivotTable drills down to the data supporting that cell's result. Excel opens a new worksheet that displays the individual data elements analyzed. Figure 21.9 shows a worksheet displaying the raw data returned by double-clicking within the PivotTable we used in previous examples.

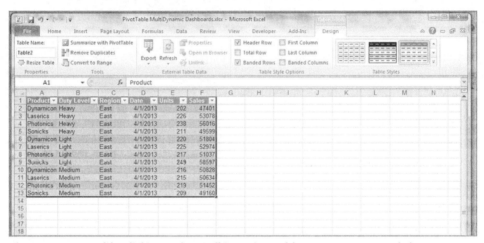

Figure 21.9: Double-clicking a data cell in a PivotTable opens a new worksheet showing the data used by that cell.

WARNING Inexperienced Excel users do not realize that when they double-click a cell in a PivotTable, the new drill-down data is displayed in a new worksheet in the same workbook. When they want to close the sheet showing drill-down data, they have a habit of either closing the entire workbook or saving the workbook with the new worksheet. This eventually produces a workbook glutted with drill-down remnants.

To turn off the drill-down feature on PivotTables, in Excel 2007 and Excel 2010, right-click the PivotTable and choose PivotTable Options. On the Data tab, clear the Enable show details check box. In Excel 2003, go to the PivotTable Options dialog box and clear the Enable drill to details check box.

TIP PivotCharts are a nice feature of Excel when you are analyzing data manually. However, if you need to present bulletproof charts that must keep their formatting as the PivotTable updates or changes, I do not recommend their use. Instead, retrieve data from the PivotTable using the GETPIVOTDATA function, as described in this chapter, and base your chart on that data. Use the form controls described in chapter 20 to enable users to easily change the table and chart. This gives you more charting options, the formatting will be stable, and you can control user interaction. You and your users will be happier!

Updating the PivotTable Linked to Internal or External Data

Dashboard users want the most up-to-date data. If they are viewing PivotTable results accessed dynamically from a database, they may need to update the PivotTable while the dashboard is open.

To update the PivotTable when it opens, right-click the PivotTable, open the PivotTable Options dialog box, and then select the Refresh on open check box. In Excel 2007 and Excel 2010, this check box is on the Data tab in the PivotTable Options dialog box.

Summary

PivotTables are incredibly powerful and deserve to be the foundation of any scorecard or dashboard linked to a database. They can retrieve selected data from a database, aggregate or do statistical analysis, group dates or products, and more. However, with great power comes great responsibility that not all users have been trained to handle.

If your scorecards or dashboards will be used by inexperienced users, I recommend first learning what type of analysis your users need the most. Then you should build one or more PivotTables containing those analyses, hide the PivotTables, and retrieve the data using the form controls such as combo boxes and the GETPIVOTDATA function. This is a very powerful tool. Once you get the hang of it, your capability will expand greatly.

CHAPTER 22

Working with PowerPivot

With great power comes great responsibility.
**—Spider-Man's Uncle Ben,
as written by Stan Lee, author, 2000**

PivotTables have been one of the best tools for the average businessperson to analyze data. However, a new and more powerful tool is available. If you have Excel 2010, you can download from Microsoft the free PowerPivot add-in. This tool is the PivotTable plus much more.

Although PivotTables and PowerPivots are similar, you need to understand major differences in their power. PowerPivot differs from PivotTables in ways that you may at first find frustrating.

You should continue using PivotTables in Excel 2010. For most single-dataset problems, they are still the tool of choice. PowerPivot expands your world of analytics because it accesses and joins very large databases and calculates much faster. This gives you a larger and more integrated view of your organization—how different parts of your organization work together. If you have used PivotTables in the past, you will definitely want to learn when to use PivotTables and when to use PowerPivots.

Basic PowerPivot Concepts

Like PivotTables, PowerPivot connects to a data source and calculates a cross-tabulation that displays on a worksheet. Unlike PivotTables, PowerPivot can analyze very large databases containing millions of rows of data. It can automatically detect when database tables have common fields and join the tables. And considering that PowerPivot can do this with databases having millions of rows, it does so very fast.

Figure 22.1 shows a sample PowerPivot table created from the PowerPivot Tutorial Sample available from Microsoft. PowerPivot joins two large data tables and creates the PowerPivot shown. You can see how the cross-tabulation and the PowerPivot Field List look similar to normal Excel PivotTables.

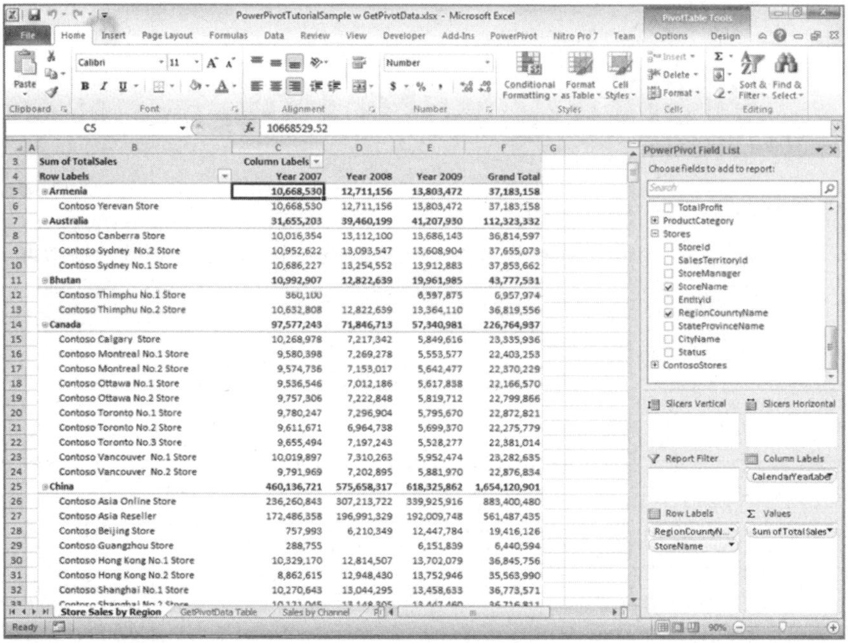

Figure 22.1: PowerPivot tables and the PowerPivot Field List look and act similar to previous PivotTables, but they are more powerful.

In addition to its ability to analyze large data files, PowerPivot contains the formula language Data Analysis Expressions (DAX). DAX uses Excel spreadsheet-like formulas to calculate new fields in the database prior to analysis. These formulas are useful for business analysts because they give them the power to do many of the database modifications or calculations they need without IT assistance and without modifying the source database. No longer will you have to plead with IT to add a field to the database to add year-to-date totals. You can do it yourself.

The following sections describe some of the advantages and disadvantages of using PowerPivot. They're worth looking over, because for some solutions you may want to use PowerPivot, and for others you can stick with the more familiar PivotTables.

PowerPivot Advantages

PowerPivot tables look similar to PivotTables, but they have major differences, advantages, and disadvantages. Here are some of the advantages:

- **You can create a single PowerPivot table from multiple databases.** PowerPivot can connect to and join multiple databases. These can even be large databases of different types.

- **You can join a wide variety of databases.** PowerPivot connects with all major databases as well as small file systems such as Microsoft Access, Microsoft Excel, and text files.

- **You can calculate quickly.** PowerPivot tables calculate fast. Even when you're working with very large datasets with millions of rows, calculations are fast. PowerPivot uses an in-memory OLAP cube that allows data manipulation, joins, and fast calculation.

- **You can connect datasets from different sources.** In Excel worksheets and PivotTables, you had to use arcane methods to link two or more sets of data. This involved using VLOOKUP or the more error-free INDEX and MATCH functions. Using these functions with the million-row datasets that PowerPivot handles is impossible. PowerPivot, however, detects fields and joins tables for you automatically. You also can manually specify which fields to join. In corporate environments this is especially useful with information stored in Microsoft SharePoint.

- **You can automatically create table and chart layouts.** As with PivotTables, PowerPivot enables you to create tables or charts. With PowerPivot you choose to use predefined layouts containing multiple charts and tables.

- **You can use slicers to filter data.** Slicers are buttons that make it easy to filter PivotTable and PowerPivot results. Slicers were introduced with PivotTables in Excel 2010 and were carried forward with PowerPivot. The slicers in PowerPivot just look better and are easier to create for PowerPivots. PowerPivot slicers can even be automatically arranged around a horizontal or vertical axis, making it easy to understand what they filter.

- **You can manipulate datasets with DAX formula language.** With PivotTables, if you needed to change a data field, you had two choices: write a worksheet formula that calculated the new field, or contact IT to change the database. Calculating new fields in a worksheet with millions of rows would seriously degrade performance. Waiting for permission (if you even get it) from IT to change the database takes time. With DAX, a mid-level Excel user can add and calculate a new data field by simply entering a formula in a worksheet.

- **You can publish to and work on SharePoint.** Many businesses, large and small, use Microsoft SharePoint as their intranet portal—a place to share information. PowerPivot is designed to work with SharePoint. You can create PowerPivot tables and charts and, by publishing them to SharePoint, make them accessible to everyone who has the appropriate role level. PowerPivot on SharePoint can be viewed through a web browser and has role-based security, work flow, and version control.

PowerPivot Disadvantages

With all that new power that PowerPivot brings, you are probably wondering what its downsides are. Well, it has a few:

- **You can't go back or even undo.** I still remember being in the room at one of the first Microsoft conventions when a product manager demonstrated Undo. The place came unglued. About half the room actually gave a standing ovation. Now we're used to it and expect it. Just don't expect it in Excel 2010 PowerPivot.

- **There is no Visual Basic.** You can't control PowerPivots from VBA. End of story.

- **There is no double-click drill-down.** Knowing how to use double-click in a PivotTable to drill down to source data can be enlightening. If you double-click by accident and don't understand what happened, you get confused. But PowerPivot does not offer double-click drill-down. Doing that on a multimillion-row database would return a huge worksheet.

- **Group with DAX, not in the PowerPivot table.** A frequent request I get when working with PivotTables is to create some type of custom grouping of products, sales information, or dates. In PivotTables you do this in the PivotTable itself. You can create groups in PowerPivot, but you need to go into the PowerPivot source worksheet tabs and use DAX functions to group data. Luckily, DAX has a powerful set of functions, especially date functions, that make this workable.

- **Months don't automatically sort in date order.** As you'll learn, months on the axis of a table or chart do not automatically sort in months order—Jan, Feb, Mar, and so on. Instead, you must go into the column sort field and tell PowerPivot which custom sort order to use. This takes a good number of clicks and should be automatic. The section "Sorting Months in Date Order with the Custom Sort Order List" explains how to set up months so that they sort in date order.

- If you are considering using PowerPivot in an environment containing different versions of Excel you need to consider this,

- PowerPivots can be read in Excel 2010 that doesn't have the add-in, but they can't be changed.

- PowerPivots can be read in Excel 2007, but you can't create, modify or interact with the tables or charts.

- PowerPivots don't work at all in Excel 2003.

POWERPIVOT OR PIVOTTABLE?

PowerPivots are incredibly powerful, but they come with some baggage. In general, PivotTables are more flexible and easier to use. For most simple analytics, use a PivotTable. If you need to analyze a large database or join multiple databases, use PowerPivot. Although you may not want to use it all the time, be glad you have it as one of the tools in your kit.

Downloading and Installing the Free PowerPivot Add-In

PowerPivot is a free add-in for Excel 2010 and more recent versions. To get this add-in, go to http://www.powerpivot.com, an official Microsoft website. This website has short videos and additional information about using PowerPivot.

After clicking the Download link, select the appropriate version of SQL Server and Excel for your installation. Microsoft SQL Server is used by PowerPivot and is available as a free companion download that installs automatically when you install PowerPivot.

PowerPivot runs on the most current version of Excel 2010. There are separate versions for 32- and 64-bit systems. (The 64-bit system takes full advantage of the extra memory and calculating performance available in PowerPivot. 32-bit systems can still run PowerPivot but may be unable to analyze extremely large datasets.)

You also need to ensure that your system has the following:

- **Microsoft SQL Server 2008 Release 2 or 2012:** This is available as a free download from the PowerPivot website and installs automatically.

- **.NET Framework 3.5 Service Pack 1:** The .NET Framework is a software framework that runs on Windows that allows interoperability between different languages. Check Programs in your Control Panel to see if you have it installed.

- **Microsoft Office Shared Features:** You may need to install this from your Microsoft Office CD if it is not already installed.

After you have installed PowerPivot, a PowerPivot tab appears in the Excel ribbon.

Downloading Sample Demos for PowerPivot

You may not have a large database readily available to use with PowerPivot. You can use any Excel list, CSV or text file, or Microsoft Access database you have. You can also use the large database samples from Microsoft that illustrate PowerPivot results.

Microsoft has created sample demos for use in learning PowerPivot. To download these sample demos, search the web for "Microsoft Download Center." In the Download Center, search for "PowerPivot samples for Excel."

Download the installation file to a folder, and then run it. Three Excel files are unzipped. Opening these Excel files opens workbooks with PowerPivot tables, charts, and the PowerPivot data. To see PowerPivot commands, open one of the worksheets and click the PowerPivot tab.

For more instructions on using PowerPivot, go to the Microsoft technical website, `http://technet.microsoft.com`, and search for "PowerPivot for Excel tutorial introduction."

This tutorial guides you through connecting to a database, creating relationships in database tables (joining), and analyzing data using PowerPivot.

REFER TO POWERPIVOT TUTORIALS FOR MORE INFORMATION

For short tutorials on PowerPivot basics, refer to the `http://www.powerpivot` `.com` **website. This website contains videos to get you started. A great deal of additional information is available on the web.**

Connecting to Data

Excel PowerPivot connects to a wide variety of data sources. If the data sources have a common field, such as account number, PowerPivot can automatically join the tables even if they are from separate data sources.

Connecting to a data source is straightforward if you have permission to access the source. If you are connecting to a database or online source, you need to check with IT for valid logon credentials. Connecting to an Excel or text file is as easy as selecting the filename.

To connect to one or more data sources, on the PowerPivot tab, in the Launch group, click PowerPivot Window to open the PowerPivot window. In the PowerPivot window, on the Home tab, you see the Get External Data group. There, you can choose the type of data connection you need.

The PowerPivot Window displays the data available from PowerPivot data connections. The data from each connection displays on its own tab, just as worksheets appear on separate tabs.

Your choices are the following:

- From Database
- From SQL Server
- From Access
- From Analysis Services or PowerPivot
- From Report
- Microsoft SQL Server Reporting Services Report
- From Azure DataMarket
  - (These are free and commercial datamarts from a variety of content providers. A link in the dialog box enables you to browse free and for-a-fee online data sources.)
- From Data Feed
  - (From an online data feed)
- From Text
  - (From a text file using column separators)
- From Other Sources
  - (From a wide variety of databases and any ODBC Connection as well as Excel)

At this point, PowerPivot activates a set of dialog boxes that walk you through the steps for authenticating the external data source and choosing the tables or queries you need. When you are done, the data from the external source appears on a separate tab in the PowerPivot window.

You can see and manage PowerPivot's existing data connections by opening a PowerPivot sheet. Then, on the Design tab, in the Connections group, click Existing Connections. You can browse, open, edit, refresh, and delete existing connections.

For information on how to create relationships between tables. The relationships between database tables define how the data between tables connect and relate to each other. If tables are not correctly joined you will get results, but it will be incorrect. For more information, refer to the online tutorials at Microsoft's support website, http://www.powerpivot.com.

POWERPIVOT COULD TAKE UP ITS OWN BOOK

Like Excel, PowerPivot has many features and a great deal of functionality. This chapter is only a brief introduction to those capabilities. The few features and work-arounds I have described, such as building free-form reports with GETPIVOTDATA and sorting month fields by date, are special techniques that I've found especially valuable when creating reports and dashboards.

Creating PivotTables or PivotCharts with PowerPivot

After you have connected PowerPivot to one or more datasets, you can create a PivotTable. When you do so using data from the PowerPivot connection, you must use the PivotTable button on the PowerPivot tab.

To create a PivotTable using PowerPivot data, on the PowerPivot tab, in the Report group, click PivotTable and select PivotTable. Select whether you want to create the PivotTable on a new worksheet or an existing worksheet, and click OK. PivotTables from PowerPivot are built the same as they are in a normal worksheet. Figure 22.2 shows a PivotTable that has been built from one of the sample PowerPivot workbooks.

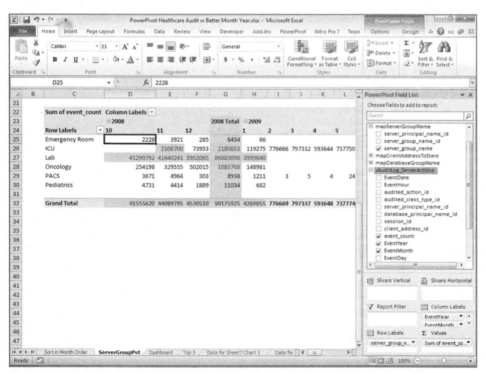

Figure 22.2: PivotTables from PowerPivot are built using the same steps as for a normal PivotTable.

Figure 22.3 shows a PivotTable and PivotChart built from PowerPivot. To build a PivotChart or a combination PivotChart with PivotTable, follow the same process described earlier in this section for building a PivotTable. However, from the PivotTable drop-down list, select one of the PivotChart or PivotChart with PivotTable combinations. Before dragging fields in the Field List, select the PivotChart or PivotTable you want to create.

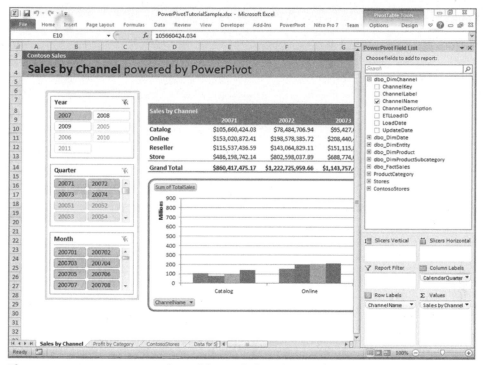

Figure 22.3: You can create PivotTables and PivotCharts using PowerPivot.

Building Free-Form Reports with PowerPivot and GetPivotData

In Chapter 21 you learned how to use the GETPIVOTDATA function to extract a single cell of data from a PivotTable. You modified the GETPIVOTDATA function so that it referred to a single cell's contents inside the PivotTable. By modifying the function references inside GETPIVOTDATA, you can extract any piece of data from a PivotTable and put it into any layout you want. You can use this same technique to create custom report layouts from PowerPivot data.

Figure 22.4 shows a PivotTable created from the Contoso sample database that you can download from the Microsoft website. Cell I5 shows a GETPIVOTDATA function that references the sum of total sales for the Contoso Anchorage store in the year 2007:

```
=GETPIVOTDATA("[Measures].[Sum of TotalSales]",$B$3,
"[dbo_DimDate].[CalendarYearLabel]",
"[dbo_DimDate].[CalendarYearLabel].&[Year 2007]","[Stores].[StoreName]",
"[Stores].[StoreName].&[Contoso Anchorage Store]")
```

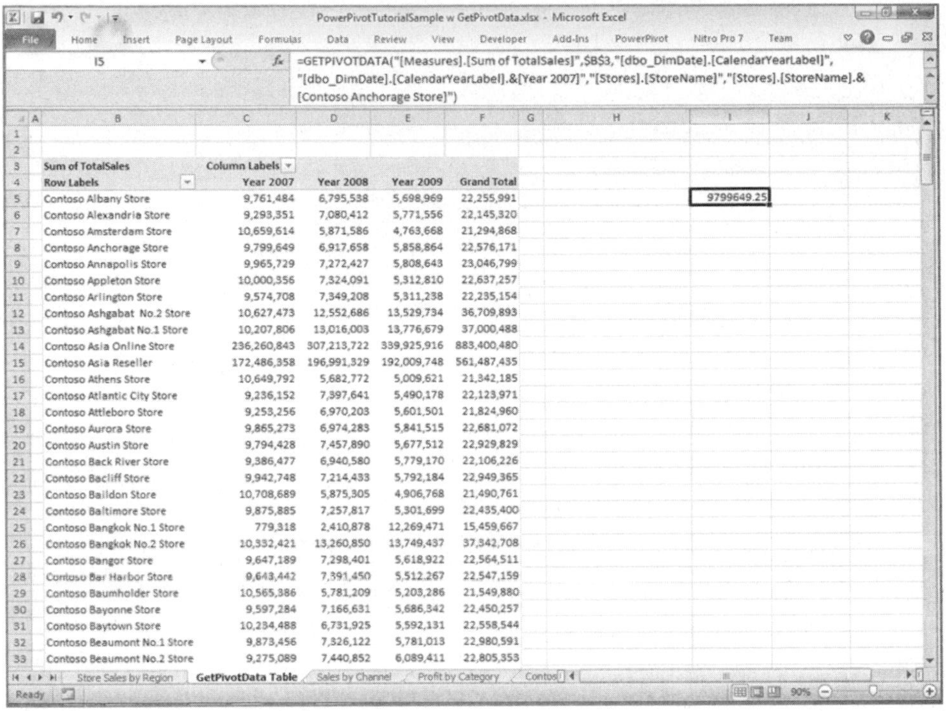

PowerPivotTutorialSample w GetPivotData.xlsx - Microsoft Excel

I5 =GETPIVOTDATA("[Measures].[Sum of TotalSales]",$B$3,"[dbo_DimDate].[CalendarYearLabel]", "[dbo_DimDate].[CalendarYearLabel].&[Year 2007]","[Stores].[StoreName]","[Stores].[StoreName].&[Contoso Anchorage Store]")

Sum of TotalSales	Column Labels			
Row Labels	Year 2007	Year 2008	Year 2009	Grand Total
Contoso Albany Store	9,761,484	6,795,538	5,698,969	22,255,991
Contoso Alexandria Store	9,293,351	7,080,412	5,771,556	22,145,320
Contoso Amsterdam Store	10,659,614	5,871,586	4,763,668	21,294,868
Contoso Anchorage Store	9,799,649	6,917,658	5,858,864	22,576,171
Contoso Annapolis Store	9,965,729	7,272,427	5,808,643	23,046,799
Contoso Appleton Store	10,000,356	7,324,091	5,312,810	22,637,257
Contoso Arlington Store	9,574,708	7,349,208	5,311,238	22,235,154
Contoso Ashgabat No.2 Store	10,627,473	12,552,686	13,529,734	36,709,893
Contoso Ashgabat No.1 Store	10,207,806	13,016,003	13,776,679	37,000,488
Contoso Asia Online Store	236,260,843	307,213,722	339,925,916	883,400,480
Contoso Asia Reseller	172,486,358	196,991,329	192,009,748	561,487,435
Contoso Athens Store	10,649,792	5,682,772	5,009,621	21,342,185
Contoso Atlantic City Store	9,236,152	7,397,641	5,490,178	22,123,971
Contoso Attleboro Store	9,253,256	6,970,203	5,601,501	21,824,960
Contoso Aurora Store	9,865,273	6,974,283	5,841,515	22,681,072
Contoso Austin Store	9,794,428	7,457,890	5,677,512	22,929,829
Contoso Back River Store	9,386,477	6,940,580	5,779,170	22,106,226
Contoso Bacliff Store	9,942,748	7,214,433	5,792,184	22,949,365
Contoso Baildon Store	10,708,689	5,875,305	4,906,768	21,490,761
Contoso Baltimore Store	9,875,885	7,257,817	5,301,699	22,435,400
Contoso Bangkok No.1 Store	779,318	2,410,878	12,269,471	15,459,667
Contoso Bangkok No.2 Store	10,332,421	13,260,850	13,749,437	37,342,708
Contoso Bangor Store	9,647,189	7,298,401	5,618,922	22,564,511
Contoso Bar Harbor Store	9,643,442	7,391,450	5,512,267	22,547,159
Contoso Baumholder Store	10,565,386	5,781,209	5,203,286	21,549,880
Contoso Bayonne Store	9,597,284	7,166,631	5,686,342	22,450,257
Contoso Baytown Store	10,234,488	6,731,925	5,592,131	22,558,544
Contoso Beaumont No.1 Store	9,873,456	7,326,122	5,781,013	22,980,591
Contoso Beaumont No.2 Store	9,275,089	7,440,852	6,089,411	22,805,353

9799649.25

Store Sales by Region | GetPivotData Table | Sales by Channel | Profit by Category

Figure 22.4: GETPIVOTDATA functions extract a single cell's contents from a PowerPivot table.

Thankfully, you don't have to enter this long function manually. Instead, click the cell you want to contain a number extracted from a PowerPivot table. Type = and then click the cell in the PowerPivot containing the cell you want to extract. Excel creates the `GETPIVOTDATA` function and includes all the arcane database, table, and field name references. Excel creates this `GETPIVOTDATA` so that you can reference specific content in a PowerPivot PivotTable even when the PivotTable layout changes.

Chapter 21 demonstrated how you can modify this `GETPIVOTDATA` in normal PivotTables to trick them into extracting data from anywhere in the PivotTable. To use the same trick here, you simply change the text references in `GETPIVOTDATA` into cell references. For example, at the end of `GETPIVOTDATA` you could change the text "Contoso Anchorage Store" into a cell reference containing that store name. When you have done that, you can enter a different store name in the cell to make `GETPIVOTDATA` extract that store's total sales.

Figure 22.5 shows the same `GETPIVOTDATA` modified to reference two cell references. The concatenate symbol, `&`, joins the text references of the original `GETPIVOTDATA` function and the new cell references you need. Changing the content of cell I4 to Year 2007, Year 2008, or Year 2009 changes the year referenced by

`GETPIVOTDATA`. Changing the content of cell H5 to a correctly spelled store name changes the store referenced by `GETPIVOTDATA`. Here's the modified formula:

```
=GETPIVOTDATA("[Measures].[Sum of TotalSales]",$B$3,
"[dbo_DimDate].[CalendarYearLabel]",
"[dbo_DimDate].[CalendarYearLabel].&["&I$4&"]","[Stores].[StoreName]",
"[Stores].[StoreName].&["&$H5&"]")
```

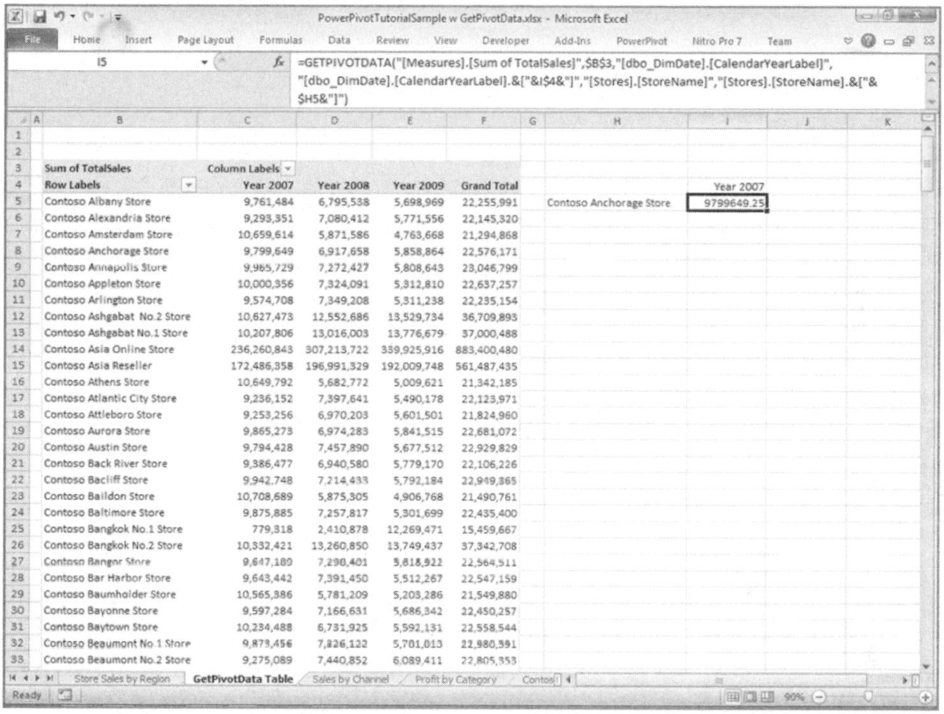

Sum of TotalSales	Column Labels			
Row Labels	Year 2007	Year 2008	Year 2009	Grand Total
Contoso Albany Store	9,761,484	6,795,538	5,698,969	22,255,991
Contoso Alexandria Store	9,293,351	7,080,412	5,771,556	22,145,320
Contoso Amsterdam Store	10,659,614	5,871,586	4,763,668	21,294,868
Contoso Anchorage Store	9,799,649	6,917,658	5,858,864	22,576,171
Contoso Annapolis Store	9,965,729	7,272,427	5,808,643	23,046,799
Contoso Appleton Store	10,000,356	7,324,091	5,312,810	22,637,257
Contoso Arlington Store	9,574,708	7,349,208	5,311,238	22,235,154
Contoso Ashgabat No.2 Store	10,627,473	12,552,686	13,529,734	36,709,893
Contoso Ashgabat No.1 Store	10,207,806	13,016,003	13,776,679	37,000,488
Contoso Asia Online Store	236,260,843	307,213,722	339,925,916	883,400,480
Contoso Asia Reseller	172,486,358	196,991,329	192,009,748	561,487,435
Contoso Athens Store	10,649,792	5,682,772	5,009,621	21,342,185
Contoso Atlantic City Store	9,236,152	7,397,641	5,490,178	22,123,971
Contoso Attleboro Store	9,253,256	6,970,203	5,601,501	21,824,960
Contoso Aurora Store	9,865,273	6,974,283	5,841,515	22,681,072
Contoso Austin Store	9,794,428	7,457,890	5,677,512	22,929,829
Contoso Back River Store	9,386,477	6,940,580	5,779,170	22,106,226
Contoso Bacliff Store	9,942,748	7,214,433	5,792,184	22,949,365
Contoso Baildon Store	10,708,689	5,875,305	4,906,768	21,490,761
Contoso Baltimore Store	9,875,885	7,257,817	5,301,699	22,435,400
Contoso Bangkok No.1 Store	779,318	2,410,878	12,269,471	15,459,667
Contoso Bangkok No.2 Store	10,332,421	13,260,850	13,749,437	37,342,708
Contoso Bangor Store	9,647,189	7,298,401	5,618,922	22,564,511
Contoso Bar Harbor Store	9,643,442	7,391,450	5,512,267	22,547,159
Contoso Baumholder Store	10,565,386	5,781,209	5,203,286	21,549,880
Contoso Bayonne Store	9,597,284	7,166,631	5,686,342	22,450,257
Contoso Baytown Store	10,234,488	6,731,925	5,592,131	22,558,544
Contoso Beaumont No.1 Store	9,873,456	7,826,122	5,701,013	22,980,591
Contoso Beaumont No.2 Store	9,275,089	7,440,852	6,089,411	22,805,353

Figure 22.5: Adding cell references inside GETPIVOTDATA enables it to extract data from anywhere inside the PowerPivot table.

To create a custom report format of PowerPivot data in any format, just create row headings of selected store names and column headings of years, like those shown in Figure 22.6. Then enter a `GETPIVOTDATA` formula at the top-left interior corner that references the row and column headings. In this example, the `GETPIVOTDATA` function in cell I5 uses the $ symbol to fix row references for I$4 and to fix column references for $H5. Copying this formula throughout the interior automatically adjusts the references for the appropriate row and column headings. Figure 22.6 shows the finished custom layout of PowerPivot data. As long as you reference the correct cells, you can create free-form report layouts containing blank areas or that mix with other data.

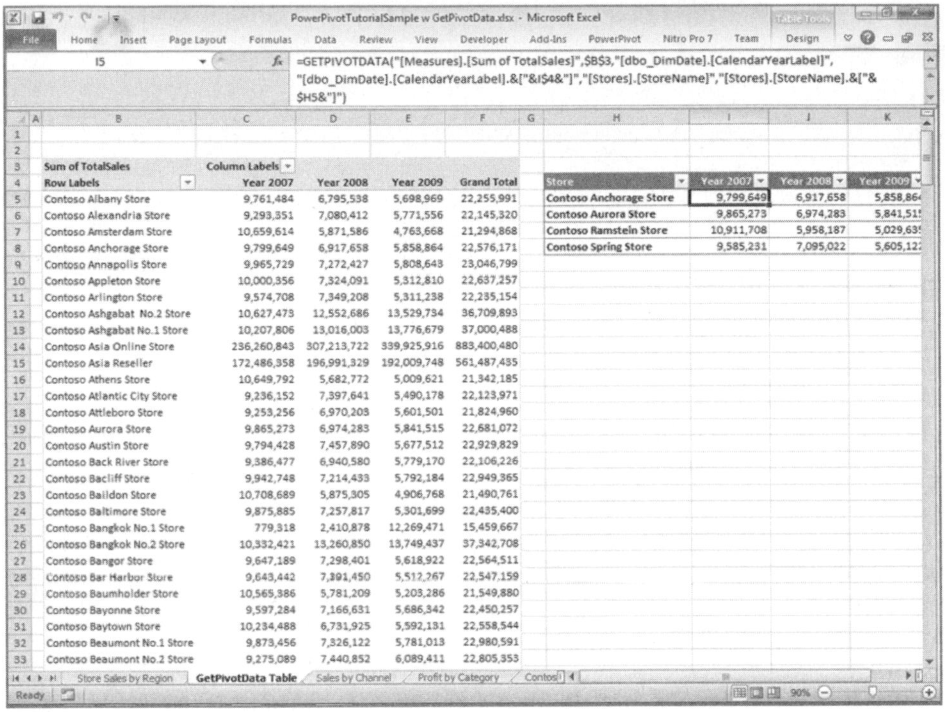

Figure 22.6: The GETPIVOTDATA function allows you to create custom and free-form report layouts.

Slicers are filters that filter data in PivotTables. They are easy to create and use, but they don't fit every need. For example, in some cases you may want to retrieve data referencing a specific store. With GETPIVOTDATA and drop-down lists you can do just that. Chapters 20 and 21 show how you can use drop-down lists to change the contents retrieved by GETPIVOTDATA. This works just as well for a PivotTable from PowerPivot. With GETPIVOTDATA you can create custom report layouts. Add drop-down lists to select report contents to GETPIVOTDATA, and you have total control over your report contents.

Sorting Months in Date Order with the Custom Sort Order List

Suppose it's Thursday evening, you're working to meet a Friday morning deadline, and everything is going smoothly. The PowerPivot has pulled out the data you need, and the tables and reports contain valid-looking numbers. Suddenly, to your horror, you notice that in all the PivotTables, the months are in alphabetical order, not date order. Figure 22.7 shows how PowerPivot tables don't sort months in date order. Search as you might, you can't find a solution.

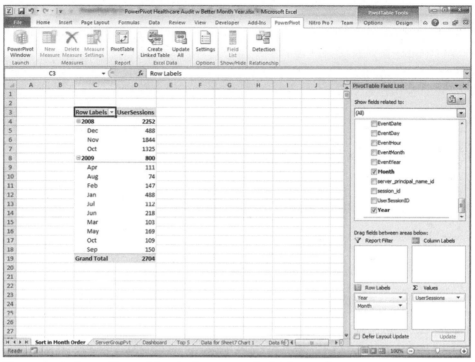

Figure 22.7: PowerPivot tables don't sort months in date order.

You could use DAX text and CONCATENATE functions to create a new field so that months look like 01 - Jan, 02 - Feb, and so on. Doing so would produce the right order, but you know that neither managers nor the accounting staff would like how it looks. And it would create more work with any Excel spreadsheet function that referenced that month.

Here's the solution. Although months don't sort in date order, you can tell them how to. Four custom sorting lists are built into Excel. One of these is Jan, Feb, Mar, and so on. You just need to let the PowerPivot know which custom sort list to use. It takes a few clicks, but it works and looks good.

Create your PowerPivot table using months, and then follow these steps:

1. Click the sort arrow in the column header for months to display the dialog box shown in Figure 22.8. Choose Month from the Select Fields list at the top. This list shows if you have years and months in the list.

2. Click More Sort Options to display the Sort dialog box, shown in Figure 22.9. Select Ascending (A to Z) by: and choose Months. Click More Options.

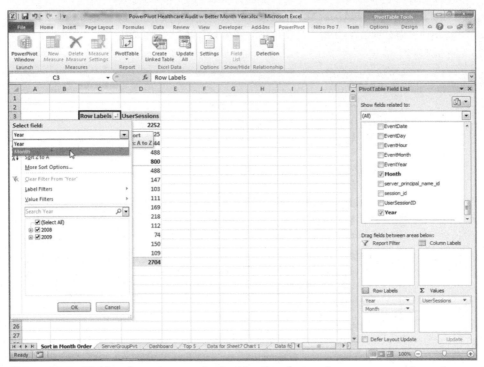

Figure 22.8: Clicking the sort arrow in the Month column gives you access to custom sort options.

Figure 22.9: Select whether you want months to sort in ascending or descending order within their years.

3. In the More Sort Options dialog box, shown in Figure 22.10, deselect the Sort automatically every time the report is updated check box.

Figure 22.10: Turn off automatic resorting and select a custom sort order.

4. In the First Key Sort Order list, select the Jan, Feb, Mar,… item. This pre-built custom sort order comes with Excel. Click OK.

5. Click OK in the Sort dialog box to return to the PivotTable.

You have applied one of Excel's prebuilt custom sort orders to this date list. Your list should now look like Figure 22.11. The list will keep this sort order even when you refresh data.

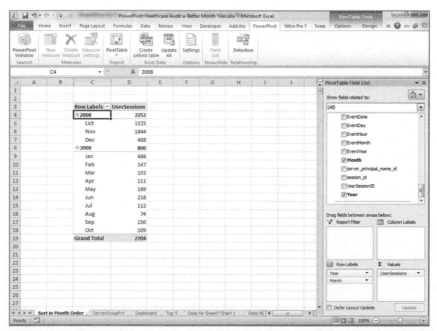

Figure 22.11: PowerPivots sort months in date order, but you must set this option in each PowerPivot.

You must set this custom sort order for months each time you create a PowerPivot. It is extra work that you shouldn't have to do, but at least it is possible to fix.

If your list did not re-sort months in date order, and years and dates are in the column, return to step 1 and make sure you select Month so that the custom sort order is applied to months.

Calculating Fields with Data Analysis Expressions (DAX)

PowerPivot connects directly to one or more databases. From that data it creates an in-memory "cube" of data that is significantly faster to analyze than data you query using SQL, as you might normally do from a PivotTable. One of the advantages of having this data in memory is that you, as a power Excel user, can create additional database fields you might need.

If you use a PivotTable and a field of data needs to be calculated or modified, such as a date conversion, you have two choices. You can add a formula to the PivotTable's list and extend that formula so that it calculates for each cell in the list. This works for lists that have hundreds or thousands of rows, but PowerPivot is designed to handle millions of rows of data. Recalculating a formula a million times would really slow down your system.

The other alternative when a data source is missing a field is to talk with the IT department and ask them to modify the source database. This is the best solution, but it could take a long time, and your request probably would be denied, because it could affect database performance.

PowerPivot offers the best solution. PowerPivot includes an extensive formula language based on Excel worksheet formulas. With DAX functions you can easily insert new columns (fields) into the PowerPivot sheet and calculate new fields in the PowerPivot's internal OLAP cube.

DAX functions are modeled on Excel spreadsheet functions, so they are easy to use. DAX functions can save you a tremendous amount of time calculating frequently used but difficult-to-calculate date periods, such as PREVIOUSQUARTER and SAMEPERIODLASTYEAR.

You enter DAX functions in the last column of the PowerPivot sheet, as you would enter a worksheet function. However, when you press Enter, the function is entered through the entire column.

To add a new calculated column to a PowerPivot table, follow these steps:

1. Click the PowerPivot tab on the Excel ribbon to display the PowerPivot window.

2. Select the tab for the PowerPivot sheet containing the data you want to work with.

3. Scroll to the far-right side of the PowerPivot sheet, and select the top cell in the last column, Add Column.

4. Type an equals sign in the formula bar, and click the *fx* button to the left of the formula bar to display the Insert Function dialog box, as shown in Figure 22.12. This dialog box displays the function and works just as it would in an Excel worksheet.

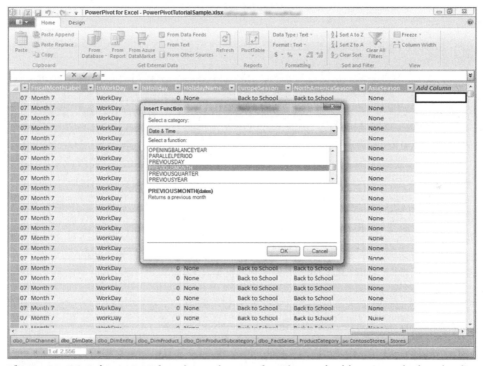

Figure 22.12: Select a DAX function to insert a function and add a new calculated column of data.

5. Select a function from the list, and click OK.

6. Complete the formula or function by entering a data column reference just as you would enter a cell reference. Click in the column, not the heading, in which you want the function to work. You must manually complete formulas with parentheses where appropriate. The PowerPivot formula bar doesn't complete them for you as the spreadsheet does. When the formula is complete, press Enter.

After you enter a valid formula in the last column, the new column calculates and appears as a new column of data. You can change the column heading by right-clicking, choosing Rename Column, and then typing the new column name.

You can drag columns into new positions. Hover the mouse cursor over the column heading until a four-headed arrow appears. Then drag the column heading left or right to the position you want.

Figure 22.13 shows a calculated data column that has been repositioned so that it is next to the column used in the calculation. The DAX function FORMAT is used here to reformat the EventDate column so that it appears with the MMM format. The FORMAT function uses custom date formats that are the same as custom date formatting in the Excel spreadsheet.

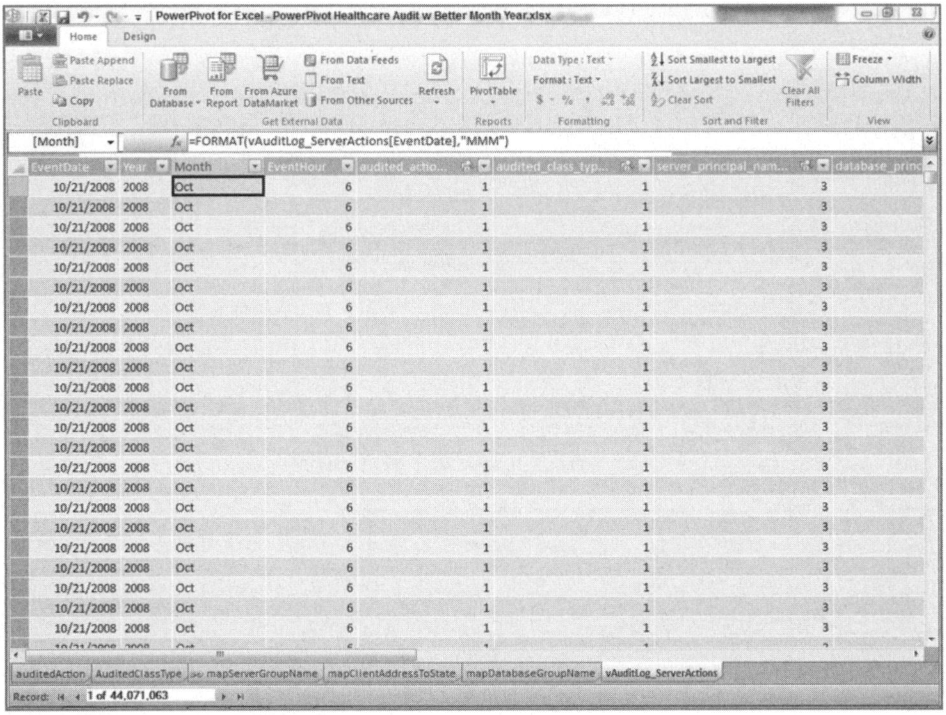

Figure 22.13: The FORMAT function reformats the EventDate column so that it appears as a three-letter month format.

> **NOTE** For more information about DAX and sample PowerPivots, go to http://www.microsoft.com **and search for "Microsoft PowerPivot for Excel 2010 data analysis expressions sample."**
>
> Two sample files in the download include a sample workbook containing DAX functions used on the Contoso database and a whitepaper on DAX functions.

Summary

Don't think that PowerPivot is just a robust PivotTable; it is far more. PowerPivot opens the world of Business Intelligence (BI) to power Excel users and business analysts. No longer do business users have to use large and expensive Business Intelligence software to find answers to common questions. PowerPivot works to solve many common BI questions.

The power you gain by learning about these additional features is the power to get a full view of your business, from one end to the other. You aren't limited to analyzing a single database, as you are with PivotTables. With PowerPivot you can link datasets from the Customer Relationship Management (CRM) system, the Human Resources Information System (HRIS), the online marketing database, and accounting and finance. By joining datasets from these different areas of the company, you can monitor customer, sales, and marketing activity from the point of first customer contact through the point of sale and onward through the customer life cycle.

CHAPTER 23

Smoothing Data and Forecasting Trends

I always avoid prophesying beforehand because it is much better to prophesy after the event has already taken place.

—Winston Churchill
Statesman
1874–1965

Humans have been forecasting ever since the first shaman squatted by a fire and cast bones to divine the future. We forecast how long it will take us to get to work based on the current traffic jams. When we get to work, we forecast product sales, marketing response rates, or budget variance.

Now we cast bones with the aid of complex algorithms built into statistical analysis programs such as SPSS. Even though few people have consistent access to SPSS and the skills to use it, you can meet your everyday forecasting needs with Microsoft Excel. Most of what you need for simple forecasting and analysis is built into Microsoft Excel and is straightforward to use.

In this chapter you learn how to smooth erratic data so that you can see and use the patterns hidden within it. You learn how to write your own formulas that work in any Excel worksheet and learn how to use the wizard in the Analysis ToolPak. If you need to forecast data that may have a linear or curving trend, you also learn how to use Excel's TREND and GROWTH functions.

There is as much art to analyzing data and developing forecasts as there is mathematical science. You must understand which mathematical method is appropriate and which parameters to use to smooth or forecast data. The qualitative art comes in knowing how far into the future you can acceptably forecast, how much you can smooth data without losing what you want to see, and how external factors such as population changes and competitive product introductions may affect your forecast.

TIP As enjoyable as you may find it to sit in your office, sip coffee, and forecast amazing profit growth, doing so can be dangerous unless you get out in the real world and apply a realistic viewpoint to your forecasts. One CEO for a technology start-up used a "hockey stick" curve to forecast the subscription-based revenue for his company. He didn't evaluate production capacity, distribution channels, or competitive pressure. After a few million dollars in angel and private investor funds had been squandered based on outrageous forecasts, the business was closed. Every forecast should come with a red title that says, "Does this look realistic?"

Smoothing Erratic Data

Business data rarely is consistent and smooth; it is erratic. Business data reflects the peaks and valleys of randomness and the whims of people's emotions in the marketplace. Whether you work for a giant corporation or a small- to midsized business, you need a way to smooth erratic data so that you can see underlying patterns.

Moving averages are used to smooth erratic data so that you can see underlying patterns. They work by taking an average of the data over a time period. That average smooths erratic spikes or dips but also "flattens" the data, causing rapid changes to be lost or delayed.

Most businesses look at data that is sampled monthly, such as sales, product turnover, and so forth. Data like this usually uses a 3-month or 6-month moving average. By averaging the data over a shorter period of time, you see more of the data's erratic nature. This also lets you see rapid shifts in movement more quickly. Averaging over a longer time period smooths erratic moves but delays the appearance of changes.

There is an art to knowing how much to smooth moving averages. If you smooth them too much, you may miss rapid shifts. If you don't smooth them enough, you may be unable to see an underlying pattern. Try different weighting or smoothing factors and different smoothing methods. This chapter describes a couple of different approaches.

Smoothing Data with Simple Moving Averages

The simplest way to smooth a data series is with a simple moving average. In moving averages, a data value is "smoothed" by averaging the current data value with a set number of preceding data values. It is averaged over time. For example, to average data over three periods, you would use a formula like this:

```
Forecast(t) = Average(Data(t) + Data(t - 1) + Data(t - 2))
```

where t is the time period for the forecast data, Data(t) is the data for the current period, Data($t - 1$) is the data for the previous period, and Data($t - 2$) is the data for two previous periods.

The time period over which you average the data depends on how much you want the data smoothed. For most monthly data, 3 or 6 months of smoothing is useful.

WARNING **Suppose you have a series of numbers in cells and you want to quickly fill in the rest of the adjacent cells with a linear or growth projection. You can select the data series and then use the right mouse button to drag the fill handle to fill the empty cells with a linear or growth projection. Although this is handy for manual work, it doesn't help in dashboards. The data created by Excel with this method is static and does not update when you change or add source data.**

Moving Averages with Formulas

Simple smoothing is easy to do with Excel formulas. You can also use Excel's Analysis ToolPak to create simple smoothing, but it is so easy to do yourself that there is little need to use the Analysis ToolPak.

In Figure 23.1, the erratic data is in the range C5:C31. A smoothing formula is used in D7:D31 to create a smoother set of values. You can see the difference in the chart.

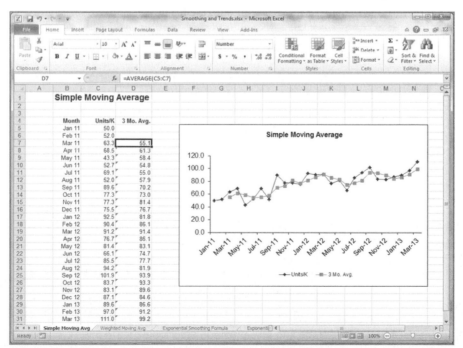

Figure 23.1: You can perform simple smoothing with AVERAGE and relative references.

Cell D7 contains this formula:

```
=AVERAGE(C5:C7)
```

This formula uses relative references to average the current data with the prior 2 months of data. Copying the formula through the range D7:D31 produces data that is smoothed over 3-month periods.

Problems with Simple Moving Averages

Although easy to use, simple smoothing can be easy to misinterpret. It can cause some issues:

- There are no data points until the first average has been calculated. Notice in Figure 23.1 that cells D5 and D6 are blank.
- Old and recent data have the same weighting in the average. This means that you won't see trends coming until they've been moving for at least half of the averaging period.
- If the data has cycles, the cycle in the smoothed data lags reality by half the smoothing period.
- More erratic data may require smoothing over a longer period, but this causes changes or cycles to be delayed and flattened.

Two other weighted average methods can resolve some of these problems.

Smoothing Data with Weighted Moving Averages

You can compensate for some of the problems in simple moving averages by using a weighted moving average. This assigns more weight to recent data and less weight to older data. All the weights must total 100 percent.

The equation looks like this:

```
Forecast(t) = Wt(t) * Data(t) + Wt(t - 1) * Data(t - 1) +
Wt(t - 2) * Data(t - 2)
```

The weight applied to data for each of the prior periods is Wt(t) for the current period, Wt($t - 1$) for the prior period, and Wt($t - 2$) for two prior periods. To smooth data while still seeing rapid shifts in data movement, you apply greater weight to current data and less weight to older. Examples are Wt(t)=50 percent for the current month, Wt($t - 1$)=30 percent for the prior month, and Wt($t - 2$)=20 percent for the second-oldest month. Putting these three weighting values in separate cells enables you to change the weighting so that you can try weights that produce the best smoothing while seeing trends.

Figure 23.2 shows three weighted values in these cells:

C4	.50
C5	.30
C6	.20

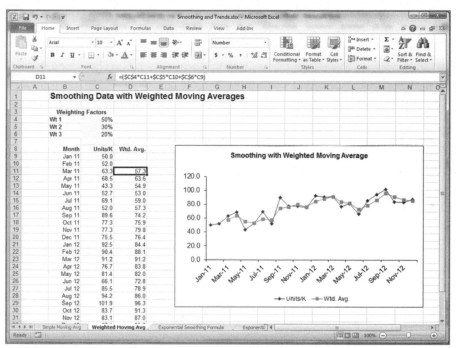

Figure 23.2: Weighted moving averages smooth erratic data while allowing you to see recent changes in movement.

Cell D11 contains this weighted average smoothing formula:

```
=($C$4*C11+$C$5*C10+$C$6*C9)
```

Copying this formula down the range D11:D32 produces a weighted average. Increasing the value in cell C4 gives more weight to current data. The total of cells C4, C5, and C6 must equal 100 percent.

Exponential Weighted Moving Average

Exponential smoothing is another method of compensating for the problems inherent in simple smoothing. Use exponential smoothing on erratic data that is not cyclical or seasonal. Exponential smoothing smooths data by including an adjustment for error in the previous forecast. To do this, it uses a *smoothing factor* called α.

The smoothing factor α specifies how much adjustment is made in the current forecast for prior error. The larger α is, the more the current forecast will respond to rapid changes.

The formula for exponential smoothing is

```
SmoothData(t) = α * ActualData(t - 1) + (1 - α) *
SmoothedData(t - 1)
```

The value of α determines the amount of smoothing and responsiveness to data movement. The appropriate value for α is based on the analyst's judgment. Usual values for α are in the range of 0.01 to 0.3, but most often they are from 0.2 to 0.3. In this formula ActualData is multiplied by the smoothing factor and is added to 1 minus the smoothing factor times the previous result of smoothing.

Exponential Smoothing with Formulas

Figure 23.3 shows data in C7:C33 being smoothed by the formulas in D8:D33. Cell D4 contains the smoothing factor α. Begin the first cell or cells in the forecast with actual data or an average of the first few data values. Cell D7 does this with

```
=C7
```

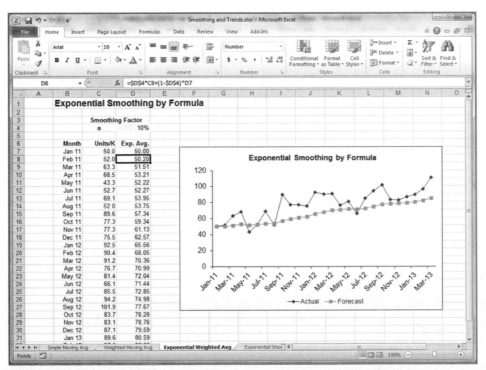

Figure 23.3: Exponential smoothing shows the underlying trend or trends in erratic data while still revealing rapid changes.

Cell D8 contains the first exponential smoothing formula:

```
=$D$4*C8+(1-$D$4)*D7
```

This formula is copied down the range D8:D33. Experiment by changing the smoothing factor in D4 to see how it smooths erratic data.

Adding the Analysis ToolPak to Excel

Excel has hundreds of built-in worksheet functions. Additional functions can help with statistics and forecasting, but you must add them to Excel with the Analysis ToolPak, a free add-in that comes with Excel. It contains tools to guide you through complex analysis.

Be aware that you may not want to use the Analysis ToolPak. Many of the analyses it produces embed static values in the formulas. This means you will probably have to manually update your dashboard when data or assumptions change. Another consideration is that any dashboard you create in which the data changes will require the end user to have the Analysis ToolPak installed.

The Analysis ToolPak is an add-in that comes with Excel, but you must install it. It contains additional statistical functions for use in Excel. One of these additional functions is the Moving Average tool.

If you are using Excel 2010, install the Analysis ToolPak by selecting File ➤ Options ➤ Add-Ins. In Excel 2007, click the Microsoft Office button, choose Excel Options, and select Add-Ins. You see a list of active and inactive add-ins, as shown in Figure 23.4. In the Manage drop-down list at the bottom, select Excel Add-ins and click Go. The Add-Ins dialog box appears, as shown in Figure 23.5. Select the Analysis ToolPak check box and click OK.

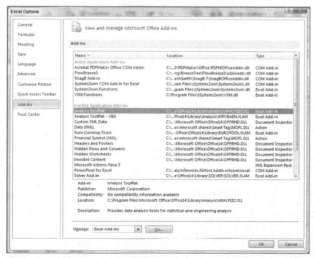

Figure 23.4: This dialog box shows active and inactive add-ins and enables you to install additional add-ins.

Figure 23.5: The Add-Ins dialog box enables you to select the Analysis ToolPak.

To install the Analysis ToolPak in Microsoft Excel 2003, follow these steps:

1. Choose Tools ➤ Add-Ins to display the Add-Ins dialog box.

2. Select the Analysis ToolPak check box.

3. Click OK.

After loading the Analysis ToolPak, you have numerous new statistical and forecasting tools available. In Excel 2010 and Excel 2007, the Data Analysis command gives you access to the ToolPak's additional functions. The Data Analysis command is on the Data tab in the Analysis group. If you do not see the Analysis group, the ToolPak is not installed. In Excel 2003, access the new ToolPak functions by choosing Tools ➤ Data Analysis.

Exponential Smoothing with the Analysis ToolPak

Excel has a built-in tool to guide you through creating exponential smoothing. To use the Exponential Smoothing tool, you must have the Analysis ToolPak installed, as described in the preceding section.

To create exponentially smoothed data using the Analysis ToolPak, follow these steps:

1. In Excel 2007 and Excel 2010, in the Data tab, in the Analysis group, select Data Analysis. In Excel 2003, choose Tools ➤ Data Analysis.

2. In the Data Analysis dialog box, select Exponential Smoothing and click OK. Excel displays the Exponential Smoothing dialog box, as shown in Figure 23.6. This figure shows the completed dialog box and the finished results in D7:D33.

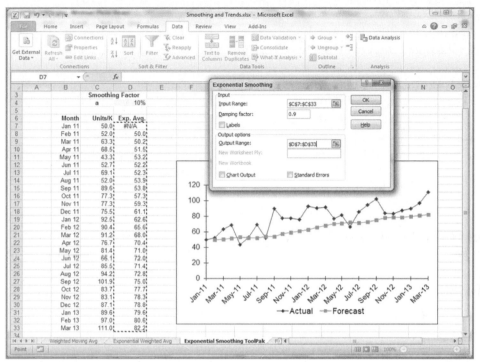

Figure 23.6: The Exponential Smoothing tool produces the same result as the manual process, but it gives you guidance.

3. Enter the data range in the Input Range box. In the figure, the data range is C7:C33.

4. Enter the damping factor in the Damping factor box. Note that you cannot reference a cell; you must type it in. Do not confuse the damping factor used in the ToolPak with the smoothing factor used earlier. They are not the same thing. The damping factor is $1 — \alpha$.

WARNING In mathematics, the term α is referred to as the smoothing factor. It is normally in the range of .01 to .3. However, Excel's Exponential Smoothing dialog box asks for a damping factor, as shown in Figure 23.6. The damping factor is 1 minus the smoothing factor, $1 - \alpha$, so it ranges from .99 to .7.

5. If the data in your input range includes a heading or label at the top, select the Labels check box.

6. In the Output Range box, select the cells where you want the smoothed data to appear. Usually this is adjacent to the input range.

7. Select the Chart Output check box if you want a chart embedded in the worksheet. The chart will not include the category (x) axis labels, so I usually create the chart myself.

The output range starts with an #N/A error because Excel doesn't have data to calculate the first smoothed data value.

One reason you may want to create your own formulas to calculate exponential smoothing rather than using the Analysis ToolPak is so that you can put the smoothing factor in a cell and reference it from the smoothing formulas. This makes it easy to test different smoothing factors. When you use the Analysis ToolPak, the numeric value for the damping factor is hard-coded in each formula, making it difficult to try different smoothing or damping factors.

Another reason for using manually created formulas is that you can use OFFSET and COUNTA, as described in Chapter 17, to create smoothing formulas that automatically adjust as the amount of data changes.

Forecasting Trends

All businesspeople wish they could see the future for their business. Although you can't see the exact future, Excel has functions that help you make estimates.

Forecasting with Worksheet Functions

Excel has a number of worksheet functions designed to help with forecasting, as shown in Table 23-1.

Table 23-1: Worksheet Functions for Forecasting

FUNCTION	DESCRIPTION
FORECAST	Calculates projected future values
TREND	Calculates projected future values for a straight-line trend
GROWTH	Calculates projected future values for exponential growth
LINEST	Calculates the formula of a straight line from data
LOGEST	Calculates the formula for an exponential curve from data

A discussion of the most commonly used functions follows. Once you understand how to use a couple of them, you will understand the others.

Forecasting Linear Trends with TREND

Humans innately make linear, or straight-line, forecasts. That is probably because doing so has been selectively programmed into our genes over the last 500 million years. Linear forecasts reflect what you expect in the physical world. If a ball is rolling in a straight line, it will probably keep rolling in that direction if nothing intervenes. If a deer runs into the brush, you look for it to reappear in a straight line from where it entered.

Be aware of how easy it is to fall into the trap of relying on linear forecasts. Psychological research shows that humans tend to expect things to continue as they have in the recent past. That explains why people do exactly the opposite of what they should, such as buying into the top of economic bubbles and selling at the bottom of downturns. It takes the emotional intelligence of a Warren Buffet to separate yourself from the emotional drive that causes you to forecast in a straight line and expect more of the same.

Even with that proviso in mind, it is probably safe to use linear forecasting for many short-term forecasts, but be aware that this is true only for the short term. Every stock and index fund prospectus warns that past performance is not a predictor of future performance. That applies to the analysis of your own businesses as well.

Excel's TREND function uses the least squares method of finding the straight line that passes through a set of data with a minimum of error. Forecasting with the TREND function is straightforward. It has this syntax:

```
TREND(known_y's, known_x's, new_x's, const)
```

known_y's are the known data values for dependent data, usually shown on the y or vertical axis of charts. *known_x's* are the independent variables, usually shown on the x or horizontal axis of charts. If you do not enter *new_x's*, Excel uses the existing *known_x's*. If *const* is TRUE, TREND calculates a linear forecast where the forecast must be 0 when the x value is 0. You will usually make *const* blank or FALSE.

Figure 23.7 shows a TREND function calculating the best fit for the data in C7:C29. The TREND function is in D7:D33, extending with forecasted results from D30 to D33. Cell D7 contains this TREND formula:

```
=TREND($C$7:$C$29,$B$7:$B$29,B7)
```

If you want to find the slope, intersect, and regression statistics, use the LINEST function or the Regression tool in the Analysis ToolPak.

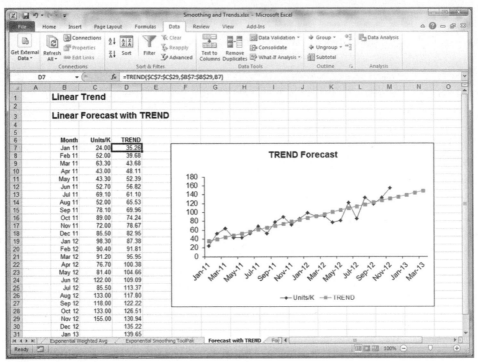

Figure 23.7: TREND calculates a straight-line forecast.

Forecasting Trends with GROWTH

Perhaps you are working with systems that are similar to those that occur in nature, such as population changes and expanding sales of new products into a fertile market. If so, you may want to use Excel's GROWTH and LOGEST functions instead of TREND, FORECAST, and LINEST. GROWTH projects the values for exponential growth, like those common to population growth. LOGEST calculates the exponential growth formula and regression statistics.

Beware of how easily the GROWTH function increases a forecast value. Many Silicon Valley businesses estimate their future growth on "network effects," the geometric expansion of users attracting more users. When that GROWTH doesn't happen, it can be fatal.

Figure 23.8 shows the same data as that used in Figure 23.7, but a GROWTH function has been used in cells D7:D33 to project future values.

The GROWTH formula in cell D7 is

```
=GROWTH($C$7:$C$29,$B$7:$B$29,B7,TRUE)
```

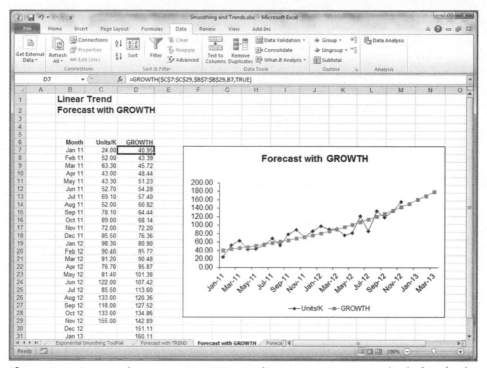

Figure 23.8: In some instances, GROWTH may be a more accurate method of projecting than TREND.

GROWTH uses the same syntax and method of entering as does TREND. If you want to calculate the exponential best-fit formula and regression statistics, use LOGEST.

Summary

Smoothing data and adding trend lines to your scorecards and dashboards can ease forecasting and decision-making. In using them, you must be aware of how easy it is to misuse trends and forecasts. Make forecasts for only short time periods, and understand that a forecast may be valid only if all conditions remain the same.

Adding trends and smoothed data to charts often creates an overloaded and visually messy chart. One way of resolving this is to allow your dashboard's users to show just the data, forecast, or smoothed series they want to see. This is easy to do. All it takes is the proper application of a check box and an IF function. To learn more about this topic, see Chapters 20 and 25.

Another topic you may want to explore is described in Chapter 24, which shows you how to add alerts that tell your dashboard users when target values have been reached or when they fall short. Alerts and targets are another useful way to help managers and executives make better and faster decisions.

Identifying Targets and Displaying Alerts

However beautiful the strategy, you should occasionally look at the results.
—Sir Winston Churchill
Statesman
1874–1965

Well-built Balanced Scorecards and operational dashboards make it easier to make good decisions. One way they do this is by putting the actual and target values in direct comparison, but this still forces the user to do the comparison. A good dashboard designer makes decisions even easier by highlighting or pinpointing the area that needs attention and focus. For example, in a column chart, if data fails to reach 80 percent of the target value, the column shows as red, which then attracts the attention of the decision-maker.

Also, when a decision is made, you want someone to take action. So you should design your scorecards and dashboards so that the viewer can generate an e-mail from within the chart. This chapter shows you how to do this in Excel.

PLAIN CHARTS AHEAD

Most of the charts in this chapter are very plain. They don't take advantage of the significant chart formatting improvements in Excel 2007 and Excel 2010. I've intentionally kept these charts with simple formatting so the trend and alert markers are more distinct.

Charting Target Values

Intermediate target values help you track your progress toward a long-range goal. Instead of measuring against a target value six months or a year away, you get better motivation and better control by tracking progress with intermediate targets. Figure 24.1 shows a simple combination chart that enables you to see monthly actual results versus target values. The actual values are columns, and the target values are markers from a line chart that look like floating dashes.

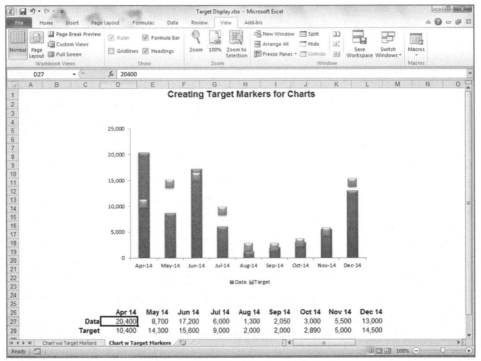

Figure 24.1: Use a combination chart to make an actual-versus-target chart.

To quickly create a chart like the one shown in Figure 24.1, begin with a column chart like the one shown in Figure 24.2. This column chart uses actual values for one series and target values for the second series. Figure 24.1 is nothing more than a column chart with an overlapping line chart. The target line is invisible, and the line's marker has been changed to a dash and increased in size. (Markers are the little symbol that appears on a line at the data point.)

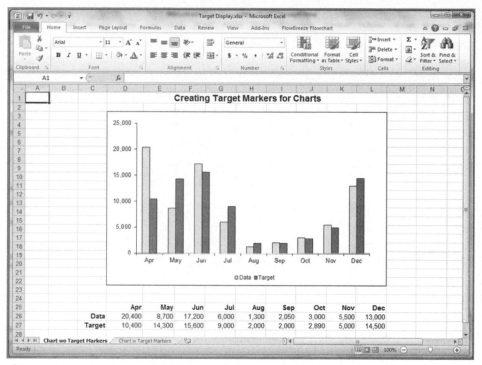

Figure 24.2: Create target markers in a chart by starting with a column chart of actual and target values like the two columns shown here and then changing one of the columns to an invisible line with markers.

To create target markers, follow these steps:

1. In Excel 2007 and Excel 2010, right-click and choose Change Series Chart Type. In Excel 2003, right-click a target column and choose Chart Type.

2. In the Chart Type dialog box, select the Line Type with Markers at each data value and click OK. This produces a line chart of target values overlapping a column chart of actual values.

3. Right-click the line and select Format Data Series.

4. Make the line invisible and the marker large. In Excel 2007 and Excel 2010, select Line Color ➢ No Line. Select Marker Options ➢ Built In and select a large dash. Use a marker size greater than 10. Click Close.

   In Excel 2003, from the Patterns tab, select a Line pattern of None. This makes the target line invisible. From the Marker pattern, select Custom and a wide line marker with a color visible over the column color. Click OK.

> ### COMBO CHARTS ARE THE TRICKSTERS OF EXCEL CHARTING
>
> Complex charts and many Excel chart tricks are accomplished through some variation on combination charts, special formatting, and selectively displayed data. To see and learn from more examples of scorecards and dashboards, go to my website: http://www.criticaltosuccess.com.

Charting Alerts with Conditional Colors

Column charts, like the ones shown in Figures 24.1 and 24.2, force managers to "eyeball" whether actual values are within the set criteria for their target. Figure 24.3 shows the same type of column chart, but the columns in the chart change color depending on what conditional criteria they have met. For example, if an actual value is within 90 percent or more of the target value, the column is green. If the actual value is between 80 percent and 90 percent of the target value, the column is yellow. If the actual value is less than 80 percent of the target value, the column is red. Conditional chart colors make it quick and easy to identify where attention should be focused. In addition to using colors, you may want to add patterns, because colors are more difficult for some people to differentiate.

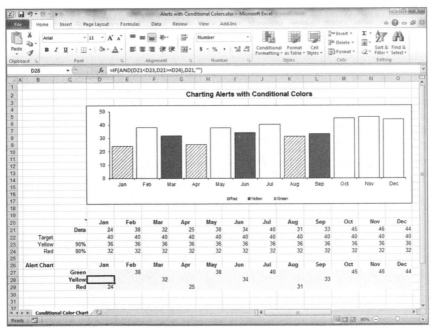

Figure 24.3: Decision-making is much easier with charts that use conditional color coding.

Conditional charts use a data series for each condition. Each of these series is given a different color or marker. Then, all the data series are displayed and adjusted so that they appear to be a single data series.

Table 24-1 shows the ranges for data, targets, and conditional criteria that appear in Figure 24.4.

Table 24-1: Definition of the Cells and Criteria Shown in Figure 24.4

VALUE	RANGE	COMMENT
Data and Dates	D20:O21	Actual dates and values by month
Target	D22:O22	Target values by month
Yellow limit	D23:O23	Yellow criteria level
Red limit	D24:O24	Red criteria level

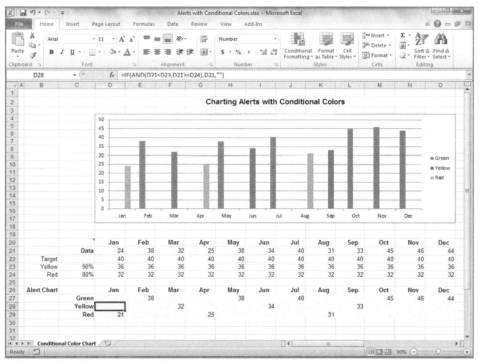

Figure 24.4: When the conditional color chart is first created it appears as three sets of separate columns, each with their own color.

The formulas in the range D27:O29 create three new data series that are used to create the colored column chart. The data in D27:O27 matches the Green condition. The data in D28:O28 matches the Yellow condition. The data in D29:O29 matches the Red condition. Table 24-2 shows the conditional formulas that define when data shows in each condition.

Table 24-2: Formulas Used to Create Colored Alerts in Column Charts

COLUMN COLOR	CONDITION	FORMULA IN COLUMN D
Green	If data in row 21 is greater than or equal to Yellow limit in row 27	D27 =IF(D21>=D23,D21,"")
Yellow	If data in row 21 is less than Yellow limit and greater than or equal to Red limit	D28 =IF(AND (D21<D23,D21>=D24) ,D21,"")
Red	If data in row 21 is less than Red limit	D29 =IF(D21<D24,D21,"")

Creating a column chart from the range C26:O29 produces the chart shown in Figure 24.4. This chart shows the same data values as the actual data, but each series has a different color. What needs to be changed for the final result is the spacing between columns. By adjusting the spacing, we can make these three data series appear in the same column positions.

To adjust Figure 24.4 so that the columns fill in the interstitial spacing and look like a single series, follow these steps:

1. Right-click any of the data series to display the Format Data Series dialog box.

2. In Excel 2007 and Excel 2010, you are in the Series Options. In Excel 2003, select the Options tab.

3. Change the Overlap value to 100 percent. Change the Gap Width to 20 percent. Click Close or OK.

This trick of dividing a single data series into multiple series of columns, bars, or lines, each with its own color, is an effective way to apply color alerts on many types of charts. Although you can make as many conditions and colors as you want, going beyond three may become confusing for the dashboard users.

MULTILINE X-AXIS LABELS

For some situations you may want a double row of labels on the x-axis. For example, due to limited chart width, you want the x-axis to have months on top and years underneath. You can't split a numeric date as a chart label, but you can if you convert the date in the cell into text.

For example, if the date is in cell D19, you can create a new text date that contains a line break character. You can then plot this text date for the x-axis. The formula to convert a numeric date in D19 into a text date for charting on the x-axis is

```
=TEXT(D$19,"mmm")&CHAR(13)&TEXT(D$19,"yy")
```

This formula converts the date in D19 to a text, three-letter month abbreviation; joins that with a line break, CHAR(13); and appends a two-letter abbreviation for the year. Using CHAR(13) in concatenated text is a useful trick in many text situations. Chapter 15 provides more examples of how to concatenate (join) text, numbers, or dates.

Charting Alerts for the Top/Bottom *n*, Quartiles, and Percentiles

A frequent request I get when creating Balanced Scorecards and dashboards for marketing, sales, and manufacturing is to show the top *n* or bottom *n* for some set of data. For example, someone may need to identify the top five production issues, or the top quartile of salespeople, or the geographic regions producing the top 20 percent of results from a marketing campaign. (A related topic is the Pareto or 80/20 chart, described in Chapter 25.)

The following example uses the functions for top *n* and bottom *n* items, but you can use the same methods for

- Minimum and maximum values
- Top or bottom quartile
- Top or bottom percentile

EXCEL PIVOTTABLES CAN AUTOMATICALLY CREATE TOP *n* AND BOTTOM *n*

Excel's most powerful data analysis features are PivotTables and PowerPivots. When you create a filter in a PivotTable or PowerPivot, the filter appears as a drop-down menu. One of the choices is Value Filters. It allows you to create a custom top/bottom *n* filter for your PivotTable or PowerPivot.

Figure 24.5 shows a simple column chart where the top three and bottom three data values are identified with different colors or patterns. Entering a different value, such as 5, in cell D6 or E6 identifies the top and bottom five data values in the chart. The Breakpoint values in cells D7:E7 show you the point where top and bottom values are included or excluded. Entering the top/bottom *n* value by using a combo box, as described in Chapter 20, is a functional feature that allows users to select their own top/bottom *n* range.

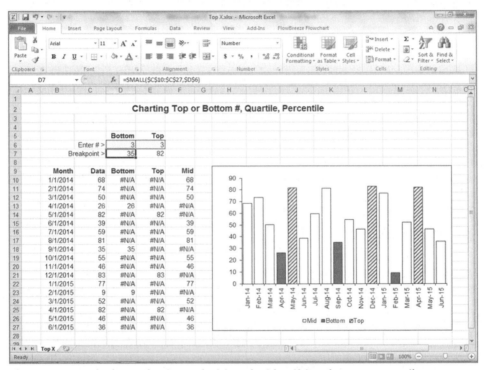

Figure 24.5: Make better business decisions by identifying the top *n*, quartile, or percentile to find where you are getting the greatest impact or where you need to focus the most attention.

The months and data are in cells B10:C27. Cell D7 calculates the breakpoint where the bottom three data values begin. Cell E7 calculates the breakpoint where the top three data values begin. The formula in D7 is

```
=SMALL($C$10:$C$27,$D$6)
```

The formula in E7 is

```
=LARGE($C$10:$C$27,$E$6)
```

You could find other ranges just as easily by using other functions such as these:

- `MIN()`
- `MAX()`
- `QUARTILE()`
- `PERCENTILE()`

You can also use a custom formula to create another statistical function or criterion.

The formulas in D7 and E7 use the values in D6 and E6, respectively, to determine how many top n or bottom n are to be included. The breakpoint for top n and bottom n is then used by formulas in D10:F27 to determine whether a data value is in the top n, in the bottom n, or in between. Table 24-3 shows these conditional formulas.

Table 24-3: Formulas to Calculate Conditional Columns

CALCULATION	RANGE	FORMULA
Bottom n	D10	`=IF(C10<=$D$7,C10,NA())`
Top n	E10	`=IF(C10>=$E$7,C10,NA())`
Mid	F10	`=IF(AND(C10>$D$7,C10<$E$7),C10,NA())`

The formulas in D10, E10, and F10 are copied down to row 27. This produces numeric values in a column when the condition is satisfied and #NA when they aren't satisfied. #NA is not plotted in Excel charts.

Now, using the technique described in the previous section, create a chart from the Month, Bottom, Mid, and Top columns. In Excel 2003, right-click one of the data series in the chart and choose Format ➢ Data Series. Select the Options tab and adjust Overlap to 100 percent and Gap Width to 20 percent. In Excel 2007 or Excel 2010, right-click the data series and choose Format Data Series, and then select Series Options to change the Overlap and Gap Width.

Charting Alerts with Line and XY Scatter Diagrams

Some data, such as clinical or manufacturing production data, is best charted with line or XY scatter diagrams. With these, you also can use a method similar to those described previously to create conditional charts. To do so, however, you need an additional formatting technique. Figure 24.6 shows a line chart with distinctive top and bottom markers. Especially when there are lots of data points, as in clinical or manufacturing scatter diagrams, you may find it hard to notice the difference between markers. If you need a better visual identifier in line and XY scatter diagrams, check the next example, which shows you how to attach a visual indicator to conditional data points.

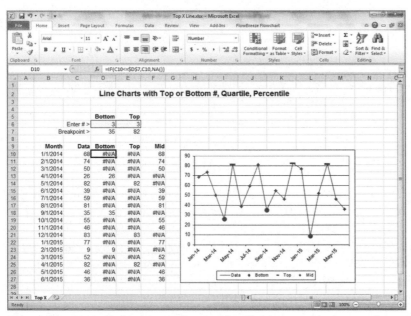

Figure 24.6: Use distinctive markers to identify top *n* and bottom *n* data points.

The previous examples explain the formulas in the Top, Mid, and Bottom columns. In the previous example, a column chart, you didn't include the data values in the chart. For this chart, you plot the Data values. Follow these steps to create a conditional line chart:

1. Select cells B9:F27 and create a column chart. This produces a chart with four columns.

   In the following steps, you will change each column into a line chart. For the Data line series, remove the line markers but leave the line. For the Top, Mid, and Bottom line series, remove the line but leave the markers. You want to make the Top, Mid, and Bottom markers distinct from each other.

2. Use the legend to identify each data series. Right-click the Data series and choose Change Series Chart Type in Excel 2007 and Excel 2010. In Excel 2003, choose Chart Type, select the Line with Markers, and click OK.

3. Right-click the Data line, and choose Format Data Series.

4. In Excel 2007 and Excel 2010, select Marker Options and None for the Marker Type. In Excel 2003, on the Patterns tab, select the color and weight you want for Line, and select None for the marker. (The markers will be shown with distinctive markers by Top, Mid, and Bottom.)

5. Return to Step 2 and repeat this sequence, but now work on each of the Top, Mid, and Bottom series in turn. Change each to a line, and then format these lines with None so that the line disappears. Use a distinctive marker for the Top, Mid, and Bottom series.

If you need greater visual differentiation for your top and bottom markers, you may want to use the technique described in the following section.

Adding a Visual Indicator to Top/Bottom *n*, Quartile, and Percentile Charts

Microsoft Excel is a powerful and versatile charting engine. It offers the little-known ability to replace data points with pictures. This means that you can make your top *n* or bottom *n* data points stand out by replacing those data markers with pictures. Figure 24.7 shows an example where the top and bottom data points use large red circles with dots at midpoint. In this example, because it is easy to distinguish the top and bottom data points, both markers can be the same. You can make the picture used by each marker different. The picture could just as easily be an arrow or even a text identifier that was captured graphically.

First, you need to create the picture to replace the line marker. For simple icons you can use Microsoft Paint, found in Windows under Start ➢ All Programs ➢ Accessories. Excel recognizes most major picture formats, so you can use any editor you are comfortable with. You can also use Excel's drawing features to create a symbol.

Here's a warning: When you replace a line marker with a picture, you can't resize the picture, but you can paste another picture over it. So, first create a couple of different-sized pictures, and then select the size that works best.

To replace a chart marker in Excel 2007 or Excel 2010, first draw your custom symbol. You can even use Excel's Insert Shape feature. Select and copy that shape or drawing. Click the data series containing the markers you want to replace, and press Ctrl+V to paste the shape or drawing.

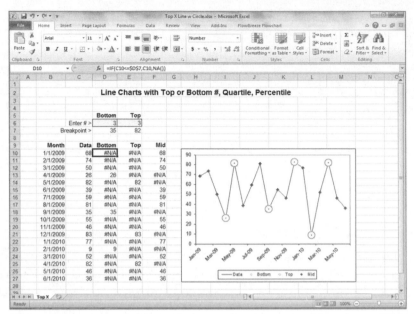

Figure 24.7: You can add any picture or drawing as a marker on conditional charts.

To replace a marker with a picture in versions of Excel prior to 2007, follow these steps:

1. Select the line on which you want to paste a picture. The picture replaces the markers on the line.

2. Choose Insert ➤ Picture.

3. Find the picture in the folder where it is saved, select the picture file, and click OK.

The picture replaces the markers for that data series.

Alerting with E-mailing

Some high-end Business Intelligence systems include the ability to send an e-mail when an alert condition is met. These systems cost tens of thousands to hundreds of thousands of dollars for the software license fees, and even more for consulting to make it work.

Although it takes a lot of work to replicate that functionality in an Excel worksheet, you can make it easy to send an e-mail when an alert condition has been met. It takes just a few minutes to add alert-driven e-mail buttons. (With the addition of some nontrivial VBA code, you can add the ability to send alert-driven e-mails from dashboards.)

To create an alert-driven e-mail system, you combine a conditional test, the HYPERLINK function, and conditional formats. The simple example in Figure 24.8 shows a condition that tests whether the actual value in D8 is greater than 90 percent of the target value in D9. In this example, the textual "buttons" appear only when the actual value is less than 90 percent of the target value.

In actual use, you would probably use a conditional IF function with AND or OR to test target conditions. When an alert condition is met, the buttons appear as shown in Figure 24.8.

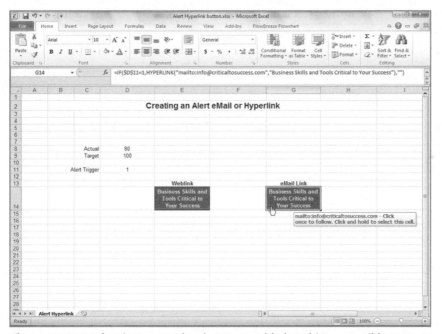

Figure 24.8: It takes just a couple of steps to add alert-driven e-mail buttons to your dashboard.

The text button in E14 uses a formula that creates a hyperlink to my website:

```
=IF($D$11=1,HYPERLINK("http://www.criticaltosuccess.com",
"Business Skills and Tools Critical to Your Success"),"")
```

When the trigger value in D11 is 1, the cell becomes a hyperlink to my website, which contains more Excel examples, tips, tutorials, and resources. When cell D11 is 0, the same cell becomes a blank cell.

The text button in G14 uses the formula that opens an e-mail message addressed to me:

```
=IF($D$11=1,HYPERLINK("mailto:info@criticaltosuccess.com",
"Business Skills and Tools Critical to Your Success"),"")
```

If you test this, please e-mail me and let me know which parts of this book have been most valuable to you.

In this case, when the trigger value in D11 is 1, the cell becomes a hyperlink that opens an e-mail message ready to send. When cell D11 is 0, the same cell becomes a blank cell.

These two cells appear as normal blank cells when D11 is 0 and appear as textual buttons when D11 is 1. This is done with a formula used in conditional formatting. In Excel 2007 and Excel 2010, create a conditional format based on a formula on the Home tab, in the Styles group, select Conditional Formatting and click New Rules. In the New Rules dialog box, select Use a formula to determine which cells to format. In the Format values where this formula is true edit box, enter the formula,

```
=$D$11=0
```

In Excel 2003, to set the conditional formats, select the cells and then choose Format ➢ Conditional Format. In the first drop-down, select Formula Is. Enter this formula:

```
=$D$11=0
```

as the condition to test for the format when the cell will have a normal format.

Assign a normal format to that cell. Do the same for the second condition using this formula:

```
=$D$11=1
```

This tests when the format should appear as a textual button with a background pattern, border, and font that make the cell appear like a button. The finished Conditional Formatting dialog box should look like the one shown in Figure 24.9.

Summary

As a dashboard designer and developer, your purpose is to help executives and managers make better decisions faster. That involves displaying the information they need for decision-making so that it is quickly accessible and memorable. But that is only part of what is needed. Your dashboards should use Excel's analytical and conditional functions to identify when a decision is needed and then use the alerts described in this chapter to identify where attention should be focused.

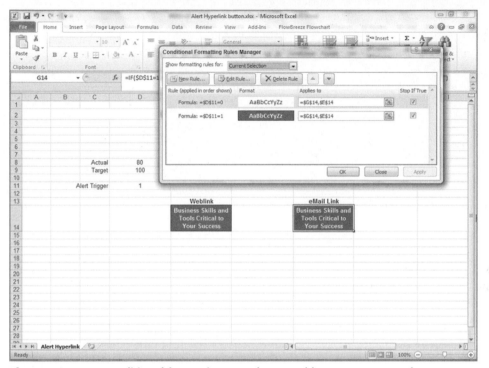

Figure 24.9: Use conditional formatting to make textual buttons appear only when an alert condition is met.

CHAPTER

25

Building Powerful Decision-Making Charts

Effective leaders help others to understand the necessity of change and to accept a common vision of the desired outcome.

—John Kotter
Harvard Business School professor

Your dashboard users want to make better decisions faster. Selecting the right type of analytics and visual presentation will help you give them what they want.

An important part of your job is understanding the business decisions that need to be made and the analysis and visual presentation that will aid the decision-making process. The charts and graphs described in this chapter are some of the more powerful charting types for business decisions.

TIP **To gain full control over Excel's powerful charting engine, you need to learn how to handle combination charts. Combination charts enable you to have two y-axes on a chart. You also can have more than one chart type in a chart—combining column charts and line charts, for example.**

In Excel 2007 and Excel 2010, you build combination charts by first creating a chart with one format, such as bar, and both sets of data. Then you select one of the sets of data by clicking one of its chart elements, such as a bar or column. The new command Change Chart Type appears in the Type group. Click Change Chart Type to open the Change Chart Type dialog box. Select the second type of chart you want, and click OK.

Usually a combination chart requires two y-axes. To add the second axis in Excel 2007 and Excel 2010, select the data series to which you want to add a y-axis. Then, in the Chart Tools Layout tab, in the Current Selection group, select Format Selection. When the Format Data Series dialog box appears, select the Second Axis option for Plot Series on. Click Close.

> In versions of Excel earlier than 2007, combination charts are found on the Custom Types tab of the first step in the Chart Wizard. Two useful combination charts are Line—Column on 2 Axes and Lines on 2 Axes. If you want to change how a data series charts, such as by changing a line to a tcolumn, select the data series and then choose Chart ➢ Chart Type and select the chart type for that data series. Any number of chart types can exist on the same chart.

SAVE TIME BY DOWNLOADING EXCEL SAMPLE FILES

Many of the Excel dashboard examples in the book take a long time to build or work with large databases. If you want free copies of more than 2 MB of sample files, go to http://www.criticaltosuccess.com and request the book's sample files.

Seeing a Full Statistical Picture with a Box-and-Whisker Plot

The box-and-whisker plot, also known as a boxplot, is a statistical carry-all. In one chart it shows the minimum value, the lower quartile (Q1 or 25th percentile), the median, the upper quartile (Q3 or 75th percentile), and the maximum value. This is a versatile chart, but it requires a few steps to create.

Figure 25.1 shows a box-and-whisker plot. Each of these box-and-whisker plots refers to a set of data, shown in the range L8:N32. The bottom and top of the box are the 25th and 75th percentiles. The band in the middle of the box is the 50th percentile, the median. The triangle marker is the mean.

The tops and bottoms of the "whiskers" in this example show the maximum and minimum values, but they also can be used to show other percentile limits, top and bottom outliers, and more. The mean, or average, is often shown as a dot or marker that overlays the box.

Although it's useful, the box-and-whisker plot is not one of Excel's predefined charts. It is not difficult to create, but it is somewhat involved. You can create a box-and-whisker plot in Excel in several ways.

The following steps show you how to make a stacked column chart to create the box. By calculating the differences between each line, you can make a box with ends at the 25th percentile, median, and 75th percentile. Making the lowest column invisible makes the box float above the x-axis. Adding a top and bottom whisker to the box using Y Error Bars finishes the appearance. Once you've created a set of these, you can copy and paste the worksheet where you need it and then plug in your own data.

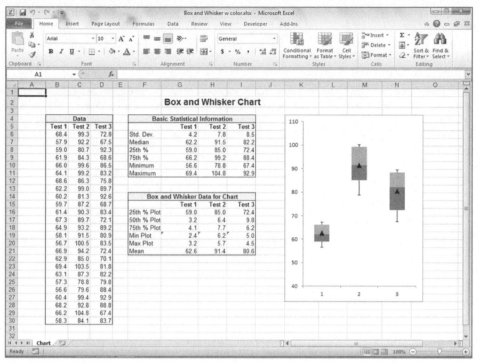

Figure 25.1: This box-and-whisker plot includes mean, median, 25th and 75th percentiles, maximum, and minimum values for a data set.

To create a box-and-whisker plot showing the median, 25th and 75th percentiles, and minimum and maximum, follow these steps:

1. Enter the three sets of data as shown in B5:D30.

2. Create a table of statistical values. These values define the top and bottom edges of the stacked columns that create the box.

LABEL	CELL	FORMULA
Std. Dev.	G6	=STDEV(B6:B30)
Median	G7	=MEDIAN(B6:B30)
25th %	G8	=PERCENTILE(B6:B30,0.25)
75th %	G9	=PERCENTILE(B6:B30,0.75)
Min	G10	=MIN(B6:B30)
Max	G11	=MAX(B6:B30)

3. Copy G6:G11 to fill H6:I11. This replicates the statistical values for Test 2 and Test 3 data.

4. Create a table of values used to plot the chart. Notice that only two of these charted values are actual statistical values; the other chart values become the heights of stacked segments in the chart. Create the following data tables for the chart values:

CELL	FORMULA	DESCRIPTION
G16	=G8	25th percentile
G17	=G7-G8	Median; height of the 50th percentile column segment
G18	=G9-G7	Height of the 75th percentile column segment
G19	=G8-G10	Lower error bar length
G20	=G11-G9	Upper error bar length
G21	=AVERAGE(B6:B30)	Average

5. Copy G16:G21 to fill H16:I21.

6. Create a stacked column chart by selecting G7:I9. Make sure you use the Stacked Column. (Do not select the 100% column.)

7. Delete the gray chart background (in Excel 2003), the grid lines, and the legend. Format the bottom column segments so that they have no fill color. Your chart should now look like Figure 25.2.

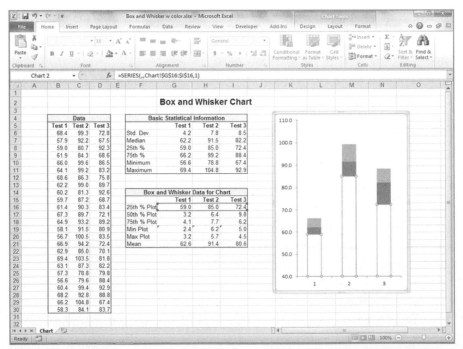

Figure 25.2: The basic stacked column chart, with 25th, 50th, and 75th percentiles.

In Excel 2007 and Excel 2010, select the top segment. In the Chart Tools Layout tab, in the Analysis group, click the down arrow next to Error Bars Options. In the drop-down list, select More Error Bars to display the Format Error Bars dialog box, shown in Figure 25.3. Select Display Direction Plus to make an error bar that goes up from the top of the segment. In Error amount, select Custom, and then click the Specify Value button. Enter the reference for the Minimum value, **G20:I20**, as the Positive error value. Clear the Negative error value. Click OK twice.

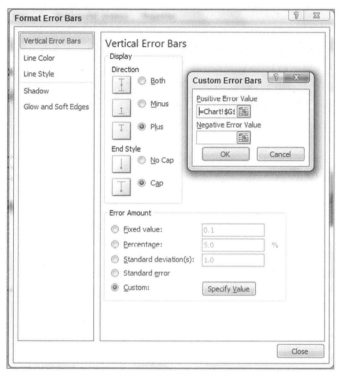

Figure 25.3: In the Format Error Bars dialog, you create the upper and lower bars.

In Excel 2003, add the top whisker for the maximum value by right-clicking the top segment, choosing Format Data Series, and selecting the Y Error Bars tab. In the Error Amount group, select Custom, and in the + (plus) reference box, enter the Max Plot data in G20:I20. In any version of Excel, you should see an error bar, the whisker, sprouting from the top of the topmost segment.

8. In Excel 2007 and Excel 2010, repeat the process described in step 7, but select the column segment touching the x-axis. Select from the Vertical Error Bars a bar in the Minus direction. In Error amount, clear the positive Error value box, and enter **G19:I19**.

In Excel 2003, add the bottom whisker for the minimum value by right-clicking the base segment touching the x-axis, choosing Format Data Series, and selecting the Y Error Bars tab. In the Error Amount group, select Custom, and in the – (minus) reference box, enter the Min Plot data in G19:I19.

In any version of Excel, you should see an error bar hanging from the top of the lowest segment.

9. Right-click the y-axis, choose Format Axis, and adjust the y-axis scale.

If the box appears too wide, right-click it and choose Format Data Series; then select the Options tab. In Excel 2007 and Excel 2010, select Series Options. Increase the Gap Width until the boxes are narrow.

To add the average (mean) as a marker on the box-and-whisker plot, you add the average as a line with markers and then hide the line. Follow these steps:

1. Copy the mean data: G21:I21.

2. Right-click the chart background and choose Paste.

3. A new segment is added to the chart. In Excel 2003, right-click this new segment and choose Chart Type. In Excel 2007 and Excel 2010, choose Change Series Chart Type.

4. Select Line with Markers as the chart type for the new data, and click OK.

5. Format the line so that it is invisible and the marker is visible with a marker shape, color, and size that work for you. Figure 25.4 shows a finished box-and-whisker plot, including 25th and 75th percentiles, median and average, and maximum and minimum.

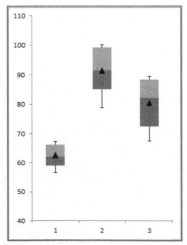

Figure 25.4: The finished box-and-whisker plot with mean or average added as a marker.

These same steps can be used to display other data, such as outliers, alert levels, and other percentile markers.

Bullet Charts: A Better Alternative to Gauges

Business Intelligence vendors seem to love to show dashboards with fancy, colorful gauges. Some of these dashboards look like they were torn from the dashboard of an expensive Italian race car. At some point in the past, vendors took the term "dashboard" too literally.

I must admit that at first executives and managers like to see these round and colorful gauges. They look cool. But you don't have to use a dashboard full of gauges too many times before you realize that all those large, colorful gauges are a waste. It is difficult to see the relationships between different values when each appears in a gauge. Gauges use large increments, so you can't see small changes. They waste space. One gauge shows one value, a target, and perhaps the alert limits. In that same space, you can fit five or six other components that let you see the relationships between values, as well as even more information.

Stephen Few, author of the excellent book *Information Dashboard Design* (O'Reilly Media, 2006), took on this problem and developed an information visualization object he calls a "bullet graph." In a small space, a bullet graph shows

- Data value
- Target value
- Easily readable scale
- Two or more easily readable alert limits

Figure 25.5 shows a bullet graph with its component parts labeled in the legend. The bullet graph in the figure is vertical, but bullet graphs can be horizontal as well. Bullet graphs are not a predesigned format in Excel and take some work to create, but once you've created one, you can plug in new data, and you're done.

You create bullet graphs by building a stacked column chart with the target, actual, and alert values as segments. (If you want a horizontal bullet chart, create a stacked bar chart.) The target value is then formatted to move independently and to appear as a dash marker. The actual value is also formatted to move independently and is thinned so that it appears over the alert value columns.

> **WARNING** Data *must* be arranged in the order shown in the figure to follow the steps for creating a bullet graph. If the data is in a different order, the column segments may be difficult to select.

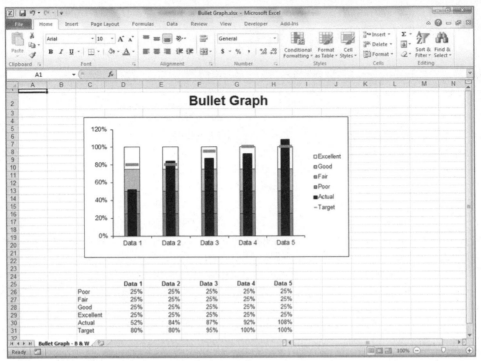

Figure 25.5: Bullet graphs display a great deal of information in a small space.

To build a bullet graph in Excel 2007 and Excel 2010, start by building a stacked column chart:

1. Enter only the data shown in Figure 25.5 in the range C25:D31. Select C25:D31. You will add more data later.

2. Insert a Stacked Column chart. Make sure you do not choose the 100 percent Stacked Column chart.

3. Select the chart, and in the Chart Tools Design tab, in the Data group, click the Switch Row/Column button. Your chart should now look similar to Figure 25.6.

To build a bullet graph in versions of Excel before 2007, first create a stacked column chart of all values:

1. Enter only the data shown in Figure 25.5 in the range C25:D31. You will add more data later to create additional bullet graphs. (You can have as many alert levels as you want. This example shows four.)

2. Select the data and labels, C25:D31, and open the Chart Wizard.

3. Select the second column type, Stacked Column, and click Next.

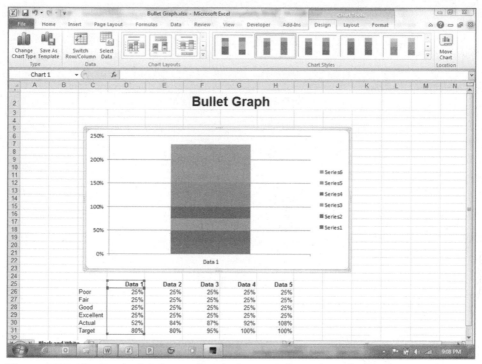

Figure 25.6: The Stacked Column chart is the start of creating a bullet chart.

4. In step 2 of 4 of the Chart Wizard, select the Series In Rows option on the Data Range tab. The Chart Wizard shows the column stacked, as in Figure 25.6. Click Finish.

5. Position the stacked column chart on the worksheet, and delete the gray background and the grid lines.

Now format the target value segment so that it appears as the independently floating marker shown in Figure 25.7. The target marker is the floating dash shown in Figure 25.7. To format this, follow these steps:

1. Right-click the target value in the top segment and choose Format Data Series. In Excel 2007 and Excel 2010, in the Series Options, select Secondary Axis and click OK. In versions of Excel before 2007, on the Axis tab, select Secondary Axis and click OK. This moves the target value to the new y-axis on the right. The chart should look similar to Figure 25.7. The secondary axis appears on the right, and the target segment covers most of the other stacked columns.

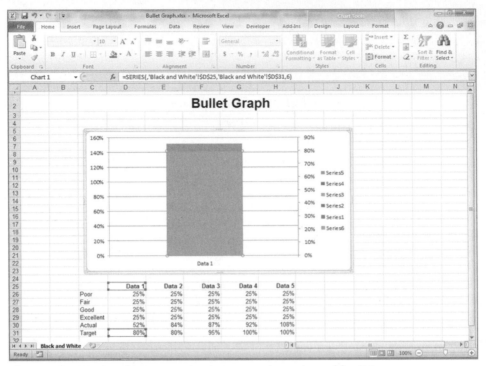

Figure 25.7: Moving the target value to a secondary axis enables it to move independently of the other segments.

Do not delete the legend. It will help you differentiate between the segments.

2. Delete the secondary axis on the right by selecting it, clicking the numbers, and pressing Delete. The target segment remains centered over the column.

3. Change the target segment so that it appears as a marker. In Excel 2007 and Excel 2010, right-click the target segment and choose Change Series Chart Type. In Excel 2003, right-click the target segment and choose Chart Type. Select Line with Marker and click OK. The target segment that was a column segment becomes a marker. There is no line, because there is only one point.

4. Right-click the marker and choose Format Data Series.

5. Format the line so that it is invisible. Doing so hides the line in the legend as well as in the chart. Format the marker so that it is a heavy dash, as shown in Figure 25.8. This formats the target marker as a heavy dash floating over the stacked columns. Click OK.

The target marker now appears as a heavy red dash floating over the stacked column chart, as shown in Figure 25.9.

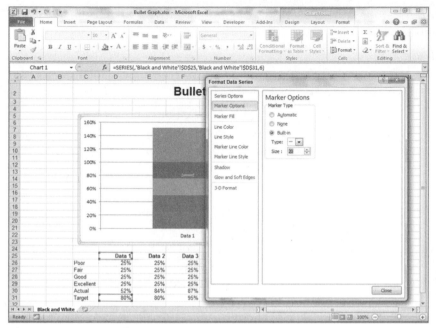

Figure 25.8: Format the target marker as a heavy bar.

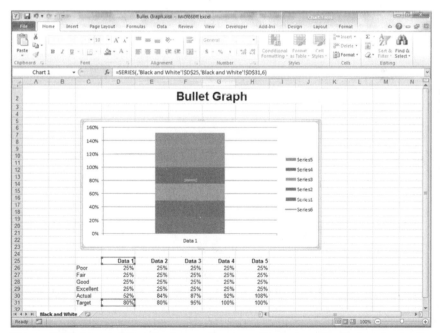

Figure 25.9: The red target value marker now floats over the alert and actual segments.

In the next steps, you will format the segment for Actual data as a column that is centered over the other columns. It will move independently of the four stacked alert column segments.

First, you must make the Actual data segment narrow so that the alert segments can be seen behind it:

1. Right-click the Actual value segment. If you're unsure which segment is the actual data, click each segment and notice which data is selected on the worksheet. Choose Format Data Series.

2. In Excel 2007 and Excel 2010, choose Series Options and Secondary Axis. In Excel 2003, select the Axis tab and then select Secondary Axis. Click OK. This makes the actual value segment independent of the left axis. If you deleted the right y-axis previously, it will not be visible. If you did not delete it, select the right y-axis and press Delete.

3. Right-click the Actual value segment, which is touching the horizontal axis, and choose Format Data Series.

4. Select the Options tab (in Excel 2007 and Excel 2010, select Series Options), and change the Gap Width to 350. This reduces the width of the actual segment so that the alert segments can be seen. Click OK.

The basic bullet graph is complete and appears as shown in Figure 25.10. At this point, you can right-click each segment and select colors to differentiate each alert level. Alert colors normally are darker at the bottom and lighter toward the top. The actual value is usually black, and the target marker uses a color that stands out, such as yellow or red.

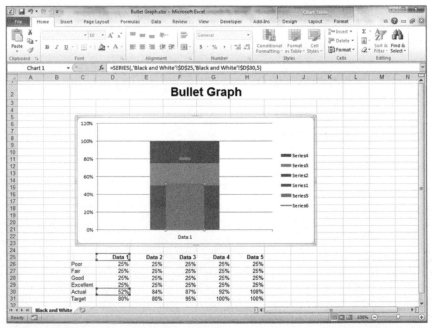

Figure 25.10: With a little additional formatting, your bullet graph will be an information-rich asset to your dashboards.

Be sure to add data by entering it to the right of the existing data, as shown in the range C25:H31. Then select the chart. This puts handles around the data, as shown in Figure 25.11. Select the data series handle at the bottom of D31 in Figure 25.11, and drag it to the right to include all data. When you release the handle, all the data series are charted as bullet graphs, as shown in Figure 25.12.

	Data 1
Poor	25%
Fair	25%
Good	25%
Excellent	25%
Actual	52%
Target	80%

Figure 25.11: Drag the data series handle to include additional data series.

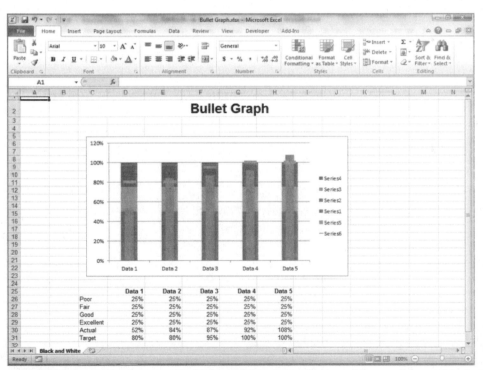

Figure 25.12: Once you have a bullet graph template, you can add more data and include it in the bullet graph.

Once you have this basic bullet graph completed, you can use it as a template for other bullet graphs by changing the data.

Pareto Charts Show What Is Most Important

Although line and column charts are used most frequently in scorecards and dashboards, the Pareto chart is one of my favorites for helping decision-makers. The name comes from Vilfredo Pareto, a 19th century economist and sociologist. He discovered the 80/20 rule, which is often stated using examples such as "20 percent of your customers bring you 80 percent of your revenue."

Pareto charts are a great way to help business decision-makers decide where to focus resources for the greatest impact. My clients have used Pareto charts to make decisions about the following issues:

- Where to focus support and quality control
- Which clients should have greater focus
- Which product features are most desirable
- Which issues cause the greatest dissatisfaction

Figure 25.13 shows a Pareto chart that calculates which 20 percent of customers generate 80 percent of the revenue. In this chart, it's easy to see that the first four customers contribute 80 percent of the revenue. In organizations with a large customer base, this type of analysis can help you identify where to focus your relationships, quality control, product features, and so forth.

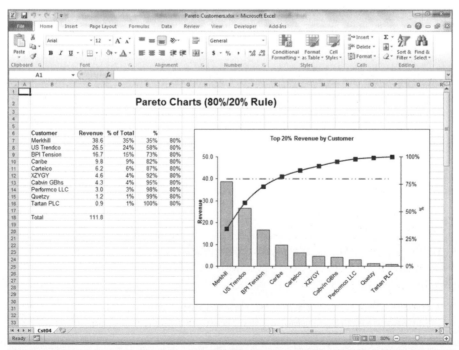

Figure 25.13: Pareto charts help you identify the 20 percent that has 80 percent of the impact.

To create a Pareto chart, do the following:

1. Enter the data as shown in B7:C16 of Figure 25.13. Notice that the data is sorted in descending order by Revenue.

2. Create a grand total for all data, as shown in C18:

   `=SUM(C7:C17)`

3. Calculate the percentage of the total for each item with the formula in D7:

   `=C7/$C$18`

   by copying it through the range D7:D16.

4. Calculate the cumulative percentage by entering this formula in E7:

   `=SUM($D$7:D7)`

   and copying it through E7:E16.

5. Enter the static 80 percent line values in F7:F16.

In Excel 2007 and Excel 2010, create a Pareto chart by following these steps:

1. Select B6:C16 and then hold down the Ctrl key as you select the noncontiguous range E6:F16. This leaves D6:D16 unselected.

2. Insert a Clustered Column chart—the first column chart in the gallery. (The columns representing percentages may be too small to see.)

3. Select the percentage columns by clicking a Revenue column and then pressing the up or down arrow key to select the Percentage column. Watch which column of data is selected to ensure that it is the Percentage column.

4. Move the Percentage column to a secondary axis by right-clicking the Percentage column and choosing Format Data Series. In the Format Data Series dialog box, in Series Options, select Secondary Axis, and then click OK.

   At this point, the chart may look confusing. Figure 25.14 shows the chart with overlapping columns. It should look like a stacked column chart with two axes.

5. Change the Percentage columns into a line with markers. Right-click the Percentage column segments and choose Change Series Chart Type. Select the line with markers, and click OK.

   Your chart should now look like a Pareto chart without the 80 percent horizontal line. To add the 80 percent line, copy F7:F16 and paste it into the chart.

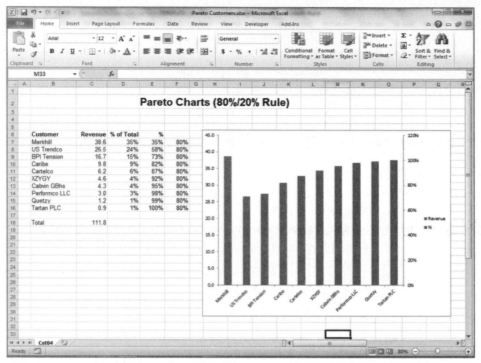

Figure 25.14: One of these overlapping sets of columns will become a line in the Pareto chart.

Your chart will now look almost like the Pareto chart shown in Figure 25.13. All that remains is a little formatting.

In versions of Excel before 2007, create the Pareto chart from this table by following these steps:

1. Select B6:C16 and then hold down the Ctrl key as you select the noncontiguous range E6:F16. This leaves D6:D16 unselected.

2. Open the Chart Wizard and select the Custom Types tab. Select Line—Column on 2 Axis. Click Finish.

This creates a double-axis chart with two column charts and one 80 percent line. All you have left to do is move the shorter of the column charts to the second axis and reformat it as a line:

1. Right-click the blue column segment representing the cumulative percentage and choose Format Data Series. On the Axis tab, select Secondary Axis

and click OK. The cumulative percentage line is now associated with the right axis and takes on the appearance of the Pareto curve.

2. Right-click the blue column segment representing the cumulative percentage and choose Chart Type. On the Standard Types tab, select Line with Markers and click OK.

Pareto charts depend on the data's being sorted in descending order. If you are doing a query from an external data source through Microsoft Query or from a SQL generated file, you can request that the data be returned in descending sort order. If you are retrieving unsorted data from an internal Excel worksheet, you may want to record a simple macro that sorts the list.

TIP I've been using Excel since before its public release in the mid-1980s, but there is still a book I keep handy on my bookshelf: John Walkenbach's *Excel Charts* (Wiley, 2002). It has methods and tips that help you create good-looking, powerful charts.

Variance Charts Make a Difference

If one of your objectives is to reduce variance from budget, you should be charting variance, not actual and budget values. If you chart actual and budget values as two lines or two columns, you force your reader to calculate the variance.

Figure 25.15 shows a human resources variance chart where the variance calculation is done in the worksheet rather than in the reader's mind. In this case, the reader can immediately see where staffing levels are ahead or behind.

In Figure 25.15, instead of charting actual and budget values, only the variance is charted, making the variance obvious. A few formatting techniques are used to make the chart more readable. The chart is based on values in row 35. The variance in cell C35 is calculated with this formula:

```
=C36/C37
```

which is copied across the row.

Figure 25.15: A variance chart makes variance from a plan more apparent than simply charting both actual and target values.

To create this chart, do the following:

1. Select B34:N35 and open the Chart Wizard.

2. In Excel 2007 and Excel 2010, insert a Clustered Column chart. In Excel 2003, select the Clustered Column type and click Finish.

3. Right-click the y-axis (right-click the numbers in Excel 2007 and Excel 2010) and choose Format Axis.

   ■ In Excel 2007 and Excel 2010, in the Axis Options, enter 1 in the Horizontal Axis Crosses At box. In Excel 2003, on the Scale tab, clear the Category (X) Axis check box, and enter 1 in the Crosses At box. This makes the horizontal axis cross the y-axis at the 100 percent mark, putting positive variance on top and negative variance underneath.

   ■ Enter a Minimum of 0.9 and a Maximum of 1.1 for scale height. Click OK.

4. Right-click the x-axis and choose Format Axis. In Excel 2007 and Excel 2010, on the Axis Options tab, select Axis Labels Low. In Excel 2003, on the Patterns tab, select Low for the Tick Mark Labels. This moves the department headings to the bottom of the chart. Click OK.

5. In Excel 2007 and Excel 2010, right-click a column.

   - Choose Add Data Labels to display numeric values at the top of each column.

   - In the Series Option tab, adjust the Overlap and Gap Width to widen and position the columns. On the Fill, select a color and then select the Invert if Negative check box so that positive and negative numbers are different.

   In Excel 2003, right-click the columns and choose Format Data Series.

   - On the Data Labels tab, select the Value check box to display numeric values at the top of each column.

   - On the Options tab, adjust the Overlap and Gap Width to widen and position the columns.

   - On the Patterns tab, select a color for the positive variance, and select the Invert If Negative check box for an opposite color for negative variance. Click OK.

Project Your Projects with Gantt Charts

If you are creating dashboards for managers and project managers, they want to see project, task, and resource data on their dashboards. However, if you are building a Balanced Scorecard and want to show completion estimates for Strategic Initiatives, it can be better to just show executives the variance from forecast. This requires two different types of project management charts. This section describes a simplified Gantt chart, and the following section shows a project variance chart more appropriate for senior managers.

In Excel 2007 and Excel 2010, do the following to create a Gantt chart like the one shown in Figure 25.16:

1. Enter the dates as shown. The end dates are the sum of the start date and duration. If a start date is dependent on another end date, link the dependent start date to the end date.

2. Select B5:D17 and, on the Insert tab, in the Chart group, select Stacked Bar Chart. Do not select 100 percent Stacked Bar.

3. Right-click the x-axis (the vertical axis showing project names) and choose Format Axis. On the Axis tab, select Categories in Reverse Order. This puts Project 1 at the top. Also, select Horizontal Access Crosses at Maximum Category. This moves the horizontal access to the bottom of the chart.

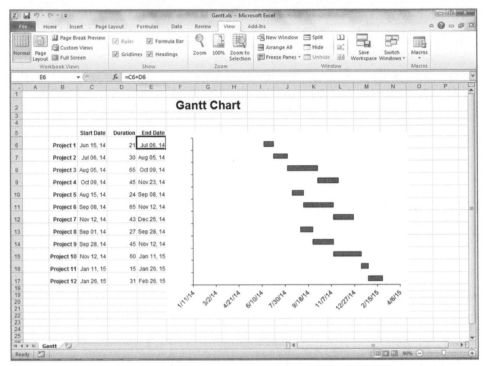

Figure 25.16: A Gantt chart is just a stacked bar chart with the first segment hidden.

4. Right-click the Start Date column segment, the leftmost segment, and choose Format Data Series. On the Patterns tab, select Border None and Area None so that the first segment is hidden and the duration appears to float.

5. Right-click the y-axis (click the dates) and choose Format Axis. Select the Axis Options tab. Apply a custom date format so that the dates display without overlapping.

To create a Gantt chart like the one shown in Figure 25.16 in Excel 2003, do the following:

1. Enter the dates as shown. The end dates are the sum of the start date and duration. If a start date is dependent on another end date, link the dependent start date to the end date.

2. Select B5:D17 and open Chart Wizard.

3. Select the Stacked Bar chart and click Finish.

4. Right-click the x-axis (the vertical axis showing project names), and choose Format Axis. Select the Scale tab and select Categories in Reverse Order to put Project 1 at the top. Select Value (Y) Axis Crosses at Maximum Category to move the horizontal axis to the bottom.

5. Right-click the Start Date column segment, the leftmost segment, and choose Format Data Series. On the Patterns tab, select Border None and Area None so that the first segment is hidden and the duration appears to float.

6. Right-click the y-axis (click the dates) and choose Format Axis. Select the Axis Options tab. Apply a custom date format so that the dates display without overlapping.

Finally, the chart is formatted for appearance and the project names along the category axis are formatted to be invisible, because they appear on the worksheet.

Project Variance Gantt Charts

Executives care about results—whether a project is on time, on budget, and within scope. One way to present this big picture is with a project variance chart. It shows where projects are ahead or behind. Using the technique described in Chapter 24, you can set different alert colors to identify variance further out of limits.

Figure 25.17 shows a project variance chart. It uses a bar chart and shows just the difference between actual and target dates. Alert limits have been used so that different levels of variance appear in different colors. The target completion date for a project is the 0 point for the axis.

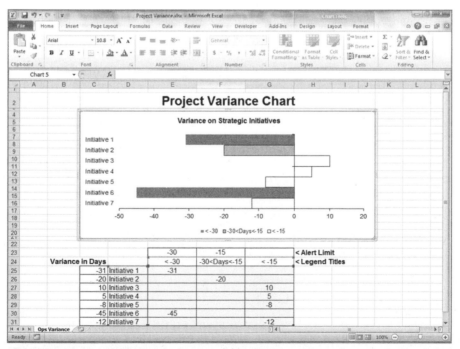

Figure 25.17: Project variance charts quickly identify projects that are not on time, on budget, or within scope.

To create a project variance chart, follow these steps:

1. Select D24:G31.

2. In Excel 2007 and Excel 2010, insert a Clustered Bar chart. In Excel 2003, open the Chart Wizard, select the Clustered Bar (the first bar chart), and click Finish.

3. Remove the background and grid lines.

4. Right-click a bar and choose Format Data Series. On the Options tab, set Overlap to 100 and Gap Width to 0. Doing so makes the three data series in columns E, F, and G appear as one series. Click OK.

5. Right-click the Category (X) Axis, displaying initiative names, and choose Format Axis. Select Low for Tick Mark Labels. This moves all the Initiative titles to the left. Click OK.

Apply color and border formats to the bars of each data series, and you have a variance project chart with conditional alert levels.

Control Charts

Six Sigma is the science of reducing variation in business processes to increase quality, reduce waste, and satisfy customers. There are many tools in a Six Sigma Black Belt's kit, but the one most frequently used to monitor and control variation is the control chart, also known as the Shewart chart. The control chart shows three things:

- A centerline, usually the average of the data
- An upper limit and lower limit within which the process should stay
- Actual data

When you use a control chart on any process, whether manufacturing, emergency room admission times, or bank processing times, it becomes visibly obvious when a process begins to go out of control. Predefined events on a control chart tell a Six Sigma professional that the process is, statistically speaking, probably going out of control. For the uninitiated, these predefined events can sound as if they are conjured out of thin air, but they have a sound statistical basis. Detecting these events can be automated in Excel, but only the basic control chart is shown here. These events indicate that processes are probably out of control:

- One data point outside the upper or lower control limit
- Six or more sequential data points steadily increasing or decreasing

■ Eight or more data points on one side of the centerline

■ Fourteen or more points alternating on either side of the centerline

The following steps show you how to create a simple control chart like the one shown in Figure 25.18. Adding different types of alerts and identifiers is covered elsewhere in this book.

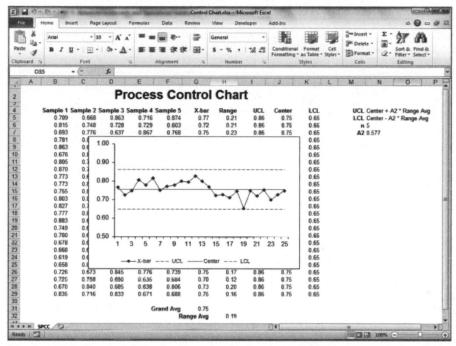

Figure 25.18: Control charts or Shewart charts are straightforward in Excel.

To create a simple process control chart like the one shown in Figure 25.18, do the following:

1. Enter the sample data in B5:F29. This demonstration has five sets of sample measurements.

2. Calculate the sample averages in G5 with

   =AVERAGE(B5:F5)

   and copy them down.

3. Calculate the sample ranges in H5 with

   =MAX(B5:F5)-MIN(B5:F5)

   and copy them down.

4. Calculate the Grand Average and the Range Average in cells G30 and H31. The Control Limit formulas are

```
UCL = Center + A2 * Range Avg.
LCL = Center - A2 * Range Avg.
```

For a sample of size $n=5$, the control chart constant for A2 is 0.577.

5. Enter the following formulas and copy them down:

NAME	CELL	FORMULA
UCL	I5	=J5+$N$7*$H$31
Center	J5	=$G$30
LCL	K5	=J5-$N$7*$H$31

6. Create the chart by selecting G4:G29, and then hold down the Ctrl key as you also select I4:K29. You should have four columns selected, but skip I4:I29.

7. Create a Line Chart with Markers.

You've created the control chart. All you need to do now is format it. You may want to apply the following formatting:

- Delete the gray chart background and grid lines.
- Reformat the UCL, Center, and LCL lines with a dashed line, without markers, and with a darker color.
- Adjust the y-axis scale size.
- Move the legend to the bottom.

Summary

A good dashboard developer needs to understand not just the software tools but also the entire business process that is being controlled. Selecting the correct analytics and visual displays is important in making fast, accurate business decisions.

If you did not read in Parts I and II how to interview executives and managers and define the critical few metrics, it is important that you do so. Chapter 12 covers tips on how to think about users' needs.

CHAPTER 26

Drilling to Detail

Never neglect details. When everyone's mind is dulled or distracted, the leader must be doubly vigilant.

—Colin Powell
Statesman, General

Scorecards and dashboards display summary results of large amounts of information. Inevitably, this forces two needs: a concise and obvious way to navigate the data and the ability to drill down from summaries and results into the original data.

This chapter describes a couple of ways to create simple navigation systems. Some are obvious, such as hyperlinks, but can take a lot of display space. Another navigation method uses a simple combo box to enable your users to jump to any named location in the workbook.

It's inevitable with Balanced Scorecards and operational dashboards that someone will find an item in the summary level that needs more examination—and that means drilling into detail. There are many ways of doing this in Excel, but the methods depend on how Excel accesses the data and the developer's experience level.

This book is written for mid- to advanced-level Excel users who usually retrieve data into the workbook. For that reason, this chapter covers methods of drilling down into data within the workbook. These usually limit drill-down to going one level deeper into data. More-advanced methods, and almost unlimited levels and views in drilling, are possible when Excel is linked to an external database such as a relational database or an OLAP cube and when it uses a PivotTable or PowerPivot to analyze data. These topics are discussed in later chapters at a level accessible by most mid-level Excel users.

Navigating

It's not uncommon for Balanced Scorecards to have 40 to 50 different displays and for operational dashboards to have three to five. Then there are the operational reports you may want to link to from within dashboards. You want to give your users a clean and simple way to navigate between this information. They need to be able to quickly move between views of data so that they can understand relationships and make strategic and operational decisions.

Balanced Scorecards created in Excel are usually presented to the executive level by encapsulating the Excel charts and tables within a Microsoft PowerPoint presentation or an Adobe PDF document, as described in Chapter 30.

If you stay within Excel for your scorecards and dashboards, you have many options for navigation and drilling into detail. In addition to normal Excel methods of navigation, I've shown you a way to make a simple drop-down menu that enables you to jump to any named location in your workbook. This makes navigation almost foolproof, even for inexperienced Excel users.

Navigating with Simple Hyperlinks

You use hyperlinks to navigate between pages on the web. Hyperlinks such as these are easy to create in Excel workbooks for navigation between worksheets, cells, and ranges. Your hyperlinks can be attached to text in a cell or to objects drawn with Microsoft Office drawing tools and shapes. (Hyperlinks cannot be attached to charts.)

Figure 26.1 shows a hyperlink button back to the Home tab at the top left of a briefing book page. Clicking this hyperlink button returns the user to the Home tab, the first page of the Balanced Scorecard.

Hyperlinks within cells are easy to create, and you can format them so that they look like buttons. Before creating a hyperlink, name the cell or range to which you want the hyperlink to jump. (You cannot name a chart, but you can name a cell or range next to the chart so that the chart will be displayed.)

To name a cell or range, select the cell or range. In Excel 2007 and Excel 2010, on the Formulas tab, in the Defined Names group, select Define Name. In Excel 2003, choose Insert ➢ Name ➢ Define. The New Name or Define Name dialog box appears. In it, type the name you want for the cell or range. Use upper- and lowercase letters with no spaces.

WARNING Make sure you name tabs using their final names before you create hyperlinks. Hyperlinks do not automatically update when a tab name changes. If you rename a tab, existing hyperlinks to that tab will produce errors.

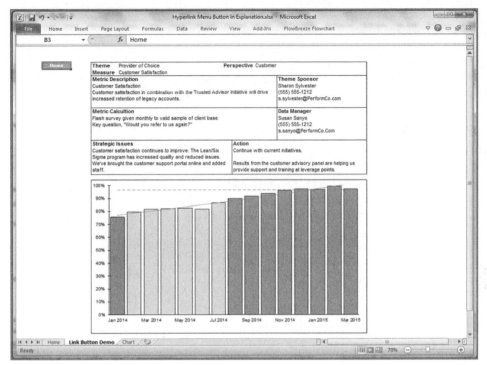

Figure 26.1: Create text menus or buttons on scorecard pages to take users to specific locations.

If you want a text hyperlink in a cell, type the text you want in the cell. If you want a hyperlink on an object, draw the object using the shape or drawing tools. Text hyperlinks in cells will convert and work in a PDF file if you use Adobe Acrobat to publish a Balanced Scorecard. Excel hyperlinks attached to a drawing object do not consistently convert in some versions of Adobe Acrobat.

To create the hyperlink, do the following:

1. Select the cell containing text, or select the object you have drawn.

2. In Excel 2007 and Excel 2010, on the Insert tab, in the Links group, select Hyperlink to display the Insert Hyperlink dialog box, shown in Figure 26.2. In Excel 2003, choose Insert ➢ Hyperlink or press Ctrl+K to display the Edit Hyperlink dialog box.

3. To link within this worksheet, click the Place in This Document icon in the left pane.

4. Type the cell location in the Type the cell reference box, or select the named range from the Place in This Document list.

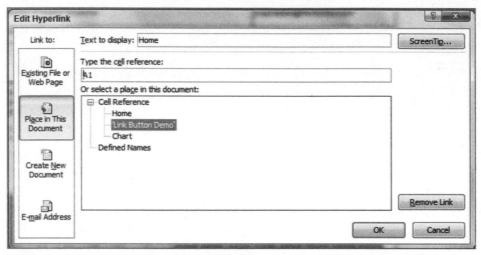

Figure 26.2: Use the Edit/Insert Hyperlink dialog box to add links to places within the same workbook or to other documents, or to open an e-mail window.

5. Click the Screen Tip button, and type any text tip you want to display when the user hovers the mouse over the link.

6. Click OK.

Your text hyperlinks will appear underlined with a unique color. Objects with hyperlinks look the same as those without a hyperlink. The mouse pointer changes to the selection hand when it is over a text or object hyperlink.

TIP Hyperlinks cannot be attached to charts in earlier versions of Excel. But you can cover a chart with a drawing object, attach a hyperlink to the drawing object, and then double-click the object and set its Fill Transparency to 100 percent and its line to none. Hyperlinks on objects in Excel dashboards work well, but issues arise with them when you convert them to PDF using some versions of Adobe Acrobat.

Text hyperlinks and followed hyperlinks (hyperlinks that have been clicked before) use formatting defined by an Excel formatting style. A style is a named collection of formatting properties. You can set these formats so that text hyperlinks appear like buttons by adding borders and a fill color behind the hyperlink.

In Excel 2007 and Excel 2010, on the Home tab, in the Styles group, select Cell Styles. In the styles gallery, right-click either Hyperlink or Followed Hyperlink and choose Modify. (Hyperlink and Followed Hyperlink do not appear until you have created and used the hyperlink.) Use the Style dialog box, shown in Figure 26.3, to modify the style of hyperlinks or followed hyperlinks so that the text box containing the hyperlink looks like a button.

Figure 26.3: Use the Style dialog box to make hyperlinks and followed hyperlinks look like buttons.

Do the following to set the formatting for a text hyperlink in Excel 2003:

1. Choose Format Style to display the Style dialog box, shown in Figure 26.3.

2. Select Hyperlink from the Style Name list.

3. Select the Style includes item you want to be included. To make text in cells look like buttons, this will include Font, Border, and Patterns.

4. Click Modify to display the Format Cells dialog box. Change the formats for how you want all hyperlinks in the workbook to appear. To make a link look like a button, you may want to add a border, a pattern to distinguish it from the background, and bold Arial text.

5. Click OK, and then click Add.

6. Repeat for the Followed Hyperlink style.

7. Click Close.

You may want to use objects you draw, such as rectangles, rounded rectangles, and arrows, as buttons with attached hyperlinks. Format the object either before or after you've attached a hyperlink. If you've already attached a hyperlink, you may find it difficult to select the object. The easiest way to select an object containing a hyperlink is to Ctrl+click the object. Double-click the edge of a selected drawing object to display its formatting dialog box.

WARNING Chapter 30 describes how to publish your Excel scorecards using presentation software other than Excel. If you are publishing in PowerPoint or Adobe PDF, be sure to read Chapter 30 before creating a lot of hyperlinks in Excel.

> **TIP** If you are not publishing your scorecards and dashboards to another application, but are staying within Excel, your users may be able to use some fast methods of navigation built into Excel.
>
> To jump between locations, press F5 and double-click a range name to jump to that name. (The following section shows a more user-friendly method of doing this.)
>
> Click the down arrow to the left of the cell reference box that is to the right of the function bar. From the drop-down list, you can select any named range to which you want to jump.
>
> Press Ctrl+Page Up/Page Down to skip between tabs.
>
> At the bottom of the Excel screen, right-click the arrows used to scroll between tabs. A list of all tabs appears. Click the tab you want to jump to.

Navigating with a Drop-Down Menu

The simple hyperlinks just described are an easy way to create a menu button or a bank of buttons. They need no explanation, but they take up a lot of screen real estate. They are also static, and they can't be manipulated using formulas. If you have had the misfortune of renaming worksheet tabs after you've created hyperlinks, you will find broken links.

Another alternative takes up little screen space and is something that users are familiar with from using web browsers. You can create a list of places to go to; when a user clicks a name in the list, the screen jumps to the corresponding location.

Figure 26.4 shows a combo box that allows users to scroll through a long list of hyperlinks. This approach works well in displays where users are navigating not between two or three pages, but between many reports, charts, or data entry areas.

This method of navigation presents users with a combo box containing a list of locations. Users select a location from the drop-down list and then click the Go To >> text to jump to the selected location.

This navigation system is built using a HYPERTEXT function in cell E6 under the Go To >> text. Selecting a name from the drop-down list builds a hyperlink address from the list in I9:K17. The hyperlink address built from the selection, shown in I25, is used by the HYPERLINK function in E6.

The function in E6 is

```
=HYPERLINK($I$25,"Go To >>")
```

Chapter 20 describes how to use the combo box. This combo box gets its list from the cell contents in H9:H17. The output from your selection goes to cell I20 as the number of the item selected.

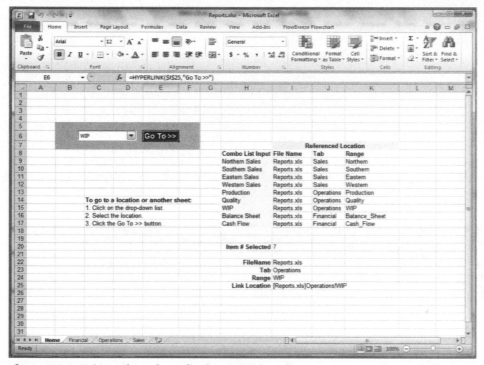

Figure 26.4: Using a drop-down list for navigation gives users easy access to cells, ranges, charts, and reports throughout a workbook.

The filename, tab name, and range associated with the selection from the drop-down list are then calculated in cells I22:I24. An INDEX function in each of these cells uses the item number in I20 to look up the appropriate text for the file name, tab, and range. The formulas are shown in Table 26-1.

Table 26-1: Index Function Formulas

NAME	ADDRESS	FUNCTION
File Name	I22	=INDEX($I$9:$I$17,$I$20)
Tab	I23	=INDEX($J$9:$J$17,$I$20)
Range	I24	=INDEX($K$9:$K$17,$I$20)
Link Location	I25	="["&$I$22&"]"&I23&"!"&$I$24

Drilling Down to Detail

Balanced Scorecards and operational dashboards are important not just for monitoring progress and alerting you to issues, but also for helping you identify where to look for solutions. This almost always requires drilling down to detailed data.

The following techniques do not allow the multiple levels of drill-down possible in very expensive Business Intelligence systems, but they do enable the display of another level of detail. The following methods assume that Excel is using data stored in a workbook. More-advanced techniques are possible when Excel accesses data in relational databases or OLAP cubes using queries, PivotTables, or PowerPivot.

DOWNLOAD SAMPLE FILES FOR THIS BOOK

Sample data files and examples used in the book, as well as many more resources for Balanced Scorecards and operational dashboards, are available for free download. For more information, see the Introduction.

ALWAYS INTERVIEW USERS ABOUT THEIR DECISION-MAKING NEEDS

Before touching the keyboard, interview the intended audience for your dashboard. Determine what data they need to make business decisions, what data is available, what data analysis they need, and what visual presentation will help them the most.

Drill-Downs in PivotTables and PowerPivots

PivotTables and PowerPivot are Excel's most valuable data analysis tools. However, most Excel users do not understand how to use them, and they baffle infrequent Excel users.

With that proviso in mind, you can use PivotTables to truly drill down from a summary into detailed data. Chapters 21 and 22 describe how to use PivotTables and PowerPivots to feed data into dashboards. With these tools you can drill down by double-clicking results and clicking Slicers to filter data. For example, with a PivotTable, if you double-click a cell containing the total sales by product for the month of June, a new sheet opens, showing you the detailed data that went into that total: all the sales, by individual product, in June.

Inexperienced Excel users often get confused by this drill-down and by the new sheet of details that opens. It is common for them to close the entire workbook because they don't realize that a new worksheet has opened, not a new workbook.

But you can turn off the ability to drill down in PivotTables. Right-click the PivotTable and choose PivotTable Options. Clear the Enable drill to details check box to prevent drilling down by double-clicking.

Another issue that occurs when using PivotTables in dashboards is that PivotTables won't work when the sheet and workbook are protected. However, without some protection, inexperienced users can accidentally create havoc in your dashboards. One alternative to having unprotected dashboards is to save your Excel dashboards with Read Only status. This allows users to open a dashboard but prompts them not to save it using its original name.

Drilling into a Data List by Clicking a Row

In some cases you can't use a PivotTable to drill down into a database. Users may be untrained in PivotTables, or you want to control exactly what they see without extensive and complex macros. In other situations, you may want to keep the sheets completely protected, something that prevents the use of PivotTables. The method described in this section works even when the sheet is protected, but if you protect this sheet you will need to allow cells to be selected but not edited.

The example shown in Figure 26.5 gives users near click-to-drill capability with the use of a few formulas and a simple macro that anyone can create. In this example, selecting a cell in the North, South, East, or West data—E27:N30—and then pressing Ctrl+D causes the cells in E24:N24 to display the data for the selected row. Because the chart displays the data in E24:N24, the chart is updated.

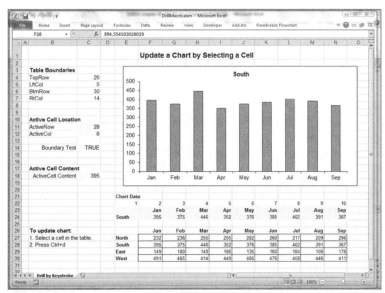

Figure 26.5: Click in any row of the regional data table, and then press Ctrl+D to see that row's chart data appear in the chart.

This works with a simple macro that retrieves the active row and active column when you press Ctrl+D (see Figure 26.6). These row and column values are stored in the range names ActiveRow and ActiveCol.

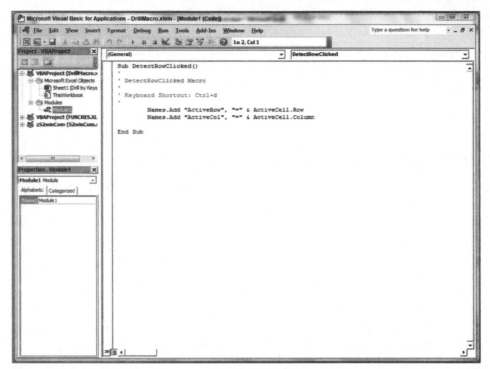

Figure 26.6: Type this simple macro into the Visual Basic for Applications (VBA) Editor to select data from tables.

After checking to ensure that the selected cell is within the clickable area, the formulas calculate the name of the product line selected. That name is then used to retrieve its East, West, North, and South data from the database.

AN ALTERNATIVE METHOD

An alternative to the INDEX method of retrieving data shown here is to use GETPIVOTDATA, as described in Chapter 21. If you create your summary table with a PivotTable, you can use the method described in this section to find the row and column names and use them to retrieve the appropriate data from the PivotTable using GETPIVOTDATA.

Table 26-2 shows the formulas to calculate the clickable area and whether the selected cell is within the boundaries.

Table 26-2: Formulas to Calculate the "Clickable" Range

LABEL OR RANGE	CELL	FORMULA
dbFruit	E26:N30	Range name
TopRow	C4	=ROW(dbFruit)
LftCol	C5	=COLUMN(dbFruit)
BtmRow	C6	=ROW(dbFruit)+ ROWS(dbFruit)-1
RtCol	C7	=COLUMN(dbFruit)+ COLUMNS(dbFruit)-1
ActiveRow	C11	=ActiveRow
ActiveCol	C12	=ActiveCol
Boundary Test	C14	=IF(AND(AND(ActiveRow>TopRow, ActiveRow<=BtmRow),AND (ActiveCol>=LftCol,ActiveCol<= RtCol)),TRUE,FALSE)
ActiveCell Content	C18	=INDEX(dbFruit,ActiveRow- TopRow+1,ActiveCol-LftCol+1)

Notice that cells C11 and C12 contain the range names ActiveRow and ActiveCol. These names are created by the simple Excel VBA macro described later in this section. When you press Ctrl+D, the values of the active row and active column are stored in these variable names. These formulas return the values from the variables in the macro and place them in cells where spreadsheet formulas can use them to select the data for the chart.

Once you know the row and column of the active cell and whether it is inside the Fruit database, formulas can calculate where the rest of the chart data is.

The content of the active cell in the Fruit database shows in cell C18 with this formula:

```
=INDEX(dbFruit,ActiveRow-TopRow+1,ActiveCol-LftCol+1)
```

This formula looks in the clickable range, dbFruit, and retrieves the cell content at the row and column clicked. To do so, the INDEX formula uses the name of the database, Fruit, and the row and column of the active cell in the database. The row and column of the active cell are calculated using the formulas shown in Table 26-2. INDEX() is a powerful function for retrieving data from a list or database. If you are unfamiliar with it, review its use in Chapter 18.

The region name of the Fruit database row containing the selected cell is calculated in cell C18 with the following formula:

```
=IF($C$14,INDEX(dbFruit,ActiveRow-TopRow+1,E$22),"")
```

This is exactly the same as the formula that retrieves the content of the selected cell, but here the content of the cell in the first column of the selected row is retrieved.

Now the worksheet needs to find the row in the database, dbFruit, that matches the row of the selected cell. The row is found by "matching" the name in cell C18 with the names in the left column of the database:

```
MATCH($E$24,$E$27:$E$30,0)
```

If you are unfamiliar with MATCH, review its use in Chapter 18. As that chapter explains, MATCH searches down the first column of the database, E27:E30, for the row with a name that matches.

Finally, the data matching each date is retrieved in cells F24:N24 using an INDEX function. The number 1 must be added to MATCH because the database, dbFruit, has one extra row for its headings. The IF function examines cell C14 to see if it is TRUE, which indicates that the active cell is inside the database. If the active cell is not inside the database, nothing ("") is displayed. Here's the formula in cell F24:

```
=IF($C$14,INDEX(dbFruit,MATCH($E$24,$E$27:$E$30,0)+1,F$22),"")
```

Figure 26.6 shows the simple two-line macro that makes this possible. Even if you are unfamiliar with macros, you can make this work.

For information on creating macros in Excel 2007 and Excel 2010, refer to the Microsoft support website, which contains detailed instructions. Go to http://office.microsoft.com, select the Products tab, and select Excel. In the search box, enter **create a macro** and click Search.

Follow these steps to prepare to create this macro in Excel 2007 and Excel 2010:

1. Select File ➤ Options. The Excel Options dialog box opens.

2. Under Customize Ribbon, select the Developer check box and click OK. The Developer tab appears, which enables you to create macros.

Follow these steps to prepare to create this macro in versions of Excel prior to 2007:

1. Open the workbook you want to contain the macro, and save it with a name.

   In the following steps you will create a macro by starting a recording. This opens a macro sheet, gives it a name, and creates a shortcut key. In this recorded shell you will later add two lines of VBA code.

2. In Excel 2007 and Excel 2010, in the Developer tab, in the Code group, select Record Macro. In Excel 2003, choose Tools ➤ Macro ➤ Record New Macro.

3. Enter the name **DetectRowClicked** without spaces in the Macro Name box.

4. Type **d** in the Shortcut Key box, and click OK.

5. Click any cell in the worksheet to record an action. Then click the square Stop Macro button on the floating toolbar, or click the Stop Macro button in the Code group on the Developer tab.

Now add the VBA code to the macro "shell" you have created:

1. In Excel 2007 and Excel 2010, on the Developer tab, in the Code group, select Macros. In Excel 2003, choose Tools ➢ Macro ➢ Macros to display the Macro dialog box.

2. Select the name you gave your macro, and click Edit to open the VBA Editor. This displays the "mini" macro you recorded and enables you to edit it.

3. Delete the black text between the Sub line and the End Sub line. This is the code for the cell you selected.

4. Type the following code between the Sub and End Sub lines:

```
Names.Add "ActiveRow", "=" & ActiveCell.Row
Names.Add "ActiveCol", "=" & ActiveCell.Column
```

5. Choose File ➢ Save and close the VBA Editor.

To test your macro, type the following into separate cells:

```
=ActiveRow
=ActiveCol
```

and press Ctrl+D. The cells containing these names should show the row and column number of the selected cell. Save the workbook.

Summary

Giving your dashboard users the ability to drill down and see the detailed data they need to solve their problems is a huge part of why you create dashboards. In most cases, Balanced Scorecards need one level of drill-down from the business unit summary level. Because these levels are predefined summaries, such as division data or regional data, you can create predefined detail views. Operational dashboards require more interactivity to help resolve issues. If you need numerous or multilevel drill-downs, I recommend that you put data into a database, either in Excel or externally, and retrieve and analyze it using

PivotTables or PowerPivots. Chapters 21 and 22 will get you started. You can make dynamic drill-downs into these pivot results using what you learn in those chapters and Chapter 20. To learn about dashboards that allow greater interaction with larger data sets, read Chapter 29.

CHAPTER 27

Using Excel Add-Ins for Extra Capabilities

The thing is, continuity of strategic direction and continuous improvement in how you do things are absolutely consistent with each other. In fact, they're mutually reinforcing.

—Michael Porter
Harvard Business School professor

Microsoft Excel is easily the world's most-used numeric analysis tool. Its analytical and charting capabilities lend power to business analysis, but there are niche areas where it could use additional capability. This chapter describes tools that work with Excel to give it even more analytical power and usability. There are too many good add-ins for Excel to describe in this chapter. For links to the add-ins described here, as well as reviews of more add-ins, see the lists at http://www.criticaltosuccess.com.

ASAP Utilities

ASAP Utilities is arguably one of the most popular Excel add-ins. It has been downloaded by more than 200,000 users and is used by 7,200 customers. That's a pretty authoritative record!

ASAP Utilities fills the gaps in Excel's feature set with features you wish were built in. It offers more than 300 new commands and functions. Even with all those features, ASAP Utilities is pretty easy to use, with its feature finder, documentation, and online video.

This add-in has been available since 1999 and works with all versions of Excel, except Excel 2010 (64-bit), from Excel 2000 upward. ASAP Utilities is available in English, Dutch, German, Spanish, and French.

A free version is offered for home, student, and nonprofit use. Businesses can receive a 90-day free trial. The price is minimal, with discounts for volume purchases.

The hundreds of tools in ASAP Utilities allow you to do the following:

- Select cells based on different criteria, such as formatting.
- Deselect cells within a selection.
- Remove leading, trailing, and extra spaces.
- Sort sheet tabs by name.
- Protect several sheets at a time.
- Utilize single dialog box control for all display (vision) settings.
- Import and export files.
- Use the 29 worksheet functions to count or manipulate text, cell formats, and file or folder names.

FlowBreeze Flowcharting

You can create flowcharts and Strategy Maps using the Drawing, Shapes, and Connector tools in Excel, as described in Chapter 13. However, it can be a lot of extra work to adjust arrows and realign connectors so that everything looks precise. (After all, when you present your work, you want it to look as precise and professional as the thinking you've put into it.) For a minimal cost you can get FlowBreeze's flowcharting and value stream mapping (VSM) software that works inside Excel (see Figure 27.1). FlowBreeze has a free 30-day trial you can download.

Because all this is created in your Excel worksheet, it's easy to create labels, tables, and charts that update automatically as worksheet data changes.

The FlowBreeze add-in displays a left pane over your worksheet. In that pane you are prompted to type captions and select the parts of your flowchart or VSM map. The add-in includes a symbol library that extends the symbols and connectors that come with Excel. FlowBreeze comes with 84 built-in symbol formats and 124 symbols (see Figure 27.2). Flowcharts can be exported in five different formats.

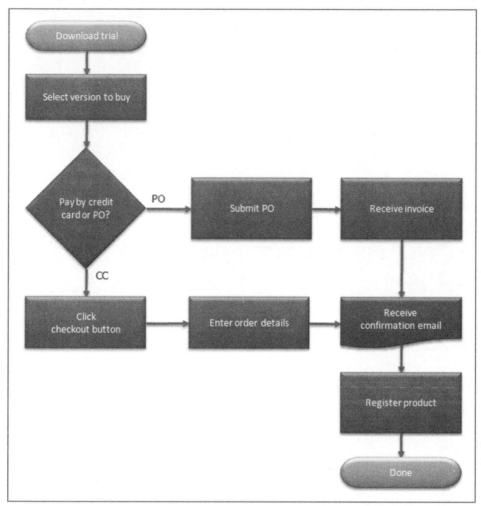

Figure 27.1: FlowBreeze makes it easy to create attractive flowcharts within your Excel worksheet.

In FlowBreeze, when the user types in a symbol caption, FlowBreeze automatically creates a flowchart symbol. Keywords you define can be used to identify the symbol FlowBreeze creates when you type the label. For example, if you add a question mark, a decision box with Y/N labels and branching is added. (FlowBreeze comes with a set of predefined, easy-to-remember keywords.) The flowchart it builds automatically adds colors and connectors and lays out symbols in an attractive way. Of course, you can go back and modify a map manually. Free templates can be downloaded for swim lanes and VSM.

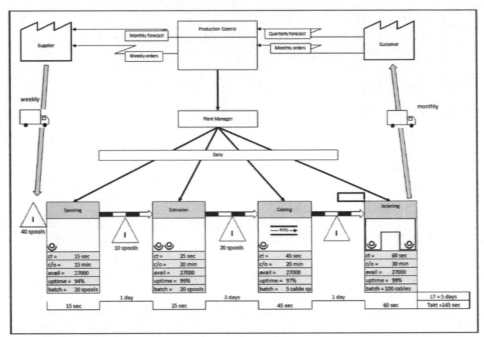

Figure 27.2: FlowBreeze also enables flowcharting using Value Stream Mapping symbols.

A number of capabilities save you time:

- Align shapes as they are created.
- Select all shapes of a specific type.
- Choose from among preset formats.
- Create a custom of list of favorite symbols.
- See and adjust for page breaks in a multipage flowchart.

FlowBreeze works with Excel 2000 through current versions. However, you need to ensure that you have the Microsoft .NET 2.0 Framework installed (which is available free from Microsoft).

Systems2Win Value Stream Mapping

Systems2Win has a website filled with Excel-based tools for Lean improvement using VSM, 5S, Six Sigma, and more (see Figure 27.3). It contains over 150 Word and Excel templates for Lean Kaizen continuous process improvement.

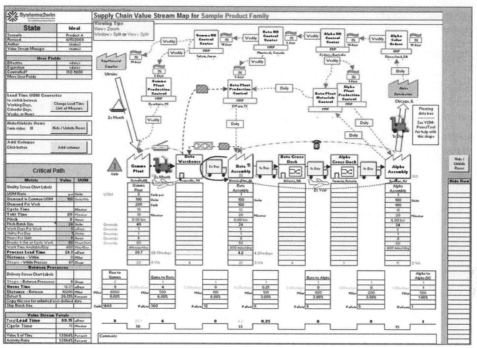

Figure 27.3: With the Systems2Win supply chain mapping tool, all of the most common supply chain metrics have been preprogrammed.

Excel-based templates and add-ins include the following:

- 5S checklists
- Layout diagrams
- Standard worksheets
- Numerous flowchart templates

Robust VSM add-ins and templates also are included:

- Answers to many Lean questions right in the templates
- The ability to hide and unhide extensive Lean metrics
- Preprogrammed Lean formulas for metrics common to most industries, such as Takt, cycle time, queue time, and more
- The ability to drill down to swim lanes and other related documents
- Free video training includes the fundamentals of Lean performance improvement, Excel mapping, and how to use Systems2Win.

Systems2Win has a free trial and a 30-day money-back guarantee.

PowerPivot

PowerPivot, shown in Figure 27.4, is the ultimate database analysis tool from Microsoft for Excel 2010. You can download it from Microsoft for free. It requires Microsoft Office 2010 and supports 32-bit and 64-bit systems.

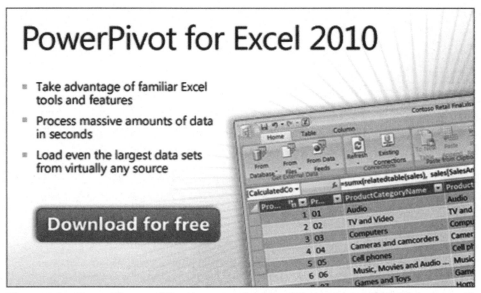

Figure 27.4: PowerPivot enables you to work with millions of rows in multiple external databases as though they were a few hundred rows in a single worksheet.

PowerPivot is a powerful PivotTable-like add-in that enables you to join, query, and analyze massive external databases—something you can't do with PivotTables. I've used it to join multiple very large MS-SQL databases with Excel worksheets, query and analyze the large database, modify the results with Dynamic Analysis Expressions (DAX)—the PowerPivot functions—and extract just the data I need for a report and chart.

Here are some of PowerPivot's capabilities:

- You can query millions of rows of external data at the same speed you'd get working with hundreds of sheet rows.

- You can use powerful DAX to manipulate data, such as grouping it by quarter, as well as to create relationships between tables.

- PowerPivot enables you to merge tables from widely used databases, websites, text files, and Excel sheets. It finds the common key and automatically creates the join. Or you can use DAX to create a new key.

- Slicers work in PowerPivot just as they do in PivotTables, so you can slice and dice to find what you want.

- PowerPivot integrates well with Microsoft SharePoint, so it is easy to publish your results.

Although PowerPivot and DAX are slightly different from PivotTables and worksheet functions, they are so close that you'll pick them up quickly. Chapter 22 shows you how to go beyond basic PowerPivots and manipulate them to get what you need for dashboards and scorecards.

Simtools

Simtools adds statistical functions, Monte Carlo simulation, and risk analysis to Excel for versions 5.0 and later. It is free and distributed by the University of Chicago. Simtools was developed to help managers perform complex decision analysis using probability and statistics.

Simtools adds 32 statistical functions in six categories:

- Inverse cumulative probability
- Correlation with random variables
- Decision analysis (risk tolerance)
- Discrete probability distribution analysis
- Regression analysis
- Randomly generated discrete distributions

It also adds three macros:

- Simulation Table displays the output from a Monte Carlo simulation model.
- Iterative Process iteratively copies values to a state range from an update range.
- Combine Rows makes all combinations from a selected range.

Instructions are not available at the University of Chicago website, but I've collected instructions from different web locations and have links available at http://www.criticaltosuccess.com.

Formlist

Formlist helps you audit your worksheets. All formulas from a selected range are output as text to a column on a worksheet so that you can examine them. Like Simtools, Formlist is made available free from the University of Chicago.

Formlist adds a macro and two lookup functions to Excel. Instructions are not available at the University of Chicago website, but I've collected instructions from different web locations and have links available at `http://www` `.criticaltosuccess.com`.

Managing Excel Add-Ins

Installing an Excel add-in usually involves little more than opening and running an installation application. Each version of Excel also comes with a set of add-ins.

After you install an Excel add-in you may find the need to enable or disable it. In cases, such as shutting down Excel while it is starting, you may find an add-in has been disabled. In other cases, if Excel determines that an add-in has caused a crash, Excel will disable the add-in. In those cases the add-in no longer appears in menus or its features are no longer available.

This section describes how you can enable or disable Excel add-ins.

To enable or disable add-ins in Excel 2007 and Excel 2010:

1. In Excel 2010, click File, Options, and select Add-Ins. In Excel 2007, click the Office button, select Excel Options, then click Add-ins.

   You can now see a list of installed add-ins and their types.

2. From the Manage list at the bottom of the Options dialog box, select the type of add-in you want to manage, then click Go.

   If an add-in has been disabled, choose Disabled Items, then click Go.

3. In the dialog box, select or deselect the add-in you want to enable or disable, then click Ok.

To enable or disable add-ins in Excel 2003, choose Tools, Add-Ins, and then select or deselect add-ins you want to enable or disable.

If Excel 2003 has disabled an add-in and you want to reenable it, choose Help, About Microsoft Office Excel. Click Disabled Items to manage add-ins that have been disabled.

Summary

Excel is one of the most widely used business tools. Special areas and special needs occasionally require additional features and tools.

This chapter has described just a few of the tools you can add to Excel. There are so many add-ins for specialized niches that they can't all be listed here. For current links to reviews and sources of some of Excel's best and most useful add-ins, check the resources at my website, http://www.criticaltosuccess.com.

Finishing Touches

God is in the details.
—Ludwig Mies van der Rohe
Architect
1886–1969

Creating a bulletproof system that shines with small finishing touches will make you look like a professional. This chapter provides you with a few useful tips.

Adding Context and Comments with Briefing Books

The Briefing Book, shown in Figure 28.1, is a supporting feature that should be behind every Balanced Scorecard and operational dashboard you distribute to others. It contains the contextual, historical, and action information that doesn't appear in a chart or table. It shows the dashboard's purpose and status, actions that have been taken, ownership of objectives, and data and contact details.

The Briefing Book you create may contain only text, or it may contain text, data tables, and charts. You can create a Briefing Book on a worksheet by copying and pasting the chart and then formatting cells so that text wraps into paragraphs. In Excel 2007 and Excel 2010, select the cells you want to act as a block. On the Home tab, in the Alignment group, choose Wrap Text.

In Excel 2003 you can create large, contiguous blocks of cells that contain word-wrapped paragraphs. Select all the cells you want to appear as a block, choose Format ➢ Cells, and select the Alignment tab. On the Alignment tab, select Horizontal (Left Indent) ➢ Vertical (Top) ➢ Word Wrap ➢ Merge Cells.

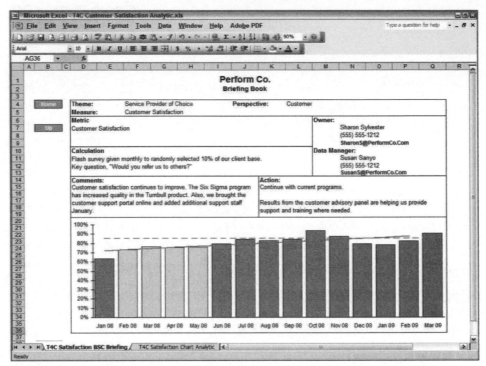

Figure 28.1: A Briefing Book shows the context, actions, and owners related to a dashboard's objective and metrics.

To protect your Briefing Book, have objective and data owners enter their text comments on a separate sheet that links to the word-wrapped cells in the Briefing Book.

Displaying Pop-Up Content and Dynamic Help

There are many ways to create in-context comments, analysis, or help in Excel dashboards, but one of the easiest and most attractive is to modify the in-cell comment box. The only disadvantage of this method is that content must be updated manually or via VBA. Figure 28.2 shows a comment that pops up with a custom shape, font, and background color.

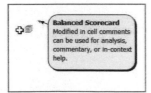

Figure 28.2: Modified in-cell comment boxes can be used as pop-ups that contain comments, analysis, and in-context help.

Before you create your first comments, you will probably want to change the username that will appear at the top of the comments. You should change it to something appropriate, such as Help, Analysis, or Commentary. In Excel 2010, choose File ➢ Info. Under Properties or Related Info, change or add a title or the author name. Right-click an item for additional options, such as removing it. In Excel 2007, click the Office button, select Excel Options ➢ Popular, and then change the username. To set the default title in Excel 2003, choose Tools ➢ Options and select the General tab. In the User Name box, enter the title you want.

Changing the username won't change the title on existing comment boxes. You can manually edit or delete the title in any comment box when the box is open for editing.

To insert a cell comment, right-click the cell and choose Insert Comment. With the comment open in editing mode, you can type and edit in it, as well as change the title. You can edit the comment by right-clicking the cell and choosing Edit Comment.

To modify the comment box to give it a distinctive appearance, right-click a cell containing a comment and chose Edit Comment. When the comment box appears, right-click its edge and choose Format Comment. You can modify the font, text alignment, colors, and lines.

Modifying the shape of the comment box takes a little more work. In versions of Excel prior to Excel 2007, make sure the Drawing toolbar is displayed so that you have access to the Draw ➢ Change Auto Shape options. In Excel 2007 and Excel 2010, you need to add the Change Shape button to the Quick Access toolbar at the top left of the screen.

To add the Change Shape button in Excel 2007, click the Office button, select Excel Options, and choose Customize. In Excel 2010, right-click the drop-down arrow to the right of the Quick Access menu and choose More Commands. In the Choose commands from list, select SmartArt Tools | Format Tab. Add the Change Shape tool, located in the left list, to the Customize Quick Access Toolbar list. Click OK. The Change Shape tool appears as a small shape icon at the top left of Excel.

Now that you have access to a shape-changing tool, right-click the cell containing the comment and choose Edit Comment. Click the edge of the comment box. In versions of Excel earlier than Excel 2007, select Draw ➢ Change Auto Shape from the Drawing toolbar, and choose a new shape. In Excel 2007 and Excel 2010, select the Shape Change tool and then choose a new shape for the comment.

To make the location of your pop-up information boxes stand out, put a symbol in the cell that indicates more information is available. In Figure 28.2, the icon indicating multiple pages is a Wingdings 2 symbol.

Controlling Dashboard Display

In most cases, you will want your Balanced Scorecard or dashboard to show a clean background without row and column headers, scroll bars, and so forth. To turn off items you may not want to show, do the following:

1. In Excel 2007 and Excel 2010, on the View tab, in the Show group, deselect these items:

   - Gridlines
   - Formula Bar
   - Headings

2. Choose File ➢ Options ➢ Advanced. In the Display section, deselect the display option you do not want.

In Excel 2003, follow these steps:

1. Choose Tools ➢ Options and select the View tab in the Options dialog box.

2. In the Show group, clear all these check boxes:

   - Startup Task Pane
   - Formula Bar
   - Status Bar

3. In the Window Options group, clear all the check boxes of items you do not want to display:

   - Page breaks
   - Formulas
   - Gridlines
   - Row and column headers
   - Outline symbols
   - Zero values
   - Horizontal scroll bars
   - Vertical scroll bars
   - Sheet tabs

4. Click OK.

Hiding Worksheets

Worksheets that contain all your formulas and analytics should be hidden from user view and protected from tampering. (You *did* separate your charts, tables, formulas, and data into separate worksheets, didn't you?) To learn more about creating a good Excel worksheet architecture, see Chapter 30.

To hide worksheets so that a user can't see them, but to still have them available for formula use, right-click a worksheet's tab and choose Hide. To display a hidden worksheet, right-click a visible tab, choose Unhide, select the worksheet you want to unhide, and click OK.

TIP When you have lots of worksheets, clicking through all the tabs gets tedious. To see a tab's name and quickly jump to it, right-click the scrolling buttons to the left of the tabs and select the worksheet you want from the list that appears.

Sending Conditional E-mails from Dashboards

The purpose of scorecards and dashboards is to change behavior and actions. A productive enhancement for getting the action started is to send an e-mail from within your dashboard to the person who can make a change in performance. You can even make an e-mail button that appears when a target value is met.

The HYPERLINK function in Excel creates a hyperlink and displays a text name in a cell. The HYPERLINK syntax is:

```
=HYPERLINK(link_location,[friendly_name])
```

Normally, the link location is a URL such as http://prefix.com, like the examples shown in Excel Help. However, you can make the HYPERLINK function send e-mail with syntax that looks like this:

```
=HYPERLINK("mailto:ron@torconsulting.com","Balanced Scorecard Consulting")
```

Typing this syntax into a cell produces a hyperlink that, when clicked, opens an e-mail window in Outlook. (You need to test this for your e-mail system.) To make this into an e-mail button that appears only when a condition is met, follow these steps that explain the example shown in Figure 28.3:

1. In cell C8, enter an e-mail address with the mailto: prefix:

```
mailto:ron@torconsulting.com
```

When you press Enter, this cell becomes a hyperlink that sends an e-mail. Notice that it has hyperlink formatting. You could put this in a hidden area of the workbook so that users do not see it. (Note: If you use this function with a web address you must start the address with http:// for the link to work.)

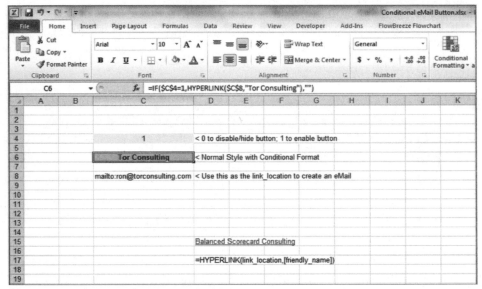

Figure 28.3: An e-mail button that appears when an alert condition is met makes it even easier to take action from within a dashboard.

2. If you keep the mailto contents of cell C8 in a visible location, you may want to change its hyperlink format style to another style to remove the underline.

3. Enter 1 in cell C4. This will be a sample condition. You can test for many different alert conditions, as described elsewhere in this book.

4. In cell C6, enter this formula:

```
=IF($C$4=1,HYPERLINK($C$8,"Tor Consulting"),"")
```

This formula displays the HYPERLINK function when C4 contains 1 and displays nothing otherwise.

Test this by typing 1 or 0 in cell C4 and watching the e-mail link appear or disappear. Notice that when the e-mail link is not visible, the mouse pointer still changes when over the cell, but it does not send an e-mail.

You can make a button effect that appears or disappears with the e-mail link:

1. Select the hyperlink cell, C6.

2. Assign cell C6 the Normal style.

3. If you are using Excel 2007 or Excel 2010, on the Home tab, in the Styles group, select Conditional Formatting. From the list of choices, choose New Rule. In the New Formatting Rule dialog box, under Select a Rule Type, choose Use a formula to determine which cells to format, as shown in Figure 28.4. If you are using Excel 2003, choose Format ➢ Conditional Formatting. In the Conditional Formatting dialog box, enter "=$C$4=1."

Figure 28.4: Use conditional formatting to make the e-mail button formatting appear or disappear.

4. Click the Format button and format the e-mail cell with patterns and borders to make it appear like a button when C4 contains a 1. Do not create a second conditional format.

5. Click OK.

TIP Combine the e-mail function you've learned here with form controls such as the combo list and concatenating text, both described elsewhere in this book, to create drop-down lists of multiple e-mail recipients.

Adding Headers and Footers

Headers and footers are critical for knowing which data is most current in printed reports or screen shots of dashboards. Believe me, this can prevent confusion. For dashboards that update daily or even hourly, this is essential for understanding differences between dashboards or report results. In addition, your header or footer might include a proprietary or confidential company message.

Locating and Removing Phantom Links

There will come a time when you open a workbook and Excel displays a dialog box asking if you want to refresh or open linked workbooks, but you can't find any links. If you are the only user of the workbook, this is annoying. But if this is a Balanced Scorecard or dashboard for executives and managers, the problem must be fixed. This section describes how to do so.

First, check for links. In Excel 2007 and Excel 2010, on the Data tab in the Connections group, select Edit Links. In Excel 2003, choose Edit ➢ Links, which opens the Edit Links dialog box. Here you can see workbooks that are linked to the active workbook. Click any linked worksheets shown in the Edit Links dialog box, and look at the workbook the link references.

One reference that is easy to forget is when chart data series link to external worksheets. If this happens, click the data series within a chart to see if the chart formula shows an external link. If the formula contains an external link, rewrite the formula so that it has a valid reference.

If you want to remove a link that no longer links to a workbook, select it in the Edit Links dialog box, click the Change Source button, and link it to the active sheet itself. Resave the workbook with a new name. If you reopen the workbook and it still asks if you want to update the link, you probably have a link within a named range.

To find a link within a named range, in Excel 2003 choose Insert ➢ Name ➢ Define. In Excel 2007 and Excel 2010, on the Formulas tab, in the Defined Name group, select Name Manager. In the Name Manager dialog box, click each named range in turn, and watch the Refers to: box at the bottom. If you find a name with an external reference or #REF! error, delete it or rewrite it.

Protecting Content, Worksheets, and Workbooks

Some of the scorecards, dashboards, and templates I have built involved hundreds of hours of development. That adds up to a lot of money and intellectual property. Your work is just as valuable to you and your organization, and you don't want untrained users accidentally messing up the inner workings.

This section shows you how to protect your Balanced Scorecard and dashboards from accidental changes and changes by untrained developers. Protecting your workbooks also sets them up so that they retain the restricted areas and display settings you have chosen.

WARNING Excel and Microsoft Office product protection methods are designed to protect the contents and display settings from inexperienced users. For a small price, anyone can buy over the Internet decryption programs that will break into the Microsoft Office protection. Therefore, do not use the Office protection to protect confidential company data.

Excel has multiple layers of protection. Cells, worksheets, and workbooks (files) each have their own protection. Each layer of protection can have different attributes, such as protecting structure but allowing data entry.

One frequent misunderstanding is how worksheet protection works. Initially, all cells in a worksheet are formatted to be protected when worksheet protection is turned on. Cells you have not formatted as unprotected become protected.

If you want certain cells to be unprotected, in Excel 2007 and Excel 2010, first select the cells you want to be unprotected. On the Home tab in the Cells group, select Format. In the drop-down list, select Format Cells. In Excel 2003, choose Format ➢ Cells. In the Format Cells dialog box, select the Protection tab and clear the Locked check box.

Whether a cell is locked or unlocked the protection does not take effect until worksheet protection is enabled. To enable worksheet protection in Excel 2007 and Excel 2010, on the Home tab, in the Cells group, select Format. In the drop-down list, select Protect Sheet. In Excel 2003, select Tools ➢ Protection ➢ Worksheet. Select the check boxes that describe which worksheet properties you want protected.

Much has been written about protection. This topic is covered in the Excel help files as well as in books and on the Internet. All these sources include tips that will help you protect dashboards.

When you set protection for the worksheet, in most cases you will want to clear all the check boxes in the Protect Sheet dialog box except Select unlocked cells.

WARNING Unprotect cells that receive input from a form control, such as a slider or combo box, or you will receive an error.

When you protect the workbook, always protect the structure. If you want to prevent your dashboard from being reduced to a resizable window, also select the Window check box.

Restricting the User's Range

For a professional appearance, you will want your dashboards to look as much as possible as if they are stand-alone applications and not Excel worksheets. In addition to turning off gridlines and row and column headers, described elsewhere in this chapter, you should limit the user's ability to move outside a range you prescribe. In most cases, you will want to limit users' cursor movements so that they can see only the tables, text, and charts in the active worksheet.

This is actually easy to do. Adjust your dashboard's formatting so that it fills the screen as you want users to see it, and then hide all columns to the right, and all rows below. The user will be unable to scroll or select beyond what he or she sees. If you have protected the worksheets, users will be unable to unhide the rows and columns.

To hide rows in Excel 2003, select the full row below the last row you want to see. Press Shift+Ctrl+down arrow to select that row and all lower rows. Now choose Format ➢ Row ➢ Hide. To hide the columns on the right, select the column to the right of the last column you want to be visible. Press Shift+Ctrl+right arrow to select that column and all columns to the right. Now choose Format ➢ Column ➢ Hide. You are left with a small worksheet area of visible cells. Users can neither select in nor scroll outside this area.

If you are using Excel 2007 or Excel 2010, select the rows or columns as just described. Then, on the Home tab, in the Cells group, select Format. In the drop-down list, select Hide & Unhide and then Hide Rows and Hide Columns.

Oops! I almost forgot to tell you how to bring back those areas. In Excel 2003, select the last row or column that is visible, and drag toward the hidden rows or columns. Now choose Format ➢ Row/Column ➢ Unhide. They reappear. In Excel 2007 and Excel 2010, under Hide & Unhide, select Unhide Rows and Unhide Columns.

Summary

When it comes to creating your scorecards and dashboards, the most important task is communicating information that aids decision-making. Your second-most important task is to make your scorecards and dashboards attractive and easy to use.

With a few finishing touches, such as those described in this chapter, you can make your dashboards look like polished, stand-alone applications rather than Excel worksheets. And it doesn't hurt to set up your scorecards and dashboards so that users can't accidentally destroy your hard work.

CHAPTER 29

Data Integration Methods

If 98% of the metrics are right, why worry about the other 3%?
—Anonymous

At every conference or workshop on Balanced Scorecards or operational and performance dashboards, I hear stories about organizations that have wasted large sums of money by purchasing a large Business Intelligence system before they fully understand how much information they need to harvest, analyze, and distribute.

The consensus among Balanced Scorecard consultants is that it makes sense to start simply, by entering data manually or linking worksheets to text files or simple relational databases. Operational and performance dashboards that have static requirements, with data that is not refreshed continuously, can also use simple data integration methods to produce great results.

Small- to midsized businesses and IT departments of large corporations usually do not have the hundreds of thousands of dollars and extensive resources necessary to implement a Business Intelligence system. In those cases, using Excel with data integration is a cost-effective solution. When expansion is needed, many midsized corporations do a great job with SQL relational databases or OLAP cubes combined with well-designed Excel dashboards.

Should You Use Manual Data Entry or Automated Data Integration?

Surveys of large corporations with Business Intelligence systems show that most scorecards or operational dashboards use six or seven different data sources. These are organizations with enterprise-wide ERP and CRM systems. My experience with small- and midsized organizations is that they have data in even more disparate sources.

There seems to be a consensus among Balanced Scorecard consultants that Balanced Scorecard software should begin with manual data entry or text file integration. Balanced Scorecard data is usually at a summary level, so it is available in summary reports that can be typed in monthly or that can be stored and integrated as text files.

One of the serious problems with using a manual data entry system, even with a Balanced Scorecard that has only 12 to 24 metrics, is that those metrics require a geometrically larger amount of raw data for calculation. Within six months to a year, the data owners become weary of collecting, calculating, and entering data. Updates soon lag. This is just one more piece of organizational inertia that a Balanced Scorecard doesn't need. I recommend using manual data entry for a few months until the system is tested. Then create a simple integrated data system like the ones described here so that data collection, calculations, and updates are automatic.

Operational dashboards face the same issues. They usually involve large amounts of data that are in someone's worksheet, but they are rarely in a form useful in a dashboard. Thus, they require reentry. This takes up personnel time, introduces error, and slows the process. If this is an operational dashboard that is critical for performance, creating a simple data integration method like the ones described here will save you time and errors.

> **TIP** Entering or importing data, targets, and alert limits in one workbook separate from the analytics and charts makes your system architecture more secure and flexible. When data, targets, and alert limits are placed in separate workbooks, the Strategic Theme sponsors can access them without having access to the Balanced Scorecard analytics and charts.
>
> As described in Chapter 30, keeping data in a separate worksheet or workbook makes it easier to make changes to the entire system, because data is not structurally involved with the analytics. For example, you should design your system so that you can point the analytics to a new data source just by changing a range name.
>
> Keeping data in a workbook separate from the analytics and charts enables the data owner or Strategic Theme sponsor to open the data workbook and make corrections without touching the analytics and charts. If you keep data in a separate workbook, you may want to keep the related user-updated targets and alert limits in that same workbook.

Manual Data Entry for Dashboards

Manual data entry worksheets are little more than tables created to allow users to enter data. You also should create user-entered tables for targets and alert levels that so users can update them.

Manual data entry tables for Balanced Scorecard and dashboards have a number of advantages:

- They can be implemented quickly.
- They don't require IT support.
- Manual data entry is perfect for new metrics requiring small calculations and those that aren't in a system, such as employee engagement survey results.
- Theme sponsors can delegate someone to update data.
- Data worksheets can be constructed for each Strategic Theme sponsor with unique passwords and data layout.
- Each data workbook can contain data, targets, and alert levels so that managers can update them easily.

But manual data entry tables for Balanced Scorecard and operational dashboards also have disadvantages:

- Initial creation can involve a painful amount of data entry.
- Operational dashboards may require large amounts of ongoing data entry to track daily operations.
- Not keeping data refreshed can lead to the failure of a Balanced Scorecard.
- There is no data integrity.
- Manual data entry introduces errors.
- There is no audit trail.

For a better user interface in your data entry worksheets, use light shading in alternating rows. Keep the top and left-side headings in view during data entry in Excel 2007 and Excel 2010 by selecting on the View tab, in the Window group, a Freeze Panes option. In Excel 2003, choose Window ➢ Freeze Panes. Doing so allows the data area to scroll while keeping the top and left headings in view. Apply conditional formatting to data areas so that data that is out of limits appears as red.

Automating Data Retrieval with Text Files

One of the easiest ways to automate and upgrade from the labor-intensive method of manually entering data is to import text files containing data into Excel. This works well when many data owners keep data in many different systems, ranging from Excel worksheets to small databases to large enterprise systems. All the data can be exported from each of these different systems into text files in a common data folder. The Balanced Scorecard or dashboards then can import the data needed. Imported data can be refreshed manually, or Excel can be set to refresh at timed intervals.

The text files created for this method may come from accounting systems, CRMs, ERPs, project management report utilities, or even Excel worksheets saved in text format.

Importing text files has some advantages:

- The process is easy.
- You can manage many disparate data sources.
- Each data owner is responsible for his or her individual data.
- Doing so reduces manual work.
- The amount of IT support required is minimal.

But, just like manual entry, it also has disadvantages:

- Extensive calculations or calculations involving multiple data sources may have to be done in Excel rather than at the data source.
- Some IT or report writer assistance may be needed to generate the reports (text files).
- Data integrity is limited, because data is not dynamically linked to the source. Rather, it is exported.

Creating Text Data Files

Most software systems include a report-writing utility. Usually this is an embedded minimalist version of Crystal Reports. A report-writing utility can create the text files you need. You may use an existing report that is printed in CSV, TXT, or PRN format. (See Table 29-1.) However, in most cases it is easier to create a new report in a simple columnar format containing just the data needed for the Balanced Scorecard or dashboards.

TIP Make sure you store dashboards, worksheets to be imported, and data source text files in the same folder. This reduces or eliminates complex links and makes it easier to find and manage files.

Table 29-1: Types of Text Formats Excel Creates

FILE TYPE	DELIMITER	DESCRIPTION
TXT	Tab-delimited	Data is separated by a tab character.
CSV	Comma-separated values	Data is separated by a comma. If the data includes a comma, such as a currency value, the value is enclosed in quotes.
PRN	Even-width columns	Data is aligned in specific columns. If it is printed in a monospace font, you will see data align in columns. Almost any software system can be set up to create a PRN file.

During development, you may want to create sample text files to reimport into Excel as a test of data integration. Figure 29.1 shows the types of text files you can export from Excel. You can create sample CSV, PRN, or TXT files from within Excel by creating an Excel list with the headers and data in columns. Format the data as you expect to receive it. When you save the data in Excel, select CSV, PRN, or TXT as the file format in the Save As dialog box.

To open these files in a word processor so that you can modify them, right-click the filename in Windows Explorer, choose Edit With, and select a text editor such as Notepad. Note that the CSV file is represented in File Explorer with an Excel icon. Double-clicking a CSV file automatically imports it into Excel. However, to create dashboards that refresh automatically, follow the text file import techniques described next.

Step-by-Step to Importing a Text Data File

Whenever possible, you should work with the IT department or the person writing reports and exporting data. You want to specify the layout so that the data will import directly into Excel. Data can be exported from most systems in Excel or CSV format.

Although Excel opens these two file formats , you may want to use the following procedure so that you can specify how frequently the worksheet should update automatically.

The Text Import Wizard takes slightly different paths for opening and parsing (separating) CSV, TXT, and PRN files. It automatically parses a CSV file into appropriate cells. TXT files, in which data is separated by tabs, also are recognized. If you import PRN files, you can drag markers left or right to mark where columns of data begin and end.

The following example walks you through the steps to import a tab-delimited text file with the extension TXT. (*Delimited* means that data intended for each cell is separated by a unique character, such as a comma or tab.) One advantage of using the Text Import Wizard is that you can set the update frequency for importing at the end of the import process. This allows the worksheet to automatically update itself when new data is available.

To follow this example, create a TXT file using the tab character to separate data, or download the sample files as described in the Introduction. To open the text files in Excel, do the following:

1. Open the worksheet into which you will import data.

2. Select the top-left cell where you want data to be imported.

3. In Excel 2007 and Excel 2010, on the Data tab, in the Get External Data group, select From Text to display the Import Text File dialog box. (This command is unavailable on a worksheet in which you already have imported data.) For versions of Excel prior to 2007, choose Data ➢ Import External Data ➢ Import Data to display the Select Data Source dialog box. Select the file you want to import and click Open.

4. Step 1 of 3 in the Text Import Wizard opens, as shown in Figure 29.1. Excel makes a best guess as to the text file format. If your file is TXT or CSV, you should select Delimited. If you open a PRN file, the wizard automatically selects the Fixed Width option. You can see what the raw data looks like at the bottom of the dialog box. Click Next.

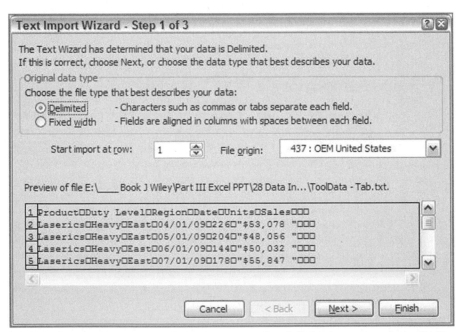

Figure 29.1: In step 1 of 3 in the Text Import Wizard dialog box, you select whether the data is delimited by a special character such as a comma or tab and whether it is formatted with each cell at a fixed column position.

5. In Step 2 of 3 in the Text Import Wizard, shown in Figure 29.2, you can change the character used to separate the data into each cell. This character is the delimiter. In the lower portion of the dialog box, you can see how your selections will affect the data to be imported.

Step 2 looks different depending on whether you are importing a CSV, TXT, or PRN file. CSV and TXT files use the comma and tab characters, respectively, to separate data. PRN files separate data into columns using space characters. The wizard selects the Fixed Width option and displays a Step 2 dialog box in which you can mark where columns should be separated. Click Next.

Figure 29.2: Excel usually makes the correct choices for Step 2 of 3 in the Text Import Wizard.

6. Step 3 of 3 in the Text Import Wizard, shown in Figure 29.3, allows you to mark which columns to ignore and to format columns in ways other than Excel's best guess. Click Next.

7. In the Import Data dialog box, shown in Figure 29.4, select where you want the new data to be inserted.

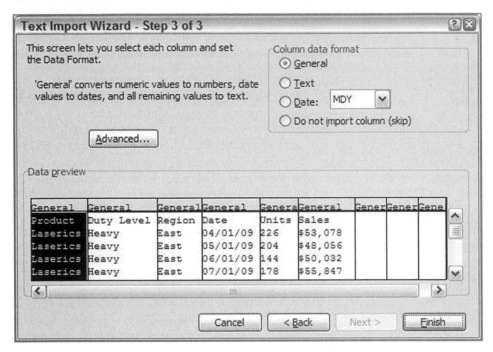

Figure 29.3: In Step 3 of 3 in the Text Import Wizard, you set column formats if Excel does not choose correctly.

Figure 29.4: Select the upper-left corner of
where you want data to import on an existing worksheet.

8. Click the Properties button to display the External Data Range Properties dialog box, shown in Figure 29.5. Here you specify how the import refreshes and how existing data is affected by new data. These settings are described in the section "Refreshing Data Automatically."

9. Click OK in the External Data Range Properties dialog box, and then click OK in the Import Data dialog box. Your data is imported into the worksheet, as shown in Figure 29.6.

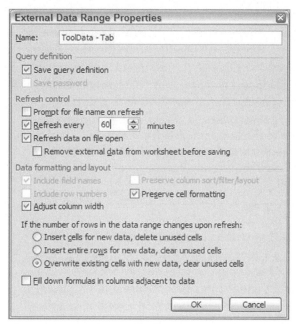

Figure 29.5: In the External Data Range Properties dialog box, you specify how data will be refreshed.

Figure 29.6: Imported text data parses into cells and formats as you specify. It updates from the text file when you click the update icon, or automatically, at timed intervals.

WARNING If you haven't run into this issue yet, you will, and it will drive you crazy, even when you are ready for it. Some systems, especially older accounting systems, export numeric data as text. When Excel imports a text file, the numeric data may remain text but look onscreen as though it is numbers. This commonly occurs with UPCs, zip codes, and credit card numbers, but I have seen it in file exports from many older financial systems. These "numbers in text clothing" cause problems in Excel formulas, in PivotTables, in charts, and during sorting.

You can adjust for this problem in the Text Import Wizard by selecting the appropriate format in Step 3 of the Wizard. If the data still does not act like a number, try creating a formula in another column, such as =D6*1, that forces the text in D6 to become a number.

TIP Data may come in looking different than how you need it for your dashboards. For example, East Coast zip codes may be missing their leading zeros, or you may need the first initial and last name of salespeople but find that a file contains full names. If you aren't under a deadline, figuring out formulas to modify the data can be fun. To create the new data, add a column to one side of the imported data and write formulas that manipulate the data. Useful functions include & (concatenation), TRIM, LEFT, RIGHT, MID, FIND, LOWER, UPPER, PROPER, and other text functions. Make sure you set the Fill down formulas in columns adjacent to the data check box in the External Data Range Properties dialog box so that your formulas are copied down as data expands. This process is described in the section "Refreshing Data Automatically."

Automating Data Retrieval from Databases

Most accounting, CRM, ERP, and proprietary software uses relational databases such as SQL, Oracle, and Access. Many of these databases allow Excel to import data directly into worksheets.

Importing from a relational database has some advantages:

- Data maintains its integrity in the source database. There is only one source of truth.
- Relationships between different data sources can be examined.
- Calculations can be made in the source database rather than in Excel.
- Updates can be made for instant examination.

Linking to relational databases also has some disadvantages:

- The process may require IT or consultants.
- Excessive data acquisition may slow system access.

Step-by-Step to Importing Data from a Relational Database

The process of importing data from a relational database follows similar steps for most databases. You will probably need assistance from IT staff to make your initial database connection if it is different from the Access demonstration that follows.

Excel can import different types of databases and sources. The following example imports a Microsoft Access database table as an example of how to use the Import Wizard. However, you can import an Access table using a simpler process.

If you have Microsoft Access on your computer, you can follow this example of how to link an Excel worksheet to a relational database. If you do not have Access, you can download the sample Northwind.mdb Access file from the author's website, `http:\\www.criticaltosuccess.com`. Download the sample Northwind.mdb file to a folder where you can access it for the following example.

To link a data worksheet to the Northwind.mdb relational database, do the following:

1. Open the worksheet into which you will import data. The example shows a workbook dedicated to data, targets, and alert limits.

2. Select the top-left cell where you want data to be imported.

3. In Excel 2007 and Excel 2010, go to the Data tab. In the Get External Data group, select From Other Sources or another appropriate icon, and then select From Data Connection Wizard. Skip to step 5. (This command is unavailable on a worksheet in which you already have imported data.) In Excel 2003, choose Data ➢ Import External Data ➢ Import Data to display the Select Data Source dialog box, shown in Figure 29.7.

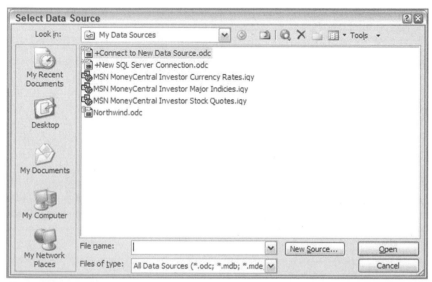

Figure 29.7: When the Select Data Source dialog box opens, you do not see the option to connect to a text file.

4. In Excel 2003, select +Connect to New Data Source.odc and click New Source to display the Data Connection Wizard, shown in Figure 29.8.

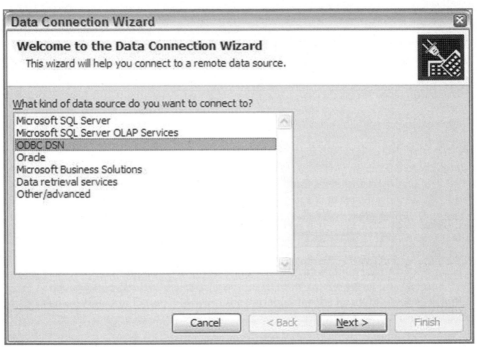

Figure 29.8: The Data Connection Wizard displays data sources to which you can connect.

5. In any version of Excel, select ODBC DSN (data source name) and click Next.

6. In the Data Connection Wizard, select MS Access Database as the data source you want to connect to, as shown in Figure 29.9. Click Next.

7. In the Select Database dialog box, select the Access Northwind.mdb database file. If you downloaded the file from Microsoft, go to the folder in which you saved it. If you have Access on your computer, you can find Northwind.mdb in C:\Program Files\Microsoft Office\Office##\Samples. After selecting Northwind.mdb, click Next.

8. In the Select Database and Table dialog, shown in Figure 29.10, you must select the tables you want to link to. If IT has built a special table containing all the data you need, select the Connect to a specific table check box. Click Next.

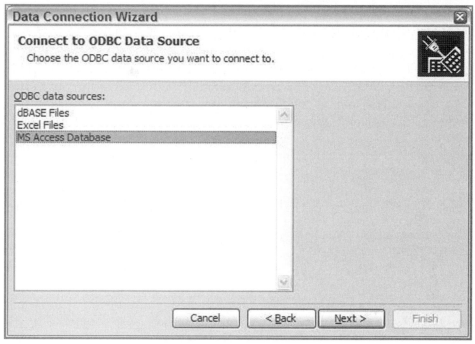

Figure 29.9: Select the ODBC source you need to connect to.

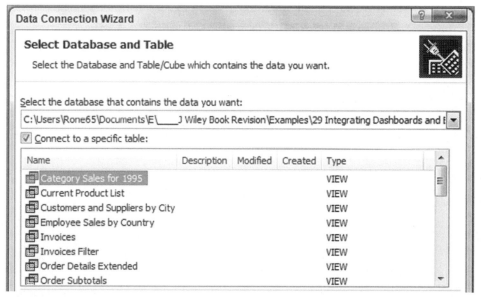

Figure 29.10: Select the tables from the database to which you want the Excel worksheet to have access.

9. Continue clicking Next until you can click Finish.

10. In Excel 2007 and Excel 2010, in the Import Data dialog box, specify where in the existing worksheet you want the new data, as shown in Figure 29.11. You also can specify whether you want the data as a table, PivotTable Report, or PivotTable and PivotChart Report. Click the Properties button to specify how frequently you want your dashboard updated. Click OK. Data appears in the worksheet.

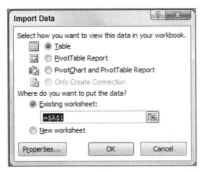

Figure 29.11: In the Import Data dialog box, specify how you want the data returned and where in the worksheet you want the data. Click Properties to specify how frequently you want your dashboard updated.

In Excel 2007 and Excel 2010, you can modify the data query by selecting a cell in the table. Then, in the Data tab, in the Get External Data group, select Refresh All. From the list, select Refresh All to refresh the data. If you want the data to automatically refresh at time intervals, select Connection Properties and choose the options you need.

In Excel 2003, clicking the Edit Query button in the Import Data dialog box enables you to modify the data query for this connection. You also can access and modify the query by right-clicking within the data in the Excel worksheet and choosing Edit Query.

Importing Data Using a PivotTable

The previous step-by-step examples resulted in flat files imported from text or relational databases. If you want to import data from a relational database and convert it into a categorized table with PivotTable-type analysis, you can use Excel's PivotTable to directly import the data from an external database and then create a PivotTable that you can update from the database.

If you have done your homework, as described in Parts I and II of this book, you will know exactly what information is needed so that your PivotTable can generate just the data your scorecard or dashboard needs. In some cases, you may want the database manager to create calculated fields in the database or create new joins between tables to give you the data you need in your dashboard.

To retrieve data into your scorecard or dashboard from the linked PivotTable, use the GETPIVOTDATA function and techniques described in Chapter 21.

Importing Data to a PivotTable

To create a PivotTable connected to an external data source in Excel 2007 and Excel 2010, follow this example using the Nwind.mdb Access database:

1. On the Insert tab, in the Tables group, select PivotTable.

2. In the Create PivotTable dialog box, select Use an external data source, and click Choose Connection.

3. In the Existing Connection dialog box, select a connection to a database if you previously created one.

4. If you did not previously create a connection to a database, click the Browse for More button in the Existing Connection dialog box. If you see a connection you want to use, select it.

5. In Excel 2010, if you do not see a data connection, click New Source to open the Data Connection Wizard. In Excel 2007, in the Select Data Source dialog box, choose +Connect to New Data Source, and click Open to open the Data Connection Wizard.

6. Choose ODBC DSN, and click Next. Choose MS Access Database, and then browse for and select your database or the sample Nwind.mdb. If you are using a database other than MS Access, select that database type. Click Next.

7. Select the tables from the database that you want to include in the PivotTable. Click Next, and then click Finish to return to the Create PivotTable dialog box.

8. In the Create PivotTable dialog box, click OK and design your PivotTable.

As an alternative to this method, in Excel 2007 and Excel 2010 you can follow the steps defined in the previous section on how to import data from a database. After you specify the data you want to retrieve, you can use the Import Data dialog box, shown in Figure 29.11, to import into a PivotTable.

To retrieve data from an external data source and create a PivotTable in Excel 2003, follow these abbreviated steps:

1. Open the data worksheet and select the cell where you want the upper-left corner of the PivotTable.

2. Select Data ➢ PivotTable and PivotChart Report.

3. In Step 1 in the PivotTable Wizard, select External Data Source, and click Next.

4. In Step 2 in the PivotTable Wizard, select Get Data.

5. Under Choose Data Source, select your database or the NWind sample MS Access Database. Click OK.

6. In the Select Database window, open the folder containing your relational database file. Select that file, and click OK.

7. In the Query Wizard Choose Columns dialog box, choose the tables you want to use in your PivotTable. Click Next.

8. The Query Wizard lets you filter and sort the data returned. Click Next until you reach Query Wizard Finish.

9. Select Return Data to Microsoft Office Excel. Click Finish.

10. In Step 2 of 3 in the PivotTable Wizard, click Next.

11. In Step 3 of 3 in the PivotTable Wizard, you can create the layout for your PivotTable. Continue creating a PivotTable from this point on using normal PivotTable methods.

Refreshing Data Automatically

Once you have imported your data from a text file or database, you will want to ensure that your dashboard reflects the most current data. You can manually update imported data or update data when the worksheet containing the data opens, or at set intervals while it is open.

To manually update any imported data, whether from a text file, relational database, or PivotTable, right-click inside the data and choose Refresh Data.

In Excel 2010, to automate the refresh of data in a PivotTable linked to an external database, select a cell inside the PivotTable. Then, in the Data tab, in the Connections group, select Properties. The Connection Properties dialog box, shown in Figure 29.12, appears. Usually you will want to select all three check boxes:

- Enable background refresh allows users to use Excel as the data refreshes.
- Refresh every ___ minutes sets how frequently data is updated.
- Refresh data when opening the file refreshes the data when you open the file.

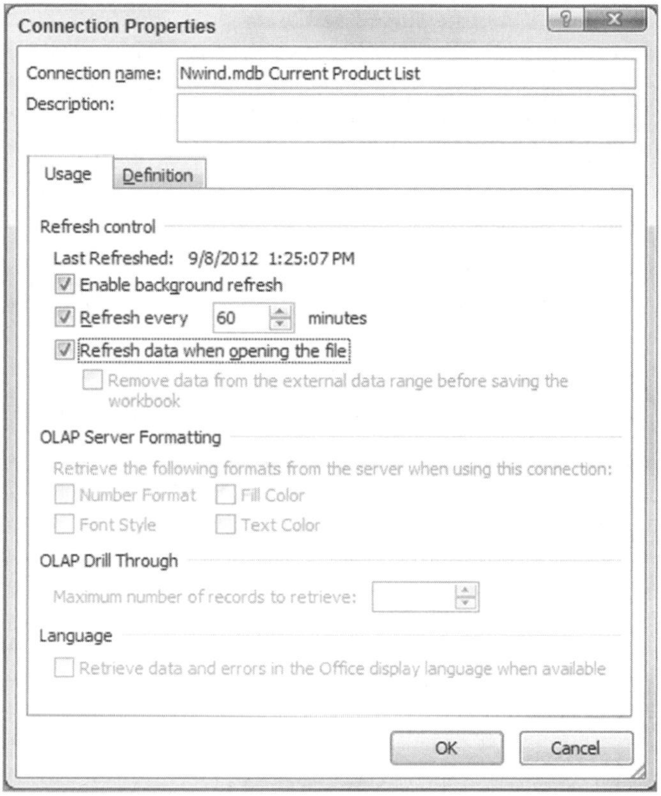

Figure 29.12: In the Connection Properties dialog box, you control how and when the data for a PivotTable updates.

In Excel 2003, to automate the refresh of data in a PivotTable that is linked to an external database, right-click within the table and choose Table Options. In the PivotTable Options dialog box, select the Refresh on open and Refresh every ___ minutes check boxes.

Linking Imported Data to Your Dashboard

You have many ways to link your dashboard analytics to imported data. These methods are covered primarily in Chapters 18 and 21.

If you have imported a flat file, insert a column to the left of the imported data and use a concatenation formula to create a unique key. Against this unique key you can use INDEX and MATCH to find data, as explained in Chapter 18. When new data is imported, the key updates to match the new data.

> **TIP** If you insert columns of formulas adjacent to imported data, you want to make sure that the formulas expand to match the number of rows of data. To ensure that this happens, open the External Data Range Properties dialog box and select the Fill down formulas in columns adjacent to the data check box. Formulas will automatically fill adjacent columns to newly imported data.

Another method of linking your dashboard to an imported data list is to use the imported list as the source for a PivotTable. Updating the PivotTable updates the data. Use the GETPIVOTDATA function, as described in Chapter 21, to extract the data your dashboard needs.

> **CREATING AN AUTOEXPANDING DATABASE NAME**
>
> The size of the data you import will probably change, but you need to refer to it consistently. To do this, use a dynamic range name to name your imported data. The section "Creating Dynamic Range Names that Adjust Automatically When the Size of the Data Changes" in Chapter 17 describes this process.

What Is OLAP, and When Should You Use It?

Relational and transactional databases work well enough when data is extracted in small amounts from smaller tables, when the databases are not under intense loads, and when data extraction does not require a lot of calculation and analysis. However, if your dashboards retrieve data from large data sets, if they require many calculations, if many transactions are hitting the database from many users, or if the database is not optimized for your data requests, you may begin seeing the following issues:

- Relational and transactional systems may be overloaded, which slows data transfer to your dashboards.
- Data requiring extensive calculations before export slows the system or the extraction.
- Users may lock each other out of files.
- You may need data from multiple sources that merge with the appearance of a common *lingua franca*.
- Business and Excel users can't understand table and field names.
- Data isn't normalized or calculated in the way that business and Excel users expect.
- Excel users are unable to develop their own queries.

The solution to these problems for many organizations is to use an Offline Analytical Processing (OLAP) cube. An OLAP cube will solve many of these problems and give you greater access and analytic ability, but there are trade-offs.

The data from an OLAP cube is not real-time; it is usually updated once a day. The OLAP cube is built from data in a relational or transaction database. This construction of the OLAP cube often occurs in the early hours. An advantage is that calculated data can be precalculated before it is needed. Another advantage is that table and field names can have names that general business and Excel users understand. A detriment can be that OLAP cubes contain analytical summaries and calculations. They do not contain the original source data. That reduces or eliminates the ability to drill down multiple levels into data.

Even so, many organizations that have well-defined metrics and that understand their needs find that they can create highly productive dashboards and performance analyses using the more cost-effective OLAP cubes with Excel.

Summary

Having the most current data in your Balanced Scorecard or dashboard can be of paramount importance. At the same time, you don't want to create an administrative nightmare requiring extra labor just to maintain data. Using the tips from this chapter, you can integrate your dashboards with your data sources so that scorecards and dashboards update automatically. It is relatively easy to export text files from disparate systems to a common folder and then build dashboards that update automatically from these text files. Similarly, you can store dashboard data in an Access or SQL database and link directly to the data.

CHAPTER 30

Publishing Balanced Scorecards and Dashboards

Knowing a great deal is not the same as being smart; intelligence is not information alone but also judgment, the manner in which information is collected and used.

—Dr. Carl Sagan
Astronomer, scientist, writer
1934–1996

Publishing your Balanced Scorecard or operational dashboards takes more thought than just sending out an e-mail or updating an Excel worksheet. Communicating your organization's performance gap requires a vehicle that can handle the analytics while being easy to develop and maintain, maintaining the security of confidential data, producing portable content for traveling executives and managers, and having great presentation quality across multiple platforms.

There are many Business Intelligence (BI) tools and vendors, but the most widely used BI tool in corporate divisions and small- to midsized businesses continues to be Excel. Within this non-BI environment, three main methods of distribution are used for Balanced Scorecards and dashboards developed with Excel. Balanced Scorecards and dashboards can remain in Excel, with distribution through an e-mailed workbook, a shared folder on a network, or a portal such as Microsoft SharePoint. Two other methods of publishing and distribution are useful for Balanced Scorecards and collections of operational dashboards. In these methods, Microsoft PowerPoint or a PDF format is used to publish a static version of a scorecard or dashboard. The pages of output are linked via hyperlinks throughout PowerPoint slides or PDF pages. In either case, hyperlinks to external Excel workbooks can be used to open related interactive worksheets.

This chapter will help you weigh the trade-offs between different methods of publishing and distributing your Balanced Scorecards and operational dashboards. In addition, you will learn to create an architecture of linked dashboards that is simple, but effective. If you create complex hierarchies of linked dashboards you can create an impressive appearance, but it will become an overwhelming burden to maintain.

EXCEL: THE DEFAULT CLIENT TOOL OF BUSINESS INTELLIGENCE SOFTWARE

All large BI software systems come with some form of query, reporting, and dashboard tool, but the vast majority of business people are devoted Excel users, not BI tool users. Not only do they have years of experience with Excel, but they also have worksheets they've spent years customizing for their specific needs. For this reason, many BI vendors include a data acquisition method so that Excel can access live data from the BI system. Some of the major vendor products that enable Excel to access BI data are Microsoft's PerformancePoint and SharePoint, Cognos's Business Intelligence Analysis for Microsoft Excel, and Business Objects' software.

Publishing Directly in Excel

Operational and performance dashboards created in Excel can often stay in Excel as long as users are trained in using the dashboard, or the dashboard is "bulletproofed." Chapter 28 describes some methods of bulletproofing a dashboard and giving it a professionally finished appearance.

Leaving a scorecard or dashboard in Excel and distributing it has some advantages:

- The business unit has an existing network or portal that can manage security for dashboard files.

- Most mid-level Excel users can create dashboards for operational needs with little training. Online video courses are available at my website (http://www.criticaltosuccess.com) to show you how to create dashboards and scorecards.

- Interactive dashboards that perform data queries or allow user interaction must be in Excel; such interactivity cannot be re-created in PowerPoint or Adobe PDF.

Using Excel as the distribution medium also has some disadvantages:

- Most dashboard developers cannot make scorecards or dashboards bulletproof, meaning that they should be used by only the developer and a small cohort.

▪ Widespread downloading of data without live links to a database can produce many versions of the truth—multiple dashboards, each showing a different result or slightly different data.

▪ Excel dashboards are difficult to scale and distribute widely throughout an organization. Many users may want their own private version of a dashboard, so they pirate it, causing havoc with version control and data integrity.

▪ Dashboards look different on different screens. If you have executives and managers using different versions of Excel on office computers and laptops and through VPNs from home, you may hear about the different appearances.

TIP Develop a naming convention and name worksheet tabs before you create hyperlinks in Excel. Hyperlinks reference the text of a tab name. The hyperlink does not automatically update when you change a tab's name, so changing a worksheet tab name may force you to re-create many hyperlinks.

Many of these disadvantages can be controlled with structure and discipline. You can manage data integrity, or prevent "many versions of the truth," by creating Excel dashboards that use data links. And dashboards should always show the data source and time of data capture. Scalability is a larger issue. Surveys have shown that, in large corporations, some dashboards have more than 100 users. Such widespread use is difficult to control.

But Excel can be used effectively, especially at the business unit level or in small- to midsized businesses that understand the contexts in which Excel works and what problems it solves.

EXCEL IS AN EFFECTIVE TOOL FOR EXECUTIVE SCORECARDS

Throughout this book, the term *scorecard* has taken on the meaning of Balanced Scorecards, but Excel also can be used to create Executive Scorecards. Executive Scorecards are multidashboard systems similar to a Balanced Scorecard, but with metrics monitoring broad operational areas or aligning functionally rather than strategically.

Workbook Architecture

Workbook architecture is one of those topics that most people want to skip over when learning about Excel, but it will save you a lot of grief. I'll make this discussion quick, so please read these tips on best practices with Excel.

Most Excel users learn basic Excel in a one- or two-day class and then learn on the job thereafter. Consequently, few workbooks have an architecture that lends itself to easy maintenance. It's not uncommon for an Excel user to create a worksheet and then return to it a year or even months later, unable to immediately remember how it works. It's like inheriting someone else's worksheets. The situation is even worse if they are no longer available to help you understand the worksheets' inner workings.

For your own peace of mind, as well as to preserve your business, use a standard architecture.

Here are a few guiding rules:

- Use range names whenever possible to self-document your formulas.

- Use dynamic range names so that database and list names expand automatically. Chapters 17 and 21 describe how to use dynamic range names that adjust as a list changes.

- Keep report display, data, target values, and alert levels on separate worksheets. Combining these on the same worksheet can make it difficult to change the structure.

- Add a worksheet tab that contains notes describing special formulas or tricks you've used. Although this might take an extra hour during a project, it can save you dozens of hours if you have to go back and make changes.

Publishing Multidashboard Systems

If your dashboards require user interaction, such as querying new data or using combo boxes to change charts, you need to distribute your dashboards in Excel. However, executive-level dashboards that have 15 to 20 dashboards with predefined queries and static charts need a different method of distribution.

The most common method of publishing scorecards with multiple static dashboards is to encapsulate the report view in a Microsoft PowerPoint presentation or in a PDF file. Encapsulating a fixed set of the most commonly viewed dashboards does the following:

- It makes navigation easy.
- It bulletproofs the system against untrained operators.
- It creates a portable package that looks good on any display.
- It keeps analysis at a strategic level rather than enabling detailed drill-down.
- It keeps data highly secure when encrypted PDF files are used.
- It lets you collect comments and post sticky notes on dashboards or scorecards when PDF files are used.

Hierarchy of Views

Systems built for PowerPoint or PDF most commonly have one main page showing the Balanced Scorecard or the executive dashboard. This main page may be a simple text dashboard, as described in Chapter 15, or it may be more robust, as shown in Figure 30.1. Pages like this are created in Excel. They can display live charts and show alert conditions and can be published and distributed in either PowerPoint or PDF.

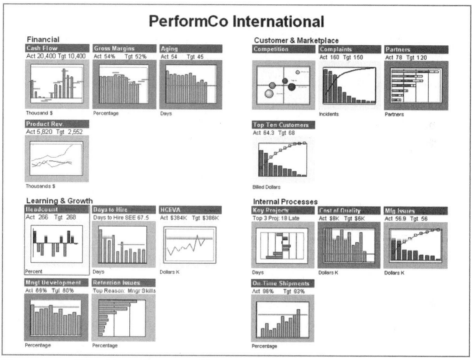

Figure 30.1: This Balanced Scorecard homepage was created in Excel and published for distribution as a PowerPoint slide or PDF page. Chart images are overlaid with a hyperlink to a page with details.

The advantage of using a main page such as this is that an executive can see the status of all metrics at a glance. Alert levels use a conditional color behind each chart. The miniature charts (described in Chapter 19) actually reflect real data.

When the scorecard reader wants more detail, she can click the chart, which has a hyperlink overlaid. Doing so takes her to the PowerPoint slide or PDF page that contains more detail. Figure 30.2 shows a detailed view presented after a metrics title on the homepage of the Balanced Scorecard was clicked. Notice the navigation hyperlink buttons at the top left. Clicking one of these buttons takes the reader down to another level of detail or to a briefing book.

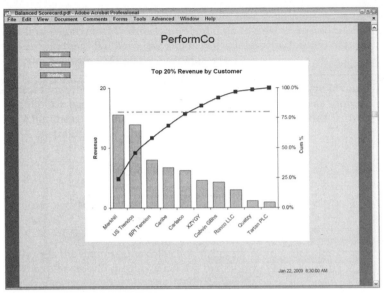

Figure 30.2: Clicking a chart in the Balanced Scorecard takes you to a detailed chart such as this.

It is difficult to drill down more than one level with Excel published in PowerPoint or PDF, because each layer adds a geometrically expanding number of static views. Here is where it is important to have done the interview and mapping work described in Parts I and II of this book. Not only do you need the right metrics, but you also need to know what level of detail and viewpoint are required for decision-making.

Figure 30.3 shows the Briefing Book, which gives your readers access to the context, contacts, and actions for an operation or objective. Chapter 28 describes how to add conditional e-mail links to Briefing Books.

Deciding How to Publish Your Scorecard or Dashboard

You can publish your Balanced Scorecard, executive dashboard, or operational dashboards in Excel, PowerPoint, or PDF. Which of the three should you use? Here are a few points to consider, along with the alternatives.

If you are developing operational dashboards that require interactive operation, such as changing chart or data orientations, or dashboards that require links to live data, do the following:

- Use any version of Excel.
- Use one of the data acquisition methods described in Chapter 29 if you need to automate data integration.

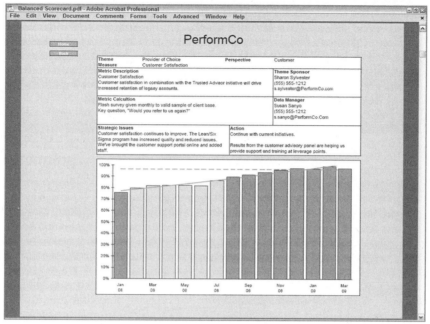

Figure 30.3: Giving your users a Briefing Book with the context, contacts, and current actions can answer their questions about problems and actions taken.

TIP There were linkage issues between Excel 2007 and PowerPoint 2007 on a network. If you have such issues, be sure to update Excel and PowerPoint with the latest software patch. If issues continue, go to the Microsoft website (http://www.microsoft.com) **and search for the error message "Some linked files were unavailable and can't be updated," or search for Article ID 927284.**

Publishing in PowerPoint

Publishing Excel tables and charts in PowerPoint is straightforward. Whether you have many Excel workbooks or a single workbook, you produce a single PowerPoint presentation that contains charts and tables linked to the original source in one or more Excel workbooks.

The result is a PowerPoint presentation with slides that are a "snapshot" of a dashboard at one point in time. If the Excel data changes, you can refresh the PowerPoint file by updating the links in PowerPoint to the Excel charts and data.

Microsoft Office applications, although they have a password-protection feature, are not highly secure. The password in Office documents prevents settings and content from being modified by untrained users; it doesn't prevent the theft of data. Utilities are available to break Microsoft Office passwords. If your dashboards contain highly confidential data, you should keep them inside a secure network or use the Adobe PDF method of publishing, described later in this chapter.

Advantages and Disadvantages of Publishing in PowerPoint

Here are the major advantages of publishing in PowerPoint:

- Accurate screen reproduction is maintained on different monitors and resolutions.
- Excel slides can be embedded into PowerPoint slides so they can be updated directly from PowerPoint.
- It is easy, but tedious, to create hyperlink buttons between PowerPoint slides.
- PowerPoint is bundled with Microsoft Office.
- It's easy to train someone to build and refresh the PowerPoint slides.
- A hyperlink on a slide can open an Excel dashboard.
- Executives and managers know how to operate PowerPoint.

Publishing in PowerPoint also has some disadvantages:

- All navigational hyperlinks must be drawn and linked manually.
- The number of hyperlinks can quickly become large and difficult to manage.
- Hyperlinks in Excel workbooks are not maintained when copied to PowerPoint.

PowerPoint Architecture

Always separate data from analytics and charts, as shown in Figure 30.4. Depending on your situation, you may have the data in a worksheet or workbook separate from the analytics and charts. This lets you relink your analytics to other data sheets. It also enables users to enter data such as targets, alert levels, and Briefing Book commentary without working with the analytics and charts workbooks.

Analytics and charts may be in separate workbooks or in a single, larger workbook. The charts, tables, and briefing book comments that you want in the Balanced Scorecard are copied out of the source workbook and pasted with Paste Special into the PowerPoint presentation.

Navigational hyperlinks in the PowerPoint presentation must be created manually in the PowerPoint presentation.

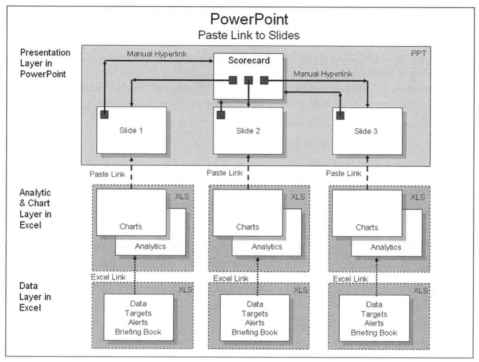

Figure 30.4: PowerPoint is the most frequently used method of publishing dynamically linked Excel charts and tables.

KEEP ALL FILES IN THE SAME FOLDER

Keeping all Excel, PowerPoint, and data source files in the same folder reduces your link complexity. Having links to files across different paths, drives, and folders can be a nightmare to maintain.

When You Should Use PowerPoint for Publishing

If you have only a few static dashboard views, perhaps up to 20 without many layers of drill-down, and if strong data security is not required, these tips will help you use PowerPoint efficiently:

- Develop and maintain in Excel and paste into PowerPoint using Paste Special. Make sure you click the Paste link option in the Paste Special dialog box, and select Microsoft Excel Worksheet Object. This enables the picture in PowerPoint to update when the Excel source changes.

- Create a table of contents with hyperlinks in the PowerPoint slides, or display the PowerPoint in Normal view so that the Preview pane appears on the left. Change the Preview pane on the left to Outline, and users can quickly navigate through slides by clicking the outline.

- When Excel data changes, update PowerPoint slides. In Excel 2010, right-click the edge of an Excel object and choose Update Link. In Excel 2003, select Edit ➢ Links or open the PowerPoint presentation and all Excel files simultaneously, and then save the PowerPoint file.

Creating the PowerPoint Presentation

Before you begin, make sure you have all Excel workbooks, data workbooks, and PowerPoint files in the same folder. This will reduce or eliminate link failure later.

To link a chart or table from Excel to a PowerPoint slide so that it can be refreshed when data changes, do the following:

1. Select the range of cells you want to show in the PowerPoint. If you are selecting a chart, select the range behind the chart.

2. Copy the range.

3. Activate PowerPoint and display the blank slide that will contain this content.

4. In Excel 2007 and Excel 2010, on the Home tab, in the Clipboard group, select the down arrow on the Paste button. You have five choices:

   - Use Destination Theme and Embed Workbook
   - Keep Source Formatting and Embed Workbook
   - Use Destination Theme and Link Data
   - Keep Source Formatting and Link Data
   - Picture

5. In Excel 2003, choose Edit ➢ Paste Special to display the Paste Special dialog box, shown in Figure 30.5. Select the Paste Link option, select Microsoft Office Excel Chart Object, then click OK.

In nearly all cases in Excel 2007 and Excel 2010 you should select Keep Source Formatting and Link Data or select Picture. Selecting the Keep Source Formatting will retain the chart formatting you used in Excel. In some cases using the Destination Theme produces a poorly formatted chart. If you select the Picture option, then you are pasting a static image of the chart. While this makes for a very small file size, you will have to manually update the chart in the slide whenever the Excel chart changes.

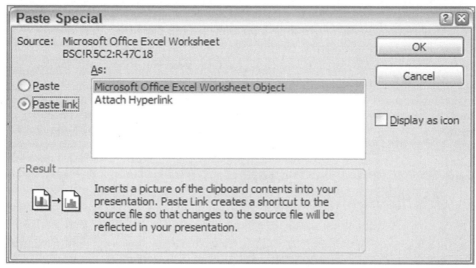

Figure 30.5: In Excel 2003, copy the Excel range or chart and then use Paste Special to create a linked PowerPoint slide.

EMBEDDING A CHART CREATES VERY LARGE POWERPOINT FILES

When you paste a chart using the Embed Workbook option you are actually including an entire copy of the workbook inside the PowerPoint slides. This can create massive PowerPoint files and it makes the original Excel difficult to manage and update. Don't do it!

After you have created PowerPoint slides with linked data, you can refresh slides when Excel files change by right-clicking the edge of the linked Excel chart and in Excel 2007 and Excel 2010 on the Design tab, in the Data group, click the Refresh Data button. In Excel 2003 right-click the object and select Update. The Excel object refreshes with the latest data.

Create navigation buttons between a slide and the Home page by drawing buttons with the Drawing toolbar. Select Insert ➢ Hyperlink or press Ctrl+K to link the button to another slide.

Publishing in PDF

Although most people who create Excel-based Balanced Scorecards publish them in PowerPoint, publishing in PDF format has some distinct advantages. PDF files are designed for high-quality production and presentation on any output device. PDF files also can be encrypted with the strongest security.

WARNING Before you begin creating navigational hyperlinks in Excel, make sure that worksheet tabs have their final names. Excel hyperlinks reference worksheet tabs as text names. The hyperlink does not automatically update if you change the tab name. If you change a tab name, you have to manually update all hyperlinks pointing to it.

Second, do not create graphical hyperlink buttons in Excel if you want to convert the file to PDF. (Hyperlinks on graphics cause problems in various versions of Adobe Acrobat.) You can create hyperlinks in the PDF file after it is created.

Advantages and Disadvantages of Publishing in PDF

Publishing a Balanced Scorecard in PDF has many advantages:

- Some PDF publishing software can preserve text-based hyperlinks in Excel.
- Adobe Acrobat has several types and levels of security, including public-key encryption and certificates.
- Certificates enable you to publish with different levels of access for different types of users.
- Readers who have the free Adobe Reader can add comments and sticky notes that others can see.
- Other document formats can be included in the PDF, enabling you to include and link to backup context and documentation originally sourced in Word, PDF, image files, AutoCAD, and so on.
- Some PDF publishing software reimports source files and regenerates the PDF file. As long as you keep the original Excel workbook structure and tab names, you can regenerate the PDF file with a few clicks. Usually you can edit the list of source files before refreshing if you want to.

Publishing in PDF has some additional advantages:

- A PDF displays consistently on any computer and screen resolution.
- A free PDF viewer, Adobe Reader, includes the ability to add comments and sticky notes.
- Links to external files can be created manually in the Acrobat document.
- Output can be of the highest print or media quality.
- Hyperlinks can open files outside the PDF, such as an interactive Excel file.

Publishing Excel worksheets to a PDF also has some disadvantages:

- Adobe Acrobat Professional is expensive. Although Adobe seems to own the corporate market for PDFs, I've found issues with every upgrade. Some lower-priced alternatives work well.

- You have to learn yet another piece of software.

- You must teach executives how to maximize the PDF size to full screen and how to add comments and sticky notes.

- You must develop the page setup settings for publication. (You need to discover which page setup settings in Excel are optimal for your PDF output.)

- You must develop the settings for customized headings, background colors, watermarks, and so on.

PDF Architecture

This is repeating what has been said before, but put your data in a separate worksheet from the presentation or chart layer. This makes charts and tables easier to maintain.After the Excel workbook is converted into PDF, it no longer has a connection or data link to the original Excel source document. However, you can easily update the PDF, because most PDF publishing software regenerates the PDF as long as you have not changed the Excel source file structure or sheet names.

Creating Complex or High-Security Balanced Scorecards in PDF

If you have more-complex Balanced Scorecards containing many slides with multiple layers, or that require very secure encryption, or if you want to bind additional documents with the scorecard or dashboard, follow these steps:

1. Develop and maintain your scorecard or dashboards in any version of Excel.

2. Keep all Balanced Scorecard worksheets or dashboards you want to publish in one folder. This will make republishing with the same settings much easier.

3. Create PDF files of all the worksheets you want displayed.

4. Create a table of contents or use the Balanced Scorecard with multiple charts. Include this page at the beginning of the PDF.

5. Bind all the PDF pages and arrange them in the correct order. Applications such as Nitro Pro and Adobe Acrobat enable you to bind pages from separate PDF documents, reorder the pages, and then save the result as a single file.

6. "Draw" hyperlinks over the table of contents items or the Balanced Scorecard charts so that users can click a topic to drill down to the detailed pages.

7. Save the PDF bound version containing the table of contents and all pages.

8. Reopen the PDF file, and add any comments or sticky notes you want for the readers.

9. If your PDF needs greater security than what is available on your network, encrypt the PDF with a secure password.

Over the years I have tried many times, sometimes with success and sometimes with frustration, to create PDF files that take in an entire Excel worksheet, convert all the hyperlinks in the worksheet, and produce a finished PDF in which all table of contents and hyperlink buttons work. The results have been so inconsistent that I can't recommend this approach. Every version and patch of Excel and Adobe Acrobat has its own set of issues. I've concluded that it's best to use the simpler approach mentioned earlier: Create pages, bind them, manually add the TOC with hyperlinks, and then publish the final PDF. This process requires more work, but it's much less error-prone.

CREATING PDF FILES FROM EXCEL WORKSHEETS

PDF files are designed to produce high-quality standardized printouts. Therefore, make sure your Excel page settings and print settings are exactly as you would want them to appear if you were printing the final version. That includes margins, orientation, page breaks, and so forth.

In older versions of Excel, you need to use PDF creation software such as Adobe Acrobat or Nitro Pro. These programs enable you to create PDFs from worksheets you select. In Excel 2010 you can save worksheets to PDF directly from within Excel. To do this, open the worksheet and choose File ➢ Save As. For the Save As type, select PDF. Select Options, and then specify the pages you want saved in PDF format. Worksheets saved in PDF file format do not preserve hyperlinks in the worksheets. You need a PDF publishing application to bind separate PDF files.

If you are using Excel 2007 you can add the ability to save workbooks in PDF format by searching the web with the terms "Excel PDF Add-in." Microsoft has released an add-in for Excel 2007 that gives it this handy feature.

Summary

As a Balanced Scorecard and dashboard developer, you walk a tightrope between executive teams, who have a strategic, long-range view, and operational teams, who have a detailed, up-to-the-minute view. The executive leadership team needs an easy-to-navigate, high-level view of the critical few strategic metrics and operational performance. They need to see only enough detail to be able to identify general issues. Usually one or two levels of drill-down along predefined queries are sufficient. When they find an issue, they will want to drill down or ask the functional manager for that area to investigate. On the other hand, operational and performance management requires the ability to drill down to lower levels and to perform interactive queries to find the cause of issues. This requires a robust Excel dashboard that may link to a database. In that case you can't publish to a PDF or PowerPoint; you must keep the dashboard in Excel.

Index